Old Cars

collector car
digest

Featured selections from OLD CARS WEEKLY

edited by John Gunnell

Published by

krause
publications

700 E. State Street • Iola, WI 54990-0001
Telephone: 715/445-2214

Library of Congress Catalog Number: 93-77545
ISBN: 0-87341-257-5
Printed in the United States of America

Contents

Introduction

There are some great stories in this book. They were written by authors who specialize in articles about collector cars. The vehicles covered are antiques such as Stanley Steamers, classics such as Bugattis and Packards, special interest cars (including the 1957 El Morocco), and muscle cars such as Chevelles and GTOs.

Cars built prior to World War II are the focus of the first section about prewar cars, which is led off by the "Veteran Motorist" features. These run the gamut of interest in early models, from developmental studies of design and technical features to essays on what it feels like to live the life of a car hobbyist.

Other topics covered by the prewar articles range from the story of the first car to climb Pikes Peak to a look at Oldsmobile's lineage. You'll learn the life story of designer Ray Dietrich, the background behind Bugatti Royales and the details of Dwight Eisenhower's military staff cars.

Then comes the postwar car section, which is loaded with facts about "fin-mobiles" and "factory hot rods." It begins with the famous "Postwar Scripts" series that traces the American car story from 1946 into the 1970s. You'll read about cult cars like the 1963 Corvette "split window" coupe, fun machines like the King Midget and misty milestones like the Edsel and the Frazer.

Additional highlights of the postwar era include tales of stock car-racing Dodge D500s, sand dune-jumping Oldsmobile ragtops and hardtop-like mid-1950s station wagons. For history buffs, questions surrounding the John F. Kennedy assassination car are answered.

Collecting, collections and collectors are featured in the book's third section, which sparkles with the kind of essential information (and inspiration) that automobile hobbyists need. Safe operation, insuring and trailering of collectible automobiles are covered. There are also articles about car collections in great museums and people who provide automotive collectibles. Toys, models, pedal cars, literature and parts are also discussed, as well as television and movie cars.

Our final "Writers' License" section is loaded with news and views from authors who write regular column-length features for old car collectors. Some of these cover particular brands of cars, while others focus on hobby happenings during a particular era or in a particular region. Some topics touched on include 1950s nostalgia, Chevrolet advertising, Ford Model T postcards, Chrysler turbine cars, "brass & gas" tours, Greta Garbo's Duesenberg, postwar Hudson memories and auto innovations.

All of the material in this book was originally presented in Old Cars, a weekly collectors' publication. We have "digested" the best stories from more than 5,000 items that originally appeared there in 1987 and 1988. The stories are not shortened or abridged. In fact, most have been updated and expanded with additional facts and photos. The design layouts and paper quality have also been improved so that you can save this "best of old cars" material in this genuine book format. Both serious collectors and casual enthusiasts will enjoy reading this first "Collector Car Digest."

PREWAR

Automobile hood designs

By Walter MacIlvain

Trivia query: What did the Dixie Flyer old Hickory truck, and Urban electric truck have common? Answer at end of article.

The engine hood, or bonnet, according to our English friends, a utilitarian piece of cover-up equipment, can also be a work of art.

The hood is always within the vision of the driver, be it the short, stubby nose of a Model T or the gracefully contoured metal expanse of a Packard Eight or a Rolls-Royce. A driver's impression of a car is doubtlessly influenced by the section of an automobile within his vision while driving the car.

The Mercedes car set the example, back in 1901, by placing the radiator in front of an inline engine. A bonnet or hood was needed to cover the power plant and to provide continuity of design with the rest of the vehicle. This became the basis of automobile design. It was quickly adopted by manufacturers of touring cars on both sides of the Atlantic, thereby separating the motor car forever from its horse-drawn counterpart.

Our manufacturers of runabouts in the Great Lakes area: Ford, Olds, Reo and Cadillac, for instance, were quick to emulate the design of the big touring cars and provide a forward hood. As these (circa 1904) vehicles carried the engine amidships, beneath the seat, the hood concealed not only the power unit, but the gasoline tank, an oil tank and sometimes a water container.

They were not engine hoods at all, but false hoods. Soon, however, even the lighter American cars adopted multi-cylinder engines with the crankshaft running parallel to the frame side rails (Model S Oldsmobile, for example) and the hood became legitimate.

The term "French hood" probably had its origin with the Mors at the turn of the century. It had a finned tubular radiator mounted low, at the front of the frame. A gracefully contoured engine cover sloped downward toward the front. This design was also used by the Cannstadt-Daimler and came to the United States in the 1903 Columbia and Locomobile. It found favor with Renault, C.G.V., Clement-Bayard and others who mounted their radiator in back of the engine, up against the dash. In this country, Franklin adopted this design in 1911 (without the radiator) and, in 1912 it was adopted by Stewart, Lippard-Stewart and Kelly Springfield trucks. Croxton-Keeton and Rayfield (1913) also used it here

The term "French hood" probably had its origin at the turn of the century. It was used by early Columbia automobiles.

and, in Scotland, the prewar Arrol-Johnston had it, too. Renault was the last to relinquish the "scuttle hood." It placed the radiator forward in 1930, but kept the sloping front for several years to maintain its traditional appearance.

The majority of American manufacturers adopted the so called Mercedes-style hood, with its low shoulders. Some of the plain hoods were made without louvers for a purpose. Utilizing fan blades cast into the flywheel, an air-tight hood, together with an under pan, would channel the cooling air from the radiator down past the engine and out through the flywheel. An example was the Thomas taxicab of circa 1909. Often, the hood contour would be a clue to the make of the car. However, Stevens-Duryea, one of the more prominent early cars, had three different radiator designs in 1906. Each had its own hood to match.

Stevens-Duryea, one of the more prominent early cars, had three different radiator designs in 1906. Each had its own hood to match.

The hoods of many cars came off in one piece for working on the engine. The three-piece styles had hinges on top and on the sides about half-way down. For several years, the hood of the Franklin hinged forward. Later, "alligator" hoods were hinged at the rear.

Moving on to the early streamline era, circa 1914-1915, many makers adopted more rounded hood designs. Part of the streamline process called for eliminating the break between hood and cowl. This entailed a blending of the radiator lines with the shape of the body at the cowl, which was possible only within the length of the engine bonnet. This was managed

William B. Stout designed the 1915 Scripps-Booth using a sharp-shouldered radiator and carrying the angle along the hood and into the cowl.

7

by the use of tapered surfaces, in some instances in connection with compound curves, in others by modifying the contour of the cowl. For example, William B. Stout in the design of the 1915 Scripps-Booth roadster, accomplished the transition of forms very neatly. He used a sharp-shouldered radiator and carried the angle along the hood and into the cowl, sweeping up to the windshield.

The same idea, with a higher-shouldered radiator, was seen in Percy Owen's 1916 Liberty Six and the Roamer, which started life as a sport model of the Halladay. It was also evident in the Murray Eight, which, like the Roamer, used the Rolls-Royce radiator as a basis. At the 1918 shows there was a proliferation of these high-shouldered designs, among them the Cole Areo Eight, the Winton Six, the Hollier and Stanley steam car. These led up to the postwar designs exemplified by the Essex, Moon's Victory Six and the Velie. The radiators became higher and narrower, with correspondingly higher hood and cowl lines. Such designs were often combined with lower body sides and beveled edges.

A second style of radiator used by Stevens-Duryea in its different 1906 models.

It must be realized that much of this is generalization; there were actually nearly as many variations as there were makes of cars. Take, for example, the disposition of the cooling louvers. The above mentioned airtight design was practically extinct in the streamline era, but a few cars still had plain hoods, notably the Dodge, Overland, Dorris, Locomobile and Pierce-Arrow. A few 1915 Dodges had four louvers on each side. Ford had similar groups of six and Buicks, and some Velies, had double groups of six with a third catch between them. The louvers were slanted backward in the Chevrolet, Haynes and Auburn and were slanted forward in the Anderson and some later Auburns. Fiat, of Poughkeepsie, New York, placed three slanted louvers high on each side of the upper hood section.

Starting with the Allied victory in World War I, there was a rash of new designs. Many had multiple narrow, closely-spaced louvers in the sides of the hoods. Horizontal louvers were an unusual feature of the 1927 Chandler. Round port holes were seen in a Chadwick speedster as early as 1910, as well as in the Dixie-Flyer of 1921 and some Daniels Eights. Of course, who can forget the venti-ports of the 1949-1957 Buicks? Several earlier cars had doors replacing the hood louvers in the 1930s, notably Packard, Lincoln and Chrysler.

In 1924, Buick, Gray, Star, Paterson and Studebaker brazenly copied the Packard break-arch hood design, which hadn't changed since 1904. Packard frowned on this, but apparently could not do much about it. Actually, this style had not been Packard's exclusive property. Check the 1903 Oldsmobile touring roadster, the 1908-1912 Elmore, the pre-1908 Thomas and, in modified format, the style used by White and Minerva.

The 1905 Grout steamer had a hood resembling a 55-gallon drum laid on its side.

Unconventional hood designs were also seen. Note the 1920-1928 Willys-Knight's two-step arch and the hood of the air-cooled Holmes. The 1905 Grout steamer had a hood resembling a 55-gallon drum laid on its side; a style also followed by Lambert Model H (1907), the Serpollet in France, and, of course, the "barrel hood" Franklin of 1905-1910.

In 1933, Chrysler products brought the back edge of the hood right up to the windshield, completely covering the cowl. In the second era of streamlining in the late 1930s and 1940s, the front end sheet metal was made to more completely enclose the exposed parts of the chassis, resulting in raising the catwalks between hood and fenders until the hood covered only the upper part of the engine. In the Chrysler Airflow models, this necessitated reaching the valve lifters from beneath the front fender.

Means had to be provided for holding the hood in place. These have taken several forms over the years, including straps, spring-loaded fasteners and screw-down clamps. One or two straps proved most effective in racing practice. Locomobile and Pierce-Arrow provided Yale locks to prevent anyone from tampering with the engine (magnetos were vulnerable to theft). When hoods first became streamlined into the car, remote-controlled catches were usually provided. Twisting a central lever would release the locks at both ends, simultaneously. Certain makes included controls actuated from inside the car.

With the universal application of the alligator (front-opening) hood, it became mandatory to provide a second safety catch to prevent the hood from opening inadvertently on the highway and becoming air-borne. These traumatic episodes actually happened, often with potentially fatal results.

In many of our modern cars, contrary to our opening paragraphs, one does not see the hood when driving. It has been lowered for better visibility of the road. Something picturesque has been lost.

Spotlighting Haynes innovations and unique features

First automotive use of aluminum, 1895.

Double-opposed engine, 1895-1905.

Planetary gearset. 1898.

Valves in head, 1895.

Aluminum cylinders and crankcase, 1896 (second car).

Roller pinion drive, 1905-1909.

One-piece axle shaft with sleeve, 1905-1909.

Freewheeling transmission, 1906-1909.

Anti-clash gearshift, 1906-1909.

Double flywheels, 1907-1909.

Roller torsion drive member, 1906-1909.

Steering gear attached to engine, 1909-1910.

Starter button on dash, 1916 to end.

Answer to trivia query: They were all made by the Kentucky Wagon Manufacturing Company, Louisville, Kentucky.

Veteran Motorist...

Evolution of the people package

• By Walter MacIlvain

Trivia query: What does the trade name "Alka-Seltzer" (no commercial intent) remind you of, automotively speaking? Answer at end of article.

Back in the days of the primitive horseless vehicle, no one but a mystic seer would have envisioned the variety of motor vehicles that would grace our highways within a very few generations.

To the pioneer working to equip a wheeled vehicle with a means of self-locomotion, seating accommodations for the driver and a passenger or two must have been a secondary matter. The main concern was to make the contraption run!

As soon as a degree of reliability had been achieved, the inventor began to think of the form that the vehicle should take, how many persons it would carry, how much merchandise, etc. Thus, the "people package" concept evolved.

Right from the start, there were two schools of design. One stemmed from the cycle and one from the horse-drawn vehicle. Carl Benz' tricycle followed cycle practice with its steel tubular framework and running gear and wire spoked wheels. His fellow countryman, Gottlieb Daimler, used wood. His 1895 motorcycle was made largely of wood and his first four-wheeler was an adaptation of a horse-drawn coach.

Thus, we see two parallel lines: One cycle oriented; the other the horseless carriage. DeDion-Bouton and Bollee went the cycle route; Panhard-Levassor, Peugeot and Daimler preferred the horse-drawn vehicle style.

Coming to America, some early prototypes and production cars were Haynes, Ford, Autocar, Pierce, Waltham, Riker and Peerless. All of these started out the cycle route. Duryea, Olds, Winton and Packard showed horse-drawn style vehicle influence. Columbia kept a foot in both camps for several years.

The followers of the cycle school made motorcycles, tricycles and quadricycles, with the operator usually sitting upon a cycle type saddle. His passengers or cargo rode ahead of him. Tubular frames with tubes for reach rods could be purchased from Nieustadt-Perry, Dayton or Baldner. Bodies could be purchased from such firms as C.R. Wilson, Frantz or Horton and, thus, the "assembled car" was born early in the century.

Those following horse vehicle practice usually employed angle steel or wood, reinforced by steel as the foundation. A piano box or other style body was firmly attached. It mattered not what motive power was used, the accommodations were the same. The whole thing was turned out much smoother in the 1901-1902 era and the machinery was better concealed. Wheels were becoming smaller, shod with pneumatics and all of the same size. Mud guards were placed over them. The guards were made of bent wood, steel or wire framed with leather sewed over the framework.

Carl Benz' first three-wheel car followed the design of the tricycle.

By 1904-1905, the car was assuming its own identity as an automobile that was unrelated to either the cycle or wagon. An exception was the high-wheeled auto buggies, just then coming into popularity in rural areas. The horse-drawn vehicle was still reflected, however, in certain body styles and particularly in their names. Thus, we had the runabout, surrey, phaeton, coupe, brougham, landaulet and others.

The earliest multi-seat car was a surrey, that of Haynes-Apperson coming to mind. Two or three bench seats seating four to six passengers were entered from the side. A surrey was incomplete without its canopy top with roll-down curtains for weather protection; features made famous by that wonderful song sung so well by James Melton, "The Surrey with the Fringe on Top."

At about the same time, the runabout or Stanhope came along. It had a single buggy seat, a folding top and an auxiliary seat that would fold down out of the dash, complete with a foot rest. As this seat was considerably lower than that of the driver, the latter had no trouble in seeing over the head of its occupants.

The years 1902-1903 saw the advent of the detachable tonneau, which would make a four-passenger machine out of a runabout. It was bolted to the sloping rear deck. The interior opened up to receive its occupants.

The simple expedient of lengthening the wheelbase next made the side entrance tonneau practical. It eliminated the necessity of backing up to the curb to take on passengers. Several foreign cars had side entrance tonneau bodies as early as 1904, as did Apperson, Peerless and Stearns in this country.

At this time, the favored open car top was the cape or folding type, although most cars were sold without top or windshield. The distinction between a surrey and a touring car was that a touring car had rear doors, while a surrey had none.

The next step was to make the wheelbase still longer and to provide auxiliary seats in the tonneau, making provision for seven passengers. Longer wheelbases necessitated stronger chassis frames. So, the so-called locomotive frame, with channel steel side members, was adopted by several progressive marques. The angle steel and wood foundation was eventually abandoned by all, with the exception of Franklin. This was a milestone in the progress of the motor car away from the horse-drawn vehicle.

The better car makers also offered enclosed cars in their lines. Peerless and Pierce, among others, offered their clients the luxury of complete shelter from the elements. But the chauffeur sat out in the open. A limousine body provided a roof over that individual's head; a brougham and many landaulets did not. Only the coupe or so-called inside drive limousine, also called a berline, provided a full enclosure for this essential individual. The latter had a partition separating the operator from those in the tonneau. Several enclosed types were offered in the Pierce Great-Arrow line as early as 1905. The electric vehicle was the development medium for the enclosed car; the silence of its mechanism provided a quieter environment for the elimination of squeaks and rattles.

Pierce was a pioneer maker of limousines.

On the other hand, the number of open car types was increasing. One man's needs were not necessarily those of his neighbor or his son. The family touring car began to acquire brothers. A runabout was found useful for a physician making house calls. A sportsman was likely to go for a speedster having a big, exposed gasoline tank mounted directly in back of the seat. Earlier, Oldsmobile, Rambler and others had made the most of their early (1907-1908) "flying roadsters" by giving them exotic flared fenders, tan leather upholstery and special paint jobs. The actual raceabout evolved about 1909-1913 and was much lower.

Then there was the person who coveted a sporting image with a bit more carrying capacity than a runabout or raceabout. For him, the toy tonneau (also known as a baby tonneau, pony tonneau or torpedo) was introduced by several makers. This was a car that usually had a cowl or "scuttle dash" and a narrow, close-coupled body. Its heyday was the 1909-1914 era, continuing into the 1920s in such cars as the Mercer Sporting, Cadillac phaeton and Hudson speedster.

Enclosed cars also proliferated, primarily for service in towns. The smaller limousines were found ideal for taxicab service, the best known being the Renault and Darracq. These were copied in this country by Thomas and others. Many coupes were preferred by doctors and professional men. The White company promoted its coupe as the successor to the electric brougham. Early with a sedan, and actually so-called, was the Case of 1911. By 1913, several sedans had appeared. Kissel Kar had a center-door sedan called a five-passenger coupe. Similarly, the Rambler was called an enclosed inside-drive car; the Lozier an inside-drive limousine.

The interior-driven limousine in the higher-priced lines, by the expedient of eliminating the partition, became a four-door sedan. This type was also anticipated by the Springfield (or open sedan) available in the 1916-1920 period. Some of these had so-called California tops with fancy rear quarter windows. The Kissel all-year car gained fame for offering cars with a pair of tops (one for summer, the other for winter) in touring, roadster and brougham styles. The latter came with a victoria top as an option.

The rumble seat roadster was named for Lord Rhumble of England. It was a direct descendent of the runabout with dickey or "mother-in-law" seat, as seen in the previous decade. Pierce-Arrow, Packard, Oldsmobile and one or two other makers developed the rumble seat into a disappearing rear deck item, making entrance and egress rather difficult. In the 1916-1922 era, the club "cloverleaf" (or chummy roadster) solved the dilemma by bringing the auxiliary seat into the body of the car. It could be entered via an aisle between the front seats and was protected by the car top. Speedwell anticipated this type, as early as 1911, with a model called a "Duck Boat."

It is surprising to find that many middle class lines of cars had in their line ups such formal types as a limousine, landaulet and brougham throughout the teens. These were phased out of such lines as Hudson, Chalmers and Chandler with the entrance into the 1920s. At that point, taxicabs were given their own chassis by such firms as Checker, Bauer, H.C.S. and Yellow Cab.

In the 1920s, taxicabs were given their own chassis.

A real epoch-making sedan was the two-door Franklin of mid-1916 to 1924 with its wide doors, fold-down front seat backs (for entrance to the rear), five windows and a V-shaped windshield. This type had few followers at the time, but evolved into the coach of the 1920s. Up to the time of the inception of the two-door family sedan or coach, the cheapest enclosed model retailed at about $1,000 more than the open cars. Hudson and Essex coaches were the catalyst that leveled off open and closed car prices. The coach was ideally suited to the family with small children. When riding in the back, the kids had no access to doors on which to swing to their probable destruction.

In the 1920s, permanent tops replaced the folding tops of many tourings and roadsters, since many people no longer folded them anyway. Collapsible tops were still popular on sport editions, descendants of the Mercers and Stutz and further back of the toy tonneau and raceabouts. A new generation of these sport models was seen in such vehicles as the

Buick 6-54 and 6-55, with maroon finish, khaki tops, nickel radiator shell and trim, wind wings and every conceivable extra of the day. The Jordan Playboy, from 1919, was one of them. Its mates were the Sport Marine and Blue Boy four-passenger jobs. In a class by itself was the Kissel speedster with its high cowl line, low-cut sides and abbreviated turtle back. Its mate, the tourister, never achieved the same popularity.

In a class by itself was the Kissel speedster.

The enclosed car era began with the advent of the coach (circa 1925). The open car, now more expensive because of smaller production, if made at all, assumed the role of a sporting vehicle in both phaeton or roadster form. The racy roadster was still with us in limited quantities. The Bearcat and the Raceabout evolved, eventually, into the Corvette.

There continued to be a demand for luxury enclosed cars. Besides the standard four-door sedans and four-passenger coupes, there evolved a more formal style of the mid-1920s. This was the four-door brougham or brougham-sedan. Usually on a long wheelbase, it was a close-coupled five-passenger job with space for a trunk at the rear and better grade interior. The rear quarters were either blind-styled or fitted with opera-style windows and landau irons. Buick had a nice example of this type, as did Chandler, Paige and several others.

Through the years, car profiles changed, too. With the coming of power steering, bodies and engines were moved forward several inches; floors and roof lines were lowered and construction was considerably altered. However, the people package still hasn't changed all that much since the 1930s.

Hudson's "step-down" design of 1951, and its followers, have given us wider seats and eliminated running boards. The seven-passenger sedan has been replaced by the station wagon and down-sizing the wagon led to the use of small mini-vans by many larger families. Slanted windshields and slippery exterior designs have led to improvements in speed and economy over the boxy sedans of yesterday. Brass trim gave way to nickel; nickel was replaced with chromium; and now automotive trim is mostly dead black. It all serves to make it more interesting to go to a car meet and gaze at the progress we have witnessed, much of it in our own lifetime. What would Carl or Gottlieb or even old Henry say now? "Well done!" or "How horrible!"

Answer to trivia query: When, in 1938, the American Locomotive Company was replacing their steam locomotives with diesels, a licensing agreement was entered into with the Sulzer firm of Germany. The resultant product was called the Alco-Sulzer diesel.

Veteran Motorist...

Acceleration figures

By Walter MacIlvain

In recent years, acceleration figures have been pretty much standardized in terms of the number of seconds required for a car to go from standstill to 60 miles per hour or of the maximum speed obtained at the end of a quarter-mile.

For example, Motor Trend for September 1987 cites various test reports on the new cars, ranging from zero to 60 in 9.61 seconds for the Mercury Cougar, in 6.69 seconds for the Mazda RX 7 Turbo II, 9.27 for the BMW M6, 10.87 for a Nissan Pulsar and 10.97 for the latest Jaguar XJ 6.

The same issue contrasts these figures (not intentionally) with its "Retrospect" section featuring a 1949 Nash. It showed a 0 to 60 elapsed time of 27 seconds. Anything under 10 seconds for today's detuned economy-type cars running on 87 octane no-lead fuel is considered very good, indeed. However, such a figure was fairly commonplace in the early 1960s using high test leaded gas, which is no longer available.

MacIlvain remembers the 1922 Jewett as a snappy light six. (Henry Austin Clark, Jr. photo collection)

In light of the above, the writer remembers the 1922 Jewett, a really snappy light six put out by the Paige firm, advertised as being capable of going from five miles per hour to 25 miles per hour in seven seconds! Not so well publicized was the figure of zero to 25 in 6-1/2 seconds attainable by the 1916 Chalmers 6-30. This was far better than the capability of the 1917 Regal four, which showed three to 30 miles per hour in 30 seconds.

Most of these old models wouldn't even reach the express train speed of a mile-a-minute! The agile 1920 Marmon 34, largely built of aluminum with a 340 cubic inch engine and weighing less than 4,000 pounds, was declared capable of accelerating from 10 miles per hour to 50 miles per hour in 15.8 or 18.8 seconds, according to whether the gear ratio was 4:1 or 3.75:1.

Pathfinder Cloverleaf Roadster

Like the hot Hudson, the 1917 Pathfinder 12 had a 5.0:1 compression ratio. (Henry Austin Clark, Jr. photo collection)

We must remember that the performance of an engine is largely reliant on its efficiency or lack of it. The compression ratio of early cars was down in the range of 3.0:1 or 4.0:1. The Hudson Super Six of 1916 was one of the first to raise it to 5:1, a figure also attained by the Weidely V-12 engine used by Pathfinder and others. Engine balancing and pressure lubrication were additional factors that raised the rpms, as was better breathing due to larger or dual valves.

The recently much-touted dual valve engine is nothing new. It was introduced in racing cars around 1912 by Ernest Henry and used very successfully by Peugeot race drivers. A Stutz racing engine had them in 1915 and that maker applied dual valves to its production models in 1917. White had a 16-valve four the same year. Starting with the 1919 Series 5, Pierce-Arrow had dual valves in its big sixes. They lasted through 1928.

Four small valves give better breathing than two large ones, as they are better able to utilize the space in the cylinder head. Being lighter with smaller springs, they can be made to open and close more quickly than the larger valves. In regard to breathing, the F-head type of combustion chamber is hard to beat. In it, one big inlet valve is placed centrally in the head and the exhaust valve is in an L-shaped pocket in the block. It was used by Chalmers as early as 1908, in the very efficient little Essex fours. The later Hudson Super Sixes, and still later the Willys, Rover and Rolls-Royce, used it, too.

The above factors, together with modern electronic ignition, fuel-injection and turbocharging, add up to tremendously quick acceleration figures, coupled with better fuel efficiency and longer life expectancy in the modern car engine.

A Stutz racing engine had dual valves by 1915 and production models got them two years later. (Paul Free-hill)

Air-cooled cars

By Walter MacIlvain

Trivia query: It is well known that the two-door Ford sedan was offered (1923-1927) under the name "Tudor." What firm built a Tudor car in 1904 and what was it like? Answer at end of article.

With the demise of the Volkswagen Beetle, the air-cooled engine has become practically extinct as an automobile power plant. That is not to say that this type of engine is obsolete. Anyone operating a power lawn mower, small tractor or snowblower can attest to that. The radial air-cooled aero engine is still very much with us, as well as air cooling being nearly universal on motorcycles.

Water cooling is not the problem that it used to be, thanks to modern anti-freeze solutions. In former days, colder climates practically obliged the motorist to drain out the water when not running his car. To keep going in winter, he could use unreliable alcohol as an antifreeze. It was subject to evaporation, due to its low boiling point.

Today's motorist can fill his car with up to a 50 percent solution of antifreeze and forget it until it's time to drain and flush the cooling system at one to three year intervals.

Water cooling has the advantage of superior cooling properties; your engine will run at roughly one-half the temperature of an air-cooled engine, thus reducing the oil break-down problem. Then, too, water jacketing will act as an insulator against sound, making for a quieter engine. Furthermore, water provides a medium for heating the interior of the car in cold weather. This is nearly impossible with air cooling, as owners of older VWs can verify.

To achieve effective cooling, an air-cooled engine must necessarily run at speed. Low speed lugging is never advisable. The blowers have to run fast enough to force a sufficiency of air around the cylinders to dissipate unwanted heat. Nevertheless, the higher the temperature at which an engine runs, the higher is its efficiency, up to a point. Therefore, an air-cooled engine is inherently more efficient than its water-cooled counterpart.

The air-cooled gasoline engine is as old as the engine itself. Gottlieb Daimler's first small, high speed gas engine of 1884 actually had no provision for cooling. As a result, it generated so much heat that the charge would ignite itself. However, this condition was not practical. When hot tube ignition was applied for more reliable operation, Herr Daimler and his engineer Wilhelm Maybach added water jacketing.

In general, it can be said that air-cooled engines have singly cast cylinders (except VWs) and are of the valve-in-head type with cooling fins either cast in or attached by means of welding or brazing.

The early French DeDion engines were air-cooled from 1895 to 1899, but when after 20,000 had been produced, water cooling was standardized by this popular maker. Several other manufacturers on both sides of the Atlantic started out with air cooling, later switching to water. They moved tentatively at first, then went all out for water-cooled engines. Converts included Knox, Corbin, Marion, Marmon, Premier, International, Chase, Brockway, Kelly-Springfield trucks and others.

The Franklin was the most persistent American car to use air to keep it from running a temperature, but its chief engineer John Wilkinson was not static in his approach to the problem. He made several radical changes in the course of Franklin's history. It was determined early that, with air cooling, a greater number of small cylinders would cool more effectively than one or two big ones. Therefore, the first Franklins were of the "cross engine" type, with four cylinders in front. Each cylinder was equally exposed to the incoming "rush" of air.

In 1904, Franklin went to shaft drive and a so-called "barrel hood" covered the four cylinders mounted fore and aft. An equalizing effect of cooling was achieved by graduating the number of cooling fins around the cylinders from front to rear. A 1905 six-cylinder design was one of the first sixes in America. In the barrel hood design there was a chain-driven fan in front for "forced draft." In 1908, the fan was gear-driven and blades were placed in the flywheel to help draw the air down and out. These blades were replaced, in 1910, by a sirocco fan in the flywheel. It proved so effective, that the forward fan was no longer required.

The 1906 Franklin's characteristic barrel hood hid four cylinders mounted fore-and-aft style. (Henry Austin Clark, Jr. photo collection)

At the same time, the cooling fins were changed from horizontal to vertical. The barrel hood was replaced by the Renault style hood in 1911, when the French patents to that picturesque style had run out. The suction cooling system was superseded by pressure in 1923, the sirocco blower was moved to the front of the engine and air was ducted up and over the engine and down around each cylinder.

This system had previously been employed very effectively by Oscar Lear in his Frayer-Miller cars and trucks, the latter becoming the Kelly-Springfield in 1910. These engines were successful in racing and some found their way into Seagrave fire trucks.

Franklins from 1921 on changed from a Renault style hood to the Fiat or "horse collar" design. Pressure cooling was continued through the De Lausse design. The front end resembled that of a water-cooled car until 1930, when side draft cooling was adopted. Air was directed against the left sides of the cylinders, again using horizontal fins. Some of this air was diverted to the carburetor intake in the 1932 models to produce a slight supercharging effect.

The 1933 and later Franklin V-12 was a veritable powerhouse, generating 150 horsepower at 3100 rpm. The Franklin engine did not die with the Franklin car. Engineers Doman and Marks made it available for use in trucks and airplanes. Air-Cooled Motors provided the White company with air-cooled, under-the-floor horizontal engines for its stand-drive "White Horse" delivery vans in the late 1930s.

Henry Gray makes an adjustment on the air-cooled motor in his 1919 shovel-nosed Franklin after a 750-mile trip. (Old Cars)

The Holmes car (1918-1923), designed by a former Franklin engineer Arthur Holmes, also employed the suction system of air cooling. This car was either ugly or beautiful (according to the eyes of the beholder), due to its frontal appearance. The louver arrangement of its radiator less grille resembled a huge bug. It was a somewhat larger car than the Franklin. The later models had three valves per cylinder.

Gun manufacturer Ansley Fox built an air-cooled car in Philadelphia (1921-1924). It had a pressure cooling system on the order of the Frayer-Miller and later Franklins. A large, powerful blower at the front ducted air over the cylinders. Like the Holmes, the Fox was designed by another former Franklin engineer, H.O. Swanson.

The usual method of cooling the individual cylinders was by means of fins around the barrels, sometimes cast-in, sometimes separate and made of copper and soldered to the cylinders. An exception was the Knox "Waterlew" made in Springfield, Massachusetts from 1899 to 1910. The Knox employed so-called "porcupine" cooling. Each cylinder had 1,500 to 2,000 one-eighth inch diameter (later 3/16 x 2 inch) steel pins screwed into the cylinder and head.

This was called "patent pin radiation." Each cylinder was equipped with its own fan blowing directly on the head. From 1908 to 1910, a choice of water or air cooling was offered.

Early International Harvester high-wheel Auto Wagons were air-cooled, as was the same firm's 1910 passenger car. The Auto Wagon had two horizontally opposed cylinders. Each was surrounded by cooling fins, with a belt-driven fan for each cylinder, and overhead valves. The 1910 models F, G and K low-wheel cars had air-cooled four-cylinder overhead camshaft engines. They changed to water cooling with the 1911 Model J. Air or water cooling was offered interchangeably in the Auto Wagon from 1912 through 1914.

A somewhat similar design to the Knox was the early Corbin air-cooled engine. It was based on the "Jones Cooling Comb," with patents that had been purchased by the American Hardware Company (which made the Corbin). J.H. Jones entered the Corbin Motor Vehicle Company with its purchase of the Bristol Motor Car Company in 1903. The Jones cooling comb comprised 56 rows of .078-inch thick sheet steel pressed into vertical grooves machined into each cylinder as vertical "cooling spines." A 16-inch horizontal fan was placed above the two cylinders. In the four-cylinder car of 1904, there were two 14-inch fans blowing directly down on the cylinder heads. The air-cooled Corbin was made through 1910, but water cooling was an optional alternate from late 1907 on.

Air-cooled Corbins lasted until 1910. Water cooling was optional on this 1908 Model R and other post-1907 cars. (Henry Austin Clark, Jr. photo collection)

The Cameron was an interesting, lightweight air-cooled car made at various addresses in the East from 1899 to 1919. It came in three-, four- and six-cylinder forms. Its cooling method was conventional enough, but innovative horizontal valves were actuated by vertical "walking beams," as they were in later Duesenberg racing engines. Although Cameron went to water cooling in 1913, the air-cooled engine was revived in 1919. It was made as late as 1948, in aero engine form, still with the horizontal valves.

E.S. Cameron and his brother, Forrest, specialized on very light cars. One of their sports models, known as the "Featherweight Flyer," did very well in competition racing and hill climbing trials (1904-1912) owing to its excellent power-to-weight ratio.

The Adams-Farwell rotary, horizontal air-cooled engine was invented, at the turn of the century, by Fay Oliver Farwell. It was used in a car marketed from 1903-1912 with the slogan "it spins like a top." It became the basis for the Gnome and LeRhone (French) aero engine used in many airplanes in the World War I era. Its counterpart was the radial engine, its first adherent probably being the French Salmson engine. This motor found much favor in the World War II years, as produced by Wright, Pratt & Whitney and others. In the rotary engine, the entire engine ... cylinders and so on ... would revolve. In the radial engine, only the crankshaft rotated (with considerably less gyroscopic effect and greater safety in the air.)

The Marion car of Indianapolis, like the early Franklin, started life as a cross-engine air-cooled job. It went to standard parallel engine design in 1906. Air cooling was superseded by water the next year. Almost the same pattern was followed by one of Marion's neighbors. The Premier, whose engineer George Weidely first built a water-cooled runabout, offered water as an alternate in 1907. The company switched to all-water cooling after that. Premier built a gigantic racing car for the 1905 Vanderbilt Cup Race. It had a 7 x 5-1/2-inch four-cylinder engine, but was overweight and never raced.

Another Indianapolis-built car, the beautifully engineered Marmon, had an air-cooled V-4 engine from its 1902 prototype through 1908. Then, an air-cooled V-8 was made in limited quantities. A water-cooled four-cylinder engine was made an option. This was standardized from 1909 on.

Many or most of the popular high-wheel motor buggies, beginning with the 1902 Holsman, were air-cooled. So were most of the cyclecars that followed.

Mention should be made of the three-cylinder, two-cycle, air-cooled engines used in several trucks, mostly made in New York State in the 1910-1914 period. These include the Chase, Brockway, Sanbert and Hatfield. These engines would run backward or forward equally well. Some interesting stories can be told about drivers inadvertently backing up in low gear or going forward in reverse. Otherwise they operated very well.

Several trucks, including this 1912 Chase Motor Wagon, utilized three-cylinder, two-cycle air-cooled engines. (Courtesy Reynolds Museum)

Even the Aerocar, so named-because of air cooling, went to water in the final year of its manufacture, 1908. The Aerocar Company had been started in 1905 by an ex-Ford executive, Alexander Y. Malcomson. He used the Reeves engine designed by F.D. Carrico and made by the Reeves Pulley Company of Columbus, Indiana. Carrico left later and went to the Speed Changing Pulley Company in Indianapolis. There he built the somewhat similar proprietary "Carrica" engines used in the DeTamble and several motor buggies.

An interesting, small air-cooled design was the D.A.C. (Detroit Air-Cooled Car Company) Twin Three of 1922. This was a 60-degree V-6 with cooling fins pressed on and ducts on both sides to carry the air from the fan to the cylinders.

One cannot leave the air-cooled scene without mentioning Chevrolet's "copper-cooled" model seen at the 1923 shows. Designed by C.F. Kettering, its four cast iron cylinders were cooled by vertical copper fins welded to them. A V-belt-driven blower at the front of the engine was designed to draw the air upward through the fins, then duct it to the blower and throw it outward from the periphery. Unfortunately, production of this innovative model was halted by Alfred Sloan, of GM, after some 800 cars had been made.

Dr. Ferdinand Porsche brought the air-cooled engine to a high degree of success as used in his rear-engined Volkswagen "Peoples Car." A horizontal opposed engine, its pair-cast cylinders were offset to provide for side-by-side connecting rods. Its cylinder heads were also pair-cast and made of aluminum. Cooling air was provided by a belt-driven blower mounted on a horizontal shaft above the engine. The sporty Porsche followed the same design.

Chevrolet's Corvair engine bore no resemblance to its predecessor, the copper-cooled model. Out in late 1959, it followed in general the configuration of the VW, but with six horizontally opposed cylinders mounted at the rear of the car. Unlike the VW, the cylinders were cast individually with their fins, only the heads being cast in blocks of three. The blower was mounted above the engine and operated in a horizontal plane, belt-driven, its shaft also carrying a horizontal generator. The Corvair was very successful, until bad publicity brought about its untimely end in May of 1969.

Air cooling is mostly now dead, as far as modern cars are concerned. But, who knows? Resurrection is possible.

Answer to trivia query: The Knox King of the Belgians side entrance open car of 1904 had a canopy top and glass front and was called the Tudor.

Veteran Motorist...

The Ford from A to A

By Walter MacIlvain

Trivia query: There were two Essex cars on the market in mid-1918. One was made by Hudson's new subsidiary, Essex Motors Inc.; the other was made by whom? Answer at end of article.

Fords are, as they should be, the most numerous of all antique cars. When this writer was a boy, at least every second car on the road was a Model T Ford. They were called "flivvers," "tin lizzies" or other derogatory names by non-Ford drivers who were annoyed by certain inconveniences caused by them: their tendency to hog the road, their slow progress climbing a steep hill, alternating between high and low (there was no second) gears and their limited maximum speed.

Prior to the Model T came the A, B, C, F, K, N, R and S models. Some of the missing letters can be found in foreign Ford catalogs. The first A was a runabout of 1903-1904, which could be had with a detachable rear entrance tonneau. The two-cylinder horizontal opposed motor (yes, it was called a motor in those days) was located amidships with a big flywheel crosswise beneath the driver's seat. You cranked it from the seat. The radiator was a coil of flanged pipe down low in front. Sometimes advertised as a "Fordmobile," it was even sold by the famous Wanamaker department stores in Philadelphia and New York. The Dodge Brothers built 650 engines for Ford in 1903. Bodies were produced by C.R. Wilson and others.

Basically, this Model A was a sound design. It sold at the low price of $850. It was steered by wheel, had a two-speed and reverse planetary transmission as developed by Ralph E. Northway and it employed a single chain drive to the differential in the center of the live rear axle.

Henry Ford had not yet settled on a single design. His "999" racing car, named for the locomotive of a famous express train, and driven by himself or Barney Oldfield, was setting records. In 1904, he showed an air-cooled four-cylinder car at the Detroit automobile show. Trouble loomed on the horizon in the form of a lawsuit for infringement of the Selden patent, brought by the Electric Vehicle Company.

The line was expanded in 1905 to include a water-cooled four called the Model B. It was a $2,000 machine with shaft drive. The Model C Ford was a development of the Model A, with a stand-up radiator in front and a false hood covering the gasoline tank. It was priced at $950. The Model F was an enlarged version of the same, with a side entrance tonneau body, priced at $1,200.

Two outstanding new models, for 1906, were the N and K. The N was assembled progressively at the Piquette plant, with a pair-cast four-cylinder engine in front and shaft drive. Selling at a mere $500, it would go 40 miles per hour. It was mounted on three chassis springs, two full elliptics in back and a single transverse semi-elliptic in front. This design was associated with Ford products until 1949. The Model N's resounding success during 1906, 1907 and 1908 gave Henry Ford the incentive to "build automobiles for the masses."

The Model K was a famous, but rare, six-cylinder Ford. It sold for $2,500 and was built largely in the Dodge Brothers' machine shops. This was Alexander Malcomson's car. Henry was against it. The weak spot in the Model K was reputedly the use of a two-speed planetary transmission in a heavy car. For 1907, the K became a seven-passenger tourer with smoother lines and more power. It was capable of 60 miles per hour. The Model N was given companions, including the Model R, with running boards and a little more luxury, and the S, which went all out with both running boards and a dickey seat on a box in the back. These low-priced runabouts gave a person everything he needed in basic transportation. Ford's profits exceeded $1 million that year.

A 1907 six-cylinder Ford roadster.

Materials used in Ford cars were now being greatly upgraded. In 1907, the N used nickel steel instead of carbon steel for gears, shafts, axles and frame. In the K, chrome-nickel forgings were generously employed. In 1908, C. Harold Wills (Ford's metallurgist who later built the Wills-Ste. Claire car) introduced vanadium steel, an exceptionally strong alloy.

The Model T was introduced in September 1908, but had been advertised as a taxicab in May. In this car, all of Henry Ford's ingenuity came to the fore. The use of vanadium steel allowed the vital parts to be made smaller and lighter without sacrificing strength. The cars looked spindly and frail, but they were not. Fairly good performance characteristics, good riding qualities, and a generous sized five-passenger body (all at the reasonable price of $850) gave Model T great family appeal.

If you think that all Ford Ts are as alike as peas in a pod, you are probably right. No two peas are exactly alike and neither were the Model Ts. Although all Model Ts had essentially the same specifications ... four-cylinder block- cast 3-3/4-inch by four-inch engine with fly-wheel magneto ignition; side valves; planetary two-speed and reverse gears; torque tube drive to a semi-floating rear axle; 100-inch wheelbase; and transverse semi-elliptic springs ... there were many subtle differences among them, other than being of different body styles. This makes for a most interesting study at a car meet where many of these marvelous little Fords are gathered. Then, too, there were so many parts and accessories in the aftermarket, that whole sections of magazines were devoted exclusively to them.

Model Ts were offered in a wide variety of body styles.

To recognize the earliest Model Ts, one must examine first, the running boards. The earliest were of wood covered with linoleum. This was soon followed by steel with long, raised ribs. The earliest Ts had hubcaps with "Ford" in block letters. The Ford script, in winged letters, appeared on the radiator. Top irons around the rear of the body and straight beaded fenders marked the 1909s and 1910s and two-lever/two-pedal controls are a sure sign. However, Ford offered a one-lever/three-pedal conversion kit later and few of the older styles are extant. For another thing, the early Ts are taller than their followers. Body panels were either of aluminum or wood.

The fenders were changed, in 1911, to a contoured pattern filling the gap between body and fender more effectively. The inner beading took on a "dog leg" curvature. The 1910 running boards had interrupted straight beads, replaced in 1911 by a diamond pattern. Bodies became steel over a wood framework. Cars came fully equipped with a brass bound windshield, top and speedometer, gas lamps and generator, horn, and three oil lamps.

Models other than the touring in the Ford line included a runabout. It came with or without a single or double rumble seat, the latter being called a tourabout. There was also a landaulet (the rear part of its top would fold down) and a town car (similarly built, except for a solid top). The driver's seat was open and many of these cars were used as taxicabs. A coupe for two completed the line.

The landaulet was omitted in 1911, and a torpedo runabout was added as a sporty job with a lowered seat and gasoline tank at the rear. Its running boards were shortened. It came with long rear fenders and a fore-door enclosure was available. Beginning in November 1911, the engine was given valve covers (this was the 1912 model, as model years ran generally from August 1 to August 1). A landmark year was 1911. That was the year in which Ford won the Selden Patent suit.

A "fore" (meaning front) door conversion kit was made available in 1912. During that year, running changes were made. The doors were made to open from the rear and the seat ridges were eliminated at the sides and back of the body. It was the final year for all-leather upholstery (the seats were still leather, leatherette was used for trim), all brass horn and lamps, brass steering wheel spider and brass-bound brass-braced windshield.

The 1913 Ford Model T fore-door touring car. (Henry Ford Museum)

The 1913 Ford bodies, now all-steel, were unique in having the doors run all the way down to the frame sills giving a squared effect. That was the last year in which buyers were offered a choice of colors: Black, red, green, blue, Pearl gray or French gray, with factory striping. The rear doors now opened from the front again and the windshield folded forward.

Built on the first moving assembly line, the 1914 Fords were distinctive in their rounded-corner doors. During the year, the seat backs (and later the seats) were made of leatherette. All cars were painted black, the bodies undergoing a dip in a tank of Japan enamel. Henry Ford declared that, if the 1915 year's production reached 300,000 cars, he would pay a rebate to every customer who bought one.

Although some early 1915 Fords had gas headlights, magneto-operated electric lights were featured that year. The bodies were given a cowl, bringing the windshield closer to the occupants. Engine hoods now had six cooling louvers per side and the rear fenders were changed from flat-topped to rounded, following the wheel contour. Later, the speedometer became an extra-cost item. Ford owners would sometimes jokingly say that they were able to tell the speed by the rattles and vibrations.

A center-door sedan was added that year. It had fold-down backs on the front seats, for easier entrance. Interiors of the sedan bodies were ornate. Bodies were built by various body makers, Fisher among them. A new coupelet was a two-passenger model with a folding top and rear deck like that of the runabout. Early 1915s had a bulb horn beneath the hood. Later, a hand-operated Klaxon horn was mounted atop the non-opening left front door.

September 1916 saw the advent of the black radiator Ford. The radiator shell was of a new contour and reflected in the new hood lines. The top now had three rectangular back curtain lights, instead of the arched design used since 1913. This was the first Model T to have the magneto-operated electric horn with its push-button, on the side of the steering column, combined with a turn switch for the headlights. The fenders were now crowned in cross section and the front ones were given a reverse curve, instead of a straight line, to their juncture with the running board. This concession to modern style was long overdue.

The 1917 Ford was continued, practically without change, through the 1922 model year. There were several subtle changes: The back of the touring car body (when viewed from the side) showed a vertical bead. In 1921, one-piece corner panels were adopted, eliminating the bead. In 1921, also, an oval gasoline tank replaced the round tank. This permitted a lowered front seat. Starting with 1919 models, demountable rims were offered as an extra-cost item. Those cars with demountables had wheels, all of the same size, taking 30-inch by 3-1/2-inch tires. The standard front tires had been 30-inches by three-inches.

During 1919, electric starters became available on enclosed models only. Those with starters were provided with dashboards carrying the lighting switch and ammeter, plus a choke-pull rod. With the 1920 models, electrical generators and equipment were made available on all models.

The 1923 Ford, which appeared in the fall of 1922, had a one-man top and slanting windshield. This was another long overdue styling change (most cars had these features in 1917 or earlier). On non-starter cars, the kerosene side and taillights were continued and demountable rims were still extra-cost items. The new tops had two, rectangular, celluloid back curtain lights arranged in a horizontal plane. In October 1922, came the luxury Fordor sedan with an aluminum body. The center-door sedan and coupe also entered the 1923 season.

With the 1924 model year, there came a taller radiator and hood. They were an inch-and-a-half higher than before. With this feature, a shield was added to surround the crank, beneath the radiator. At this time, the oil pan of the engine was extended beneath the fourth connecting rod bearing, whose cap formerly required a double offset wrench for its adjustment.

A new Ford sedan was the Tudor. It had wide doors at the forward end of the body replacing the center-door model. The price of the runabout without starter or demountables dropped to a record $290. On some days that year, a total of 10,000 Fords were turned out. The coupe also was given wider doors (now hinged at the front) and a wider rear deck.

In 1925, Ford offered 4.40-inch by 21-inch low-pressure (balloon) tires. At the same time, the automaker increased the steering gear ratio to compensate for harder steering. This was an extra cost feature. Quick-change speed bands were also provided that year.

The best-looking Ford Ts were the final 1926-1927 models. Lower in build, these cars had new one-piece paneled fenders of graceful contour, wider doors, and the left front door actually opened. Tops had plate glass back curtain windows. The coil box was moved to a position on top of the engine and the gasoline tank was relocated beneath the cowl (except Tudor models) and filled from beneath the cowl ventilator. After April 1926, the headlights were bracketed to the fenders with a tie-rod between them. Rear brake drums were now lined with asbestos, instead of the former metal-to-metal design. The car frame was lowered an inch and a half.

During 1926, optional colors, in lacquer, were offered, as well as steel spoked (wire) wheels with drop center rims. Radiator shells, on enclosed models, were nickel-plated and wood-wheeled cars were provided with a three-arm tire carrier at the rear. Natural wood wheels were an option and balloon tires were standard.

For 1927, wire wheels became standard. A wealth of special equipment items were offered including bumpers, gypsy curtains, top boots and wind wings. Despite the new styling, Ford sales continued to decline. In May 1927, production of Model Ts ended with car number 15,007,003. Then, the changeover to a new Model A began.

Answer to trivia query: The 1918 Paige Model 6-55 seven-passenger touring car was called the Essex. It was built by Paige-Detroit Motor Company.

Veteran Motorist...

S-S-S-Steam

By Walter MacIlvain

Steam car aficionados are in a class by themselves. A steam car is as different from its internal combustion engine contemporary as a diesel-motor ship is from a windjammer.

The steam car takes off from a standstill with no engine to start, no gears to shift and no clutch that grabs. The driver just advances the throttle lever beneath the wheel and, silently, the steam car is in motion. Then, there is a rapid exhaust sound, accompanied by the thumping of the pumps. You are underway. If it is a Stanley, the full elliptic spring suspension yields a surprisingly soft ride for a 1911 car.

This Model 62 Stanley steamer had smooth torque, limited vibration and no gears to shift. (Carnegie Institute photo by Howard P. Nuernberger)

Steam locomotives had been on the rails approximately 100 years before the automobile took to the road. Therefore, the most reliable early motor cars were those driven by steam. The Stanley-designed Locomobile found worldwide acceptance before the turn of the century, at a time when the Oldsmobile and Ford long-distance runabouts were graduating from one- to two-cylinder engines and thinking, haltingly, about four cylinders. Already, the Stanley/Locomobile steamers found two cylinders to be enough, as a double-acting bi-cylinder steam engine produced the same number of power impulses per revolution as an eight-cylinder explosion engine.

There were dozens of steamers in the first decade of the 20th century. The Stanley brothers were responsible for the Locomobile and Mobile and were back in the field with their own marque in 1901. Many others (Marlborough, Reading, Grout, Clark, etc.,) were more or less based on the Stanley design using a fire-tube boiler. Next to Stanley in popularity was the White, based on the Serpollet of France. It used a water tube or flash steam generator.

The Stanley's boiler consisted of a large number of tubes arranged, vertically, in a cylindrical case that was wound about with piano wire to give strength to the structure. This would be tested to 1,000-pounds steam pressure, although the operating pressure in these cars would be from 250- to 600-pounds. This pressure was kept stored up in the boiler until needed, allowing sustained road speeds up to about 45 miles per hour on the level.

The White's flash boiler, on the other hand, would generate steam instantaneously as the car ran along. The generator was roughly a coil of tubing into which the water entered at one end. It flashed into steam as it came out the other end. The White steam car was a tool maker's precision job, made to close tolerances. After 1905, a "climbing gear" or two-speed transmission was incorporated. Their cost was approximately $1,000 more than the Stanley and a wide range of body styles was offered.

The U.S. Army was interested in testing the capabilities of the 1909 White steamer. (Alfred Maticic)

Historically, Leon Serpollet of France was first to develop a steam car that could be operated by one man alone. Previous to his time (he died in 1907), two men were needed. A steersman/operator and a stoker (chauffeur to the French) were required. By means of the flash boiler, the entire operation could be handled by one individual. Thus, the word chauffeur entered our language as a car driver.

When the White family imported a Serpollet steam car, the men liked it so well that they adopted the flash boiler principle. The White car was a steamer until 1912, although gasoline powered vehicles were added in 1909. These were based on another French design, that of the Delahaye (see "The Rape of the Delahaye" by Alec Ulmann in the Bulb Horn for January, 1962).

Fred Marriott broke the world's speed record, in 1906, by driving a Stanley 107.66 miles per hour on the sands of Ormond Beach in Florida. A sportsman of the old school, the late Fred Marriott once told the author that he started with a head of 1,000-pounds of steam. The threat of blowing up the ends of the cylinders with all that pressure caused several false starts when trying for the record.

The Stanley boiler was placed under the hood, in front, and the two-cylinder engine was arranged horizontally (except in the very first models). It was in direct connection with the axle at the rear.

The White boiler was located beneath the driver's seat, with the compound cylinder engine under the hood in front. Shaft drive was located rearward, as in a gas car. As it was not necessary to build up a head of steam, a White would start from the cold more quickly than a Stanley. A condenser would turn the exhaust steam back into water and permit using it over again. Stanley did not use a condenser until 1915. The condenser resembled a gas car's radiator at the front of the vehicle.

Millionaire Howard Hughes owned this 1925 Doble steam-powered roadster pictured here at Long Beach, California in 1950. (Bob Graham)

The queen of all steam cars was the Doble. Abner Doble was Stanley's chief engineer. He left in 1913 to build an advanced car of his own in a neighboring garage. He continued in various locations until 1931. A luxurious car, it mechanically resembled a Stanley with more sophistication. Doble used a water tube boiler and electric pumps. The pilot coil operated electrically. With only 28 moving parts, 15 of them were in the engine. The semi-flash boiler was located in front. It was tested to 7,000-pounds. The Doble provided breathtaking performance.

Photo shows the Doble steam engine.

Veteran Motorist...

Slogans we have liked

By Walter MacIlvain

Certain automobile slogans were loaded with snob appeal. For example, the American Underslung was depicted as "The car for the discriminating few." The Norwalk, also with an underslung chassis models, was called "The car of absolute exclusiveness." The British Alvis was "the car of the connoisseur." For years Daimler was "The royal car," until it was dethroned by Rolls-Royce. The same phrase described the Hispano-Suiza, patronized by royalty of other lands. Benz, of Germany, titled itself "The car for emperors, the emperor of cars." The name King implied royalty, but the car was actually named for the company's founder, Charles B. King. Other emperors can be discerned in "Pathfinder the great, king of twelves," Austin's "The highway king" and Moline's "the king of the road."

The aristocracy was a favorite theme, exemplified by Isotta-Fraschini: "The aristocrat of automobiles" (in Italy, of course). On a lower scale, the original Empire runabout was promoted as "The little aristocrat."

On the other end of the scale, the Orient Buckboard was advertised as "The cheapest automobile in the world" in a day (1903) when cheapness had a lightly different connotation. Durant's Star stressed "Low cost transportation," too.

The idea of worldwide acceptance was implicit in the Curved Dash Oldsmobile's "The sun never sets on the Oldsmobile," and also in Ford's "The universal car." Herbert Austin's little Seven was "Famous the world over," while the Mors was "Known all over the world." Studebaker called itself "Vehicle makers for the world." The Gobron-Brillie's "The finest automobile in the world" and Duesenberg's "The world's finest motor car" implied universal appeal.

Some makers expressed provincialism, such as Rover, "One of Britain's fine cars"; the Roamer, "America's smartest car"; Bliss, "The finest American car;" and Simplex, "Made in New York City." An extreme example of provincialism was the Marathon, "Built in the South for the South."

Somewhat optimistic guarantees were spelled out in such cases as Rainier, "Guaranteed free of repairs for one year" and the Tincher, "Guaranteed for three years." The Bianchi, in 1923, was "Guaranteed for 50,000 miles" and the British H.E. was "Backed by five years guarantee." The Gardner was known as "The guaranteed car." The best waranty of all was that of Acme, "Guaranteed for life." Own an Acme? You're covered!

Mechanical perfection was often expressed, such as the Elgin, "Built like a watch" and "The car of the hour." "The full-jeweled Corbin" referred to generous use of ball bearings. "The mechanical masterpiece" was the original Marmon. The word "Acme" meant "The highest degree of mechanical perfection." Cleveland was, optimistically, "The car without a weak spot," and Elcar was "A well built car, tuned to the times."

The 1916 Metz Model 25 roadster was advertised as "The quality car." (Henry Austin Clark, Jr. collection)

Locomobile was "Easily the best built car in America"; the Mora was "Mechanically right"; and the Stuyvesant was "The car of precision." We all know that "No Rolls-Royce ever wore out."

Certain slogans reflected features of the product, i.e., "The waterless Knox"; the "No clutch to slip, no gears to strip" Metz; the "It spins like a top" Adams Farwell rotary engine; Enger, the "Twin unit twelve;" "The white line radiator belongs to the Stearns"; American Simplexes "The valveless two-cycle car" (later Amplex); and "The car that has no valves"; the two-cycle Elmore. Knight-engined cars were also valveless in the usual sense. If the radiator insignia of a Panhard contained the letters S-S, it meant "Sans Soupapes" (without valves). The short-lived Handley-Knight boasted "America's finest Knight motored car," and the Willys-Knight advertised "The engine that improves with use." Simplicity of control gave the Oldsmobile driver "Nothing to watch but the road."

Longevity was expressed by such phrases as "Peugeot, the everlasting car;" Velie, "Long life;" Marion, "Built to run and last for years;" the Corbin "Never wears out;" and the Aerocar, "The car for today, tomorrow and for years to come." Incidentally, the Renault was titled "The car" (or Le Car) early on.

A bit of history turned up in "Lambert, the father of friction drive;" Selden, "Built by the father of them all;" the Panhard, "Famous since 1889;" and Riley, "As old as the industry, as modern as the hour."

Others we liked were, "There's a touch of tomorrow in all that Cole does today"; "The quality goes clear through," Dort; "Toujours Pret," Bernet; and "The first real successor to the horse," Reliable-Dayton. But, when the little Metz runabout was advertised as "The quality car," me thought they protested too much!

To end this on a positive note, we give the honors to "The superlative Spyker, guaranteed forever!"

Veteran Motorist...

The starter

By Walter MacIlvain

A gasoline engine does not start by spontaneous combustion. It must be rotated by some extraneous means in order to get it firing.

The earliest and most direct means was the so-called "arm-strong starter," a strong arm applied to a crooked handle at the side or front of the vehicle, according to the position of the engine. The crank was a dangerous instrument that accounted for many broken arms and an occasional broken jaw, especially if the operator neglected to retard the spark.

The self-starter came in about 1912. However, Winton had an air starter in 1906, along with other devices operated by compressed air. This maker continued its air starter right up to 1915, when it finally acceded to the demand for an electrical device, which was first offered as an option.

The starting crank disappeared from some cars in 1913, notably Cadillac and Haynes. However, it could still be found in the tool box for emergency use. Packard left it in place until 1913 and Ford until 1927. In the 1930s, most automakers had sufficient faith in their electrics to dispense with the handle altogether, to the consternation of the backyard mechanic.

In the 1910-1915 era, some fearful and wonderful starting devices appeared. They ranged from a handle on the floor (resembling a detonating device for dynamite) on the InterState, to a push-button on the dash. There were acetylene starters, air starters and spring wind-up mechanisms which, when released, rotated the engine once or twice. It was an inventor's paradise until 1911. Then, "Boss" Kettering of Dayton Engineering Laboratories, with the cooperation of Henry and Wilbur Leland of Cadillac, arrived at an electrical assembly that really worked time after time after time. The Delco single-unit starting, lighting and igniting system was placed on the 1912 Cadillac production model. It made feasible the ownership and operation of automobiles by women.

Immediately, nearly all the other manufacturers mounted the band wagon with some form of electric starting. Some of these involved the replacement of the engine flywheel by a gigantic starter-generator. Some used the Dyneto system operated by a silent chain.

For a few years, the inexpensive cars stayed with the hand crank. Then, Maxwell, Chevrolet and others offered electric starting (electric lighting usually went along with it) as an extra-cost option. Ford held out the longest, until 1919. However, at the $290 base price in 1925, the Ford runabout still had no electrics beyond the magneto-operated headlights. Certain big cars disdained offering an electric starter for a short period, reasoning that their owners could well afford chauffeurs to crank their cars.

Ah, yes, the thrill of an automobile ride for many of us youngsters began with the whir of the starter. Remember the high-pitched sound of the early Studebaker starter? Contrast this with that of the four-cylinder Dodge, which made no sound at all. Also remember the 1913

Oakland, the sound of which would slowly rise and fall, accompanied by intermittent dimming of the lights until the engine finally caught.

Many and varied were the aftermarket devices available to the owner of the Model T Ford. They ranged all the way from spring-wound contraptions to those allowing you to crank it from the seat. MoToR's yellow pages were full of them.

The starter pedal of my dad's Buick was a long one. Pushing it down would first advance the starter pinion into the flywheel. At this point, the electric motor was activated and began to rotate the engine. Known as the manual shift, it was virtually impossible to strip the flywheel gear teeth. And there were no springs to break, as was the case with Bendix drives.

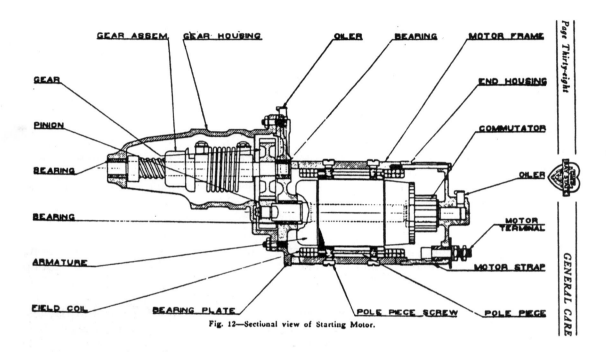

Fig. 12—Sectional view of Starting Motor.

Illustration showing Bendix drive and Delco-geared starter.

The Bendix drive was invented by Joseph Bijur and developed by Vincent Bendix. It was licensed to the Eclipse Machine Company, which marketed it starting in 1914. It became popular on cars equipped with separate unit starting-lighting systems. All the operator had to do, was push a button and the starter motor did the rest. It automatically advanced a pinion into engagement with the flywheel gear by means of a patented spiral tooth arrangement. With much wear, sometimes the pinion would jam and lock up the engine. An experienced driver would turn off the ignition, put his car into high gear, and gently rock the car, principally backwards, until the locked gear would release with a click.

Hoping that the Bendix spring was not broken, he would then climb back into the car and try again. The lock-up was undoubtedly a sign that one or more of the flywheel teeth were chipped and no further trouble would be experienced until the engine happened to stop with that particular flywheel defect in line with the Bendix gear again.

Flywheel teeth, in the cheaper cars, were cut right into the iron casting itself. In the better cars, a steel ring gear was shrunk onto a groove machined into the flywheel for the purpose. The best method of repairing broken teeth was to mill a groove into the casting and shrink on a ring gear. Such a steel gear was practically good for the life of the car.

The alternate manual shift and Bendix drive reigned supreme for many years. The solenoid came along to replace the manual shift and the Bendix drive was enhanced by the Folo-Thru device. It allowed continued cranking when only one cylinder caught. And that's about where it stands today.

Veteran Motorist...

Life with a veteran car

By Walter MacIlvain

The care and feeding of an antique automobile is a matter of (1) getting to know it and how to cope with its eccentricities, (2) acquiring confidence, (3) learning how to shunpike in getting from place to place and (4) learning how to handle your public.

The act of moving the spark lever sometimes fires one of the cylinders, but often only if conditions are just right. (Old Cars)

First of all, how do you start the thing? My antique or veteran car was built before the self-starter era, so first we had to learn how to grasp the starting handle so as not to get hurt if the car kicks or backfires. You simply place the thumb on the same side of the handle as the four fingers so when you pull up and it backfires, the crank will slip out of your hand without taking the arm with it. Do not push down on the crank unless you have absolute confidence that no backfire can take place, as you could break more than your arm! We know one man who pushes down on his crank with his foot. Apparently, a broken leg would be more acceptable to him than a broken arm.

One starting procedure is like this: Give the car a full choke for as many pull-ups as you have cylinders, before you turn on the switch (no backfire is possible with the switch off). Adjust the throttle to a moderate idling speed, enrich the mixture slightly, then turn on the switch and retard the spark all the way. The act of moving the spark lever will sometimes fire one of the cylinders and, if conditions are just right, the engine could start. In this case, you quickly advance the spark to keep it running. In case it didn't "start on the spark," one or two half-turns of the crank should have it running. Then, after advancing the spark, switch it from "BAT" to "MAG" and it should smooth right out.

Acquiring confidence is just a matter of practice. The more you drive your antique, the more confident you become. These old cars, especially from 1908 on, were fairly reliable. Breakdowns seldom occurred in day-to-day driving. The biggest bugaboo was with the tires, but that anxiety has been practically eliminated. Spring breakage was another, but modern roads have greatly diminished that hazard. If you have no magneto, of course, you have to keep the battery in mind. Also, check for gasoline in the tank, oil in the crankcase and air in the tires.

If an engine should refuse to run or stop on the highway, there are two things to look for: The car is not getting gas or not getting ignition. Look for a broken or plugged fuel line, absence of fuel in the tank or a faulty vacuum tank, if so equipped. If you have gasoline in the carburetor, then it must be the ignition. A broken wire, loose connection, short circuit, points not functioning properly or condenser or coil burned out could cause problems.

A broken wire, loose connection or short circuit could cause problems. (Larry Caverns)

Shunpiking is a fine art. It starts with a study of your maps. If your car will do the minimum speed limit comfortably and traffic is light, the highway will be the quickest way to go. Just hug the right side of the road and watch your mirror. If not, then country roads and traffic lights will be your lot. One eye should still be in the mirror. A periodic pull-over to let other cars pass is a must. Some people really might be in a hurry and it's a sin to block traffic. Cars in a group must keep well separated from one another to allow drivers to "duck into line." At stake here is not only our own safety, but the future of the hobby.

Sad as it seems, not everybody respects antique cars. Some even resent being held up by them. Thus, we must conduct ourselves accordingly. It is best for all concerned not to give any offense. Many will show appreciation and wave and toot the horn good naturedly. We respond in kind. It is most helpful to have someone along who will do the honors and answer questions intelligently, in case you are stopped by the roadside.

Everyday mechanical maintenance, more important than cosmetics if you drive your car, consists of keeping all reservoirs filled, screwing down the grease cups or refilling them, changing the oil frequently, using the of can where needed and listening to what the car has to tell you. A knock or slackening off of the engine speed means loose connecting rods. Light tapping sounds will be heard if the valves are healthy. A heavy thump in the motor, under power, indicates loose main bearings. Undue smoking usually means the car needs piston rings, although other causes in later cars include fuel pump diaphragm failure or plugged oil drain holes (if the valves are in the head). Oil can also seep by loose valve stem guides (hot oil will go where there is no hole). If you are using more than a quart in 200 miles, you'd better look into it.

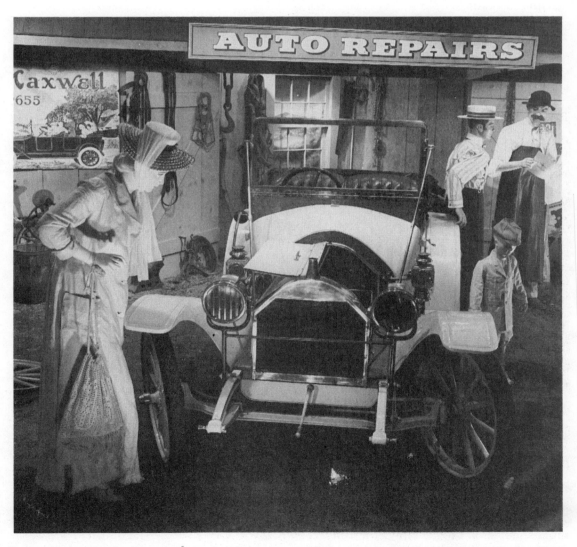

Owning and caring for an antique car can give you no end of amusement; it is ideal therapy for loneliness or depression.

Owning and caring for an antique car can give you no end of amusement; it is ideal therapy for loneliness or depression. There is always something constructive to do to improve a car's operation or appearance. Brass polishing can take a full eight-hour day at the beginning of the season, after which one can easily brighten it as required. Polishing brass is merely removing the oxidation to allow the natural shine of the metal to come through. Small parts, such as curtain fasteners, can be cleaned with very fine steel wool, but don't let anyone catch you polishing the lamps that way! Plastic curtain lights (windows) can be brought back with acetone or lacquer thinner. Natural wood can be made presentable with furniture polish.

A buzz or rattle tells us something. Perhaps a hole in sheet metal needs a rubber grommet or the re-routing of a copper tube. Noisy foot boards can often be couched in thin rubber.

Then, too, you can carefully play with the ignition system. A magneto is a marvelous unit containing a complete ignition system, but if it hasn't been rebuilt for many years, it may seize after running hot and cooling down again. The newer insulating materials will obviate this. New wiring is a must, particularly the leads to the spark plugs, as they carry thousands of volts. This pressure will easily cause shorts between wires or between a wire and adjacent metal. The trembler points of the spark coils will need periodic adjustment. Use the lightest possible, pressure on the adjustment that will keep it firing.

And have fun!

Veteran Motorist...

Tired wheels

By Walter MacIlvain

The boy was Charles Goodyear. Using his mother's kitchen as a laboratory and her cooking utensils as tools, he discovered the art of curing rubber in 1844 in his home in Woburn, Mass.

Molded rubber products soon proliferated. By a few years later, Goodyear was making such items as poker chips, horseshoe pads and solid rubber tires for bicycles, racing sulkies and the like.

Making an early Goodyear tire was hard work.

When the automobile came along, rubber tires were chosen over steel for their cushioned ride and better traction on the cobblestone streets of the day. But, not until 1888 did pneumatic tires appear. J.B. Dunlop, in England, devised them to cushion the ride of his invalid son's wheelchair. Their use quickly caught on for bicycles and horse racing sulkies. They were patented for automobile use in December 1892.

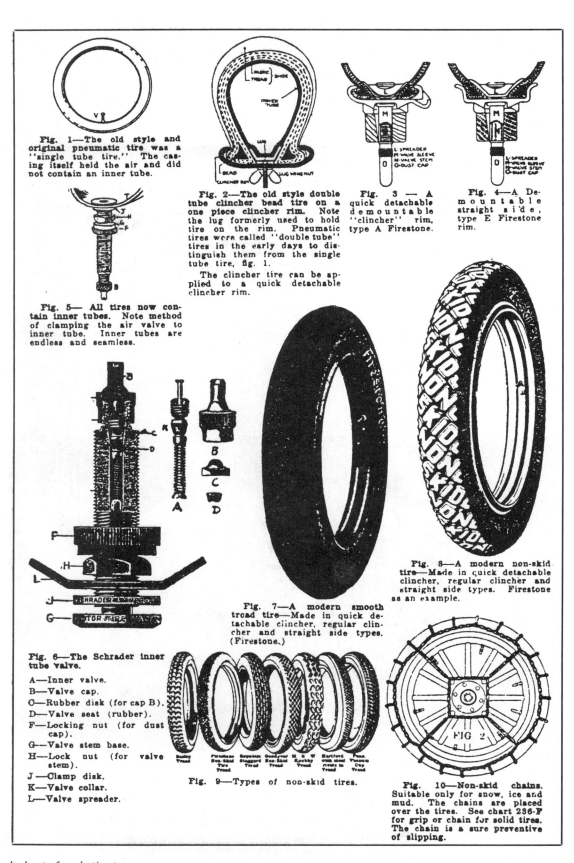

Fig. 1—The old style and original pneumatic tire was a "single tube tire." The casing itself held the air and did not contain an inner tube.

Fig. 2—The old style double tube clincher bead tire on a one piece clincher rim. Note the lug formerly used to hold tire on the rim. Pneumatic tires were called "double tube" tires in the early days to distinguish them from the single tube tire, fig. 1.

The clincher tire can be applied to a quick detachable clincher rim.

Fig. 3 — A quick detachable demountable "clincher" rim, type A Firestone.

Fig. 4—A Demountable straight side, type E Firestone rim.

Fig. 5— All tires now contain inner tubes. Note method of clamping the air valve to inner tube. Inner tubes are endless and seamless.

Fig. 6—The Schrader inner tube valve.

A—Inner valve.
B—Valve cap.
C—Rubber disk (for cap B).
D—Valve seat (rubber).
F—Locking nut (for dust cap).
G—Valve stem base.
H—Lock nut (for valve stem).
J—Clamp disk.
K—Valve collar.
L—Valve spreader.

Fig. 7—A modern smooth tread tire—Made in quick detachable clincher, regular clincher and straight side types. (Firestone.)

Fig. 8—A modern non-skid tire—Made in quick detachable clincher, regular clincher and straight side types. Firestone as an example.

Fig. 9—Types of non-skid tires.

Fig. 10—Non-skid chains. Suitable only for snow, ice and mud. The chains are placed over the tires. See chart 236-F for grip or chain for solid tires. The chain is a sure preventive of slipping.

A chart of early tire types.

Firestone Pneumatic Tires and Tubes

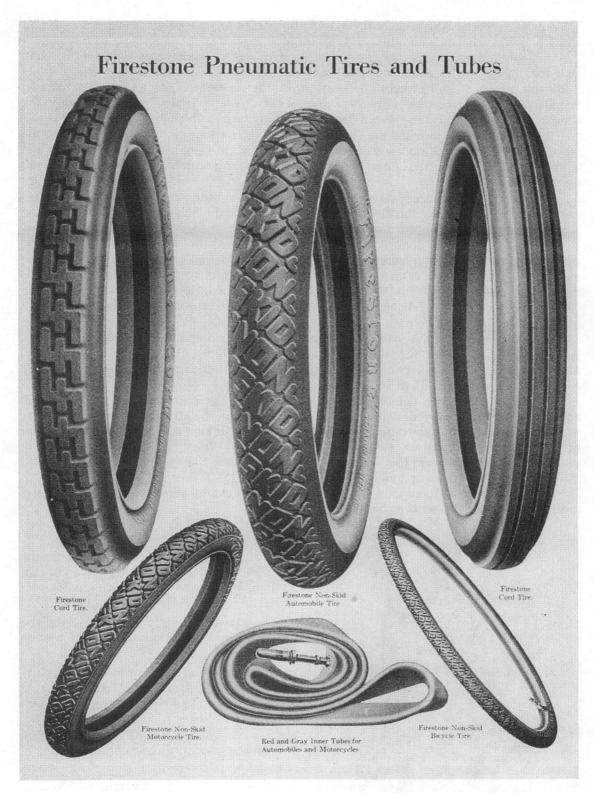

Firestone pneumatic tires and tubes.

August Schrader was already there with the pneumatic tire valve. It was first used, in 1844, for sea divers' suits and then, in 1891, for bicycle tires.

Michelin, of France, claimed priority for production of pneumatic automobile tires and, also, for ring-type rubber molds. Their tires were used on the winning Peugeot in the Paris-Bordeaux race in 1895. However, the Hartford Rubber Company, in the United States, had installed pneumatics on one of Charles Duryea's cars in March 1895. They were used on the winning Duryea in the Times-Herald Thanksgiving Day race in Chicago.

Thomas B. Jeffery patented the clincher tire and rim on June 16, 1891, assigning it to the bicycle making firm of Gormully & Jeffery Company. An associated G & J Tire Company was later to be absorbed by the United States Rubber Company, which continued the G & J tire for many years.

Single tube bolt-on tires were used on the earliest motor vehicles. Double tube tires came along in 1902, using the clincher rim adapted from the bicycle trade. Even then, the mushroom-like early casings wore out in a few days usage.

Another Englishman, John F. Palmer invented the cord tire. It was first known as the thread tire, to distinguish it from casings made from a woven piece of cloth fabric. The first machinery for these was set up at the Silvertown Rubber Company in England. The cord tire came to the United States with Diamond Rubber Company and the B.F. Goodrich Company in 1910. When Goodrich advertised the Silvertown Cord tire to be guaranteed for 3,000 miles, a milestone had been reached,

Goodrich claims to have made the first pneumatic truck tire in 1911, although it was Paul W. Litchfield, of Goodyear, who developed it for trucks and buses. The Goodyear "Wingfoot" Akron-to-Boston Express service was inaugurated in 1916. Prior to that, most trucks were governed to speeds of 12-15 or so miles per hour.

The demountable rim dates back to the early 1900s, but was not adopted as standard equipment until several years later. The clincher rim came the straight-side rim and, along with that, the Q-D (or quick-detachable). This had an outer ring that would take a clincher tire when turned one way and a straight-side when turned the other. The inner, solid part of the rim could be converted to straight-side by using rubber filler pieces or by simply filling the clincher part with a length of half-inch rope.

The split rim of the teens gave the motorist a new set of annoyances, but with the proper tools, was a boon to faster tire changing.

An early auto wheel and straight side rim.

A gentleman named C.A. Shaler developed a method of repairing tires by the vulcanizing process using electricity or steam. He also marketed a kit, lit by a match, that enabled a motorist to vulcanize a patch to a tube.

Goodyear claims to have pioneered the use of rayon in tires, followed by nylon, then polyester.

Our old friend, the Rambler, had an early version of the modern idea of wheels detachable at the hub in 1908. However, their large wheels were heavy to-handle and, when the Jeffery car superseded the Rambler in 1914, the idea became dormant until its revival in the 1920s.

The struggle of man versus tires continued. Flat tires were the bane of early motoring. One hesitated to accept the offer of a ride from his neighbor out of fear that a tire might blow and that he would be expected to pay the $40 to $60 for a new one. This conversation, during a ride through the country, would be frequently punctuated by a reference to a spot where a puncture had been repaired or a blow-out took place. May the day of the "uncertain pneumatic" be gone forever!

The balloon tire was pioneered in England by Dunlop and Palmer. This happened back in 1909, when fat, low pressure (30 pounds versus 60-80 pounds) tires appeared briefly. They raised such a ruckus with steering geometry and clearances that the idea was abandoned until the mid-1920s. Then, with improved science and knowledge, balloons and four wheel brakes came along at about the same time. Moon and Cole were early birds with them. Balloons were made standard by Buick in 1925. They were optional with Ford and others.

The demountable rim was superseded by the drop center type in the late 1920s. During World War II, it was reported that, in Washington, D.C., several cars were running around with no tubes in their tires. A few years later, tubeless tires were the "in" thing. To accomplish this, it was necessary to seal the valve mountings to the inside of the rims. They were welded air-tight.

Steel belted tires came to us from Europe. Goodyear had them in 1977. Modern tires are either bias ply, bias belted or steel belted. Bias means that the cords run diagonally around the casing. Radial means that the cords run from the center outward, at right angles to the perimeter. Bias belted tires are similar to bias ply, but with the addition of two or more strips or belts wrapped around the perimeter, beneath the tread. Radial belted are wrapped around the outside with fabric or steel belts, giving better riding and handling qualities, as well as improved mileage.

Size markings are in centimeters for width and in inches for wheel diameter. The Department of Transportation (DOT) requires safety markings in code; letters A, B or C indicate the safe maximum speed. A = 115 miles per hour, B = 100-110 miles per hour and C = 85-95 miles per hour. Numbers indicate life expectancy of the tread (10 points = 3,000 miles). A 120 rating indicates a life of 36,000 miles.

The famous Firestone Non-skid tire tread.

The "schoolmaster": R.E. Olds

By Ralph Atkinson

There is one man in the early history of the automobile industry who had such an influence that he was called the "School Master of Motordom."

Ransom Ely Olds, like any good schoolmaster, taught the fundamentals of his profession. In this case, he taught the rudiments of automobile production. His classroom was the automobile factory itself. He founded both Reo and Oldsmobile. The latter firm was founded 90 years ago and celebrated its 95th anniversary on August 21, 1992.

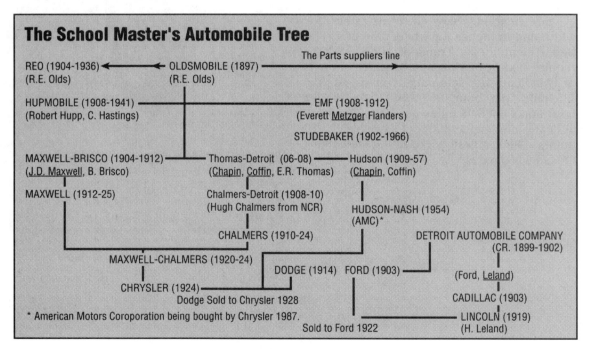

The School Master's Automobile Tree

The Parts suppliers line

REO (1904-1936) ◄——— ◄— OLDSMOBILE (1897) ————————————————
(R.E. Olds)   (R.E. Olds)

HUPMOBILE (1908-1941) ——————— EMF (1908-1912)
(Robert Hupp, C. Hastings)   (Everett Metzger Flanders)

STUDEBAKER (1902-1966)

MAXWELL-BRISCO (1904-1912) ——— Thomas-Detroit (06-08) ——— Hudson (1909-57)
(J.D. Maxwell, B. Brisco)   (Chapin, Coffin, E.R. Thomas)   (Chapin, Coffin)

MAXWELL (1912-25)   Chalmers-Detroit (1908-10)   HUDSON-NASH (1954)
                                (Hugh Chalmers from NCR)   (AMC)*

                                CHALMERS (1910-24)   DETROIT AUTOMOBILE COMPANY
                                                                  (CR. 1899-1902)

MAXWELL-CHALMERS (1920-24)   DODGE (1914)   FORD (1903) ———   (Ford, Leland)

CHRYSLER (1924)   Dodge Sold to Chrysler 1928   CADILLAC (1903)

* American Motors Coroporation being bought by Chrysler 1987.   LINCOLN (1919)
                                Sold to Ford 1922   (H. Leland)

A chart showing the "family tree" of R.E. Olds and the firms that he worked for and within the automobile industry.

Olds, along with his pupils and auto parts suppliers, learned how to build automobiles so well that his basic techniques or methods are still used today.

The "schoolmaster" is directly or indirectly responsible for at least nine major marque name plates or makes, several of which are still being manufactured today. In fact, there is at least one marque which he had an influence in creating in each of the "Big 3" line ups today. He is also indirectly responsible for American Motors Corporation, if one counts one old the parent companies of the 1954 merger that became AMC.

The automobile had been around for a little over a decade in Europe (since 1886) when Olds opened his "school" (along with his factory) in the late 1890s. Production of automobiles at that time was still an extremely slow, cumbersome and meticulous process. Olds had already built a few horseless carriages, ranging from steam to electric, and finally concentrated on building gasoline-powered cars. One wonders, why did he build steam and electric cars when his family's business was building gasoline engines?

There is also a question as to when he first started producing automobiles to sell and when he officially founded his first automobile company. Some say it was as early as 1896. Others say it was in the spring of 1897. However, the most accepted date is August 21, 1897. No matter what date you choose, R.E. Olds did not leave much of a mark until his first real big break came when his factory burned down.

He had wanted to build an automobile without using highly skilled laborers or craftsmen, since the best skilled craftsmen in the United States at the turn of the century were halfway across the country. Most lived in industrial New England. Olds thought that anybody who was somewhat competent could build the kind of automobile he wanted to build. It was simple in design, easy to assemble, lightweight, inexpensive and powerful enough to meet the needs of the typical motorist.

The car that made R.E. Olds a household name was the famous Curved Dash model. Could that be R.E. Olds at the tiller?

The idea of an inexpensively priced car went against the grain of his financial backers. They wanted Olds to build expensive cars. Since they controlled the purse strings, they also controlled Olds' business. However, after that disastrous fire, they had no choice, but to produce his inexpensive car.

With most of his troubles behind him, Olds implemented several new and fresh ideas for building automobiles. His approach was a methodical one. He invented this country's (if not the world's) first true automobile factory. Back then, automobile factories were usually slightly worked-over barns. The Olds works was totally different.

Olds also assigned workers specific tasks or duties. Then, he obtained outside suppliers to ship certain items, such as transmissions and additional engines, to his factory for assembly. In simple terms, the "schoolmaster" farmed out part of the building process to other concerns. His factory was merely an assembly center of all the major components. This saved time, money and space. This process, by the way, is still very much in use today.

Olds was directly responsible for two major brands of automobiles himself. His former pupils and main parts suppliers, along with some of their business associates, were responsible for at least seven other marques.

There were many people who were trained by this man. Most likely, more of the influential people in the auto industry of his day received their training under him than from any other auto pioneer. Among them were Johnathan D. Maxwell, a mechanical engineer who earlier worked with Elwood Haynes and the Apperson Brothers on their first car. He later got involved with Benjamin Brisco and they formed Maxwell-Brisco, which later became Maxwell. Maxwell ultimately evolved into Chrysler Corporation.

Another student, Robert Craig Hupp, was the engineer who founded Hupmobile and invented the fuel gauge. Charles D. Hastings, the businessman who became head of Hupmobile, was also a protege of Olds. Another was Howard B. Coffin, an engineer and designer who co-founded Thomas-Detroit (Chalmers) and, more importantly, Hudson Motor Car Company. Coffin was the first person who stressed standardization of parts in the automobile industry. Another associate engineer, Roy D. Chapin, co-founded both Thomas-Detroit and Hudson. He later became president of Hudson. Chapin also served as Secretary of Commerce. He was in charge of road construction in President Herbert Hoover's cabinet. Chapin learned the practical aspects and the business end of the automobile industry from Olds.

Finally, William Metzger was probably among the most important and least remembered students of the schoolmaster. He was the first true car salesman! Metzger would later go on to sell Cadillacs and EMFs (Everitt Metzger Flanders), which were marketed by Studebaker dealers.

Other people who learned from the schoolmaster included his parts suppliers. Henry M. Leland supplied the majority of engines for Olds' cars. Leland would later go on to form Cadillac and, later, Lincoln. Leland is best remembered as the master of precision and the father of standardization in the automobile industry. The Dodge brothers, John and Horace, built mostly transmissions for Oldsmobiles. They would move on to Ford, before forming their own motor car company.

Many people paid visits to Olds' school/factory. It has been said that a young Henry Ford paid frequent visits. It is even possible that Henry Ford pulled the first corporate raid. Ford may have raided the Olds school to take some of its main suppliers away (the Dodge Brothers and Henry Leland among others).

The Ford/Dodge Brothers legacy is basically well known. However, the Ford/Leland association, during one of Ford's first two automobile ventures (the Detroit Automobile Company), is unfortunately cloudy. It was very brief, due to a conflict of egos. Leland gained control of Ford's company and transformed it into Cadillac.

There truly was no single person in the entire automobile industry's early days who contributed more to the beginning of the industry itself than Ransom E. Olds. He was the "Father of Mass Production"; the first producer of low-priced horseless carriages; the builder of the first true automobile factory and training grounds; and the inventor of an early motorized lawn mower.

Mrs. Bernice Olds Roe of East Lansing, Michigan, the daughter of Ransom E. Olds, at a display honoring her father. (Automotive Old Timers)

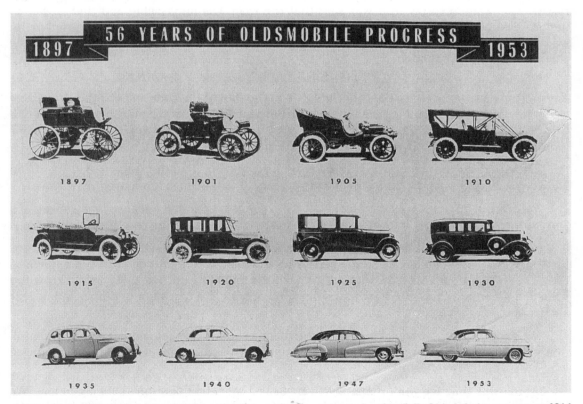

A sampling of the "schoolmaster's" namesake products, some made after R.E. Olds left the company. (Oldsmobile Motor Division)

Locomobile was first up Pikes Peak

(This story was originally published by Locomobile to publicize the first ascent of Pikes Peak by automobile on August 12, 1901. W.B. Felker and C.A. Yont were those involved. Fifteen years elapsed between the time of their climb and completion of the Pikes Peak Auto highway. The Locomobile which made the ascent was restored to perfect operating condition and factory-new appearance by James B. Howell of Denver. It was then displayed at the Colorado Car Museum in Manitou Springs, until it was sold to a Denver car collector. The story of the climb is in the words of Mr. Felker. The photos are Mr. Yont's. The material was supplied by Byron and Lois Akers, who operated the Colorado Car Museum for many years.)

"Ever since reading about the failure of an attempt to climb Pike's Peak with a motor carriage, I had wanted to try it. It was said that the road was impassable and that it was an impossible undertaking. My companion, Mr. C.A. Yont, was a good amateur photographer. He was not in the habit of starting anything which he could not finish; even his style of handling a camera gives you confidence.

"The ascent is 17 miles long and the altitude reached is 14,147 feet. We left Denver Sunday morning and steamed to Cascade, which is at the foot of the pass and 86 miles from Denver. While filling our gasoline tanks, preparatory to an early morning start, some of the old-timers had considerable fun at our expense, guessing how far up we would get. We wore our most determined air, but it seemed to make little impression.

"They told us that since the cog railroad was built in 1891 the wagon road has been allowed to go to ruin and, that for the last two years, it had been seldom used by wagons.

"We started up at six o'clock, August 12. The date is mentioned because I may speak of a snowstorm later on and it may have been hot in some sections of the country.

"We had gotten about one-quarter of a mile when I saw the only signs of weakening in our photographer. The road had been washed by the rushing waters into gullies deep enough to roll a barrel. We would straddle one with the wheels and start up. The gully would grow too wide and we would drop into it, perhaps being hung high and dry on our compensating gear and front axle.

"We spent three hours in going the first two miles and no horse could excite our admiration more than that steam engine did. She would snort, spit steam and kick back the rocks; why, we just couldn't give up.

"About this time we were reminded that our last meal had been the evening before. We ate three sandwiches and a pickle, which was all we had until we were within 40 rods of the top.

Taking water at the Halfway House. (Photo courtesy Colorado Car Museum)

"We reached the Half-way House about 11 a.m. We thought that the worst part of the climb might be over, but a lady in charge pointed up the mountain about two miles and said she was afraid we might have some trouble at Windy Point and on the W. From where we stood, that W looked about as savage a piece of scenery as a crooked piece of lightning. I just took off my coat and crawled under the wagon and felt of every bolt and nut and piece of machinery about it. We were cheered on our start from here by a very beautiful piece of bridge work. I threw the steering lever over to the outside, put on a full head of steam, and then helped one rear wheel with one hand while holding the steering lever with the other. Yont put his shoulder to the back of the machine, and at the word, we did business with that bridge. We pretty nearly had a runaway right here. Yont was kicked by a log thrown up by the steering wheel and, when the machine jumped, I was straightened out like a flapping flag. I hung on and managed to get the steam shut off. Yont is an engineer by profession, but his eyes popped when we made it. It was the worst bridge he ever saw. I lived in Leadville for nine years and have seen some rather bogus bridges, but that beat me.

"Grand View is what the name implies. If you get off the road a few feet, you can drop 4,000 feet and not bump any on the way down. Our picture could not do it justice.

"It is not necessary to put up any signs at Windy Point. One knows when they get there. I understand that Old Boreas got his start in business there. He may not have been there when we arrived, but the man left in charge was certainly keeping things moving and business must have been good.

"Of course, when you get above timber line, there is no surface soil in sight. There may have been some that high up, but nature has kindly put it aside and covered it with sharp rocks, all the way in size from a hen's egg to a box-car. When your rear wheels slip on the hen's egg size you wish they were box-car size and, when you have to lift your machine over them, you wish they were the hen's egg size.

"The W did not prove as formidable as it looked from below, but we realized why the lady at the Halfway House smiled when she said we might have trouble. I know the man who built the Pike's Peak road. He is mild mannered and kind, but he wasn't worrying much about people's safety when he built that W. Turn a letter W sideways and you have an idea how it looks, but that don't give you an idea of how you feel when you are on one of the points of the W about 13,000 feet up in the air.

"About a mile from the top, when everything, but our spirits, was high, one of those good old north westerners you read about struck us. How it did blow and snow! We put on overcoats and huddled about the fire-box to keep from freezing, hoping it would blow over. We finally decided that it would be safer to climb up above it and get next to the sun again. This we did, but it was miserable, cold work; the top side of a snowstorm is not only better looking, but more comfortable.

"All this time our Loco had been responding to every call; no distended nostrils and tired droop of a head; no sympathetic rubbing of bruised hoofs or mental reservations as to large measures of oats; just a pressure on the throttle and a cheerful choo! choo! that knew no tired feeling. Like good horsemen, we had taken every care that our steed should have plenty of food. We now began to realize that man's machinery requires fuel and that we had not properly calculated the amount of steam that can be gotten out of three sandwiches and a pickle. The air is rare at 14,000 feet and hard to get. A few minutes' tussle with a bad place in the road makes you think you have asthma, pneumonia and all kinds of lung trouble. We struggled to within 40 rods of the top, where Mr. Yont succumbed to the altitude and lack of food.

It looked like a hard proposition, but, as sick as Mr. Yont was, he insisted that we could make it. Luckily, a Mr. Bigger, of Cascade, came along on horseback and offered to go to the signal station at the top and get food for us. With this help, we rushed the last few rods and came bumping around the corner of the U.S. signal station in a cloud of steam. The crowd just leaving on the cog road were not as surprised at seeing us as we thought they ought to be.

"We stopped long enough to take pictures and food. It took three cups of hot coffee a piece to thaw us out.

The Locomobile at the summit of Pikes Peak, 14,147 feet above sea level. (Photo courtesy Colorado Car Museum)

"The return trip was perhaps more dangerous, but not such hard work. If our brake had given out, we certainly would have broken all records for the down trip, but would not have lived to claim it. We were tired and impatient to get down out of the clouds and cold before dark and so took many chances that perhaps might not have been exactly prudent. There seemed no limit to the abuse which the Loco would stand. Once in a while, a bunch of rocks would throw us up into the air and we would come down with the brake jammed hard and the engine reversed, not altogether certain whether we could stop her or not. One of these drops broke a leaf to the front spring. This was the only accident we had and it did not inconvenience us. Coasting downhill on a smooth road is exciting, but coming down a grade 17 miles long, pitched and tossed about like a small boat in a storm, is hard work. You get tired hanging on. At the Halfway House we lit our side-lights and came the balance of the way in the dark. We had gone over the road so carefully in the morning that we thought we knew every inch of it, but we found many bumps that we had missed going up. Our brake became so hot that we could smell the burning leather and the metal parts could not be touched by the hand. We used about seven gallons of gasoline going up, coming down we used nothing but nerve. We had no horse to sympathize with, but we felt so proud of our Loco that our feelings had plenty of exercise.

"We reached Cascade at 9:30 p.m. We were too tired to stand around and brag much and the way we hustled to bed made some of the summer resorters doubt that we had just taken our Loco to the highest altitude ever reached by an automobile.

"Leaving Cascade, early the next morning, we had a beautiful coast down through Ute Pass to Manitou. Taking breakfast at Colorado Springs, we jogged along, arriving at Denver at four o'clock. Our extra tire, which we had tied on in the front, broke loose and was torn to pieces by the rocks. We did not have to make a repair of any kind on the trip."

The car rolls over a characteristic piece of land above the timber line. (Photo courtesy of Colorado Car Museum)

Oldsmobile before World War II

By Dennis Casteele

Oldsmobile dates from the organizational meeting of Olds Motor Vehicle Company on August 21, 1897, in Lansing, Michigan. R.E. Olds brought a great deal of mechanical experience to the formation of Olds. His partners, mostly prominent Lansing businessmen, supplied financial and organizational backing. The board of directors said "build one carriage in as nearly a perfect manner as possible."

At least four carriages were built. One survives in the Smithsonian collection and is now, fittingly, on loan to the R.E. Olds Transportation Museum in Lansing.

A 1900 Curved Dash Oldsmobile represents the first mass-produced domestic automobile. (Old Cars)

By 1899, Olds Motor Vehicle Company was merged into the larger Olds Motor Works, based at Detroit, near Belle Isle. A fire destroyed the plant in the spring of 1901. Intense lobbying brought construction of a new Lansing plant.

In 1900, notices of a special runabout with an Oldsmobile nameplate appeared in the press. Dubbed the "Curved Dash" (due to its unique frontal design) this machine put America on wheels. Changes in the Curved Dash came as they were needed, not by model-year. It remained in the Olds catalog until 1907, by which time it was a much changed car.

The Model R was the first Curved Dash conceived in the late 1800s. Prototypes were made before the fire. Production cars reached the public in the summer of 1901. About 425 were built that year. They were two-passenger runabouts with optional back seats. The Model 6-C, introduced in April 1904, looked similar to the R, but had great differences. The body was larger, with more reinforcing. The running gear was heavier and stronger and the colors varied.

The Model B Curved Dash was introduced at the beginning of 1905 and remained through 1906. A heavier engine was fitted and larger leaf springs ran front to rear. Two brake pedals were used.

Curved Dash production exceeded 12,000. Many survive today. In 1906, a straight ("piano box") front was available alongside the Curved Dash style.

By 1904, R.E. Olds left his namesake firm to found Reo. The Olds Motor Works expanded its line. Based on Curved Dash running gear were light delivery trucks and rail inspection cars. In 1905, came a new twin-cylinder touring for $1,400.

By 1906, Oldsmobile fell to sixth in sales and concentrated on the upper end of the market. New that year was the four-cylinder Model S Palace Touring and a Gentleman's Roadster. They rolled on 106-inch wheelbases and had $2,250 price tags.

In 1907, Oldsmobile introduced nickel plating on some cars, including open and closed versions of the four-cylinder Models A and H (Flying Roadster). A year later, the firm became a cornerstone of General Motors. A new six, the Model Z, joined the line. In 1909, a few sixes were made, but the bulk of production was of fours called the 20, D, DR and X models.

People-packed 1908 Oldsmobile touring was used in Boston-to-New York-to-Boston endurance run. (Davis B. Hillmer)

One of Oldsmobile's most memorable machines, the Limited, bowed in 1910. It was powered by a 500 cubic-inch six and rolled on 42-inch wheels. The limousine sold for $4,600. In 1911, the Autocrat, a four-cylinder car, joined the Limited. It was followed by a smaller four-cylinder, called the Defender, in 1912.

An interesting year for Oldsmobile was 1913. Defenders were offered again, plus a new, less expensive six called the Model 53. Charles W. Nash became general manager at Oldsmobile that season. In 1914, the six-cylinder Model 54 was the mainstay product. Late in the year came the Model 42, which returned to four cylinders in a lightweight chassis. 1915 saw a continuation of the 42, plus a revised four-cylinder Model 43 and a six-cylinder Model 55. The division's first V-8 came in 1916. In 1917, the six-cylinder Model 37 was added and, in 1918, a revised V-8 called the Model 45, was offered.

A new page was turned in the Oldsmobile product book, in 1919, with the Economy Truck. This 3/4-ton commercial vehicle had a 128-inch wheelbase and four-cylinder engine. Production continued through 1923.

A 1922 Oldsmobile touring car carried these travelers on their Florida vacation. (Old Cars)

Oldsmobile continued to offer sixes and V-8s in 1919-1920. An all new four-cylinder called the 43-A, was offered in 1921, along with V-8 Models 46 and 47. Again for 1922-1923, it was fours and V-8s for Oldsmobile buyers. The 1924 model-year brought a six that would be Oldsmobile's bread and butter car into the next decade. New Fisher bodies were built in a Lansing plant and came as standard closed car equipment.

From 1925 to 1927, Oldsmobile offered its six-cylinder series 30 cars with letter suffixes C-E. The letters did not conform to model-year changes. In 1925, the division offered chrome plating on some cars. By 1927, the E-designated cars came with four wheel brakes.

In 1928, Oldsmobile stayed with just one series. These F-28s were powered by a six-cylinder engine and offered in seven body styles with deluxe equipment options. The 1929 model F-29 continued with a slightly more powerful engine and Fisher bodies on all models.

The short-lived Viking companion car came to Oldsmobile in 1929-1930 as an entry-level model. It was powered by a 260 cubic-inch V-8 and rode a 125 inch wheelbase. It came in just three body styles: A pair of four-door sedans and a convertible.

The mainstay of 1930-1931 was the tried and true F-series. For 1932, this line was joined by the new L-series, with a straight eight that lasted until the postwar Rocket V-8.

In 1933, a completely restyled Oldsmobile greeted buyers. An eight served as the Indy 500 Pace Car. Hydraulic brakes were new in 1934. An exterior restyling, came in 1935, as Oldsmobile's sales rose to 126,768 for fifth place on the charts. The two series format carried into 1936.

Once again, Oldsmobiles were completely restyled in 1937 and a semi-automatic transmission was new. Production passed 200,000 for the first time. The optional "Safety Automatic" gearshift was carried over in 1938. Model-year 1939 was one of expansion, with three series powered by sixes and eights.

The last prewar Oldsmobile was the 1942 model. This is a series 98 four-door touring sedan. (Old Cars)

Oldsmobile played the role of GM innovator once more, in 1940, with a new option. It was the first fully automatic transmission: Hydra-Matic Drive. This was also the first year for the 98 model designation and for a wood-bodied station wagon. The 1941 model-year was virtually, a mirror image of 1940, with sales of more than 270,000 cars. This was an all-time high and good for a sixth place industry ranking. The three Oldsmobile series were known as Special, Dynamic Cruiser and Custom Cruiser. Production in 1942 carried just into the month of February, and 1942 models (B44s) are considered rare.

Oldsmobile had no official vehicle production during World War II, but its plants kept busy making tank and aircraft cannon, rocket shells, aircraft engines and tank components.

Bugatti felt Royale could sell itself

By John A. Gunnell

When the Bugatti Royale Type 41 Kellner coupe was put on sale by Christie's auction company, the owners expected to realize over $10 million for it. Only six Royales were originally constructed by the Bugatti Works in Molsheim, France. This car was the fifth example. Both its chassis and engine bear serial number 41141.

Intended for sale to royalty, the Type 41 Bugattis proved to be too expensive even for the wealthiest people during the worldwide depression of the 1930s. Of the half dozen built, none were ever owned by a person of regal blood. In fact, it's been noted that "Pizza King" Tom Monaghan is the only king who ever owned one.

Ettore Bugatti once told a prospective buyer, Prince Mohamed Abdul, about his approach to promoting Royale sales. "For such a chassis, I have never considered it necessary to publish a catalog," he said. "There is, in fact, no need whatsoever of advertising such a model."

Later, however, the deepening depression led Bugatti to change his tactics. Forced to seek buyers outside royal circles, he decided to exhibit the Kellner coupe in the 1932 Olympia Motor Show in England. It was a hit of the show, attracting considerable attention, but no buyers. Bugatti took the car home.

The 1931 Bugatti Type 41 Royale Kellner coupe was part of the Briggs Cunningham Collection since the 1950s. (Old Cars)

He gifted the vehicle, which was then painted black and yellow, to his daughter L'Ebe Bugatti. It remained in the family until Briggs Cunningham purchased it in the early 1950s. Since the Royale had received excellent care from the day it was built, no major restoration work was required. It was refurbished with no modifications other than painting the body blue and black.

While the first Royale's engine displaced 846.6 cubic inches, the remaining five cars, including the Kellner Coupe, had slightly smaller straight eights. Bore remained at 4.92 inches, but the stroke was decreased from 5.91 to 5.12 inches. This made the displacement 778.7 cubic inches. In comparison to the original's 180-inch wheelbase, the Kellner coupe has a 170-inch stance.

Historians have, over the years, attributed these changes to the fact that Bugatti built the first Royale as his personal car. The belief is that he made it a bit larger and more powerful for this reason. In 1931, he wrecked the original, although it was ultimately rebuilt, later, with modifications.

The Kellner coupe's engine is aluminum, with the head and block cast as one piece and the cylinders extending almost full depth. The mainshaft for the crank is mounted in the block (rather than in a crankcase) in the bottom of the cylinders, each of which is surrounded by a water jacket. Full weight of the assembled engine is a modest 720 pounds, of which 238 pounds represent the block casting and 220 pounds the crankshaft.

Rated horsepower is 300 at 1700 rpm, enough to propel the car to 135 miles per hour. According to published articles, the Type 41s could be started in high gear and lugged at three miles per hour. From there, the Royales could accelerate to 125 miles per hour without shifting gears. This speed required only 2,000 rpm.

Transmission attachment is a three-speed, sliding-pinion type with direct drive on second, the gear assembly being integral with the rear axle unit. Drive ratios are 2.5:1 overall: 1.8:1 in low, 1.0:1 in second and .6:1 in high (an overdrive).

Depending on the type of coach work selected, Royales weigh some 5,000 to 7,000 pounds with 3,000 pounds representing the weight of the chassis. A 42-gallon fuel tank is fitted and gas mileage in the 10-12 miles per gallon range has been reported.

The Kellner coupe has a simple and clean interior finished in leather with few luxurious frills. The mechanical brakes are cable operated and leaf springs are mounted at all four corners.

Styling on the car is very understated. Behind the characteristic horse-collar grille is a long hood with 11 louver doors which, with the cowl, run nearly to the mid-point of the wheelbase. The cabin is approximately the same length as the radiator/hood/cowl, with the rear of the body sitting above the center of the rear wheels. A large trunk and rear-mounted spare sit behind the body.

In back of the cowl, a slanted windshield post runs at roughly a 30-degree angle to the roof. The doors take up approximately half the length of the body, with thin, vertical posts at their trailing edge. A prominent molding treatment encircles the rather narrow windows. It has a heavier bead along the belt line, which is slightly below the level of the top of the hood. Opening at its top, the trunk is a bin-like structure.

The car has large U.S. Royal tires mounted on the wheels, which are large, plain-looking castings with finned openings around the rims. The rear spare has a bright cover in the center, with a down-pointing lever-type handle. "Cunningham's" coupe, now part of the Collier Museum collection, is believed to be in probably the best mechanical condition of the four Royales remaining in the United States.

This 1987 photo of Kellner coupe suggests a bit of detailing had been done. (Christie's)

The christening of the Essex Terraplane

By Jack Miller

July 21, 1932 was a memorable day for the Hudson Motor Car Company. It was the day the Essex Terraplane was introduced to the nation amid much publicity surrounding the christening ceremony and with a national radio hook-up via WJR radio, a major Detroit radio Station.

A great risk was taken by the Hudson Motor Car Company in spending the money to develop a totally new car during such economic hard times as the depression era of 1930-1933. The car was to be a small lightweight auto that was stylish, comfortable, economical and reliable. The Essex Terraplane was all of this, plus it had excellent performance for a six-cylinder car.

Two thousand Hudson-Essex dealers and salesmen were invited to Detroit for the July 21, 1932 christening ceremony with Amelia Earhart, the premiere aviatrix of the time, doing the honors. The event was staged at the factory shipping terminal, located on Connor Avenue near Mack, four blocks north of the main plant. This area was chosen as there was plenty of room for the huge tents, stage and storage for the new Essex Terraplanes.

The dealers were given tours of the factory, road tests of the new car and complete product information on the car in meetings held in the huge tents. The dealers and salesmen were also treated to a luncheon at factory expense. They were shuttled around Detroit in buses rented for this occasion.

D.J. Kava did a White Triangle News interview with George W. Kropp, who was Hudson's manager of Body Engineering Specifications. It provides a very interesting insight to the Terraplane christening ceremony with Amelia Earhart.

"Engineering also became involved with the Amelia Earhart christening. There was going to be a big ceremony, followed by a large dealer driveaway. Someone in engineering got the idea that she should christen the car with a champagne bottle. A tripod affair was built and a bottle was hung on it so it swung true. Of course, it was too heavy and would have broken the very delicate bird radiator ornament. So someone got the idea they should etch the bottle with acid. I had to take a bottle to the lab for etching but they said, 'We have no way of holding the acid in a given place,' and suggested that the outside of the bottle be coated with wax. I went upstairs again, to the woodshop, and they coated it with wax and cut grooves in it. Then back to the lab, where they etched it to what they thought was the correct depth. When we tried it on the tripod, it swung true and broke the bird off completely.

"The next bottle, I told them to etch a little more. That was done and it was felt it was etched as thinly as possible. It was given to one of the experimental trimmers to cover with red, white and blue quarter-inch wide ribbon in a basket weave pattern. He broke it. So off I had to go again, with another bottle. This time, we got it done perfectly, ribbon and all.

"At the christening, instead of using the tripod, the bottle was given to Amelia Earhart and she broke the bottle at the base of the bird without incident."

In another related event during all of the ceremonies, the first Essex Terraplane that came off the assembly line (a special coupe), was dedicated and presented to aviation pioneer Orville Wright, who also attended the Hudson-Essex Terraplane christening ceremonies. There were 16,581 Terraplane automobiles and 412 Terraplane commercial models produced in calendar year 1932.

Two thousand Hudson-Essex dealers and salesmen were invited to Detroit for the July 21, 1932 christening ceremony with Amelia Earhart, the premiere aviatrix of the time, doing the honors. (Jack Miller photo collection)

As the story goes, at the final event of this great occasion, the dealers and salesmen were organized into a huge parade. They went through the streets of Detroit in their new bronze Essex Terraplane demonstrators, all 2,000 of which were alike. The parade proceeded south on Connor, past the main plant complex, and turned onto Jefferson Avenue for the trip downtown to Woodward Avenue. It then turned north through the heart of downtown Detroit. At this point, the cars dispersed for their home towns. Hudson Essex Terraplane Club member Bill Bade of Newark, New York was among those salesmen who attended the christening ceremony.

The parade not only benefited the Hudson Motor Car Company. It also served as a tremendous morale boost to the people of the Detroit area, since the depression was still first in the minds of everyone. Many were still without jobs.

This great new car, plus the pageantry and the parade, showed everyone that the Hudson Motor Car Company was willing to take a chance to help the economy recover from the depression and to signify that prosperity was just around the corner.

The effort was well rewarded, as can be seen in an excerpt from the biography of Roy D. Chapin, written by J.C. Long in 1945. (This rare biography was commissioned by Mrs. Chapin, after her husband's death, and was given to close family friends and business associates of Mr. Chapin.):

"The Introduction of the Essex Terraplane: Chapin had some very definite 'productive' plans in mind. Earlier in the year he had been encouraged by improved business at the automobile show and had written to Mr. Tiedeman (Tiedeman was Roy D. Chapin's father-in-law, in whom he confided a lot about business decisions). "It may be that this industry of ours really will be the one that gets things moving once more. We did it in '22 and I hope we can in '32.

"The low-priced closed cars of Essex and Hudson had promoted the sensational recovery of Hudson in 1922 and now Roy (Chapin) had another car idea under wraps. He was planning to produce a very light car in the bottom price class, a vehicle which should combine style, comfort and reliability. These qualities were claimed for all makes of cars, to be sure, but Roy believed that the Hudson-Essex factories, which were noted for production efficiency, could more than meet all competition. Furthermore, he was convinced that he had found a name with great public appeal, namely, the Terraplane. The name was designed to link the popular interest in aviation to a new, swift car which would travel as with wings.

Tearing up Pikes Peak in a promotional run is a new 1932 Terraplane convertible. (Jack Miller photo collection)

"To launch any new car at this time was a daring move. The improvement in business at the start of the year had not continued. Moreover, the automobile industry was profoundly discouraged by the increased taxes on motor vehicles. In June 1932, they had lost their battle on the issue. Various elements where Chapin and his colleagues had hoped to find support, especially after a favorable vote in the Ways and Means Committee of the House of Representatives, had failed to lend support at the final hour. The slogan of balancing the budget had swept aside the appeal of the automobile makers against discriminatory taxes. Both administration Republicans and most of the Democrats had voted for the levies. The chief blow to the industry had come from Senator James Couzens of Michigan, who had promised to vote against the motor taxes, but who, in the final showdown, had changed his position.

"Roy, however, was not to be discouraged and the plans for introducing the Terraplane went forward with sensational vigor, the great event taking place on July 21, 1932.

"Accounts of the affair appeared in newspapers throughout the United States. It was, in fact, one of the notable events in automobile industry history, and it demonstrated that Chapin's remarkable gifts for salesmanship on the grand scale were undimmed by the depressing condition of the times. Of all the reports, the one in the July 20, 1932, issue of Automotive Industries was so clear, so brief and so succinct as to deserve a place in the permanent record."

The account printed in Automotive Industries read as follows: "A Wow of a Christening: That Hudson announcement of a new Essex Terraplane must have been a wow. It just simply stopped Detroit, according to all accounts. One cynical and hardened editor who has been going to announcement parties for 15 years came back from this one to say that 'it was the hottest announcement of any new model in many years.'

"And Athel Denham, our own Detroit editorial representative, got all worked up about the demonstration himself. He unleashed his prying camera, took some snapshots which were so interesting we just have to give them space here, and then wrote us the following in a confidential memorandum: Enthusiasm Higher Than Thermometer ... The Hudson Motor Car Company really deserves an editorial break on their introduction yesterday of the Terraplane, here. With a temperature well up in the 90s, ceremonies were short and to the point, run off like.'"

Raymond Dietrich, designer of Classics

By Tom LaMarre

Raymond H. Dietrich's career spanned the time from the early days of the auto to man's landing on the moon. Although car collectors might picture him as drawing Classic cars until his death, Dietrich never locked himself in the past. He enjoyed the recognition that was given to his early work, but as a designer he always lived in the present. Perhaps this philosophy was best reflected in one of his later projects, designing an electric car that would generate its own power.

Born in Brooklyn, New York in 1894, Dietrich's first job was as an apprentice engraver for a subsidiary of the American Bank Note Company. Next came a stint with a maker of piano hammers. To pay for art lessons, Ray pitched for a semi-pro baseball team.

Baseball's loss was the auto industry's gain when Dietrich was hired as an apprentice in Brewster Body Company's design department. While earning $9 per week, he studied body construction and engineering at the Mechanics Institute in New York.

After graduating in 1917, Dietrich worked briefly in Chevrolet's engineering division until Brewster lured him back. There he met Tom Hibbard and, in February 1920, they formed LeBaron Carrossiers in New York. Three years later, the company merged with the Bridgeport Body Company, in Connecticut, and its name was changed to LeBaron, Incorporated.

Orders poured in as a result of the firm's successful impact at the annual New York Salon (car show), where it displayed custom body work on domestic and imported chassis.

Detroit took notice of LeBaron's success. Edsel Ford was particularly impressed with LeBaron's work and ordered eight customs to be built on Lincoln chassis. At the same time, Ford used Murray Body president Allan Sheldon, as an intermediary, to convince Dietrich to move his operations to Detroit. Under this arrangement, Dietrich would receive everything he needed through the Murray Body Company. In return, LeBaron was to design and build prototypes for the Lincoln Motor Car Company.

When the officers of LeBaron balked at the offer, Dietrich went to Detroit alone. In 1925, Dietrich, Incorporated was established. It occupied space in the Murray Body Company. Edsel Ford made sure Dietrich received all the help he needed, yet he didn't object to Dietrich building bodies for other companies. As Dietrich, Incorporated expanded, its customers included Packard, Chrysler, Franklin and Pierce-Arrow.

As Dietrich, Incorporated expanded, its customers included Packard, Chrysler, Franklin and Pierce-Arrow. Ray Dietrich designed the body for this 1929 Packard model 645 dual-windshield phaeton.

Orders declined during the depression. Ray Dietrich then resigned from the company bearing his name in 1931. He joined Chrysler, in 1932, as a designer of passenger cars and trucks. He also taught drafting at the Chrysler Engineering Institute. In 1938, he left to work as a consultant. During the war, he supervised production methods for radar units, mobile units and 45-ton tank retrievers.

In 1949, Dietrich organized another company in Grand Rapids, Michigan. However, aside from a Lincoln parade car, there wasn't much call for custom bodies. His later projects included a gas turbine jet design for Lincoln Mercury and designs for office furniture and trailers. In 1963, Dietrich designed the Firebird electric guitar for the Gibson company. It was one of his last commercial projects.

Ray Dietrich died, at age 86, on March 19, 1980. "Ray had a wonderful creative life," said Mrs. Dietrich, "and to be recognized in his own time is very gratifying."

At least one Dietrich design has been produced since his death; Gibson has reissued the Firebird guitar several times, due to collector demand. It would have pleased Ray, a man who always designed products for the present and the future.

Shown in the 1931 Packard catalog as style number 2072, was the Dietrich Convertible Victoria. (Old Cars)

Innovation and quality characterized the 1936 Packard 120

By Gerald Pershbacher

"Well, we've done it," C.R., a Packard engineer, said as he patted the first 1936 Packard 120 off the assembly line in August 1935. "They said it couldn't be done, that we couldn't build a medium-priced car and still call it a Packard. But we did it, and the sales prove it." He knew that the sales of the 1935 edition, the first 120, almost reached 25,000 units compared to the senior cars, which did not total even 7,000 cars.

As C.R. walked to his office, he recalled the meeting the engineering staff held with the sales staff on Monday, November 19, 1934. It was an uphill climb then to even help Packard's own staff understand the importance of the innovative 120.

The 1936 Packard 120 four-door touring sedan against a backdrop of a lake full of sailboats. (Applegate & Applegate)

"One of the most important factors in reducing tire wear is the rigidity of the frame itself," it was explained. "In that respect, we have a frame construction that is better than any of the other frames from the standpoint of rigidity that we know of today. The type of suspension used on Chevrolet and Pontiac was outstanding for tire wear, while the type used on Cadillac, Oldsmobile, Buick and LaSalle was not an offender. Our geometry (in construction) is more nearly like the Cadillac type," he recalled, as the conversation unfolded in his memory.

Of the 120's stately, smooth ride, a cohort said, "For normal carrying position on the boulevard ride, the rate is softer than it would be if we did have the rubber mountings in the system. I do not know just how to express that to you. The point I am trying to make is that there is a very soft spring for the normal riding position, because the rubber increases the rate of action and increases the ability to hold the car up out of a chuck-hole when the wheel movement is at maximum."

A stately new home fits the image sought for the 1936 Packard 120 four-door sedan. (Applegate & Applegate)

He recalled how the sales managers were puzzled with the high-tech talk. "Well, does that mean that the person riding on this type of suspension will get fewer jolts in the car than he will on the other one?" one of them asked. "You see, we do not have to give the explanation; in fact it is desirable if we do not give the explanation on the advertising. The things we want to do is to give the results of this engineering, what it means to you. We can say, 'less jolting,'" said an ad man as he reduced the matter to the lowest common denominator.

The high-pitching ride and "galloping" of Chevrolet was brought out. The new 120 was promoted as, not only reducing tire wear with its fine suspension, but the ad men said, "We can say they won't get out of alignment, too." The engineers agreed.

On servicing, one engineer explained, "The points that I think of that should be serviced regularly would be knuckle pins and rear spring shackles, about every 2,000 miles or something like that." To which the sales force replied, "If we could say that, someplace along the line, only four points or six points require monthly attention, it would be good." But, the engineers said that monthly wasn't so good, either. "Well, I think that can be worked out along a little bit less definite lines," an ad man said, jotting some notes. It was an interesting encounter of detailed technology with practical sales appeal.

C.R. chuckled as he thought of how advanced the 1935 Packard 120 was and how many of the same characteristics carried over to the 1936 version. He knew it was hardly an update on the design, structurally and cosmetically, although the new version did have both wheelbase and horsepower matched at 120. He recalled how the meeting tacked the matter to true horsepower for the 1935.

Both staffs called the 120 the "X" car in late 1934. It was more of a code name than anything, although the 120 designation hadn't been settled on yet. The 1935 model came close to the magic number in horsepower: "We know it has a straight eight motor, but what horsepower does it develop?" asked the sales and advertising executives. One engineer said 110. Another said 111. A top manager settled the point, because it sounded better "One-hundred ten; you had better use that."

Although the car's top was not all-steel, something that produced "a lot of ballyhoo coming from the other camp," it was decided to say the car carried an all-steel body construction, as if the roof were a separate thing. "People who are sold on the all-steel body are sold up to the hilt and they believe that anything else is taking death in their hands and riding forth to it. So, to all intents and purposes, this is an all-steel body. We'll call it the Packard safety-plus body, an improvement on the all-steel body," said an ad man and the matter was closed.

But one major question remained in the meeting: Was this new car truly a Packard?

"Packard has had its finer and smaller car since 1909; we began with the old Packard 18 and then went into the model 38s. We were actively planning on building a smaller car when the World War came," said one historian. "At least for a quarter of a century, we have had the smaller and finer car in the picture. Today the level of all car prices is down, way down, and we are going to come out in 1935 with our smaller car at about 50 percent of the price of our cheapest big car; exactly what we did in 1921 and 1922."

"Every part had been built to Packard standards - isn't that true?" someone asked. "When you say 'every part according to Packard standards,' that is a sort of indefinite thing," answered an engineer. "But," said a sales-pitch man, "it is sufficiently indefinite to be correct."

A restored 1936 Packard 120 convertible sedan with optional side-mounted spare tires. (Old Cars)

Then C.R. piped up, "We have naturally cut corners where we felt they could be cut and still give us what we considered a Packard. Our standards of performance are higher than other manufacturers. We have built far greater endurance into units, such as transmissions, where we can actually subject them to endurance tests."

"As soon as we can compare them against the new cars, as we said this morning, we can soften them with this ad and, then, we can soak them with our right, when we get facts on the 1935 cars," said an ad man, un-Packardly.

"Max Gilman, vice president of distribution said, "If you don't do anything else over the weekend, think about the price of this automobile. I think there might be more suspicion in $985 than $1,035, just to quote figures. The public will approach this car in a spirit that they hope its Packard strong points are true. They are going to be skeptically inclined, but, this car has the benefit of all that Packard has been doing for 35 years in building quality cars," a top official said.

C.R. agreed. And he knew that Packard was set for a great year in 1936, building the car America wanted and needed; a car with class, good price and nice looks and a heritage that was proud.

SPECIFICATIONS

1936 Packard 120

Series: .... 120 B Series
Model: .... Five-passenger touring sedan (built-in trunk), body #992
Factory Price: $1,115
Number One Value Today: $23,000
Wheelbase: .... 120 in.
Tires: .... 7.00 x 16 in.
Weight: .... 3,560 lbs.
Engine Type: .... L-head eight
Bore: .... 3-1/2 in.
Stroke: .... 4-1/2 in.
Displacement: .... 282 cid.
Compression Ratio: .... 6.5 standard; 7.0 optional
BHP: 120
Carb: .... Stromberg
Transmission: .... selective synchromesh, three forward speeds, one reverse
Options: .... Single sidemount, radio, clock, sidemount cover, heater, radio antenna

A short history
of Duesenberg

The Duesenberg family came from Lippe, Germany. Fred Duesenberg, who became a self-taught engineer, was born in 1876. He came to America in 1885. Raised on a farm, he made a living as a farm implement mechanic.

August Duesenberg, the great organizer and younger brother, helped Fred open a garage in Des Moines, Iowa. In 1903, a race car was built. The brothers then teamed with lawyer E.R. Mason to build Mason cars. F.L. Maytag, the appliance-maker, purchased Mason in 1910.

Augie and Fred formed Duesenberg Motor Company in St. Paul, Minnesota during 1913, supplying auto and boat engines to other companies. During World War I, they produced a variety of aero and marine engines. They included the Duesenberg H, a 900 horsepower V-16 and a 16-cylinder Bugatti power plant of 1,500 horsepower that was built in a new Edgewater, New Jersey plant.

An outstanding Duesenberg designed engine of this period was the horizontal valve "walking beam" power plant, as used in Roamer and Meteor cars. Rights to this engine were sold to Rochester Motor Company and the Edgewater factory was purchased by Willys-Overland.

A love of racing brought the brothers to Indianapolis, Indiana where the Duesenberg name became famous as the manufacturer of cars that won the 1921 French Grand Prix and the 1924, 1925 and 1927 Indy 500s. In 1920, the Duesenberg Model A had been introduced for the passenger car market. Its 90 horsepower engine, lightweight construction (lots of aluminum) and four-wheel hydraulic brakes were racing-inspired.

The speedway was a testing ground for many developments found in the car. Its 260 cubic-inch 100 horsepower straight eight, with single overhead cam, could propel it to 90 miles per hour in stock form. In 1923, a sedan averaged 62 miles per hour for 50 hours at Indianapolis Motor Speedway.

Priced at $6,500, the Model A failed to earn financial success. By 1924, the firm was in receivership. Chet Ricker, an Indy timekeeper and scorer and a consulting engineer, took over managing Duesenburg. He was named co-receiver with W.T. Rasmussen. In 1926, they sold out to E.L. Cord. Fred Duesenberg became Cord's engineering vice president at the small Duesenberg shop in Indianapolis.

Cord had wanted to build "The World's Finest Motor Car" as a prestige car-line for his auto empire. An interim Model X was produced. Then, in December 1928, the Model J bowed at a New York auto show. It went into production for deliveries in April or May 1929.

The 1926 Duesenberg Model A roadster. Priced at $6,500, the Model A failed to earn financial success. (Old Cars)

Lycoming, another Cord firm, built the J's 420 cubic-inch 265 horsepower rated twin overhead cam straight eight designed by Fred Duesenberg and draftsman W.R. Beckman, with some degree of input from E.L. Cord. It used two valves per cylinder, a 5.25:1 compression ratio and a two-barrel Schebler carburetor. Top speeds of 119 miles per hour were claimed, plus a 13 second 0-to-60 miles per hour time. Actual Duesenberg performance has been debated since.

Duesenberg built chassis-only using two wheelbases: 142.4 inches and 153.5 inches, with the longer ones being rarest. Prices started at $8,500, later climbing as high as $10,000. Some 23 custom coach builders, here or in Europe, produced the bodies. About half of the cars were designed by Duesenberg's own Gordon Buehrig.

Duesenberg built chassis-only on two wheelbases: 142.4 inches and 153.5 inches. Prices were $8,500-$10,000. Some 23 custom coach builders made bodies. This is a 1934 Duesenberg Murphy roadster. (Applegate & Applegate)

E.L. Cord maintained rigid factory control over designs to ensure a somewhat uniform image of luxury. Some cars were, however, re-bodied later. Coachwork was usually $4,150 to $6,500 extra, although some finished cars ranged to $20,000 during the Great Depression! As planned from the start, production was limited. It's believed that about 481 J/SJ models were made. Amazingly, 250 were sold by mid-1930.

In May 1932, a supercharged version of the J was released as the SJ. Around 35-36 of these cars were built before production closed in 1937. Some Js also had superchargers added. On July 2, 1932, Fred Duesenberg was driving an SJ that skidded off a mountain road in Pennsylvania. Although seemingly in good shape after the accident, he died 24 days later of medical complications.

The SJ was largely a carryover model. It was not greatly updated and has even been called "outdated," since there was little avant-garde about its engineering. But, old-fashioned or not, the crank-driven Schwitzer blower, with larger crank bearings, stiffer valve springs and tubular steel con rods, made it special. The maximum boost of 5 psi helped push output ratings to 320 horsepower. Performance claims included 0-to-l00 miles per hour in 17 seconds and a 130 miles per hour top speed. Eight cars had special one-piece stainless steel exhaust headers and the rest used an external exhaust system covered with flexible pipe. Though frequently thought of as an SJ characteristic, the flex pipes were also made an extra-cost option on Js.

Some SJ bodies were built by Cord's Central Manufacturing Company, according to designs by stylists like Gordon Buehrig, Franklin Q. Hershey and others. Custom coach work was supplied by Derham, Murphy, Walker-LeGrande, Bohman & Schwartz, Rollston, Judkins or Willoughby. A few roadsters were built on special 125-inch wheelbases.

In March 1932, E.L. Cord stepped down as president of Duesenberg. Sales executive Harold T. Ames took that title. August Duesenberg was a vice president. Production ended in 1937 when Cord got out of the auto industry. Augie Duesenberg attempted a revival in 1947 and died eight years later, after the effort had proven unsuccessful.

All Duesenbergs are considered full Classics under Classic Car Club of America guidelines. Of the approximately 480 Models J and SJ cars built, the latest research indicates that over 50 percent are still operational and that as high as 75 percent survive today in some form.

A tale of two Cadillacs

By Bill Siuru

Dwight D. Eisenhower and George S. Patton Jr., are probably the most well-known personalities of World War II. Besides being famous United States Army generals, they had something else in common. They left behind Cadillacs with interesting stories.

While Patton is usually depicted as riding across France and into Germany in a Jeep, he also had a 1938 Cadillac at his disposal. The story has it that the car had been shipped to France prior to the war and was taken captive by German occupation forces when they over-ran France. It was left behind as the Germans retreated and was subsequently commandeered by Patton. The Cadillac was a Series 75 Fleetwood Model 7533 seven-passenger Imperial sedan with a sliding glass partition. Records show that some 479 of this model were produced in 1938.

Patton was the ultimate soldier and faced the prospects of a postwar career in civilian life with great uncertainty. Indeed, he often said, "The proper end for the professional soldier is a quick death inflicted by the last bullet of the last battle." However, Patton met his fate not by that last bullet, but while riding in the 1938 Cadillac.

General Eisenhower on running board of the ex-General Patton 1938 Cadillac Series 75 Imperial sedan. (Photo courtesy Eisenhower Library)

Patton's view of his postwar future took on an almost death wish aura, which on several occasions in 1945 was almost fulfilled. These brushes with death included near misses when his Piper Cub was mistakenly attacked by an inexperienced free-polish pilot flying an RAF Spitfire; when his speeding Jeep nearly collided with an ox cart; and when a car accident (from which he escaped with minor injuries) took place.

On December 9, 1945, Patton was riding in his Cadillac, on his way to do some pheasant hunting in the German countryside. His driver momentarily took his eyes off the road to look at some demolished vehicles that Patton was pointing out to another general riding in the car. In that instance, the truck the Cadillac was following slowed down to make a turn. General Patton's driver saw the truck and slammed on the brakes, swerving to miss the truck. But, it was too late. The Cadillac collided with the truck. While it was a rather minor accident with only the front end of the Cadillac suffering damage, Patton did not fare so well. He was severely injured. A broken neck left him paralyzed from the neck down. On December 21, Patton died from his injuries.

A militarized 1939 Buick was also part of General Eisenhower's wartime fleet used overseas. (Photo courtesy Eisenhower Library)

After the accident, the car was repaired. It was used by military VIPs until 1951. The repairs were quite interesting. While the Cadillac was a 1938 model, the front end was restored using parts from a 1939 Series 75 Cadillac that was found in France. Thus, the car that now is displayed at the Patton Museum of Cavalry and Armor at Fort Knox, Kentucky is deceiving. It looks like a 1939 model. However, Cadillac buffs will quickly see that it is really a 1938 automobile and that the repairs do not duplicate a 1939 Cadillac, either.

When Dwight D. Eisenhower was running the show in Europe, he used a 1942 Cadillac 75 sedan. The car was painted the typical army olive drab for camouflage. It included a siren and a red warning light on the left side. The siren was seldom used because of Eisenhower's dislike of sirens.

After the war, the car served Eisenhower when he was chief of staff of the United States Army. When he was president of Columbia University, it was still at Ike's disposal. As a five-star general, he was still on active duty, but without a specific assignment. When Eisenhower later became the Supreme Commander of Allied Forces in Europe, that car was shipped to his Paris headquarters. Its O.D. paint was replaced by a shiny black paint job. Finally, in 1956, the car was retired and put up for auction. By now, it had 200,000 miles on the odometer and there was 67,000 miles on its third flathead V-8 engine.

A soldier poses with Eisenhower's 1942 Cadillac during World War II. Ike did not like the siren on the fender. (Photo courtesy Eisenhower Library)

Knowing Ike's endearment to the car, it was purchased anonymously at auction by some of his friends. It was then shipped back to the Cadillac plant in Detroit and restored to its original condition, including the O.D. paint scheme. On March 13, 1957, the car was presented to Eisenhower on the steps of the White House. On seeing the car, Ike remarked that the car looked like it was ready for a 50,000 mile journey. The scratches he had remembered on last seeing the car were gone. The car was then shipped to its new home at the Dwight D. Eisenhower Library in Abilene, Kansas.

General Eisenhower's favorite 1942 Cadillac was restored and presented to the president on March 13, 1957. (Photo courtesy Eisenhower Library)

Frank Lloyd Wright's unique Lincoln

Frank Lloyd Wright was a lover of fine cars. In the early years of the century, he owned a series of large, brass cars. During the 1930s, he chose a Packard phaeton and then an L-29 Cord.

Wright was instantly attracted to the 1940 Lincoln-Continental when it was introduced late in 1939. He ordered cabriolet number H092816, a rather early production model. Evidently, he didn't like convertibles.

The 1940 Lincoln-Continental coupe had not yet been introduced. So, Wright had his cabriolet converted into a town coupe with open chauffer's compartment. Peculiar half-moon or arched rear quarter windows were added. The rear window was eliminated completely.

The architectural genius had the car painted Cherokee red, perhaps to remind the world that he was proud to be part American Indian. Some would call the color brick red.

Frank Lloyd Wright's 1930 Cord L-29 is also painted brick red. It still exists and was seen on the cover of the 1987 Old Cars calendar courtesy of owner Len Weiss. (Old Cars)

There's an interesting story about this car that went around Chicago collector car circles for many years. Frank Lloyd Wright had two homes and architectural schools. Taliesin North was in Spring Green, Wisconsin and Taliesin West was in Scottsdale, Arizona.

Throughout the World War II years and up until the mid-1950s, Wright made winter and spring migrations in his customized 1940 Lincoln-Continental.

Wright told people he had the rear window eliminated because he did not believe in looking backwards. He wanted to see where he was going, rather than where he had been. This was certainly true of the great architect's life and architecture. Did the philosophy apply to his Lincoln-Continental, too? Well, it made a good story.

Wright owned a 1941 Lincoln-Continental coupe. It was also painted Cherokee red, but was not as radically customized as the cabriolet. A Lincoln-Continental coupe was not offered until the spring of 1940. Had it been available at the time Wright customized his cabriolet, he might never have made his custom.

Wright seemed to like the coupe pretty much the way Edsel Ford designed it. It is not known whether or not Wright bought the 1941 coupe new or what happened to it. Proof that he did own both cars for quite some time can be found in the March-April 1954 issue of Lincoln-Mercury Times. It featured a story about Wright and a color photograph of both cars shot at Taliesin North.

By 1955, Frank Lloyd Wright and his two Lincoln-Continentals were growing older. He bought a new, white 1955 Lincoln Capri sedan. The 1940 model was simply stored in a shed at Taliesin North. It slowly fell into a state of decay and remained there for several years after Wright's death. He died April 9, 1959, in Phoenix, at the age of 91.

In 1963, the car was purchased from the Wright Foundation by Pat Thym, of Dodgeville, Wisconsin. He was known for his car collection and restaurant in Dodgeville. Thym restored the car to its original custom condition and kept it for many years.

In more recent years, it has gone through several owners. The exact "history" of the vehicle is uncertain until 1987. Then, it was purchased by Tom Monaghan of Domino's Pizza.

Tom Monaghan and George Crocker with Frank Lloyd Wright's personalized 1940 Lincoln Continental. It is not known if Monaghan still owns the car. (Photo courtesy Cars & Parts magazine)

There is no doubt it was Frank Lloyd Wright's car. Both the original title and the peculiar customizing prove it. There may be other facts surrounding the purchase of the car from the Wright Foundation and its restoration. To date, Thym's ownership history has the most documentation behind it.

What happened to Wright's 1941 coupe remains a mystery. The 1955 sedan was seen, at Taliesin West, in 1973. There is a good chance it's still around.

Frank Lloyd Wright was an incredible man. He revolutionized American architecture as much as Henry Ford revolutionized transportation. In his eighties, Wright was designing buildings so fresh and unique that they immediately inspired wild acclaim or total antagonism. Nobody could be neutral toward his work.

His last great (and controversial) architectural achievement was the Marin County Civic Center in California. This and many other Wright buildings repeat the half-moon or arched window of his 1940 Lincoln-Continental.

Today, you can't argue with the greatness of Frank Lloyd Wright's architecture or his preference for the prewar Lincoln-Continental. You can argue with his style of customizing.

Like Raymond Loewy's pair of similarly customized Lincoln-Continentals, the Wright car's changes did nothing to enhance the original beauty of Edsel Ford's timeless masterpiece. The changes made personal statements about two great men who altered their cars to suit individual tastes. Now, with both the great designers gone, the cars have gained historic significance and serve to keep the original owners very much alive.

Industrial designer Raymond Loewy also customized a 1940 Lincoln Continental that looked similar, but not identical, to Wright's car. (Old Cars)

POSTWAR

From the Home of the Golden Hawks

Postwar Scripts...

There was lots new for 1962

By R. Perry Zavitz

There was a time when everybody was excited to see the new cars at introduction time. The manufacturers, the dealers and the public all could hardly wait for the unveiling of the new models.

It seems strange, today, when new cars make their debuts and no one, not even the industry, bothers to yawn. But, back then, there seemed to be more to get excited about. The year 1962 was a good example of why "new" created excitement at new-car time.

Pontiac led the parade of 1962 cars to be unveiled. Not only were there fresh styling refinements, but its new line up included a new model called the Grand Prix. Sportiness combined with luxury was the in thing then and the Grand Prix successfully mated those qualities in a full-size package. It was a like an upgraded Catalina two-door hardtop. The 120-inch wheelbase, the shorter of the two full-size Pontiac wheelbases, was used.

The first Pontiac Grand Prix appeared in the 1962 line up. It combined sportiness and luxury in a full-size car. (Pontiac Motor Division)

Standard power train consisted of a 303 horsepower V-8 with three-speed manual transmission. Transmission options included Hydra-Matic and four-speed manual gear boxes. Whatever the transmission choice, it was controlled from a console between the bucket seats. Every Grand Prix had bucket seats, which were growing in popularity at this time, (Bucket seat equipped cars more than tripled during 1962.) A tachometer added to the sporty image.

The interior of the Grand Prix was upholstered tastefully and uniquely. The exterior was equally tasteful. There were slight differences to the grille. Most chrome side trim was omitted, but across the rear, extra bright trim made the Grand Prix easily identifiable.

With a base price of $3,490, the Grand Prix sold for about $140 more than a Bonneville two-door hardtop. It was a popular model, with production totaling 30,195 for its initial production year.

The day after Pontiac's debut, Oldsmobile went on display. It too had a new model to show off. Added to the top of its not-so-compact F-85 line was the Jetfire. It was a two-door hardtop that featured a turbocharger on its 215 cubic inch V-8. What was a novel way of squeezing out more power then, has now become a common engine accessory. The Jetfire developed 215 horsepower or one horsepower from each cubic inch of displacement. That gave this little Olds an excellent power-to-weight ratio.

Making its appearance the same day as Oldsmobile was Studebaker. Among the Lark models was a new top series introduced for 1962. The Daytona was available with either six or V-8 power. Two-door hardtop and convertible body types were offered. It was a Daytona convertible, driven by Sam Hanks, that paced the Indianapolis 500 in 1962.

Next to make its 1962 entrance was Buick. Added to its Special series was an upgraded two-door hardtop and convertible that revived the Skylark name. These neat little models were powered by an aluminum version of the 215 cubic inch V-8 used by their sister cars the Pontiac Tempest and Oldsmobile F-85. The Skylark did not have a turbocharger, yet developed a very respectable 185 horsepower.

Lincoln's introduction took place simultaneously with Buick's. However, after its total change in design and image of the previous year, there was no great difference for 1962. Lincoln was stressing quality and backed it up with a two-year or 24,000 mile warranty. Because other 1962 warranties were for just 90 days or 4,000 miles, this triggered the warranty wars that sprang up in the era.

The day after Buick and Lincoln bowed, the entire Chrysler line was introduced. New in Plymouth's Valiant line up was the Signet. Unique to the Signet was its black grille with a large Valiant emblem in the center. This two-door model was the first of the Big 3 compact hardtops on the market. Dodge had a comparable model in its compact Lancer series. It was called simply Lancer GT and had a bit less chrome on the front.

New among the larger Dodges was the Polara 500. Using the 116-inch wheelbase of the Dart series, the Polara was priced between the Darts and the big Custom 880. It was distinguishable from the Dart models by a grille with most bars blacked out and some bright work added on the rear flanks. Comparable full-size Plymouth luxury two-door hardtop and convertible models were also added for 1962. They were labeled Sport Furys.

DeSoto was conspicuous by its absence in the 1962 model year. The final year of the marque had been 1961, when production was abbreviated.

Chrysler made some styling changes that improved its appearance. The fins were blunted considerably. That made sense. What did not make sense, to most of us, was a shuffling of model names. The middle series Windsor name was done away with and was replaced by the 300 name. No, it was not a whole series made up of the former 300 high-performance models. It was just a confusing change of nomenclature; confusing because there was still a 300H muscle Chrysler offered, as well. Hence, the need arose to refer to the super-powered models as the "300 letter-car series." By the way, the new 300H continued with 380 standard horsepower.

On the 1962 Imperial, fins all but disappeared. Placed on top of the rear fenders were long lens taillights, which would have looked just as good as hood ornaments.

The day after Chrysler introduced its cars, Chevrolet did likewise. That was the debut of a whole new line of compact cars ... the Chevy II. Three trim levels were offered: 100, 300 and Nova 400. There were two- and four-door sedans and a four-door station wagon in each series, plus a two-door hardtop and a convertible in the top Nova sub-series.

Brand new engines were used. Most were equipped with a six-cylinder motor of 194 cubic inch that developed 120 horsepower. Also available, except in the Nova, was a 153 cubic inch four-cylinder motor rated at 90 horsepower. It was the first Chevy four since 1928. The four had not quite become extinct among North American cars and it was the Chevy II that marked the start of its return to popularity. At the time, though, the V-8 was taking over from the six as the most popular American car engine.

The Chevy II was more comparable to the compact cars of the other manufacturers than the Corvair. But, the Corvair was not about the go the way of the DeSoto, at least not yet. A full complement of models was still offered by Corvair for 1962. And to add some excitement to the series, the Spyder option was offered on the top-line Monza coupe and convertible. In addition to the expected nameplates, the Spyder featured a turbocharged engine. With it, a Corvair developed 150 horsepower from its 145 cubic inch flat-six rear-mounted engine.

The Chevy II 300 sedan seen in the middle of this stack was an all-new type of car in 1962; not compact like the Corvair (top), but smaller than the Impala (bottom).

A new V-8 engine was on the option list for the full-size Chevrolets. In addition to the 283 cubic inch motor, there was an enlarged version of 327 cubic inches. It developed 250 or 300 horsepower. A bigger V-8 with 409 cubes was also available. It produced 380 horsepower ... as much as the much heavier Chrysler 300H.

The 409 was not available in the Corvair, but the 250 and 300 horsepower 327s were. Exclusive to the Corvette were 340 and 360 horsepower versions of this engine. The 1962 Corvette was the last of the first generation. It had a blacked-out grille and no two-toning in the side coves.

Full-sized Fords appeared on the same day as Chevrolet. There was a realignment of model names. The big Fords were called Galaxies, but they were offered in three levels of trim from the straight Galaxie through the Galaxie 500 to the new top-of-the-line Galaxie 500XL.

Concurrently, Mercury introduced its full-size models. The Monterey came in standard, Custom and S-55 versions. Like the Ford 500XL, the S-55 was available only in two-door hard-tops and convertibles.

Falcon offered more models for 1962, but they were little more than a variety of trim packages ranging from standard through DeLuxe to Futura. The Futura offered two two-door coupes and a four-door sedan. Mercury's Comet almost duplicated the Falcon. The top model was the S-22, but it came only as a coupe.

For 1962, a fiberglass tonneau cover transformed the open Ford T-bird into a sleek two-passenger car, much in keeping with the original Thunderbird concept.

Although rumors had the Studebaker Hawk flying into history, it made a spectacular mid-October return as the Gran Turismo Hawk. It sported a (1958-1960) T-bird-like roof and other little styling improvements here and there. This Brook Stevens' restyling made it a more popular model. Standard engine in the GT Hawk was a 289 cubic inch 210 horsepower V-8, while a 225 horsepower edition was optional.

Not until November did Ford introduce its new Fairlane line of mid-size cars. (Hence the renaming of the full-size Fords to free the Fairlane name for these new welter-weight models.) On a 115-1/2-inch wheelbase, this new mid-size car was 197.6 inches long. This was 16-1/2 inches longer than the Falcon and about 12-1/2 inches shorter than the Galaxie. Both the Fairlane standard and Fairlane 500 models had a choice of a 170 cubic inch 101 horsepower six or a new 221 cubic inch 145 horsepower V-8. The V-8 introduced a thin-wall casting process for engine blocks.

Almost two weeks after the Fairlane made its debut, Mercury introduced its comparable Meteor. The Meteor was actually a bit larger than the Fairlane. Wheelbase was one inch longer and overall length was some six inches greater. The same engine choices were available, though. In keeping with the other Mercury series, Meteor was available in standard Custom and S-33 sub-series. The latter was a two-door sedan with a fancy interior.

Mercury's mid-sized model was the Meteor. Like its Ford counterpart, the Fairlane, it had an optional 221 cubic-inch V-8. (R. Perry Zavitz)

Postwar Scripts...

Spyder and Jetfire were the turbo pioneers

By R. Perry Zavitz

Has there ever been a more innovative car produced by a major American manufacturer than the Corvair? It had its engine located in the rear. That engine was a horizontally-opposed six. It was made of aluminum. All this in a new (compact) size car.

But, technical innovations did not stop there. For 1962, Corvair made a turbocharger available in its top-of-the-line Monza models. Superchargers had been offered sporadically by various cars since 1906. Incidentally, almost all of them had disappeared: Chadwick (the first with a supercharger), Duesenberg, Auburn, Franklin, Cord and Kaiser dropped them.

As you already know, the purpose of supercharging is to get a bigger shot of fuel into the cylinders. That is done by forcing the charge into the cylinders under pressure. The result is a more powerful explosion. Consequently, more horsepower and torque is developed from a given displacement. In superchargers, the increased pressure of the fuel charge was obtained from a mechanical blower, but that drained power from the engine and was somewhat self-defeating.

The Corvair had a different type of supercharger. It used the escaping exhaust gases to turn the blower that produced the extra pressure. In the Monza, pressure was increased 10 to 11 pounds. From the 145 cubic inches of the Corvair engine, the turbocharger increased the normal output of 102 horsepower to 150; and torque from 134 pounds-feet to 210. That is an increase of 47 percent in horsepower and 57 percent in torque.

Although it sounds simple, it is a somewhat complex mechanism. And to enable the standard Corvair engine to withstand the greater power, the turbo versions had revised pistons, connecting rods, crankshaft and exhaust valves. Also, a lighter cooling fan was used, as well as a stronger clutch pressure plate. This option (RPO 690) cost $317.45 extra. That was not a bad price, especially in light of the results.

The turbo Corvair engine weighed a mere two pounds per maximum horsepower developed. That little motor developed more power than the potent 1951 Hudson Hornet, but from an engine that had less than half the displacement of the Hornet. Even in the 1962 crop of cars, the Corvair turbo was the most powerful six and more powerful than some of the small V-8s.

For 1962, Corvair offered a turbocharged engine as an option in its Monza convertible and coupe models. It developed a generous 150 horsepower. (Courtesy Chevrolet Motor Division)

Performance-wise, the turbo Monza could do 0-to-60 in just a hair over 11 seconds. It could do the quarter-mile sprint in just under 18 seconds at 80-plus miles an hour. Top speed was 110 or a bit better. At a steady 60 miles per hour, fuel consumption was practically 25 miles a gallon, which was excellent 25 years ago.

As already mentioned, turbocharging was available only in the Monza series, but just on the coupe and convertible. In other words, turbocharging could not be had in the Monza sedan or wagon. Turbocharged Monzas were called Spyders. The turbocharger required the four-speed manual transmission, sintered metallic brakes and heavy-duty suspension.

There were 6,894 Spyder coupes and 2,574 convertibles made during the 1962 model season. For 1963, production totals nearly doubled for coupes and tripled for convertibles, as word of these hot little cars spread.

Production of 1964 Spyders was down considerably. The introduction of Ford's Mustang can be blamed for much of that drop. While displacement was increased to 164 cubic inches, the horsepower rating was unaltered. However, the torque figure rose to 232 pounds-feet.

With an all-new body, the 1965 Corvair placed the turbocharged models in their new top-of-the-line Corsa series. Standard horsepower for the Corsa was 140, but with the turbocharger option, the rating was 180 horsepower. This situation was repeated for 1966, which was the final year for turbocharging in the Corvair.

Moving back to 1962, we find that, along with the Corvair Monza Spyder, Oldsmobile introduced a new model in its F85 line. It was a two-door hardtop named Jetfire. Like all F85s, it used an aluminum 215 cubic-inch V-8. But, that V-8 was unlike all the other Olds V-8s. It was turbocharged.

Pressure for the fuel charge was only five pounds, so the extra power was not as great, relatively, as in the Monza Spyder, despite the fact that the Jetfire's turbine reached a maximum speed of 90,000 rpm, compared to 70,000 for the Spyder. The normally aspirated Olds 215 V-8 with 10.25:1 compression developed 185 horsepower and 230 pounds-feet torque. Under the same compression, the Jetfire's engine developed 215 horsepower and 300 pounds-feet. The increases were 16 percent and 30 percent, respectively. While the output was substantial, it was relatively less than the Spyder achieved.

One of the problems in turbocharging is to overcome the increased tendency for detonation. Jetfire did it in an unsophisticated manner. A tank with a methyl alcohol and water mixture was mounted on board and its contents spiked the fuel charge.

The Jetfire's acceleration from 0-to-60 was in the eight to nine second range. A standing quarter-mile took 17-1/2 seconds and maximum speed was 110. Those latter two figures were about the same as the Spyder, but the Jetfire was a 13 percent heavier car.

1963 was the second and last year Oldsmobile produced the Jetfire, which featured a turbocharged version of the 215 cubic-inch aluminum V-8. (Courtesy Oldsmobile Motor Division)

Priced at a reasonable $3,049, the Jetfire was produced in a modest quantity of 3,765 copies. The total rose to 5,842 during the 1963 model run. However, the price fell by a whole dollar! After 1963, no Jetfires were made. In fact, no turbocharged Oldsmobiles were made until the last few years.

While Oldsmobile has the reputation of being an innovator, they left the turbo business to Buick and went off in a different direction (to diesel engines). However, more recently, they created a four-valve, four-cylinder engine, which had a turbocharged version.

Today, turbocharging is becoming more common as a high-performance feature. However, it seemed amazing, a quarter century ago, when the Jetfire had an engine that developed one horsepower for each cubic inch of displacement. And the Corvair Spyder even exceeded that magic plateau.

Postwar Scripts...

Recycled names

By R. Perry Zavitz

During the postwar years, a number of automobile nameplates or model names were "recycled." In some cases, the same name was brought back by a second manufacturer, after being dropped by its original user. In other cases, the original automaker revived the same name.

The first situation was the case in 1975, when the Dodge Charger SE (Special Edition) debuted. It was the Dodge version of Chrysler's Cordoba. A rare Charger SE was the Daytona, which was not given much publicity until the following year. The Daytona was a dressed-up edition of the Special Edition featuring a partially blacked-out grille, two-tone paint and nicer upholstery.

The name Daytona obviously came from that Florida community where racing has taken place since almost the dawn of the automobile. But, as far as the Daytona nameplate is concerned, Dodge lifted it from a Studebaker. It was in their 1962 line up that Studebaker added new top-of-the-line hardtop and convertible models in the Lark series. Called Daytonas, they were a bit more elaborate than the Regal hardtops and convertibles.

Daytonas were Studebakers in the marque's late 1950s years. In more modern times, Dodge used the name. (Studebaker)

Yet, the Studebaker Daytona was available with either the 112 horsepower Skybolt six or the 180 horsepower V-8. Incidentally, the six underwent some major changes for the 1962 models. The old L-head was replaced by an overhead valve engine for peppier performance. The V-8 had a 259.2-cubic-inch displacement. A longer stroke version with a 289 cubic inch displacement and 210 horsepower was optional in the Lark Daytonas.

A rather unique feature Studebaker promoted at the time was the Skytop sliding roof. It was a sun roof, but with a cloth cover instead of steel. This was a Daytona option on the hardtop.

Exactly how many Daytonas were made in the 1962 model year is not clear because production figures are combined with Regal hardtops and convertibles. However, the reported totals were up considerably over the year before, so the Daytona probably was a major factor in that increase.

Daytona base prices were $2,308 for the hardtop and $2,679 for the convertible. That was $90 more than for the Regal editions.

Studebaker Daytona hardtops and convertibles continued in 1963. For 1964, the Daytona name appeared on a series of cars that were priced above the Commanders. The Daytona line was offered in four-door sedan, Wagonaire (the station wagon with the sliding roof for sky-high cargos) and convertible models. All were available with either six or V-8 power. A Daytona convertible was offered, but only with a V-8.

As you well know, 1964 was a crucial year in Studebaker history. The South Bend, Indiana factory was closed and all car production was transferred to Hamilton, Ontario, Canada. That change brought the end to the Daytona convertible. No Studebaker convertibles were ever made at Hamilton.

The Canadian-sourced Studebaker cars for 1965 included the Daytona line, but there was no four-door sedan either. All 1965 Daytonas were V-8 powered. The engine was no longer the Studebaker motor. (Hamilton never built engines either.) The General Motors-McKinnon engines used were based on Chevrolet's 283 cubic-inch 195 horsepower V-8.

In what turned out to be Studebaker's final model year, the 1966 Daytona was a two-door sedan only. The four-door sedan was called the Cruiser and the Wagonaire was a separate line. The Daytona sports sedan, as it was sometimes called, could be ordered with either a six or V-8 engine again. The six was also a Chevrolet engine. It was the smaller one, used in the Chevy II, with a displacement of 194 cubic inches and 120 horsepower.

The recent Buick Skyhawk is a namesake of a 1956 Studebaker model. The earlier Sky Hawk was overshadowed by the Golden Hawk. (Studebaker)

Another 1975 model receiving more promotion than the Dodge Charger Daytona was Buick's Skyhawk. A sleek new fastback version of the Chevrolet Vega called the Monza 2+2 was introduced. But, the same car was offered with Oldsmobile or Buick badges. The Buick version was called Skyhawk. This was another name that came from Studebaker.

The 1956 Studebaker drew a lot of attention when it hatched a flock of Hawks. The Packard-powered Golden Hawk was the most remarkable of this unique series. But, often overlooked because of the much celebrated Golden Hawk, was the Sky Hawk. It was quite outstanding in its own right.

Like the Golden Hawk, the Sky Hawk was a hardtop, while the other lesser Hawks were pillared coupes. The Sky Hawk was powered by the four-barrel carburetor version of Studebaker's 289 cubic-inch engine with a 210 horsepower rating.

For those not turned on by tailfins, the Sky Hawk deserves attention. It did not have fins atop its rear fenders (a borderline liability for the Golden Hawk). The Sky Hawk also did not bother with the wide chrome piece along the sill, which the Golden Hawk sported. Some considered too much chrome a liability, too.

At $2,529, the Sky Hawk was priced about $530 less than the Golden Hawk. For people interested in rarer models, take note that there were 3,610 Sky Hawks made. That made it the scarcest of the 1956 Studebaker Hawks. And that was it. Studebaker trimmed the Hawk population down to just two models the next year. The Sky Hawk was a casualty of that cut.

In mid-1977, Pontiac supplanted its Ventura with a new car they called the Phoenix. It was scarcely more than a Ventura SJ with improved grillework. The Phoenix name was resurrected from a Dodge model introduced for 1960.

1960 was the year when compact cars made the biggest news, but Dodge slightly downsized some of its cars for that year. Actually, Dodge did much the same as had been done successfully, in Canada since 1934; it offered a Plymouth-sized series of models. However, it did not adapt Dodge styling to the Plymouth body, as was done in Canada. Instead, it offered styling similar to that of the bigger Dodges, yet distinctively different, too.

Phoenix was the top-of-the-line down-sized Dodge 17 years before Pontiac used the nameplate on its cars. (Chrysler)

These new down-sized Dodges were called Darts. They came in three sub-series which were labeled Seneca, Pioneer and Phoenix. The most luxurious was the Phoenix. It corresponded to Plymouth's top-of-the-line Fury and cost only about $20 more than a Fury.

As a Dart, the Phoenix had a 118-inch wheelbase and measured 208.6 inches overall. Plymouth was about three-quarters of an inch longer, but had the same wheelbase. Like the Fury, Phoenix was offered with either the new 145 horsepower slant-six or 318 cubic-inch 230 horsepower V-8. The 361 cubic-inch 295 horsepower V-8 was an option. A further Phoenix option, not obtainable in the Fury, was the 383 cubic-inch 325 horsepower V-8.

For its second year, the Phoenix was basically the same (except for the annual styling facelift). It remained the top Dart model with the same engine choices. Again, the line consisted of a four-door sedan, two- and four-door hardtops and the convertible.

Rather extensive name changes were made for 1962 Dodges. The Phoenix title was discarded, but the philosophy of marketing a Plymouth-sized car has continued right through to the present.

Two Fiestas seemed to be over-priced. The first one was a 1953 Oldsmobile model. The other was a 1970s Ford import. (Blackhawk Auto Collection)

Production of Dodge Phoenixes, in rounded totals, amounted to 70,700 of the 1960 models and 37,300 for 1961. The 1960 model run exceeded the Plymouth Fury by one-third, but production then fell nearly 30 percent short of the Fury's total for 1961.

A new entry in the car market for 1978 was the Ford Fiesta. It was a German made econobox. Since it cost about $1,000 more than a Pinto, it is a bit hard to understand the "econo" claim. However, that Fiesta name brought back memories of another car of the same name. Oldsmobile offered it 25 years earlier.

The 1953 Olds Fiesta was a far more exciting car than the little Ford, though it, too, seemed overpriced. The $5,715 tab for that big convertible was twice the price of its sister, the Super 88 ragtop.

Basically, it was an upscale version of the already upscale 98 convertible. Two styling features differentiated the Fiesta from the 98. It had a wraparound windshield and a slight dip in the belt line, at about the midpoint. Both of these features were to be incorporated on all Oldsmobiles the following year.

The normal 165 horsepower Rocket V-8 of the 98 was tweaked slightly to get 170 horsepower for the Fiesta. The fact that Hydra-Matic transmission, power brakes, power steering, a deluxe radio, an Autronic Eye headlight dimmer, a heater/defroster, back up lights and whitewall tires were standard was no surprise, in view of the Fiesta's hefty cost.

Only 458 of these models were produced for 1953 and it did not return. However, the name was revived by Olds on its 1957 and 1958 station wagons. Most of the Fiesta wagons had pillarless hardtop styling, which is a rarity among station wagons.

Along with the Ford Fiesta, the 1978 season saw the debut of an AMC model called the Concord. It was a Hornet with a new name and not-too-drastic restyling. Earlier, AMC had used the SST designation on some of its cars. This implied Super Sonic Transport, a label for "jumbo" jet planes of the day. Likewise, the Concord tended to inspire thoughts of the latest in high speed travel and comfort, as exemplified by the huge Anglo-French jet liner (spelled Concorde, with an "e" on the end). But, before the English and French were using many planes for trans-Atlantic flight, Plymouth was already using the Concord name.

A mild restyling marked the 1951 Plymouth. After two seasons of its first postwar redesign, Plymouth altered the front end shape and grille of its cars. The company then introduced new model names. Instead of the previous Deluxe and Special Deluxe titles, the 1951 Plymouths had Concord, Cambridge and Cranbrook designations.

The Concord cleared up some confusion that had existed regarding the DeLuxe models. There were really two lines of DeLuxe Plymouth in 1949 and 1950. The larger version was a standard edition of the Special DeLuxe, but the other line was built on a 111-inch wheelbase. That made it 7-1/2 inches shorter than the other DeLuxe models. Without explanation, DeLuxes came in both sizes. The 1951 Concord name identified the shorter line of Plymouths. They were really compact cars, though seldom recognized as such.

Mechanically, Concords were identical to the other Plymouths. The engine was the reliable 217.8 cubic-inch L-head inline six rated at 97 horsepower. It had hardly undergone any changes since the restyled 1949 models were introduced.

Concord was the first name used exclusively for Plymouth's short wheelbase models of the early 1950s. AMC used the name later, in the 1980s. (Chrysler)

As before, this series consisted of a three-passenger business coupe; a slope-back two-door sedan; and a two-door all-steel station wagon. All three models were interesting, because each one was a bit out of the ordinary.

The coupe revived the once popular three-window style. The sedan was a unique shape for Plymouth, since all their other cars (except wagons) had a decidedly notch-back shape. The Concord wagon, also called the Suburban, scored a sensational breakthrough in the station wagon area by offering a practical all-steel vehicle. Its 1949 predecessor was not the first all-steel wagon, but its price put it within the reach of almost all new-car buyers. The Suburban's popularity was outstanding. It was the best-selling wagon in 1951. During 1952, it lost first place to Ford. Yet, by itself, the 1952 Concord Suburban's sales almost equaled the sales of all wagons built by all General Motors wagons combined.

All Chrysler lines were scarcely changed for 1952 and that applied to the Concord, of course. There was a slightly altered emblem on the hood, a new hood ornament, and the Plymouth nameplate on the back was changed.

The Buick V-6 took an "oddity's odyssey"

By R. Perry Zavitz

Along with the arrival of smaller cars in the early 1960s came the need for smaller engines. The whole purpose of compact cars, at least at the beginning, was to lower costs. This meant both initial price and operating costs. So, big V-8 engines were frowned upon. The Falcon and Valiant used scaled-down versions of their big brothers' six-cylinder motors. The Corvair was a one-of-a-kind car and required a totally new engine. But, the next crop of compacts, such as the Buick Special and Pontiac Tempest, created the need for something in the power range between the little sixes and the big V-8s.

Pontiac met this challenge by amputating one bank of its V-8 to make a slanted four-cylinder engine. Buick did something similar, but it made the cut crosswise, instead of along one side. In other words, Buick made a V-6. That sounds simple enough, but there were a lot of problems to overcome. The greatest was the fact that a V-8 engine has a 90 angle between the banks. That works out fine for balancing the firing cylinders of a V-8, but take away two cylinders and the remaining six are thrown way out of balance, causing serious vibration.

Normally, V-6 engines used a 60-degree angle between the cylinder banks to bring the firing back into balance. This is what the Italian Lancia had been doing with its V-6 since about 1950. Actually, the V-6 had already made its American debut in the 1960 model year. Certain GMC trucks were available with V-6 engines. They were offered in 305, 351 and 401 cubic-inch displacements. Each had a 60-degree angle between the cylinder banks. So, there was little help Buick engineers could get in this regard from their GMC counterparts.

Buick designed a new crankshaft and a firing order of 1-6-5-4-3-2 was used. That firing order is not very complicated. If you start counting with cylinder number 6, the firing order is simply backwards. Anyway, this eliminated much of the chopped-off engine's vibration. Since the remaining vibration was lateral, much of it was absorbed by special rubber engine mounts at each side. Interestingly, Pontiac's half V-8 had vertical vibration, which was much more difficult to overcome.

Many of Buick's V-8 components were used on the V-6. Items such as the generator, starter flywheel (with automatic transmission), valves, fuel pump, and flywheel housing (with manual transmission) interchanged. However, the bore and stroke of Buick's V-8 was altered. With a 3.625 inch bore and 3.2 inch stroke, the V-6 had a displacement of 198 cubic inches. That was about four cubic inches larger than the Tempest's four-cylinder engine or the Chevy II six.

A V-6 uses a very compact configuration. It is half the length of an inline six, of course. It is shorter than either a V-8 or a four. Amazingly, Buick's V-6 weighed just 362 pounds, about the same as the Chevy II's little four-cylinder motor. Debuting concurrently with the V-6, Ford's new thin-wall 221 cubic inch V-8 was 80 pounds heavier.

Buick's V-6 developed 1.35 horsepower and 205 pounds-feet of torque. That was significantly more power and torque than any of the other 1962 engines in its displacement class. The V-6 was standard in the standard line of 1962 Buick Specials, but was not available in Deluxe or Skylark models. However, the next year, it did become available in Deluxe Specials.

From management's decision to actual production, this engine was developed in the amazingly short time of six months. When it appeared, it was greeted by an enthusiastic press. Performance was excellent. Zero-to-60 acceleration took as little as 12.4 seconds. Top speed was 100 miles per hour.

Popular Mechanics magazine took a V-6 powered Buick with automatic transmission on a 1,100 mile test run. They compared it with a manual-shifted Buick V-6 and five other competitive cars. The V-6 automatic averaged 19.3 miles per gallon. In shorter runs, the manual V-6 reached 23.25 miles a gallon, which was better than any of the other cars.

The first American car to offer a V-6 engine in production models was the 1962 Buick Special. It had adequate power and good economy. (Buick)

Improvements were made to the V-6 as they developed and, for 1964, the bore and stroke were increased to match Buick's 300 cubic inch V-8. With 225 cubic inches, the enlarged V-6 produced 155 horsepower. That was practically three-quarters of the output of the V-8, so there appeared to be equal efficiency in the eight and the sawed-off six.

V-6 availability was extended to the Skylark for 1964, except Sport Wagons. The enlarged V-6 gave excellent fuel economy. In the 3,244-mile Mobilgas Economy Run, from Los Angeles to the New York World's Fair, Buick led its class of intermediate six-cylinder cars with a 25.2986 miles per gallon average. In fact, it was fourth best overall. Only the Rambler American, Dodge Dart and Plymouth Valiant were able to better it.

Yet, economy was not a serious goal for most people in the mid-1960s. Many more buyers were looking for power instead. Block-busting V-8s were squeezed into cars like Buick's Special and Skylark. As interest shifted to the muscle cars, Buick's interest in its V-6 faded. For its 1968 models, Buick dropped the V-6 in favor of Chevrolet's larger inline six, which was offered for the few customers who abhorred eight cylinders.

From 1962 through 1967, six model years, Buick installed over 302,000 V-6 engines in its cars. Some 66,100 of them were built for the 1964 model year alone. That was the peak, but 1963 marked the biggest percentage of V-6 powered Specials and Skylarks. Two out of every five Buick Specials and Skylarks had V-6 power. However, the ratio fell to one in 10 by 1967.

Happy combo! Racy and rugged. Holy Toledo, what a car!

Leave ordinary, garden-variety driving behind...in this 'Jeepster' Convertible. The rugged rascal only Toledo could build—because that's where 'Jeep' ruggedness comes from.

Settle back in those bucket seats. Take the wheel. And *go!*

You'll be noticed...thanks to snazzy features like that continental spare. Now, hit the highway and open 'er up! What a smooth performer...specially if you choose that hot new V-6 with automatic transmission.

Then flip one lever...you're in 'Jeep' 4-wheel drive! You've got excitement ...and safety, too...you just won't find with ordinary sports cars. What's your idea of fun? This baby will get you there!

Or, maybe you'd rather choose from the 'Jeepster Commando' models. Roadster. Station wagon. And the sportiest pick-up ever!

The 'Jeepster' family. It's tough. Terrific! You've

got to drive it to believe it! See your 'Jeep' dealer. Check the Yellow Pages.

KAISER Jeep CORPORATION

'Jeepster'
Family of fun cars

A LIMITED NUMBER OF FRANCHISES ARE AVAILABLE IN SELECTED AREAS. IF YOU ARE INTERESTED, WRITE TO: DEALER DEVELOPMENT MANAGER, KAISER Jeep CORPORATION, TOLEDO, OHIO 43601

This ad promotes the use of the V-6 in the 1967 Jeepster. Kaiser-Jeep purchased the engine tooling from Buick. Buick later bought it back.

The Buick V-6 did not disappear, though. Kaiser-Jeep found that Buick's compact engine would fit nicely in some of their models. So, an arrangement was negotiated with Buick to buy V-6 engines. The Kaiser-Jeep people liked this engine so much that, eventually, they bought the rights and tooling from Buick. Jeep's V-6 was virtually unchanged from Buick's specifications, except that developed horsepower was rated at 160, an increase of five.

Jeep used this engine as an option in their Jeepster Commando and related models, as well as in the Universal Jeep. It was not available in the larger Wagoneer models. Jeep offered the V-6, with little or no change, in the 1967 through 1971 model years.

In February 1970, American Motors purchased Jeep from the Kaiser-Jeep Corporation. Probably, that takeover was a factor in dropping the V-6, which was soon replaced by AMC's inline six. Then, something else, much more important, was falling in place. The fuel crisis of the early 1970s renewed Buick's interest in the economical V-6 and history repeated itself in reverse. Buick negotiated with Jeep and bought its V-6 engine rights and tooling back.

After further vibration dampening and a slight enlargement to 231 cubic inches, Buick was back in the V-6 business with a 110 horsepower motor. That rating is down from before, but by this time net horsepower figures were published instead of gross horsepower.

The V-6 made its comeback in the 1975 model of the Skylark, where it had its home before. The Apollo, which was really a four-door version of the Skylark, could not be ordered with a V-6 until midway in the model year. The reason was probably a matter of building production volume to a level to meet the demand.

There certainly was a big demand for the V-6. In all, there were 113,000 V-6 powered 1975 Buicks. The new Skyhawk used the V-6 exclusively, in place of Chevrolet's questionable four-cylinder engine. The V-6 was also offered in the mid-size Century. The 45,174 V-6 Centurys actually accounted for more than any of the other Buick lines. The quantity of 1976 Buick V-6s rose 110 percent to 238,300. Of that total, 9,651 of the motors were installed in full-size LeSabres.

V-6 popularity leveled off for 1977 models, but then took another sharp rise to 342,059 installations in 1978. That was far more than the entire Buick V-6 total during the 1960s.

Several different versions were made available for the first time in 1978 models. There was a mini V-6 of only 196 cubic inches (smaller than even the original 1962 engine). This 90 horsepower motor was not available for the Skyhawk or Skylark, as one might expect. Instead, it was the standard engine for Centurys. The regular 231 cubic inch V-6 was a Century option.

An option in the Regal sport coupe was a turbocharged edition of the 231 engine rated at 150 horsepower with a two-barrel carburetor or 165 horsepower with four-barrel carburetion. The restyled 1979 Riviera could also be ordered with a turbocharged V-6. It was rated at 185 horsepower. There were 36,038 turbo V-6 Buicks built during the 1979 season.

In the 1980s, the V-6 has taken off. It's becoming the most popular new type of engine since the high-compression short stroke V-8s of the 1950s. It has been embraced by many other car makers. Buick supplied Oldsmobile and Pontiac with V-6 engines beginning with 1977 models and Chevrolet starting with 1980 models. This was done even though the other divisions at GM were getting their own V-6 programs rolling.

Improvements have been continually incorporated and output has been raised. The turbo Buick Regal Grand National broke the 200 horsepower barrier with 245 horsepower. For awhile, it was the most powerful American production engine. Next, that honor went to the hopped-up GNX version, rated at 300 horsepower. Both used the small 231 cubic inch V-6.

The V-6 has come a long, long way since its shaky beginning 25 years ago. It has grown from a dubious novelty to a forgotten oddity to an inevitable necessity.

Dodge's counter-trend luxury car

By R. Perry Zavitz

The Chrysler Corporation has its share of ups and downs, as we all know. It seems that the downs are remembered most. But, let's look at an upscale car during one of those down periods.

The Big Three entered the compact car arena with 1960 models. Chrysler did so with its Plymouth Valiant. The most distinctively styled compact, it did not enjoy the sales rush that the Falcon, Corvair or even the Rambler Classic scored.

But, Chrysler was committed to an extensive down-sizing program. They altered the 1960 Dodge to the point that its new Dart was a Plymouth with a different grille. For 1961, the Valiant compact invaded the Dodge camp in the form of the Lancer.

Medium-priced cars were sent into a sales tailspin by the 1958 recession. In late 1960, Chrysler announced DeSoto's demise. With trouble in the medium price area and the rapid rise of compact car popularity, it seemed to be the right thing for Chrysler to move strongly into reduced size cars. The idea had a great deal of merit, except that, by 1962, it was no longer such a good idea. The economy had recovered. Fewer new-car buyers were looking for smaller cars. They wanted the large ones they were so used to and were looking for luxury too.

So, down-sizing did not work for Chrysler at this time. As all the full-size Plymouth and Dodge models were shrunk seven to 10 inches for 1962, sales also shrunk. The public was not yet ready for standard size cars to be made smaller.

The 1962 Dodge Custom 880 four-door hardtop was a midyear model. (Phil Hall)

To counter their misjudgment of public taste, in mid-1962 Dodge introduced the Custom 880. It was the result of a simple trick, for which Chrysler had great talent. They introduced a new model which was little more than a composite of existing and earlier models. They brought out a new and bigger Dodge without taking the time, or spending the money, to completely retool a new model. (Chrysler's most interesting composite car was their Australian Chrysler Royal of about this same time. Its hood and front fenders, the cabin, and the trunk and rear fenders were each based on previous Plymouth components of differing years and the result was a fine-looking, up-to-date car.)

The midyear Dodge Custom 880's 122 inch wheelbase Chrysler chassis was actually the same size chassis as Dodge used the year before. They used the Chrysler body, but with a slightly fancier 1961 Dodge Polara grille. That grille made the new car look like a Dodge, instead of a Chrysler.

The Custom 880 was nearly a foot longer than the down-sized Dodges, but about one inch shorter than the Chrysler. It was powered by a 361 cubic inch V-8 that developed 265 horsepower. That engine was also used in the Dodge Polara 500 and Chrysler Newport.

Tipping the scales at about 3,600 pounds, the Custom 880 weighed just 35 pounds less than the Newport. That indicates not much was missing from this Dodge that the Chrysler model offered. Prices started at $2,964, right where the shorter Polara 500 left off. Actually, that was the same price as the Chrysler Newport four-door sedan, but most other body types were less than comparable Newports.

Buyers liked the Custom 880. Despite its late start, by year's end it was Dodge's fourth most popular series. During calendar 1962, 18,754 people bought Custom 880s. Dodge sales for the year were up more than five percent, while Plymouth, which had no large size model, gained less than half a percent.

Part of the reason that the Custom 880 improved Dodge sales was probably that it took up some of slack caused by DeSoto's withdrawal from the market. But this Dodge offered more body types than DeSoto had for several years.

Because it used the Chrysler body, the Custom 880 was offered in the same body types: Four-door sedan, two- and four-door hardtops, convertible and two- and three-seat station wagons. But, the station wagons were not the average type of cargo carriers. They were pillarless four-door models. Only a few car-makers bothered to build hardtop station wagons.

The Custom 880 returned for 1963 and attracted more buyers by its expanded range of models. A lower priced 880 sub-series offered a four-door sedan and six- or eight-passenger wagons. These 880 wagons were pillared models, unlike those of the Custom 880 line. Prices of the 880 models were about $150 less than similar Custom 880 models, which had not changed from 1962.

Another addition for 1963 was the 305 horsepower version of the 383 cubic inch V-8, which was previously reserved for Chrysler Windsors and Sport 300s. For people wanting more power, the 360 horsepower version of Chrysler's 413 cubic inch V-8 could be ordered.

Styling of the 1963 Dodge 880 and Custom 880 was mainly limited to a new grille. It consisted of many thin vertical strips, which was less attractive and too bland for a car of its status. This was improved somewhat with a new grille for 1964. It had thin horizontal elements forming a more intricate pattern.

The same 880 and Custom 880 models were available for 1964, but prices were increased $13. The engines (361 cubic inches standard and 383 cubic inches optional) continued to be offered with the same power ratings as before. According to "The Specification Book for U.S. Cars 1930-1969" (Motorbooks), the 413 cubic inch V-8 was also optional in Dodge 880s and Custom 880s in 365-, 415- and 425-horsepower forms. Four-on-the-floor gear shifting was optional.

The 1965 Dodge Custom 880 continued on a 122 inch wheelbase. (Dodge)

For 1965, totally new styling appeared, along with a rationalization of model series and sizes. By this time, most automakers recognized a need for three sizes: Compact, mid-size and full-size. Dodge adopted this approach and its full-size cars became known as Polara, Custom 880 and Monaco. So, the Custom 880 was no longer the top-of-the-line Dodge. Nor did it have the distinction of size and appearance it had enjoyed in the previous three model seasons.

During the 1962 to 1964 model years, Dodge produced a total of 77,351 Custom 880 and 880 cars. Approximately 14,600 were 880 sedans. Station wagons totalled 14,200. There seems to be no breakdown of 880 and Custom 880 wagon totals, so the number of hardtop wagons cannot be ascertained.

1962 DODGE CUSTOM 880

Engine type:	V-8
Bore:	4.125 inches
Stroke:	3.375 inches
Displacement:	361 cubic inches
Compression:	9.0:1
H.P. @ R.P.M.:	265 @ 4400
H.P. per cubic inch:	0.73
Torque @ R.P.M.:	380 pounds-feet @ 2400
Rear Axle Ratios:	2.93:1 (automatic)
	3.23:1 (manual)
Overall length:	213.5 inches
	215 inches (wagon)
Overall width:	78.7 inches
	80.0 inches (wagon)
Overall height:	55.2 inches
	55.9 inches (wagon)
Wheelbase:	122 inches
Tread:	60.9 inches (front)
	59.7 inches (rear)
Weight:	3655 pounds (sedan)
Tire Size:	8.00 x 14
	8.50 x 14 (wagon)
0 to 60 time:	13.2 seconds
1/4-mile time:	18.4 seconds
Top speed:	105 miles per hour
Original price:	$3030 (hardtop coupe)
Current #1 Value:	$7000 (hardtop coupe)

Grand Prix was the greatest Pontiac

By R. Perry Zavitz

Subtle changes made a significant difference when Pontiac introduced a new addition to its 1962 line of cars. Called the Grand Prix, it featured several little styling differences, but all of them made a cleaner-looking car.

It had a two-part grille of thinner ribs than on the other Pontiacs. At the rear, the normal Pontiac Star Chief design was used, but with a chrome-ribbed panel added between the taillights. A Grand Prix logo was affixed to the right ends of both the rear trim and the grille.

Less chrome side trim was tacked onto the Grand Prix than on its siblings. A common Grand Prix option was a set of distinctive 8-lug aluminum wheels with prominent lugs. Catalina's 120 inch wheelbase two-door hardtop body was used for the Grand Prix. It was the shorter of Pontiac's two full-size Sport Coupes.

Inside, the Grand Prix featured luxurious single-tone decor. A center console between the bucket seats was standard, as well as a tachometer and full instrumentation.

Standard engine in the Grand Prix was the 303 horsepower version of Pontiac's 389 cubic inch V-8. Three-speed manual transmissions were standard, but Hydra-Matic and four-speed manual transmissions were available with any engine offered.

The first Pontiac Grand Prix was the 1962 model. (Pontiac)

Four other engines were on the option list. All were dual exhaust 389s. Horsepower ratings were 318 and 248 with two-barrel carburetors or 333 and 348 with three two-barrel carbs. Surprisingly, there was an economy model that developed 235 horsepower.

Grand Prix was intended to be a high-performance luxury car. Except for the economy model, it would do 0-to-60 in under 10 seconds. Actually, there were a few with a big 405 horsepower 421 cubic inch engine installed. So equipped, the Grand Prix could do 0-to-60 in six seconds or even less.

Although it was the size of the smaller Catalina, the Grand Prix's price was more than the Bonneville hardtop. In fact, the $3,490 price was the highest of any 1962 Pontiac, except the Bonneville convertible and the top Safari wagon.

Evidently its price did not scare away the buyers. They snapped up the 30,195 made in the 1962 model year. That was almost as many as all Bonneville two-door hardtops of the same model year. Production shot up almost 2-1/2 times for 1963 when 72,959 were made.

Vertical headlights were introduced on 1963 Pontiacs. The Grand Prix had these, along with a grille of it own. The grille design was not greatly different from that of the other senior Pontiacs. Across each side of the two-part grille was a chrome bar with round parking lights mounted on the outer ends. This placement of the parking lights became a Grand Prix trademark.

Also new on the 1963 models was a slightly concave shape in the back window. Another distinctive styling touch was the taillight treatment. Eliminating the normal Pontiac taillights, the Grand Prix placed its lights behind the horizontal rear panel trim. Except when illuminated, these lights were scarcely noticeable.

The Grand Prix had become a very distinctive automobile with its little unique styling features and minimal use of chrome add ons. In fact, it had a simple beauty at this time, which places it on a par with a few Classics such as the Cord and the Continental Mark II.

The 1964 Grand Prix underwent the customary annual model change, but came through unscathed. Detroit has a terrible habit of not leaving well enough alone. Their changes usually spoiled the product. Pontiac stylists maintained a good degree of restraint in this case. A simpler Pontiac-type grille containing rectangular parking lights, the concave rear window, hidden taillights and limited use of side chrome maintained the Grand Prix styling theme.

No less than seven engines were available in the 1964 Grand Prix. (It almost seemed there were more engine choices than color choices.) Standard was the 306 horsepower 389 cubic inch V-8. The 230 horsepower economy edition was still offered. There were two other 389s on the option list. In addition, the 421 cubic inch V-8 could be ordered in three different potencies up to 370 horsepower.

Production of the 1964 Grand Prix fell about 10 percent below 1963. Yet, it was Pontiac's best-selling individual body/model, except for the four-door sedan and the two-door hardtop in the Catalina line.

To the end of 1964 production, Pontiac produced almost 168,000 Grand Prix two-door hardtops. That marked the end of its first generation Grand Prix. After introduction of a new body, production continued to drop annually through 1968.

A Grand Prix convertible was offered in 1967 only. (Pontiac)

The all-new 1969 Grand Prix had the biggest hood ever. (Pontiac)

New styling began with the 1969 models, when a semi-classic type of square grille was integrated with the front bumper. A special mid-size 118 inch wheelbase chassis was created for the Grand Prix. That GP package caught the public's fancy so well that nearly 112,500 copies had to be built for 1969.

Subsequently, the Grand Prix's popularity led to other GM divisions climbing on its band-wagon. First, Chevrolet introduced the Monte Carlo for 1970. It shared the Grand Prix body. A little later, Buick's Regal and Oldsmobile's Cutlass Supreme muscled in on the same basic body.

Celebrating its 30th anniversary in 1992, the Grand Prix ranks among the most durable car nameplates. Of particular credit to the GP is the fact that it has stuck to its original concept quite closely, in spite of the rapidly changing economic and other conditions the last 30 years have hurled at the industry.

The Grand Prix's popularity peak was reached during the years 1976 to 1978. While not remembered as an outstanding time for automotive engineering, styling or sales, Grand Prix chalked up three consecutive 200,000-plus sales years. Well over 288,000 were built in the 1977 model year. That accounted for just over one-third of all Pontiac production and more than three percent of all cars built in North America that model year.

With around 2-1/2 million made since 1962, obviously the GP is firmly established. We look forward to seeing it remain for many more years. And it will, as long as it continues to appeal to the buying public by offering a stylish, not-too-big, not-too-small performance model. Viva Grand Prix!

Don't forget the Frazer

By R. Perry Zavitz

When we think of Howard "Dutch" Darrin-styled postwar cars, we usually think first of the 1951 Kaiser. Later, we may recall the previous Kaisers, some of which bore Darrin's name on the trunk lid as an acknowledgement of his design work. Actually, the car he styled was not the Kaiser. It only borrowed the styling already set for the Frazer.

Frazer was a new nameplate on the American automotive scene at the end of World War II. Frazer, the man, had been in the auto industry since 1912 when he started as a mechanic's helper at Packard. But, more recently, he had begun to earn a reputation of taking control of floundering car makers, getting them back on their feet (or wheels) and rolling again.

Joe Frazer once worked at Chrysler and suggested the name for a new car they were about to launch. Plymouth, he said, was a name known by every farmer in the country. He was referring to a brand of binder twine, not the landing site of the Pilgrims. His suggestion helped make the Plymouth a success.

In 1939, Frazer suddenly left Chrysler to become president of Willys-Overland Motors. He revised the Willys compact car into the pleasant-looking American. But, the war stopped car production. He turned that roadblock into a wonderful opportunity with the Willys Jeep. Consequently, Willys-Overland was a thriving auto company again.

Encountering difficulties with chairman Ward Canaday concerning Willys-Overland's future, Frazer moved out. He managed to get financial control of the Graham-Paige company, which was seriously planning to get back in the car business as soon as the war ended.

Frazer hired Howard Darrin to style the car which would be the postwar Graham-Paige. Darrin's daring design was a full-width car with the fender line flowing straight from front to rear just below the belt line.

Meanwhile, a new name entered the auto industry. Henry J. Kaiser, a successful West Coast shipbuilder, was also preparing to make cars after the war. He and Joseph Frazer got together and the Kaiser-Frazer Corporation was established.

Though new to the auto industry, Kaiser had definite ideas of what his car was to be like. It would be smaller than the junior-Packard-sized Frazer and more the size of a Plymouth. It would have front-wheel drive, like the Citroen Kaiser owned. Other features were to include a unique suspension system Kaiser-Frazer called Torsionetic and unit-body construction.

When the war ended, Kaiser-Frazer was scrambling to get its car on the road. The sprawling Willow Run factory, located a short hop from Detroit, was where Ford made bombers during the war. It was purchased from the government. Manufacturing and assembly gear was rapidly installed. A few prototype cars were made, but the front-wheel drive was a knotty problem which caused delays.

Frazers (and Kaisers) were made in a factory in Willow Run, Michigan.

The Graham-Paige, renamed Frazer, was ready for production. But, the Kaiser was still a long way from reality. Since the Frazer was ready, it actually went into production, but not at Willow Run.

Willow Run Frazers came off the assembly line along with Kaisers. In the meantime, Kaisers had been considerably changed from former plans. Henry Kaiser was simply too eager to see his name on all the streets and highways of the country to patiently wait for the engineering bugs to be designed out of his car. He was probably also chagrined to face the probability of his partner's name on the roads before his.

Consequently, the front-wheel-drive idea was abandoned. Then, to speed things along more, the Kaiser became a clone of the Frazer. In other words, it was changed to be the same size as the Frazer and similar in all other ways, except for minor details and grille design. So, Kaiser-Frazer was in business. The dream of mass-producing cars was now a fact.

Kaiser-Frazer did not make its own engines. These were purchased from Continental Motors, a Muskegon, Michigan manufacturer of automotive and industrial engines. The one chosen by Kaiser-Frazer had a displacement of 226 cubic inches, which was the same as the Ford six. Output was rated a bit higher than Ford at 100 horsepower. Yet, it was commonly believed that Kaiser-Frazer's rating was conservative. Frazer offered no engine option. Actually, no one else did at this time either. Some companies made overdrive available and Frazer did likewise.

Of course, this was just the start. There were no two-door sedans, coupes or convertibles. And hardtops were still in the future. There was not even a standard and deluxe choice for Frazer buyers.

However, that was the situation only at the beginning. After a few months, a deluxe model was introduced. Also added was a four-door sedan called the Manhattan. Mechanically, it was the same as the base Frazer, but it could be easily distinguished from it. Two-tone exteriors and colorful interiors were the Manhattan's main features.

Kaiser-Frazer was very fortunate to have the talented Carlton Spencer as their color consultant from the beginning. The 1947 Frazer Manhattan was the first of several outstanding cars which strongly bore his tasteful influence. A countless variety of two-tone paint combinations were offered on the Manhattan. Spencer was also a master at giving his colors descriptive and exciting names.

Cardinal red, Horizon blue, Bermuda tan, Turf green, Doeskin, Airway blue, Saddle bronze, Pine tint, Copperdust metallic, Aloha green, Wedgewood blue, Caribbean coral metallic, Oakwood brown metallic, Cape Verde green and Cerulean blue were just a few of his imaginative names. Even the drab shades were given appealing appellations like Onyx (black), Claypipe gray, Adirondack gray, Polar gray, Speedway gray, Coral sand and Sportsman beige.

The Manhattan's interiors were perhaps even more exciting than the exteriors. While the industry largely knew of nothing other than dull grays and browns for upholstery, the Manhattan triggered a revolution with color-coordinated interiors. They matched or complemented the exciting exterior finishes. Even the many new types of improved upholstery materials coming into use after war Spencer used. This moved Kaiser-Frazer cars beyond the limits of automotive tradition in this regard.

Spencer has said that he was in Grand Rapids more than Detroit. Grand Rapids, the furniture capital of the country, was where he learned about the latest materials and what colors were the most popular.

The Manhattan's list price was $2,711. It is a bit difficult to understand that this was a rather hefty price 40 years ago. In 1947, the base Frazer, priced at $2,294, was a little higher priced than the Buick Roadmaster sedan. But, the Manhattan was in a price range between the Cadillac Series 62 sedan and the Sixty Special.

The 1947 Frazer Manhattan helped to "bridge" the gap between prewar and postwar car design.

Despite that apparent price disadvantage, Frazer sold very well. The 1947 Manhattan's production totalled 32,655; almost equal to both Cadillacs mentioned above combined. It appears as though this new kid on the block had some things going for it. It did very well, compared to the long-established and highly desired Cadillac.

The colorful interiors and exteriors were an attraction, no doubt. Availability was perhaps the most important factor, though. Kaiser-Frazer had the production capacity to supply its dealer network generously. Other dealers operating right after the war faced a flood of orders, but a trickle of cars. This caused long waits for delivery. Those shopping around found that there was no waiting for a new car at a Kaiser-Frazer dealer. Getting a new car, no matter what make, was more important right after the war than waiting for a favored make.

So, Kaiser-Frazer did amazingly well in its early years. During 1948, for instance, they sold more cars than any company except those in the Big 3. The new firm was the largest independent car maker.

That being the case, where was Joseph Frazer, whom we praised earlier? He had the deep-rooted experience and wisdom Kaiser-Frazer needed. But, more and more, he was overruled by an aggressive and automotively inexperienced Henry Kaiser. Frazer quietly withdrew in frustration from the company around 1950.

The Biltmore Manor made the perfect setting for the clean-styled 1948 Frazer Manhattan sedan.

Kaiser-Frazer achieved the enviable position of the best-selling independent in 1948, but it was largely by default. As industry production caught up to the pent-up demand and other automakers introduced their postwar designs, Kaiser-Frazer sales tapered off. Brand loyalty returned. Kaiser-Frazer had neither the time nor the major ingredient to develop brand loyalty. The main ingredient, of course, is quality. Kaiser-Frazer took a short term view of this. They were more interested in producing cars to sell now, than in building them better to entice repeat customers. This, unfortunately, was another policy that was more consistent with the Kaiser, than the Frazer, side of the management team.

Substantiating this problem were surveys made by Floyd Clymer. From 3,000 Kaiser and Frazer owners in 1947, he found 34.7 percent rated their cars excellent, 32.7 percent very good and 20 percent good. So, a total of 87.4 percent owners thought their Kaiser-Frazer cars were better than average. He made another smaller survey of Kaiser-Frazer owners in 1949. He found 53 percent said their cars were excellent, 21 percent very good and 13 percent good, for a total above average 87 percent rating.

An 87 percent better-than-average rating by owners seems good. But, compare that with other car owner surveys that Clymer conducted in 1949. Excellent, very good and good ratings totalled 90.2 percent for Chevrolet, 94.2 percent for Ford, 94.4 percent for Mercury and 95 percent for Studebaker. So, Kaiser-Frazer cars, apparently, did not have as high quality as these other cars attained.

Kaiser-Frazer cars were changed only imperceptibly for 1949. The Manhattan continued, but it was produced at a much slower rate. A total of 18,591 were built. The price rose moderately to $2,746.

Some face-lifting took place for 1949 in an effort to compete with the newly restyled cars from the Big 3. The simple, horizontally-slotted grille was replaced by a larger one filled with bold criss-crossed chrome pieces. Horsepower was increased to 112, without any change to compression or displacement.

By the way, Frazer introduced an interior feature that quickly became standard practice. With the relocation of the gear shift lever to the steering column in the 1930s, a rod had to be placed along the steering column to connect with the gear box. It was not exactly a thing of beauty and became an annoying dust collector. Between the steering wheel and the dash, the first Frazer placed a cover enclosing both the steering column and the gear shifting shaft. This cover was extended, on the 1949 Frazer, almost to the floor.

Against Joe Frazer's advice, Henry Kaiser insisted on increased production for their 1949 models. The result was such a surplus of cars that 1950 models were nothing more than re-serialized 1949 leftovers. So, 1949 and 1950 Frazers are considered together. Production of Manhattans amounted to an estimated 10,223.

There was a new Manhattan model added for 1949, however. It was a four-door convertible priced at $3,295 (about $200 less than the two-door Cadillac convertible). Along with the Kaiser version, it was the first four-door convertible made after the war. Only a handful were actually built ... about 82 for 1949 and 1950 combined.

With Joseph Frazer virtually out of the company, the final year for the car bearing his name was 1951. While the Kaiser was completely restyled for that year, Frazer kept the old body, albeit substantially revised.

The Manhattan series continued with two models, but no sedan. The four-door convertible was available, along with a vinyl-covered, steel-roofed four-door hardtop. This model had been available before as the Kaiser Virginian, but not as a Frazer. Both these Manhattans were priced at $3,073. The engine was re-rated at 115 horsepower. For Manhattans, GM's Hydra-Matic drive was standard. It seems that only 152 hardtops and 131 convertibles were made during the 1951 production run.

The base Frazer offered a sedan, as well as a model called the Vagabond. The latter was nearly a hatchback model and was also a Kaiser exclusive in 1949 and 1950. The rear seat folded down and the back end opened up (like a station wagon does) to receive large objects. But, with the seat and seat back in their usual positions, the car appeared to be a normal sedan.

Too bad the Frazer did not remain longer. Like its human namesake, it was outstanding. Unfortunately, it was overshadowed by its Kaiser running mate.

New Era station wagons

By R. Perry Zavitz

Chevrolet made a steel two-door station wagon called a Suburban in the mid-1930s. Though never popular, it heralded future wagons. There were a few Chevy woodies as well, but they were made by outside firms. That was common.

Ford was the only car maker producing its own wagons then. Owning large forests and a wood body factory in northern Michigan, Ford was the understandable station wagon production leader.

Of the 31,800 wagons built in 1946, Ford made 14,194. Combined with 2,299 Mercury woodies also made, Dearborn accounted for 52 percent. Prices started at $1,565 for the eight-passenger six-cylinder model. But, Ford's leadership in wagon production was challenged by an unlikely competitor.

After making Jeeps during World War II, Willys-Overland offered a station wagon version. In its first full year in the civilian car market, Jeep took top place in wagon sales away from Ford.

Using Chevrolet's two-door steel station wagon concept, Willys-Overland produced a variation of their military Jeep. Styled by Brooks Stevens, it cleverly blended a Jeep front with relief steel side panels painted beige and tan to simulate wood. Jeep's reputation, a durable steel body and a price of $1,608 made Willys' station wagon a winner.

Seven-passenger Jeep station wagons led body style production in 1947, as 33,336 were built. Though Ford's production rose 62 percent, to 22,984, it was second.

But, in 1948, Jeep's lead was usurped by the least likely source. It was another two-door steel wagon ... the midget Crosley. About the size of today's Chevrolet Sprint, it was a four-passenger wagon with scarcely more room than the trunk of a normal-sized sedan.

It seems impossible, but the largest producer of station wagons in 1948 was Powel Crosley. His tiny wagon sold for less than $1,000.

Crosley's narrow 49 inch body won no beauty contests. No wood was used in the wagon, but imitation woodgrain panels on the back half covered up some of Crosley's blandness. At a mere $929, it attracted so many buyers Crosley was the most popular wagon of 1948.

With 23,489 built, Crosley nosed Jeep out of top place in station wagon production. Ford fell to fourth place with only 15,346 wagons, because it was in the middle of a postwar styling changeover. While still peddling its prewar styles, Chevrolet passed Ford for third place with 18,570 woodie wagons.

Chevy and Ford kept their relative positions in 1949, while Crosley plunged to sixth place. Even though it was a flash-in-the-pan, it is phenomenal that such a little car, from such a little company, actually out-produced all the big ones.

Jeep regained its wagon production leadership in 1949, but another new entry took over the number two post. It was Plymouth. Plymouth woodie wagons were available for many years and continued. But, it was not this limited- production model that pushed Plymouth into prominence. Instead, an all-steel two-door Plymouth model became the next station wagon sensation.

Called a familiar name (Suburban), it was mounted on Plymouth's new shorter 111 inch wheelbase chassis. Unlike other popular wagons, it avoided the wood look, although early examples were painted only in a dark walnut color.

The Suburban was slightly more stylish than a cement block. However, being well proportioned and having the same front end as the other Plymouths, the six-passenger Suburban looked the most like a conventional steel car of any station wagon yet made.

The $1,855, the Suburban featured a couple of innovations which quickly became commonplace. The rear seat folded down to form a level floor. Out of sight and out of the way, the spare tire was placed under the floor.

After a spring start, 24,795 Plymouth Suburbans were built. Had it been in production at the beginning of the year, the total might have exceeded the wagons Jeep made for its first place showing.

Introduced in 1949 and competing with its own woodie wagon, the Plymouth Suburban was an innovative car. In 1951, the Suburban was number one in wagon sales.

Top place among wagons changed again in 1950. This time, it was no newcomer that won the sales race. The familiar Chevrolet took the lead. Its production rose 64 percent to 37,100 units. Why such a jump when there seemed to be very little difference from the 1949 models?

Actually there was a major difference, although it was hardly visible. The redesigned 1949 Chevrolet wagon began with wood, but ended the year as an all- steel car. The price of either eight-passenger wagon was $2,267. In 1950, the appeal of the Chevy wagon included its durable body, which had virtually the same appearance as the previous wooden one. Termites tell us wood Chevrolet wagons were those with the angular joints formed by the lighter trim on the rear side panels. The lighter trim formed rounded joints on the steel-bodied wagons.

Similar steel bodies, with imitation wood graining, were used by Pontiac, which was 1950's fifth biggest wagon builder, as well as by Oldsmobile.

Nash was not a station wagon producer until the Rambler came along. The Rambler wagon sold better in 1951 than Ford's wagon.

While Chevrolet wagon production remained steady in 1951, Plymouth took over top spot by building 45,300 Suburbans and Deluxe Savoys. Chevrolet was second with 38,000 wagons made. In third spot, making 29,261 wagons, was yet another newcomer named Rambler.

Nash's compact Rambler convertible, introduced in the spring of 1950, was joined by an $1,808 station wagon later in the year. Of more modest capacity than the Suburban, the five-passenger Rambler applied imitation woodgrain around the windows on some models. Rambler's wagon was styled by the late Don Butler, who actively researched automotive history and wrote several authoritative articles and books.

Ford's 1949-1951 station wagon (dubbed Country Squire after 1950) was unique. The spare tire mounted on the tailgate was a slight continental hint. Also unusual was the two-door body. Few other two-door woodies were made. Despite its uniqueness, the rather bulky-looking station wagon had limited success. Ford had to settle for fourth rank in production.

With Ford's new 1952 styling came new station wagons. These stylish models lifted Ford to top place in the wagon market after a five-year absence.

That suddenly changed when Ford introduced new styling for 1952. Three wagons were offered. The famous Ranch Wagon, selling at $2,079, was the lowest priced. It had two doors, while the Country Sedan and Country Squire each had four doors. The latter was premium-priced and featured attractive artificial wood panel appliques.

These were beautiful-looking wagons, retaining all the stylish flair of Ford sedans thanks to Gordon Buehrig's design skill. His remarkable designs did not end with bodies for Duesenbergs and the 1936-1937 Cord.

Despite slow initial production, Ford built 58,546 wagons in 1952 to secure top spot again. Ford also stayed on top for many years to come. Production totals amounted to 111,230 for 1953, 174,400 in 1954 and 286,241 during 1955. Onward and upward Ford went in the burgeoning station wagon market, as industry production exceeded one million wagons in 1953 and grew annually. This trend even ignored the 1958 recession, when wagon output climbed. It rose again, to 5.4 million total units, in 1959.

By this time, Ford was the undisputed "wagon master." From the end of the World War II to the end of 1959, Ford built over 1.7 million of these cars, or nearly one-third of all domestic station wagons.

Chevrolet ranked second, accounting for almost 25 percent of all wagons in the same period. Plymouth was third, Rambler was fourth, Pontiac was fifth, Jeep came in sixth and Mercury placed seventh. Dodge, which began making wagons for 1950, was eighth. Buick scored ninth. Studebaker, after a late start in 1954, was 10th. Mysteriously, Oldsmobile vanished from the wagon market from 1951 to 1956 and was only 11th. Crosley, from 1948 to its 1952 demise, ranked 12th. After their strong 1950 beginnings, Chrysler and DeSoto were 13th and 14th, respectively. Edsel, 15th, was not the rarest. That honor went to Packard which, from 1947 to 1949, built 3,864 of the most prestigious wagons (called Station Sedans) of the early postwar years.

Postwar Scripts...

A glimpse into 1963

By R. Perry Zavitz

In our annual look into the quarter century rearview mirror, we'll review a few of the 1963 highlights.

The only totally new car introduced that year by any of the Big 3 was Buick's new Riviera. Although the name had been used by Buick since 1949, the 1963 model was an additional model that had no history.

The fact that Ford could sell up to 90,000 four-passenger luxury Ford Thunderbirds naturally caught the attention of its competition. So, General Motors planned a car to muscle in on a share of that segment of the market. Buick was the division selected to offer this car.

The Riviera's styling was original, bearing very little family resemblance to other Buicks or GM cars. It was one of an all too scarce group of cars that had simple, but elegant, styling.

At its introduction, the new Riviera was a two-door hardtop that rode on a 117 inch wheelbase. Overall length was 208 inches, which was shorter than the other Buicks, except the Special and Skylark. However, it was equipped with the same 401 cubic inch V-8 found in the Wildcat, Invicta and Electra lines. It developed 325 horsepower. Even though that was larger and more powerful than the Thunderbird, Riviera buyers could order a 340 horse-power version of the same motor.

The base Riviera tipped the scales at almost an even two tons and carried a base price of $4,333. That undercut the Thunderbird by more than $100.

Creating almost as much public interest as the Riviera, was the restyled Chevrolet Corvette. Although the shape of the lower rear was predicted in the 1962 model, the rest of the fiberglass body was quite different. The front was unique, with its hidden headlights. Only the 1936-1937 Cord, the Graham-Hollywood and the 1942 DeSoto had hidden headlights before. By reviving that feature, Corvette began a trend that has remained almost constantly to the present.

Most important, though, was another styling feature the Corvette revived. As well as the convertible, Corvette offered a coupe for 1963. It was a fastback; a shape which had disappeared at least a decade earlier. The divided rear window of the 1963 Corvette was another former styling item that had fallen by the wayside even before the fastback. Despite the use of these older styling characteristics, the Corvette looked as modern as the minute in 1963.

Of course, performance was what the Corvette buyer really wanted. To satisfy the varying demands of the sports driver, Corvette had three optional engines to offer. They developed 300, 340 or 360 horsepower. The latter was fuel-injected. All these, as well as the 250 horsepower standard V-8, were variations of Chevrolet's 327 cubic inch engine.

Interestingly, the Corvette's new styling brought a lower price. The convertible was $4,037, down a buck from 1962. However, the coupe was $4,252.

Not only GM, but Studebaker too, offered a totally new model and a revision of an existing model. The new Studebaker was the Avanti. The first new car introduced by Studebaker in a long time, the Avanti was a two-door coupe. Although it looked like a hardtop, it had a pillar which was actually part of a built-in roll bar.

Styling for this car was done in a very short time by Bob Andrews, John Ebstein and Tom Kellogg, who were working for Raymond Loewy. He sequestered this trio to a remote ranch house in a California desert. The result was a somewhat controversial design. However, the Avanti II, which emerged after Studebaker quit making cars, is still more or less alive with very little change. This should remove all doubt regarding the style's acceptability.

Standard Avanti engine was a 289 cubic inch V-8 rated at 240 horsepower. Optional was a supercharged version that was rated at 289 horsepower. The Avanti's base price was $4,445, matching the base Thunderbird.

The other 1963 Studebaker to gain attention by its newness and uniqueness was the station wagon. Named Wagonaire, it featured a sliding roof over the cargo area. If anything needed to be hauled that was higher than the 30-1/4 inches between the floor and roof, the roof could be slid forward. Thus, the sky was the limit for any cargo in the Wagonaire.

Among the independents, American Motors was the only company to present new styling for an entire line of 1963 cars. The Rambler Classic and Ambassador donned new suits. The styling was not a great deal different from before, but was noticeably cleaner. The big change in the bodies was the curve in the side windows, which allowed the roof to be a bit narrower. It also tended to decrease light reflections at night. Today, this is so commonplace we seldom give it a thought. But, in 1963, it was a rarity, especially among cars in the Rambler price range.

The smaller Rambler American only received superficial styling changes. However, a two-door hardtop was added to the top line. Actually, there were two versions of the hardtop; the 440 and the upgraded 440-H.

Available with overdrive-equipped American and Classic models was a twin-stick transmission control. This allowed the driver to shift in or out of overdrive, rather than try to control such shifting by uncertain foot pressure on the gas pedal.

The restyled 1963 Chryslers included the Town & Country station wagon in either Newport or New Yorker trim. Both were pillarless hardtop wagons.

Another car that introduced new styling for 1963 was Chrysler. The trapezoidal grille gave the new bodies a Chrysler identity. The Town & Country station wagon was available in either Newport or New Yorker trim. Of further interest, the Town & Country, in either Newport or New Yorker version, was of pillarless design. They were hardtop station wagons. It was a Chrysler 300 convertible driven by Sam Hanks that paced the Indianapolis 500 for 1963.

The already mentioned Corvette, with a fastback, initiated a return of that body style. While there were no other such cars in the 1963 model year, Ford took a step in that direction by offering a Sports hardtop. It was a full-size two-door hardtop with a long sloping rear window. Mercury did likewise, calling its model the Marauder. It was in sharp contrast to the other full-size Mercurys. All of them, except the convertible and station wagon, featured a backward sloping rear window. Some would even roll down electrically.

The most noticeable change in the 1963 Mercury full-size models was the reverse angle of the rear window, which could be lowered electrically.

During 1963, a number of records and milestones were noted. A record number of cars were built: 7,346,845. Also, 7,556,717 was a record number of sales. One in every eight cars built was a station wagon. Over 61 percent of the cars sold were V-8s. That was up from 55 percent the year before.

The 49 millionth Chevrolet was built on February 14 in St. Louis, Missouri, followed (on June 10) by the 50 millionth Chevrolet made in Tarrytown, New York. Meanwhile, the Ford Motor Company made its 60 millionth vehicle. It was a Mercury S-55 hardtop.

Postwar Scripts...

A tale of two wagons

By R. Perry Zavitz

Station wagons became very popular after World War II. It was then that manufacturers realized station wagons need not have traditional varnished wood bodies. These looked great, but deteriorated fast.

When Jeep, Plymouth and others offered steel-bodied wagons, sales shot right off the charts. Station wagon production went from less than 32,000, in 1946, to almost one million, in 1959. Station wagons grew from less than 1.5 percent to almost 17 percent of total car production in the same period. Then, their popularity leveled off.

Wagon styling became much more car-like, instead of resembling a small shed turned inside out. Also, handy features were developed for wagons, such as fold-down rear seats and roll-down rear windows. Such items were soon considered basic wagon equipment.

When Studebaker announced its 1963 wagon, it had an interesting new feature. The rear half of the roof could be slid forward. This opened up the cargo area to accept objects too high to fit into other wagons. As far as height was concerned, the sky was literally the limit in this new Wagonaire (as it was called). Otherwise, Studebaker wagons could not handle anything more than 10-1/4 inches high.

The 1963 Studebaker Wagonaire could be used as a passenger car, a pickup or a convertible. Its sliding roof was quite a unique feature.

There was not even a support across the back end of the roof, which would have hampered the loading of tall objects. So, in effect, the Wagonaire was just about as handy as a pickup truck, but came without a truck's utilitarian and commercial appearance. In addition, the open/close transformation was a simple matter. It took very little effort and just a few seconds. This also made the wagon into a "convertible" for the third-seat passengers.

Interior cargo space was 75 cubic feet in the Wagonaire. That was appreciably more than either the Rambler or Valiant wagons.

All 1963 Studebaker station wagons were known as Wagonaires. They were four-door, six-passenger models. Listed options included a rear-facing fold-down third seat, a folding ladder step on the tailgate and a roof rack.

Like the Lark passenger models, Wagonaires were available in Regal or Daytona trim. Similarly, 112 horsepower six-cylinder or 180 horsepower V-8 engines were offered. Three-speed manual transmission was standard, but overdrive, automatic or four-on-the-floor were optional.

Base prices ranged from $2,550 for the Regal six to $2,835 for the Daytona V-8. That was quite competitive with Ford's Fairlane wagons.

The 1964 Wagonaire came in three series: Challenger, Commander, Daytona, which were offered as the result of new model line ups by Studebaker. The Lark name was gone. Wagonaires could still be ordered with six or V-8 power. But, in midyear, production was halted. Studebaker decided to shut their South Bend, Indiana factory and concentrate car manufacturing at Hamilton, Ontario, Canada. The Wagonaire got lost in that shuffle.

The Wagonaire is not to be confused with the Wagoneer. About six weeks after the 1963 Wagonaire was introduced in showrooms across the country, the Wagoneer made its appearance in other dealerships. It was completely restyled station wagon from the Kaiser-Jeep Corp.

That was the new company name for the former Willys Motors Incorporated. Actually, there had been several name changes since the Jeep first went into production during World War II at Willys-Overland Motors. At war's end, civilian Jeep production continued. In 1946, a station wagon with Jeep styling was added. It remained in the line, with little exterior changes, through 1964 (after the Wagoneer arrived).

The first postwar auto merger took place when Kaiser bought Willys in 1953. Because Kaiser and Willys cars were unsuccessful in the North American market, production was transferred to Argentina and Brazil, respectively, to cater to those markets. However, Jeeps and Jeep wagons were still built in Toledo, Ohio. They had found a comfortable corner in the North American market and, indeed, in the world market.

The first major styling change for the wagon came with the 1963 model. Like the original, the new wagon bore a strong frontal resemblance to the familiar military Jeep.

The Wagoneer shed much of the boxy appearance of its predecessor partly by becoming 5-1/2 inches longer and almost 20 inches lower. It was also over seven inches wider than the earlier model. However, the new shape did not yield as large a cargo area as the former wagon. The Wagoneer had 78 cubic feet for cargo ... 20 inches less than before. But, a new trick was added to give as much as 107 cubic feet. The front seat was divided and the right one-third of the seat could be folded down to make extra room.

Mechanically, there was a lot about which the Wagoneer could boast. It had an overhead cam engine, new the year before, that developed 140 horsepower. "The only American-made automotive engine with overhead cam design" claimed the catalog. (And none of us ever thought of Kaiser as an engine innovator!) This six-cylinder motor had a displacement of 230 cubic inches. Although Chevrolet's six also had a 230 cubic inches, the Kaiser-Jeep engine was actually about a quarter of a cube bigger. Both were rated at 140 horsepower. Testers comments about that being a conservative rating were made concerning the Wagoneer, but not the Chevrolet. Regardless, there were no other six-cylinder engines with higher power ratings that year.

The 1963 Jeep Wagoneer had an overhead cam engine and options included four-wheel drive (with or without automatic transmission) and Powr-Lok rear differential.

One unique item available on the Wagoneer came as no surprise. Being a member of the Jeep family, four-wheel drive was an expected option. But, there were some surprises available with this feature. An automatic transmission was available with either two- or four-wheel drive. This automatic 4x4 was a first. Also new, with four-wheel drive, was a Powr-Lok rear differential so the Wagoneer could go places and do things no other vehicle could.

The Wagoneer had no-nonsense styling, yet it was neither austere nor utilitarian looking. Perhaps it seemed more at home in front of a posh country club than climbing out of a gully. But, the Wagoneer could do its job well in either location.

It was available in either a two- or four-door body and with standard or Deluxe trim. Chrome window moldings marked the Deluxe models. Neither a third seat nor other engines were offered. Prices ranged from $2,546 for the two-door 4x2 to $3,526 for the Deluxe four-door 4x4 model.

After a couple years, the Jeep-style grille disappeared. The Wagoneer was soon known as a rugged, dependable vehicle in its own right. It no longer needed the Jeep appearance to convey that message.

Also, V-8 power was offered, simulated wood trim was made available and, occasionally, a special model featuring unique trim packages showed up.

While the Studebaker Wagonaire disappeared in 1964, the Jeep Wagoneer has survived to modern times. It became known as the Grand Wagoneer. This nameplate was sold at your nearby Jeep-Eagle dealer; a division of Chrysler Corporation.

Yes, corporate changes have continued. In early 1970, American Motors bought the Jeep division from Kaiser. Then, Chrysler bought AMC. The Wagoneer has been a dependable and durable vehicle. The fact that it has survived, basically unchanged, through 25 years (six years longer than the highly acclaimed Model T) and three corporate ownerships, pretty well proves a point.

Olds "rocketed" industry into new performance age

By R. Perry Zavitz

It was September 15, 1948, when Oldsmobile introduced something quite sensational. Not only was a new model launched on that date, but the car itself "rocketed" the industry into a new age of performance.

Because the Olds 88 was so impressive, the entire American auto industry soon was cranking out thousands of cars following its lead.

What made this car so special was not that it was the first "Olds 88" ever produced, but its all-new V-8 engine. The same engine powered the top-of-the-line Oldsmobile 98, but the 98 was a big, heavy car. It needed a powerful engine.

Placing this powerful engine in the small Oldsmobile body was comparable to dropping a big, powerful Pontiac engine into a mid-size body to create the GTO, which marked the start of the muscle car era. The first Oldsmobile 88 caused similar repercussions in the industry.

This new engine was not Oldsmobile's first V-8. It had offered V-8 power in its 1916 to 1923 models and again in the 1929-1930 Viking. Since that time, technology had progressed, so the 1949 V-8 was very different from its early predecessors.

The valves were situated in the head. The stroke was short in relation to the bore. And compression was considerably higher. In fact, it was the goal of much higher compression that led Oldsmobile to develop this overhead valve, short stroke V-8 engine.

A 1949 Oldsmobile Rocket 88 ragtop paced the 69th Indy 500 with famous race car pilot Wilbur Shaw behind the wheel. (IMSC)

The L-head design slowed the flow of incoming fuel, so the more efficient valve-in-head configuration was used. The centrifugal forces of the fast rotating engine were reduced by shortening the stroke. Other advantages included smoother operation, less piston wear per engine revolution and a physically lower engine, which the design people cheered.

The much greater stresses of the higher compression and power were better handled by a short V-8, instead of a long straight eight block. The crankshaft, about half the length in the new Oldsmobile engine, had five main bearings. There was no weight saving in the V-8 over its straight-eight predecessor. In fact, the new motor was slightly heavier, but lighter per horsepower developed.

Called the Rocket engine, the new V-8 had a displacement of 303.7 cubic inches. It developed 17 percent more horsepower than the one it replaced; 135 versus 115 horsepower. And that was the whole reason Oldsmobile was going for higher compression. The higher the compression, the more power could be extracted from the fuel. The more power developed per gallon of fuel, the less fuel burned per mile of travel.

A 1950 Oldsmobile 88 rips down a dragstrip. (Old Cars)

The factory issued an optional plexiglas hood. (Old Cars)

Hershel McGriff won the 1950 Mexican Road Race in a 1950 Oldsmobile.

Oldsmobile's aim was to produce an engine with 8.0:1 compression. However, their 1949 V-8 had only 7.25:1 compression. They missed their target, but mainly because of inadequate fuels. This and the 7.5 compression of the new Cadillac engine put a great deal of pressure on the oil industry to develop and make universally available higher octane gasolines.

In anticipation of increasingly higher octane gasoline in the forthcoming years, Oldsmobile designed their engine so higher compression could be reached easily and inexpensively. Their Rocket V-8 could go as high as 12:1 compression.

Many other car makers joined the high-compression V-8 club. Cadillac introduced their high-compression V-8 simultaneously with Oldsmobile. Within three years, Chrysler, Studebaker, DeSoto and Lincoln were using new V-8 power. One exception was Hudson, which chose to compete by using a six-cylinder inline motor. The 1951 Hudson Hornet's six was larger and developed 10 more horsepower than the 88's engine.

It is no surprise that the 1952 Oldsmobile engine got an increase of power. Compression had been raised to 7.5:1 for 1951, but with no change in the power rating was seen then. The 1952 Oldsmobile 88, however, was rated at 145 horsepower. Since 1951, Oldsmobile offered a Super 88. This was an upscale 88. The 1952 Super 88 had a hotter version of the engine than the lesser 88. It boasted 160 horsepower, thanks to a four-barrel carburetor.

The horsepower race was on. It seemed just as important at this time for car companies to increase their engine power each year as it was to design a new grille. Oldsmobile was not going to let the others pull out and pass.

For 1953, Oldsmobile raised its compression to 8.0:1, as originally planned. The 88 engine was consequently rated at 150 horsepower. The Super 88's motor developed 165 horsepower.

The competitive urge to increase horsepower was growing faster than the practical limits of compression would permit. For 1954, compression was raised to 8.25:1. But, to gain further output, Oldsmobile used the easiest trick in the book ... increased engine size. The bore was made one-eighth inch longer. Displacement grew to 324.3 cubic inches. Rated horsepower jumped to 170 for the 88 and 185 for the Super 88.

Their high-performance reputation made 88s popular as pace cars. This one handled starting duties at the Milwaukee Mile. (Phil Hall photo collection)

Compression was raised, for 1955, to 8.5:1 with horsepower increasing to 185 and 202 for the 88 and Super 88, respectively. Actually, the hotter Rocket was offered in the 88 for a modest $35. Then, for 1956, a big jump in compression to 9.25:1 helped increase the rating to 230 horsepower in the 88 and 240 in the Super 88.

Still another rise in compression, to 9.5:1, was made for the 1957 Oldsmobile. But that in itself was not enough to be competitive in the horsepower race. Displacement was enlarged by increasing both bore and stroke. The 370.1 cubic inches resulted from a one-eighth inch larger bore and one-quarter inch longer stroke. The new rating was 277 horsepower. It is noteworthy that this rating was more than twice that of the original Rocket engine.

There was only one standard version of the engine used in all 1957 models. However, there were some rare examples of J-2 versions which had three carburetors.

The year 1958 was a year of recession. Car sales fell 22 percent. Oldsmobile was affected by the recession, but not to that extent. Its sales fell only 17 percent.

Although compression was hiked up to an even 10.0:1, horsepower receded to 265. Perhaps this was the result of a more honest rating. The 265 horsepower engine was used in the Dynamic 88, the bottom line series of 1958. But, the less popular Super 88 and 98 lines got a 305 horsepower version of the engine.

The 1959 Oldsmobile 88 had some engine surprises. After six consecutive years of compression increases, it dropped a notch to 9.75:1 for 1959. In the Dynamic 88, power was nudged up to 270 horsepower. But, the Super 88 had a different version. With a one-eighth inch larger bore, displacement grew to 394 cubic inches. Compression, as in the smaller edition, was 9.75:1, but horsepower rose to 315.

Oldsmobile's engine development was an industry pace setter. It helped put Oldsmobile higher on the sales charts, too. Production of the 88, Super 88 and Dynamic 88 during its first 10 models years amounted to a total in excess of 2,500,000.

Oldsmobile was successful in significantly improving the efficiency of its engine. As compression rose from 7.5:1 to 10:1, power rose dramatically. The original Rocket V-8 developed .445 horsepower per cubic inch of displacement. Surprisingly, that was slightly less than its old straight eight predecessor. However, by 1959, the horsepower per cubic inch figure was pushed up to .840, almost double. That was progress.

Postwar Scripts...

In defense of the "pregnant" Packards

By R. Perry Zavitz

Even though Packard underwent extensive styling changes from the 21st Series to the 22nd Series (1947 to 1948 models), these cars were very little different in profile. Obviously the new shape was mostly in the sides.

The 1948 body became a full-width body. It was widened between the front and rear fenders. That was just about what all the car makers were doing then; making slab-sided cars. Packard kept in step with the times.

Probably, the biggest mistake in this design was not making the greenhouse wider as well. Had the car been wider from the belt line up, it would not have looked like the "pregnant elephant" critics compared it to. Check the convertible and see how much better it looks, compared to the closed cars. With the top down, there is nothing above the belt line to make the lower sides look bulgy.

Whether you liked it or not, Packard's new styling was good enough to be awarded the "Fashion Car of the Year" gold medal from the New York Fashion Academy. Other styling awards were received in Switzerland, Rome, Monte Carlo, Bulgaria and even Colombia.

Speaking of the convertible, that was exactly what Packard began building first in their 23rd Series. There had not been one built by Packard since the war, so great emphasis was placed on it by introducing it in July 1947. Closed models were not introduced until several months later.

Packard was not so dumb as to build just convertibles during that time. The 21st Series cars remained in production until the 22nd Series sedans and coupes were ready.

There were three model lines: Standard Eight, Super Eight and Custom Eight. The Standard Eight and Super Eight models were very much the same, except for the motor.

Both motors were straight eights, of course. For the Standard Eight, a 288 cubic inch engine developed 130 horsepower. The Super Eight's engine had a half-inch longer stroke, giving it 327 cubic inches and a 145 horsepower rating. The Standard Eight and Super Eight were the same size. Wheelbase was 120 inches and overall length ran 204-5/8 inches.

Touring sedan was the label Packard put on the four-door trunk sedan and club sedan was the label for the two-door fastback. The Standard Eight offered these body types in standard and deluxe versions. Exclusive to the Standard Eight was the station sedan ... a wood station wagon.

Both the touring and club sedans were available in the Super Eight line. A deluxe edition did not offer the club sedan, though. However, there were two stretched models. Riding on a 141 inch wheelbase was a touring sedan and seven-passenger limousine. The convertible, called a Victoria, was a standard Super Eight model.

The ultimate Packard of the time was the Custom Eight convertible. This 22nd Series edition boasted a 127-inch wheelbase and a 356 cubic inch 160 horsepower straight eight engine.

Topping the Packard lines was the Custom Eight. It was larger than the other Packards, with a wheelbase of 127 inches and overall length of 211-3/4 inches.

Body types included the touring sedan, club sedan and Victoria convertible. Using an extended wheelbase of 148 inches was another touring sedan.

Powering the Custom was a 356 cubic inch straight eight rated at 160 horsepower. This was the largest and most powerful motor used in a 1948 domestic car. The Custom Victoria listed for $4,295 or just $450 less than the Lincoln Continental cabriolet.

The trim set the Custom apart from all other Packards. The 22nd Series had a very nicely styled grille consisting of two sections. The upper section was narrow with the top edge retaining the traditional Packard yoke. In this section were three horizontal chrome bars. Below it were more horizontal bars running across the entire front, from fender to fender. The bumper was even designed with a couple of ridges, to blend into this horizontal motif.

The Custom grille had both horizontal and vertical bars, giving an egg-crate appearance. Nowhere on the Custom did the name Packard appear. If you did not know it was a Packard, then forget it. At the low end of the Packard spectrum was the six. Two body types were made ... a four-door sedan for export and a long-wheelbase model for taxi service.

Packard stubbornly ignored the calendar, bringing out new models when it felt like it. The 22nd Series spilled well into 1949, which was Packard's "golden anniversary" year. Some celebration seemed in order. So, in the spring of 1949, the 23rd Series was announced. The cars were hardly changed.

The grille, indeed the whole front end, was unaltered. However, the Super Eight models received the Custom grille; the one that the Custom used. The Custom no longer had the front bumper that matched the criss-cross grillework. Instead, it had a plain bumper like the other models.

The side and rear trim made the 23rd Series identifiable. About halfway up each side, a chrome strip ran nearly the whole length of the car. This chrome piece ended on the taillight, on the Super and Super Deluxe models, and just short of the taillight on the Standard Eight models. The taillights themselves were totally different. Instead of being the flush rectangles of the 22nd Series, they were oval chrome protrusions.

Despite the common grille, there was a slight difference between the Super Eight and the Custom Eight. This was the chrome strip along the belt line. On the 22nd Series, it ended about two-thirds of the way down the trunk lid on all models. However, on the 23rd Series, it usually ended where it met the trunk lid at the top, except on Custom Eights. Then, it surrounded the sides and even the bottom of the trunk door.

The Packard name appeared on the front fenders, above the chrome strip, on all models including the Custom. However, no changes were made to the Station Sedan.

There was an additional change in the 23rd Super Eight line. It used the same 127 inch Custom wheelbase, which brought the total length to 211-3/4 inches ... identical to the Custom Eights.

The 23rd Series Packards are most easily distinguished from their predecessors by the chrome strip midway up the side, as seen on this Standard Eight Club Sedan.

Some fine-tuning to the engine raised the output of both the Standard Eights and the Super Eights five horsepower (to 135 and 150, respectively). The Custom Eight stayed at its plentiful 160 horsepower, allowing Cadillac to play catch up with its new V-8.

Several models did not appear in the 23rd Series. The six was dropped right after the start of production. Missing entirely were the long-wheelbase Custom Eight models. Even the Super Eight stretch models disappeared during the model run. But, none of this was very exciting for a 50th anniversary.

The excitement was a $225 option. It was a torque converter automatic transmission and appropriately named Ultramatic. It had a reputation for reliability. With this, Packard became the only independent American car-maker to engineer and manufacture its own modern automatic transmission. Even Ford could not muster that much effort until later.

One feature that made the Ultramatic unique was its lock-up design. At speeds between 15 and 50 miles per hour, the final gear would connect directly to the flywheel. This eliminated fuel-wasting slippage. This is a feature the other automakers are just recently beginning to incorporate. Was Packard 40 years ahead with this kind of transmission or were the others 40 years behind?

The 23rd Series ended in the summer of 1950. Packard sales amounted to 77,843 during 1948, a record 97,771 in 1949, and 73,155 for 1950. Packard far outsold both Lincoln in each of these years. It also outsold Cadillac in 1948 and 1949.

The hardtop's first decade

By R. Perry Zavitz

It was called the hardtop, but not because it was the first type of car with a hard roof.

The full term was hardtop convertible, but it was not a convertible. The roof was fixed and would not open. However, with the windows rolled down, the sides were as open as a convertible with the top up.

What really made this body style different from other cars was that the doors had no window frames and there was no center post to support the roof. It looked almost like a convertible with the top up.

There were sporadic attempts to make cars like this as far back as the 1920s, but it was not until 1949 that the idea finally caught on.

General Motors generated the greatest interest when, in mid-season, they introduced the hardtop in the top series of Buick, Cadillac and Oldsmobile. Chrysler took exception to GM's claim of introducing the hardtop, because they had made hardtops in their Town & Country line in 1946. However, only six of them were built and they were not offered for public sale. That made GM's boast technically correct.

The 1949 Buick Roadmaster Riviera was the first postwar production hardtop to be introduced to the public. It was followed, shortly after, by the Cadillac and Oldsmobile hardtops. (Buick)

The Buick Riviera, Cadillac Coupe DeVille and Oldsmobile Holiday were two-door models. But, in the same year, another hardtop was introduced. It came from the new kid on the block: Kaiser-Frazer. They had a convertible in their 1949 line up and they also added a model that was based on the convertible's appearance, but had a fixed steel roof.

Called the Virginian, this Kaiser was different in an important respect from the hardtops of any other manufacturer. Kaiser was making only four-door cars then, so the Virginian was a four-door hardtop. Also enhancing the Virginian's top was a vinyl covering. It was among the industry's first vinyl-covered roof, although some earlier cars had leather or "simulated leather" roof coverings.

Only 10,000 hardtops were built in 1949. But, this new type of car was popular enough that production continued in 1950 and sales expanded considerably. General Motors produced more hardtops in the lines already offering them and added them to lower priced series: Buick's Super, Cadillac's Series 61 and Oldsmobile's 88 and 76 series.

Pontiac used the name Catalina to identify the hardtop that it introduced in 1950. (Pontiac)

Hardtop availabilities were also extended to the remaining GM divisions. Pontiac made the Catalina hardtop in its Chieftain Deluxe and Chieftain Super Deluxe lines and Chevrolet's Styleline series included the Bel Air hardtop.

This brought the hardtop within the reach of more car buyers. The Bel Air was priced at $1,741. This compared to $2,973 for the Oldsmobile Holiday, the lowest priced 1949 hardtop.

Chrysler did not let the hardtop idea die after their first six prototypes. The Newport was introduced in the Windsor, New Yorker and Town & Country lines of Chrysler. Also, the Sportsman hardtop was offered as a DeSoto Custom and the Diplomat hardtop joined Dodge's Coronet series.

Ford's first real hardtop came along in 1951. Prior to that, the company offered a two-door sedan-coupe with special Crestliner trim features. (Old Cars)

Ford was caught unprepared for the hardtop era. They quickly cooked up the Ford Crestliner, the Mercury Monterey and the Lincoln Lido and Capri. These 1950 and 1951 models were two-door cars with fancy finishes and trim. They were not true hardtops.

Then, in January 1951, Ford put a real hardtop on the market. Resurrecting the Victoria for its name, Ford made up for lost time by producing over 110,000 hardtops by year's end. The Victoria led hardtop production for calendar 1951, being the first to exceed the 100,000 level.

At the end of March, the Plymouth Belvedere hardtop made its debut. The independents joined the trend with the Nash-Rambler Country Club coupe, the Packard Mayfair, the Hudson Hollywood and the Frazer Vagabond. The latter was made from carryover Kaiser Virginian four-door hardtops, which Kaiser could no longer use after its radical redesign in early 1951.

Studebaker offered no hardtop until the Starliner was introduced, with their other 1952 models, in December 1951. A month later, Willys premiered its first postwar passenger cars. They included the Aero Eagle hardtop. Shortly after, the Mercury Monterey and Lincoln hardtops made their first appearance. The only automakers not building hardtops were Henry J and Crosley.

Through calendar-year 1952, the American auto industry produced over half a million hardtops. They had quickly become very sought after cars.

It was 1955 when a significant development occurred. Although four-door hardtops had been offered earlier by Kaiser and Frazer, it was not until now that the others made such body types available. In January, Buick and Oldsmobile offered four-door hardtops in addition to their two-door models.

Even though 470,500 four-door hardtops were built during 1955, they seemed not to have cut into sales of two-door hardtops. For the first time, two-door hardtop production shot past the million mark, reaching a total of almost 1.7 million. Together, two- and four- door hardtop production reached 2.1 million.

The long-awaited Lincoln Continental Mark II appeared on October 5, 1955 as a 1956 model. This $10,000 car was offered only in two-door hardtop configuration, except for a pair of experimental convertibles built.

After Oldsmobile and Buick introduced four-door hardtops in 1955, just about every other make had them ready in 1956. This Dodge is one such example. (Chrysler)

In 1956, Rambler's all-new body design was limited only to four-door models. Hardtops were included. Among them was the industry's first hardtop station wagon.

As early as their second year of production, Buick and Oldsmobile produced more four-door hardtops than two-door hardtops. Pontiac achieved that distinction in 1957. Combined two- and four-door hardtop production exceeded assemblies of four-door sedans, for the first time in history, in 1957.

Also noteworthy among the 1957 hardtop cars was Mercury. All of its station wagons, whether two- or four-door models, were of the pillarless hardtop style. Production data counts most hardtop station wagons simply as station wagons, not as hardtops. However, they cannot be ignored in a hardtop survey.

The next new hardtop to appear was in the 1958 Edsel line up. Two- and four-door hardtops were offered in each of the series, except the station wagon series. The recession of 1958 caused car production to fall by almost one-third. That was reflected in hardtop production, too. It plunged 57 percent. The public was slow to buy in 1958. When they did, they were inclined to choose conventional sedans. The market rebounded somewhat in 1959 and hardtop production increased, but not quite proportionally.

About one car in four built in 1959 was a hardtop. In 1957, the ratio was one-in-three. The percentage of hardtops produced in each calendar-year grew annually from 1949 (0.2 percent) to 1957 (33.3 percent). Then, hardtop popularity slumped to a low of 22.7 percent in 1960. However, it took off again thereafter, increasing annually, and climbing to 58.2 percent in 1969. A slow decline followed after that, with a drop to 41.9 percent by 1976. After that, hardtop production quickly dropped out of sight.

Of course, we are primarily concerned with the hardtops made before 1960. During those years, Chevrolet turned out the most; nearly two million. However, Ford produced more two-door hardtops to lead the industry with 1.4 million. Ford was the two-door hardtop leader during 1956, 1957 and 1959. Buick was the four-door hardtop leader for 1955 and 1956.

As hardtop production was on the increase, the following cars scored the greatest increase over the previous calendar year: Dodge in 1951; Nash in 1952; Plymouth in 1953; Dodge in 1954; DeSoto in 1955; Lincoln in 1956; Plymouth in 1957; and Studebaker in 1959. No one increased production in 1958, but Chevrolet suffered the smallest drop.

From the end of 1949 to the end of 1959, an aggregate total of nearly 11.8 million hardtops were built. That accounts for one out of every five American cars made. The hardtop's popularity was truly phenomenal in the 1950s and it grew even more during the 1960s. In the 1970s, new safety-oriented structural requirements lead to the demise of this good-looking, sporty body style.

What's in a name?

By Bill Siuru

Marketing people agonize over long periods to find suitable names for new automobile models. Choosing the right name can be almost as important as styling and engineering in determining the success of a car.

Prior to the 1950s, lots of cars went around with mundane names like Deluxe, Custom and Special. In the 1950s, the automakers started to see the importance of picking the right name as a way to enhance the image of a particular model. Let's look at the names of many of the General Motors cars of this period to see when particular names were first used and where they came from.

At Buick, the names Special, Century, Roadmaster and Limited were used well before World War II. After the war, Century and Limited were not used for several years. The Century reappeared, in 1954, on a Buick muscle car. It used the large Super/Roadmaster 195 hp V-8 in the lighter weight Special body.

In 1958, the year that chrome reached its peak use, the name Limited reappeared for a single year. This time it was used on the biggest and gaudiest cars in the Buick line up. In 1959, Buicks had a complete change in nomenclature, as well as major changes in body styling. Specials became LeSabres, Centurys became Invictas and Super and Roadmasters became Electras and Electra 225s respectively. The title Special would appear again, on Buick's compact car, in 1961.

The Wildcat name first appeared on a mid-1962 Buick with "wild" performance. Seen here is the 1964 Wildcat Sport Coupe. (Buick)

Riviera was originally a name associated with Buick hardtops, the first one appearing in 1949. It was used on both two- and four-door hardtops. In 1963, the name was transferred to Buick's personal/luxury car, which was designed to compete in the Thunderbird and Eldorado arena. Naturally, the name Riviera comes from the French resort area and is associated with fun-loving luxury.

The title Wildcat first appeared on a production car in 1962. It was used on a special model in the Invicta series; a luxurious hardtop with bucket seats, distinctive exterior trim and a vinyl-covered roof. In 1964, Wildcat replaced Invicta as a designation for Buick's middle series. Wildcat was Buick's contribution to the list of fierce-sounding animal names that were used as car titles in the 1960s.

For most of the time, Cadillac has used numerical designations, such as Series 61, Series 62, Series 60 and Series 75. When Cadillac did choose names for its models, they were chosen to connote the elegance and affluence associated with the marque. When Cadillac introduced its hardtop in 1949, it was called the Coupe DeVille after an elegant body style of the custom body era. Later, the DeVille (sometimes spelled deVille) title was applied to several other Cadillac models, such as the Sedan DeVille four-door hardtop. Finally, there was an entire DeVille series.

Eldorado is another expensive-sounding title that has been used by Cadillac for many years, starting with the 1953 limited-edition convertible. In 1954 and 1955, the Eldorado nameplate was used on special top-of-the-line convertibles. In 1956, a two-door hardtop was added to the Eldorado series and the additional name Seville was tacked on. At the same time, the name Biarritz was also added to the Eldorado nameplate. Seville came from the Spanish town, while Biarritz is a French beach community.

In 1957, Cadillac brought out its limited edition four-door hardtop to compete with the Continental Mark II. It was given a rich-sounding name: Eldorado Brougham. In 1965, Cadillac called its lowest priced series the Calais, named after the French town on the English Channel.

Like the other GM divisions, Chevrolet's first use of a name with real character came with its first hardtop in 1950. The name Bel Air, associated with an affluent Southern California community, was chosen. In 1953, the name was used for all the top-of-the-line Chevrolets. By 1959, Bel Air was relegated to second place, being surpassed by the Impala designation. The Impala is an African antelope known for its speed. In 1958, when the Impala name first appeared on convertible and two-door hardtop models, they were still part of the Bel Air series.

The Biscayne that Chevrolet introduced in 1958 was named after upscale Biscayne Bay, although it was a low-rung model. (Chevrolet)

On several occasions, Chevrolet has also used geographical places that suggest fun and pleasure. These have included Biscayne, for Biscayne Bay in Florida; Malibu, for the Southern California Beach; and, naturally, Monte Carlo. It has also used names that have no meanings or very odd meanings.

Rumors had it that Chevrolet's Mustang-fighting "pony car" of 1967 was to be called the Panther. This was a macho-sounding name like Cougar, Marlin and Mustang. Instead, Chevrolet chose Camaro. It was a name that did not mean anything, but sounded good. When Chevrolet picked the name Caprice for its flagship models in 1966, they probably did not look up the word in the dictionary. If they had, they would have found it means, among other things, "a head with hair sticking out" or "a sudden change of mind or whim."

For the deluxe version of the Chevy II, it used the name Nova, implying the car was a star of supreme brilliance. The Corvair Monza had the famous Italian racecourse as its namesake.

The names Dynamic, and its derivative Futuramic, appeared in Oldsmobile titles for several years to highlight Oldsmobile's advanced engineering and styling. Oldsmobile's first hardtop, in 1949, was called a Holiday coupe. From then on, most Oldsmobile hardtops were designated as Holidays. Likewise, through the years, Oldsmobile station wagons were titled Fiestas. However, the name Fiesta first appeared, in 1953, on a limited-edition convertible that was Oldsmobile's counterpart to the original Buick Skylark and Cadillac Eldorado.

The 88, Oldsmobile's bread-and-butter car, has had a proliferation of adjectives placed before the numerals 88. They have ranged from Dynamic and Futuramic, to Delta and Delmont. One interesting numerical designation was given to the Oldsmobile muscle car, the 442. At first, the first 4 stood for the four-speed transmission, the second stood for the four-barrel carburetor, and the 2 stood for the dual exhaust. Later, the first 4 meant that a 400 cubic inch V-8 was under the hood, while the other numbers meant the same.

Pontiac's 1951 two-door hardtop was again named after Catalina Island. Until 1959, the terms Catalina and hardtop were synonymous to Pontiac buyers.

When Olds started producing a compact, in 1961, a title was chosen that had a United States Air Force fighter ring to it ... F-85. Actually, the designation was inspired by Oldsmobile's own F-88 show car, the numbers 85 being chosen to distinguish it from the full-size 88. Deluxe versions, and later the whole line up, were designated with Cutlass, a seafaring name. When Oldsmobile wanted to get into the bucket seat action of the 1960s, it chose names like Starfire, Jetfire and Jetstar. These were very "space age" names, quite fitting for the space generation that was just getting underway.

Oldsmobile introduced its personal luxury car in 1966 and called it Toronado, a name that did not mean anything, but does suggest speed and power. The name had previously been used on a one-off Chevrolet show car, in 1963. Starting in 1966, certain station wagon models were built with a portion of the roof raised in the rear and included a "windshield" to improve the view for the back seat passengers. Thus, the panoramic rail-car name Vista Cruiser was quite appropriate.

Since Pontiac's namesake is a famous Indian chief, it is logical that Pontiac picked titles like Chieftain, Star Chief and Super Chief for its cars between 1950 and 1966. As a point of history, when first introduced in 1926, Pontiacs were billed as the "Chief of the Sixes." Of course, care should be taken to avoid Pontiac references that might be insulting to Native Americans.

Carrying a jet-like designation, the first modern small Oldsmobile was the 1961 F-85. The Cutlass was the fancy version. (Oldsmobile)

When Pontiac brought out its own pony car, in 1967, it was called Firebird after the legendary Indian symbol, which implies action, power, beauty and youth. (The name had also been used on prototype GM gas turbine cars.)

When the first Pontiac hardtop appeared in 1950 it was called a Catalina after the island off the California coast. In 1959, the name was given to Pontiac's entire low-priced line. The name Ventura also had a Southern California flavor.

In 1962, Pontiacs started taking on a youthful, performance-oriented image and names were chosen to complement this image. The name LeMans, after the famous French road race, first appeared on specially-quipped Tempest convertibles and sport coupes. Then there was the GTO, an abbreviation for Gran Turismo Omologato. To officially qualify for this title in international motorsport circles, a car must have high speed potential and good road manners, while still being capable of carrying people and their belongings. The GTO certainly fit the bill.

For its personal luxury car, Pontiac chose the name Grand Prix, another title associated with motorsports. The nameplate Bonneville came from the Bonneville Salt Flats, in Utah, where Pontiac set a 24-hour endurance record in 1956.

Names are important in selling cars and the people at GM know this. They spend a lot of time and effort in selecting the right names.

Gm Series and Sub-series Names 1946-1970

BUICK

Caballero (1957-1958)	Century (1954-1958)
Electra (1959-1970)	Estate Wagon (1946-1964 and 1970)
Gran Sport & GS (1966-1970)	Invicta (1959-1963)
LeSabre (1959-1970)	Limited (1958)
Special (1946-1958 and 1961-1968)	Riviera (1949-1970)
Roadmaster (1946-1958)	Skylark (1953-1954 and 1961-1970)
Sport Wagon (1964-1970)	Super (1946-1958)
Wildcat (1962-1970)	

CADILLAC

Biarritz (1956-1964)
Calais (1965-1970)
Eldorado (1953-1970)
Imperial (1946-1954)
Series 60 or Sixty (1946-1970)
Series 62 (1946-1964)
Seville (1956-1960)

Brougham (1957-1960 and 1966-1970)
DeVille (1949-1970)
Fleetwood (1946-1970)
Park Avenue (1962-1963)
Series 61 (1946-51)
Series 75 or Seventy-Five (1946-1970)
Town Car (1961-1962)

CHEVROLET

Aerosedan (1946-1948)
Bel Air (1950-1970)
Brookwood (1958-1961 and 1970)
Caprice (1966-1970)
Chevy II (1962-1969)
Corsa (1965-1966)
Corvette (1953-1970)
Fleetline (1946-1952)
Greenbrier (1961-1965) and (1969-1970)
150 (1953-1957)
Impala (1958-1970)
Lakewood (1961-1963)
Monte Carlo (1970)
Nomad (1955-1961) and (1969-1970)
Parkwood (1959-1961)
Styleline (1948-1952)
Super Sport or SS (1961-1970)
Yeoman (1958)
700 (1961-1964)

Beauville (1955-1957)
Biscayne (1958-1970)
Camaro (1967-1970)
Chevelle (1964-1970)
Concours (1967-1970)
Corvair (1960-1969)
Del Ray or Delray (1954-1958)
Fleetmaster (1946-1948) and (1960-1961)
Handyman (1953-1957)
210 (1953-1957)
Kingswood (1959-1960) and (1970)
Malibu (1964-70)
Monza (1960-1969)
Nova (1962-1970)
Spyder (1962-1963)
Stylemaster (1946-1947)
Townsman (1953-1957) and (1970)
500 (1960-1969)

OLDSMOBILE

Celebrity (1958-1966)
Custom Cruiser (1946-1947)
Delmont (1967-1968)
Dynamic (1946-1948) and (1958-1966)
Fiesta (1953) and (1957-1963)
Golden Rocket (1967)
Jetfire (1961-1962)
Luxury (1963-1970)
Scenic/SceniCoupe (1959-1960)
Supreme (1966-1970)
Toronado (1966-1970)
Vista Cruiser (1964-1970)
442 (1964-1970)
68 (1947-1948)
78 (1946-1948)
98 (1946-1970)

Cruiser (1946-1947)
Cutlass (1961-1970)
Delta (1966-1970)
F-85 (1960-1970)
Futuramic (1948-1950)
Holiday (1949-1970)
Jetstar (1964-1966)
Royale (1969-1970)
Starfire (1954-1956) and (1960-65)
Super (1951-1964)
Town Sedan (1961-1970)

66 (1946-1948)
76 (1946-1950)
88 (1949-1970)

PONTIAC

Bonneville (1957-1970)
Chieftain (1949-1958)
Executive (1966-1970)
Formula 400 (1970)
GTO (1964-1970)
LeMans (1962-1970)
Sprint (1966-1969)
Streamliner (1946-1951)
Tempest (1961-1970)
Trans Am (1969-1970)
Vista (1959-1965)

Catalina (1950-1970)
Espirit (1970)
Firebird (1967-1970)
Grand Prix (1962-1970)
Judge (1969-1970)
Safari (1957-1968)
Star Chief (1953-1965)
Super Chief (1957-1958)
Torpedo (1946-1948)
Ventura (1960-1961)
2 + 2 (1965-1968)

Oldsmobile after the war

By Dennis Casteele

After its sedate prewar history, Oldsmobile exploded with postwar excitement. A factor in this was growing popularity of Hydra-Matic. Buyers were opting for the self-shifting gear boxes about as fast as GM could build them. By 1941, Cadillac offered it, too, increasing demand.

Oldsmobiles for the shortened 1946-1947 period resembled prewar offerings. Then, in 1948, the Oldsmobile "revolution" began. An-all new look came with that season's "98." A February introduction delayed this top-of-the-line model's debut, but it was worth the wait and introduced the longer, lower "Futuramic" look on machines that were showroom traffic builders nationwide.

By 1949, the rest of the package was in place with the announcement of the high-compression, overhead valve Rocket V-8. It set performance standards for years to come. Created to power the heavy 98s, Oldsmobile engineers stuffed the new motor in the lighter Seventy-Six chassis to make the legendary Rocket 88. These and the plusher 98s were a hit. Oldsmobile took half of the 1949-1951 NASCAR race wins.

A 1949 Rocket 88 ragtop was the Indy Pace Car. The Seventy-Six series was dropped. A restyled wood wagon appeared, in 1949, to be replaced with a similar all-steel version later. It was carried over to 1950. Then, Oldsmobile dropped wagons until 1957.

The refined Rocket 88 and smooth-shifting Hydra-Matic quickly became a desirable motoring combination. In 1951, over 285,000 sales were achieved and a Super 88 appeared. Oldsmobile had solid years in 1952-1953 and, in the latter season, took its Fiesta show car into production. Just 458 Fiesta convertibles were made. For years, their $5,715 sticker price was top dollar for an Oldsmobile. Every option on the list was standard, as was a curved windshield.

A 1956 Oldsmobile Holiday 88 coupe. (Oldsmobile)

Sales of over 354,000 units vaulted Oldsmobile to fourth place in the industry for 1954. A whopping 583,000 cars sold in 1955. The 1956 model-year brought a slight restyling to the 88, Super 88 and 98 series. The hard-running Rocket V-8 got a boost in 1957-1958 with a tri-carb J-2 package.

By 1959, the performance image had faded a bit. Chrysler had its hemi and Chevrolet had fuel-injection. Oldsmobile breathed its last gasp, for a while, on the race track. Lee Petty topped the Daytona 500 in an Oldsmobile. For the next few years, Oldsmobile stressed luxury and comfort.

At Oldsmobile, 1961 was a significant year for several reasons. A long-awaited small car, the F-85, was introduced early in the model run. A special mid-year version bowed with the name Cutlass, taken from a mid-'50s dream car. A revived Starfire also appeared in mid-year, as an option-laden convertible.

By 1962, Oldsmobile looked back to the high-performance market and introduced its turbo charged Jetfire, which carried over into 1963. The program took a decided leap forward, in 1964, with the first 442 package. It had a special handling suspension coupled with underhood goodies. The 442 lasted into the 1980s and, for a time, achieved series status.

A variety of 88 nameplates appeared on Oldsmobiles in the 1960s including Dynamic, Delta and Jetstar. The 98 continued to offer luxury. Cutlasses, including 'S' and Supreme versions, became stars of the 1960s and 1970s. Station wagons regained popularity and the Vista Cruiser was offered in 1964.

In 1966, Oldsmobile dropped a bombshell with the first domestic front-wheel drive car since the Cord. The Toronado looked and drove different and began a GM trend that continues today. It quickly replaced the Starfire as Oldsmobile's personal/luxury car. A GT version, of 1970, gave enthusiasts something. In 1968, Oldsmobile and Hurst Performance Products Company teamed to offer the first Hurst/Oldsmobile. The H/O name also appeared in 1969, 1972, 1974, 1975, 1979, 1983, 1984 and 1988.

Lower and wider lines marked the 1960 Oldsmobile 98 hardtop. (Oldsmobile)

Competition Oldsmobiles were seen again as well. Oldsmobile set the pace at the Indy 500 in 1970, 1972, 1974, 1977 and 1985. A number of Oldsmobiles performed well on dragstrips and won again in stock car racing.

By 1973, Oldsmobile worked its way back into number three sales position with production approaching one million annually. Pushed to compete on the fuel economy front with inhouse V-8s, Oldsmobile engineers scrambled for a diesel powered V-8. A number of diesels were produced in the next few years.

In 1987, its 90th year, Oldsmobile continued as the auto industry's third best-selling nameplate. Since that time, Oldsmobile product highlights have included the 20th Anniversary Hurst/Olds of 1988 and the re-issue of the 442 nameplate in Quad Four format.

The 1954-1956 Ford Skyliners: Another better idea?

By Bill Siuru

Today, moon roofs are a popular automotive accessory. Like almost everything else automotive, this feature was tried years ago. In the case of a glass "window" in the roof, the most interesting early attempt was from the Ford Motor Company in 1954-1956.

The 1954 Ford Crestline Skyliner was the first Ford to have a transparent plastic window in the roof. Almost one-half of the two-door hardtop's roof was transparent. When you wanted to keep the sunshine out, there was a thin nylon sun shield that could be snapped into place from the inside.

The transparent top first appeared on the 1954 Crestline Skyliner.

The man behind the Skyliner roof treatment was L. David Ash, a Ford interior stylist. The 1954 Mercury Monterey Sun Valley hardtop also had this feature. Because the Mercurys were introduced a short time before the Fords, they got most of the early publicity.

The 1954 "bubble-tops" turned out to be reasonably good sellers. The 13,344 Skyliners accounted for over 12 percent of Ford's 1954 two-door hardtop sales, and the 9,761 Sun Valleys represented almost 10 percent of all Mercury Monterey hardtops sold. The Ford and Mercury "moon roof" models cost $110 and $130 more, respectively, than their solid roof counterparts. Based on the relative success of the 1954 editions, the idea was incorporated into the completely redesigned 1955 Ford and Mercury models.

The premier model in the 1955 Ford line up was the Crown Victoria. It had many ideas taken from Ford's experimental idea car, the Mystere. Besides a multi-tone paint job set off by a check-mark chrome strip (that would be featured on 1955 and 1956 Fairlanes), the Mystere had a heavy stainless steel tiara separating the two halves of the roof. It was often called a "basket-handle." This tiara would be the Crown Victoria's most distinguishing feature. The Mystere also had a transparent front roof, plus a bubble, aircraft-like canopy behind the tiara.

A close-up look.

Contrary to how it appeared, the Crown Victoria's tiara did not serve a roll-bar function. It added little to the actual strength of the roof. To get the needed strength, the Crown Victoria used a beefed-up frame from Ford convertibles. The Crown Victoria was offered in two models. The plain Crown Victoria came without the bubble-top and the Crown Victoria Skyliner had this plexiglass front section. For more conservative buyers, there was also a conventional two-door hardtop simply called the Victoria.

The regular 1955-1956 Victorias (1955 shown) were attractive and popular.

Crown Victorias, especially the Skyliner version, were not a sales success. Of the 148,536 Ford hardtops made in 1955, only 35,164 were Crown Victorias and, of these, only 1,999 had transparent tops. It wasn't the prices that held sales down, either. The Crown Victoria was only about $100 more than the Victoria and the bubble-top cost just $70 more. So, more likely, it was the car's unusual styling that hurt its popularity.

Placed in the context of 1955, it was considered way out. Added to this was the fact that people were buying hardtops to combine the open-air features of a convertible with the creature comforts of a sedan. With the chrome basket-handle in the way, the Crown Victoria was not really a hardtop.

Interestingly, when hardtops were phased out, in the mid-1970s, and replaced by cars with solid pillars and opera windows, many of the new designs bore a faint

The 1955 Ford Crown Victoria bubble-top.

resemblance to the Crown Victoria. Could it have been another case of an idea arriving before its time?

An even greater disaster awaited Crown Victoria sales in 1956, despite Ford's skyrocketing hardtop sales. Ford added a four-door hardtop called the Town Victoria Sedan and a two-door Victoria hardtop to its Customline series. When final totals were in, Ford had sold 272,788 hardtops in 1956. However, only 9,812 were Crown Victorias and, of these, only a mere 603 had glass tops.

The 1956 Ford Crown Victoria steel-top.

The handwriting was on the wall for 1957 when the Crown Victoria and Skyliner disappeared. However, the Skyliner nameplate lived a few years longer on Ford's newest "better idea" ... the retractable hardtop.

In more recent years, Ford resurrected the Crown Victoria nameplate for some its top-of-the-line sedans. Sales of these cars were stronger than sales of their namesake.

Back at Mercury in the 1950s, things were even more dismal. Mercury did not market a car equivalent to the Crown Victoria. Instead, the Sun Valley name was used on a 1955 Montclair two-door hardtop with a plexiglass roof. With only 1,787 sales in 1955, it was dropped at model year's end.

While the bubble-top was relatively well received by the public at first, its downfall can probably be attributed to stifling hot interiors caused by the direct rays of the sun. Made of one-quarter inch thick tinted plexiglass, the "glass" roof was supposed to filter out 70 percent of the sun's glare and 60 percent of its radiation. Nevertheless, the rays that got through made things very uncomfortable. There was a sun shield that had an aluminized outer side, but its use defeated the purpose of the roof ... seeing the sky on those nice sunny days. Plus, it did not block all the sun's heat.

A prototype Ford with landau-style roof.

The moon roof of today is much smaller in size and has special glass to reduce the sun's heat. Perhaps the most important change from Skyliner days is that cars can be air-conditioned. In 1954-1956, air-conditioning was a rare option on low-priced cars. It was not available on Fords until 1955 and that year, only 22,575 air-conditioning units were installed in FoMoCo products. Most of those went in Lincolns or Mercurys.

In the late 1970s, Lincoln again offered a bubble-top. It was very similar to the Skyliner's plastic sliding sun screen. The section that covered half the roof area was made of tinted and reflective glass. It did not open, like a normal moon roof.

Interestingly, if you peer inside any 1955 Ford, you will see a miniature "sun roof" over the instrument cluster. The Ford people said there was no tie-in between this styling and the real sun roof. They insisted that it was only design coincidence. Some folks find this hard to believe.

Olds ragtops went "dancing on sand"

By Dennis Casteele

A fleet of red and white 1956 Oldsmobile Super 88 convertibles was used to transport tourists through the white sands of Sleeping Bear Dunes, near Glen Arbor, Michigan. By modifying the manufacturer's name, they became known as "Dunesmobiles."

In March 1983, one of these cars surfaced. It belonged to Oldsmobile Club of America (OCA) member Eddy Garver of Harrison, Michigan. Garver's car bore a windshield decal indicating that it was the number 5 car in the original fleet. He had almost totally rebuilt it, to original condition, during his seven years of ownership.

Garver researched the car's background extensively, going as far as discovering the owner and operator of the Sleeping Bear Dunes attraction. He also located men who worked there, as drivers, when the Oldsmobiles were in service. "I was told a great many facts about the dunes and the cars by the owner, the drivers and many others," Garver said. "I have gone back to the dunes with my Oldsmobile, many times, to find out as much as I could about the history of the cars."

A fleet of red and white 1956 Oldsmobile Super 88 convertibles was used to transport tourists through the white sands of Sleeping Bear Dunes, near Glen Arbor, Michigan.

The Oldsmobiles came along in 1956, but the story of these genuine "dunes buggies" starts back in 1935. That's when a young man named Louis C. Warnes equipped a vehicle with a special motor and giant tires for personal pleasure trips over the vast, sandy lands near his home. His friends begged him to take passengers. Soon, he added other cars and trained drivers and the dunes tours began.

Warnes' first fleet consisted of late 1930s Ford convertibles and one Mercury. These were replaced, in the late 1940s, by a fleet of 10 Ford convertibles. One of these cars still exists today. The Fords were used until 1956. Then, the new fleet of Oldsmobiles made the word Dunesmobile famous. All 10 Oldsmobiles used were stripped-down Super 88 models with no heaters, radios or power brakes. They had only power steering.

The unusual thing about Warnes selecting Oldsmobiles was the fact he had always been a devoted Ford fan. Later, he did buy a 1957 Ranchero, with a matching red and white color scheme, for his personal car. It, too, still exists.

Warnes told Garver he bought the Oldsmobiles because they were flashy and dependable. He claimed that he never had a major breakdown with any of them. His worst problem was front end bearing failure, caused by sand cutting the bearings apart. A third advantage of the Oldsmobiles was that they inspired the catchy name Dunesmobile, which helped the business develop an image, and grow.

All the Dunesmobiles had two problems in common. Before too long, their front bumpers were dulled and their windows were pitted by the "sandblasting" that resulted from so many trips across the dunes. They went up and down bluffs that were up to 50 feet high.

A restored Dunesmobile.

After the 10 cars were put in service, word spread about the new Oldsmobiles on the dunes. Many people traveled there and rode in the Dunesmobiles. One man reported that he took his family there each weekend, for an entire summer. He said it was "just for the thrill of riding in the beautiful new cars."

As business increased, Warnes bought five more 1956 Oldsmobiles. However, he didn't custom-order them. Instead, he took whatever cars they had and painted them red and white to match the others. The last two were four-door models. Their tops were removed and the bodies were lengthened. The tops were put in storage, until the late 1960s. Then, they were replaced and the cars were retired from service.

Garver once photographed his car in front of the Sleeping Bear gift shop, where all the trips started and ended. "There are still many pictures of all the dunes cars inside the old gift shop," he reported. Warnes kept some of the Oldsmobiles around for a long time after they were retired from service. Eventually, they all disappeared. Some were sold, some were traded in and some were given away to his nieces.

In the late-1960s, the cars were replaced by a fleet of lengthened pickup trucks. Later, the dunes became part of a national park. This meant that vehicle rides were not allowed on the sand. However, one of the Dunesmobiles was sold for one dollar and displayed at the national park center just down the road from the dunes. It was one of the four-doors. Soon after it was put on display, it was driven away and not seen again.

The Oldsmobiles were originally used from the first part of June until mid-October. They were then parked for the winter. Each had its own, numbered stall in a huge garage a few hundred feet from Lake Michigan.

Warnes and his wife worked at the dunes for decades. They loved both the dunes and the hundreds of thousands of people who rode across them. "The Warnes' are special people and I owe a lot to them for the way they cared for the cars when they owned them and for being so kind to my wife and I when we went to see them," Eddie Garver wrote in Journey With Olds. "They even gave me the original Sleeping Bear decals used on my Oldsmobile."

(Story based on information supplied Eddy Garver, member no. 5888 of the Oldsmobile Club of America. Original photo courtesy Dr. Art Burrichter, Deerfield Beach, Florida. Special thanks to Helen J. Early of Oldsmobile public relations department.)

Collector car dealer Art Burrichter, of Florida, obtained one of the Dunesmobiles and had it for sale at his dealership in Boca Raton.

A total of 15 of the 1956 Oldsmobile Dune Rides cars were ordered. This one survives. (Old Cars)

Hardtop station wagons:
The best of two worlds

By Bill Siuru

In the late 1950s and early 1960s, station wagons were among the most popular models offered by United States automakers. The hardtop was also at the peak of its popularity. So, several automakers offered station wagons that not only could haul the load, but also gave "open air" driving. These were the hardtop wagons offered by American Motors, Chrysler, Ford and General Motors.

Several automakers offered station wagons that not only could haul the load, but also gave "open air" driving. This is the '57 Buick Caballero. (Old Cars)

While all hardtop wagon makers probably had designs on their drawing boards by 1956, Nash can be credited with introducing the idea to the public with its 1956 hardtop wagon in the Rambler series. Interestingly, since badge-engineered Ramblers were also offered under the Hudson marque for that year, some Hudson hardtop wagons were made. The difference between Nash and Hudson Ramblers was minimal. When American Motors offered stretched Ramblers, calling them Ambassadors, the hardtop wagon was offered under this nameplate, too. While American Motors lead the way, it was by far the smallest producer of these models.

In 1957, Buick, Mercury and Oldsmobile offered their versions. While GM produced the wagons for only two years, Mercury keep a version in its line up until 1960. They also made the greatest number of them. In fact, all Mercury wagons in these years were of the hardtop variety. It was also the only marque to offer a real two-door hardtop wagon.

While AMC lead the way, it was by far the smallest producer of hardtop wagons. This is the 1959 Ambassador version. (AMC)

While the 1955-1957 Chevrolet Bel Air Nomad and its sister, the Pontiac two-door Custom Safari are sometimes called hardtop wagons, they are not truly representative of this body style. Only the front door windows were frameless on the Nomads and two-door Custom Safaris.

Chrysler was a latecomer into the hardtop wagon field, with its Town & Country wagons appearing in 1960. It offered only hardtop wagons between 1960 and 1964. Because of body sharing between Chrysler and Dodge in 1963 and 1964, Dodge was also able to offer its version of the hardtop wagon. By 1965, the hardtop wagon was gone, even though two- and four-door hardtop coupes and sedans would be popular for many more years.

Chrysler was a latecomer into the hardtop wagon field, with its Town & Country wagon first appearing in 1960. A 1961 model is shown. (Chrysler)

The hardtop station wagon is a desirable collectible for people who want unique styling combined with load-carrying ability. These wagons should appreciate in value in the future, because of their good looks and historical significance. They are also quite rare, especially those examples in good condition. Like most wagons, many took a beating in their early days.

Almost without exception, the hardtop wagon represented the top-of-the-line for each manufacturer. Notice that the low-priced three didn't even offer the model. Station wagons tended to be a company's most expensive models, and the hardtop wagons were the most costly of all.

The fact that each of these models was luxuriously appointed and usually came equipped with the largest engine, also adds to their collectibility. They often were ordered with many accessories and creature comforts, too.

The original owners were usually after luxury in their cargo carriers. Otherwise, they probably would have purchased the more economical conventional wagons. The hardtop station wagon is currently a sleeper in the collectible car market.

Most hardtop wagons, like this 1958 Olds Super 88 Fiesta, were luxuriously appointed and equipped with large engines. This adds to their collectibility. (Oldsmobile)

HARDTOP STATION WAGON PRODUCTION
(Four-door models, unless noted otherwise)

AMERICAN MOTORS

1957 Rambler Custom Cross Country - 6 passenger	402
1958 Rambler Custom Cross Country - 6 passenger	182
1958 Ambassador Custom Cross Country - 6 passenger	294
1959 Ambassador Custom Cross Country - 6 passenger	578
1960 Ambassador Custom Country - 6 passenger	435
TOTAL AMC	**1,891**

* Does not include Hudson for which production figures are not available.

BUICK

1957 Special Riviera Estate Wagon 6 passenger	6,817
1957 Century Caballero - 6 passenger	10,186
1958 Special Riviera Estate Wagon - 6 passenger	3,420
1958 Century Caballero - 6 passenger	4,456
TOTAL BUICK	**24,879**

CHRYSLER

1960 Windsor Town & Country - 6 passenger	1,120
1960 Windsor Town & Country - 9 passenger	1,026
1960 New Yorker Town & Country - 6 passenger	624
1960 New Yorker Town & Country - 9 passenger	248
1961 Newport Town & Country - 6 passenger	1,832
1961 Newport Town & Country - 9 passenger	1,571

1961 New Yorker Town & Country - 6 passenger 676
1961 New Yorker Town & Country - 9 passenger 760
1962 Newport Town & Country - 6 passenger 3,271
1962 Newport Town & Country - 9 passenger 2,363
1962 New Yorker Town & Country - 6 passenger 728
1962 New Yorker Town & Country - 9 passenger 793
1963 Newport Town & Country - 6 passenger 3,618
1963 Newport Town & Country - 9 passenger 2,948
1963 New Yorker Town & Country - 6 passenger 950
1963 New Yorker Town & Country - 9 passenger 1,244
1964 Newport Town & Country - 6 passenger 3,720
1964 Newport Town & Country - 9 passenger 3,041
1964 New Yorker Town & Country - 6 passenger 1,190
1964 New Yorker Town & Country - 9 passenger 1,603
TOTAL CHRYSLER **33,326**

DODGE

1963 Custom 880 Hardtop Wagon - 6 passenger 3,292
1963 Custom 880 Hardtop Wagon - 9 passenger 3,407
1964 Custom 880 Hardtop Wagon - 6 passenger 3,305
1964 Custom 880 Hardtop Wagon - 9 passenger 3,420
TOTAL DODGE **13,424**

MERCURY

1957 Commuter two-door - 6 passenger 4,885
1957 Commuter four-door - 6 passenger 11,990
1957 Commuter four-door - 9 passenger 5,752
1957 Voyager two-door - 6 passenger 2,283
1957 Voyager four-door - 9 passenger 3,716
1957 Colony Park four-door - 6 passenger 7,386
1958 Commuter two-door - 6 passenger 1,912
1958 Commuter four-door - 6 passenger 8,601
1958 Commuter four-door - 9 passenger 4,227
1958 Voyager two-door - 6 passenger 568
1958 Voyager four-door - 6 passenger 2,520
1958 Colony park four-door - 6 passenger 4,474
1959 Commuter two-door - 6 passenger 1,051
1959 Commuter four-door - 6 passenger 15,122
1959 Voyager four-door - 6 passenger 2,496
1959 Colony Park four-door - 6 passenger 5,929
1960 Commuter four-door - 6 passenger 14,949
1960 Colony Park four-door - 6 passenger 7,411
TOTAL MERCURY **101,272**
[2] A few two-door 1959 Voyagers may have been built.

OLDSMOBILE

1957 88 Fiesta - 6 passenger 5,767
1957 Super 98 Fiesta - 6 passenger 8,981
1958 88 Fiesta - 6 passenger 3,323
1958 Super 88 Fiesta - 6 passenger 5,175
TOTAL OLDSMOBILE **23,246**

1957 El Morocco:
low-priced luxury

By Tom LaMarre

"The Chevrolet has long been recognized as a serviceable, economical car by the American auto-buying public," said Automobile Topics magazine. "Likewise, the 1957 Cadillac Brougham is believed by many to be the epitome of automotive styling. Put them together and what do you have? The first car that might be termed a low-priced luxury car."

The April 22, 1957 issue of Automotive News explained, "Called the El Morocco, it will be basically a 1957 Chevrolet, but from there the similarity is slight." They weren't kidding!

The man behind the car was Ruben Allender. He said that market studies and advance orders indicated "tremendous" demand for his customized Chevrolet. The El Morocco featured a rear fender section patterned after the Cadillac Eldorado. It came complete with stainless steel side trim and vertical wind splits. Other Cadillac touches were an egg-crate grille, parking lights integrated into the bumper and black-tipped bumper guards.

The El Morocco was patterned after the Cadillac Eldorado. It came complete with stainless steel side trim, vertical wind splits, an egg-crate grille, parking lights integrated into the bumper and black-tipped bumper guards.

Three body styles were available: A two-door hardtop, four-door hardtop and two-door convertible. Here's the two-door hardtop.

Three body styles were available ... a two-door hardtop, four-door hardtop and two-door convertible. "All cars customized from brand new Bel-Air (sic) Chevrolet," said the El Morocco brochure, misspelling Bel Air. The Chevrolet name did not appear anywhere on the vehicle. Color choices were limited to black and silver, bronze and white or solid blue. All models were equipped with Powerglide, Power-Pack, power steering, power brakes, white sidewall tires, push-button radio and heater. In addition, the buyer's name was stamped into the leather steering wheel hub. Not bad for less than $3,000.

Ads for R. Allender & Company, located at 1966 East Forest in Detroit, promoted franchises as well as the car. An inquiry to the address in June 1957 elicited this response from J.J. Allender: "In reply to your postal card of recent date regarding our El Morocco car. We have two distributors in the state of California and...we suggest that you contact either one of them and they will be glad to give you any information you desire regarding the El Morocco car." Those dealerships were N.E Druley Chevrolet in Redlands and Bates Chevrolet in Arcadia.

Literature says all of the cars had the Power-Pack engine option, but this one appears to have single exhausts, indicating a standard V-8 was installed.

A follow-up letter from Druley (who was also a Packard dealer) illustrated one of the weak links in the El Morocco marketing chain. It stated, "In reply to your inquiry of R. Allender (sic) regarding El Morocco: Are you a new car dealer or an individual? If dealer, what dealership are you connected with? If you are an individual, what is your California dealers resale number?

Please send a picture of your business and information regards (sic) financial (sic) status. Thanking you for your inquiry and upon information received will be glad to give you information regards (sic) El Morocco car."

At least "El Morocco" was spelled right. Automobile Topics showed it as the El Morroco. The trade publication said, "It is expected that demand will exceed even the most optimistic forecast. However, Allender's sales, service and parts facilities assure complete satisfaction to all owners. What R. Allender and the El Morocco have started may well signal a trend to luxury cars in the low-priced field."

Instead, production of the Cadillac clone ended during 1957. This happened after only an estimated eight to 15 of the 1957 models had been built.

This 1957 El Morocco appeared at the Chevy Vette Fest in Chicago in the fall of 1991 (Ron Kowalke)

Rare haulers

By Bill Siuru

We have all heard the Edsel story many times; about how the marque flopped because of some faulty market research. Between 1957 and 1959, some 110,087 Edsels were built. Of this total, only about 13 percent were station wagons. This makes this body style the rarest Edsel model after the convertible. Considering the abuse station wagons usually suffer, it is indeed a rare occasion when you see an Edsel station wagon today.

When the 1958 Edsel first appeared, in 1957, there was an abundance of series, with several models in each car-line. The station wagon was offered in three versions, the two-door Roundup, the four-door Villager and the top-of-the-line four-door Bermuda.

All the 1958 Edsels were built on the 116 inch wheelbase chassis used for the 1958 Ford wagons. Indeed, there was a relationship between the Edsel and Ford lines. The Roundup corresponded to the two-door Del Rio, the Villager paralleled the Ford Country Sedan and the Bermuda's equivalent was the Country Sedan.

All 1958 Edsels were built on the 116-inch wheelbase chassis used for the 1958 Ford wagons. The Villager paralleled the Ford Country Sedan. (1959 model shown.)

Since the new make was aimed at an upscale market niche, the prices of the Edsels ran about $250 more than their Ford counterparts. Not surprisingly, the total number of 1958 Edsel wagons sold was less than even the least popular Ford wagon (the Del Rio) by some 6,217 units. Even the higher priced Mercury wagon accounted for over 22,000 sales in 1958.

The 1958 Edesl station wagon was offered in three versions, the two-door Roundup, the four-door Villager and the top-of-the-line four-door Bermuda.

To produce the Edsel wagon, the Edsel Ranger/Pacer front sheet metal was grafted on to a Ford wagon body from the cowl back. The rear fender and tail treatment was from the Ford wagons and was quite different from the rest of the Edsels. The taillight bezels, while Edsel-specific, were made to fit Ford sheet metal. The Bermuda featured simulated wood grain paneling.

The only engine available was the 361 cubic inch, 303 horsepower V-8 used in the Edsel Ranger and Pacer models. There were no wagons in the upscale Mercury-based Edsel Corsair and Citation series.

For 1959, all Edsel station wagons were called Villagers.

When the 1959 Edsels appeared, only Ranger and the Corsair models remained. Now, even the Corsair was based on Ford products. The Villager was the only wagon offered. However, this turned out to be the best year for Edsel wagons, if you can call less than 8,000 units "best."

Once again, the front sheet metal from other Edsels was used and rear end treatment was taken from Fords and adapted to the Edsel. This gave the Edsel Villager station wagon a unique appearance.

It corresponded most directly to the Ford Country Sedan. The standard engine was now a 332 cubic inch, 225 horsepower power plant used in the Corsair models. Edsel Rangers used a 292 cubic inch V-8, that wasn't offered in a wagon. A six-cylinder 223 cubic inch and 145 horsepower engine was also available as a delete option. For the performance-minded, there was an optional 361 cubic inch "Super Express" V-8.

The Edsel marque made its swan song with the 1960 model, which was discontinued well before the end of the model year. Of the 2,846 Edsels made to 1960 specifications, just 275 were station wagons. The Ford influence on all the Edsels, and especially the wagons, was even more pronounced. The 292 cubic inch V-8 was now standard, with a new 352 cubic inch 300 horsepower Super Express V-8 available. The 223 cubic inch six was also optional again.

Of the 2,846 Edsels made to 1960 specifications, just 275 were station wagons. (Phil Skinner)

EDSEL STATION WAGONS	PRICE	PROD.
1958		
Roundup 2-door/6-passenger	2,841	924
Villager 4-door/6-passenger	2,898	2,054
Villager 4-door/9-passenger	2,955	1,735
Bermuda 4-door/6-passenger	3,155	892
TOTAL		**5,605**
1959		
Villager 4-door/6-passenger	2,971	5,687
Villager 4-door/6-passenger	3,055	2,133
TOTAL		**7,820**
1960		
Villager 4-door/6-passenger	2,989	216
Villager 4-door/9-passenger	3,072	59
TOTAL		**275**
GRAND TOTAL		**13,700**

The ultimate in visibility

By Bill Siuru

Automotive styling seems to go in cycles. Today the emphasis is on cars with very good visibility, coupled with sleek aerodynamics. This follows the "closed in" look from Detroit, which was characterized by formal roofs and opera windows. If you look back a couple of decades, to 1959 and 1960, some General Motors cars offered the ultimate in visibility, especially at the rear.

They were the four-door hardtops, introduced in 1959 by all five General Motors marques. Their thin roof pillars and "steamboat-bridge" rear windows were new then and still look unique today.

The 1959 model year initiated General Motors' new emphasis on a common thread between marques. Therefore, all five lines used basically the same four-door hardtop body with common design and construction.

Chevrolet called its version a Sport Sedan. The radically-curved backlights caused some visual distortion. *(Chevrolet)*

Chevrolet offered the unique "greenhouse" four-door hardtop in both the Bel Air and Impala series. Chevrolet called it a "Hardtop Sport Sedan." Pontiac called its version the "Vista Sedan" and offered it in all three of its series: Catalina, Star Chief and Bonneville in 1959. Then, in 1960, a Ventura Vista Sedan was added to the line up. Like all Oldsmobile hardtops from day one, the Oldsmobile version of the new pillarless four-door body was titled a "Holiday" model, in this case a Holiday Sedan. It was available in Dynamic 88, Super 88 and 98 versions.

Cadillac offered the "four-window" hardtop sedan with cantilever style roof and wraparound backlight treatment in 1959 only. (Old Cars)

At Buick and Cadillac, two four-door hardtop models were included in both model line ups. The greenhouse type, often called a four-window hardtop, was available from Buick for LeSabre, Invicta and Electra buyers. Electra 225 buyers had a choice of the four-window hardtop or a more conventional six-window hardtop called a Riviera sedan. Cadillac used four-door hardtops exclusively and had both four- and six-window versions in its 1959 Series 62 and DeVille car-lines. The Series 60 Special Fleetwood used the alternate six-window styling. In 1960, use of the wraparound or greenhouse style rear window was dropped by Cadillac.

The 1960 Buick LeSabre four-door hardtop featured the wraparound rear window glass. (Ron Kowalke)

The greenhouse styling did have some drawbacks. There was some visual distortion, due to the extreme wraparound format of the rear glass. Of course, these 1959 and 1960 General Motors cars had equally expansive front wraparound windshields, so there were problems seeing out of both ends of the cars.

In addition, the rather fragile roof structure didn't give much protection in the case of a roll-over crash. And, because of all that glass, interior heating on sunny days was a problem. Tinted glass, as a minimum, or air-conditioning, were needed to be really comfortable. A set of visors for the rear window was offered as an accessory for some models, but didn't solve the heat problem entirely.

The roof line looked very racy in profile view, as depicted here on a 1960 Oldsmobile Ninety-Eight Holiday Sedan. (Oldsmobile)

Four-door hardtops were extremely popular in those days. They appealed to about 30 percent of Buick, Oldsmobile and Pontiac buyers. In these lines, they were either the best-selling or second best-selling models. Over 50 percent of the Cadillac buyers opted for either four- or six-window four-door hardtops. However, the latter style was more popular with Cadillac buyers by a substantial margin. At the opposite end of the GM price spectrum, the conventional four-door sedan was purchased most often by Cherolet buyers.

By 1961, the sales trend moved toward more closed-in styling. However, the greenhouse rear window theme was retained on some General Motors models for a few more years. The most obvious application was on 1960-1964 Corvair four-door sedans.

Pontiac offered the four-door Vista hardtop in all of its car-lines from Catalina to Bonneville. It went well with the new and highly-promoted "Wide-Track" stance. (Pontiac)

Chevelle: 1960s super car with choices

By Linda Clark

In 1964, Chevrolet introduced a full line of mid-sized cars under the name Chevelle. Chevelles were 11 inches longer than Chevy IIs and 16 inches shorter than Chevrolets. Many buyers thought it was the ideal sized car.

From the start, the Chevelle could be tailored to one's needs. Chevelle buyers had their choice of 14 different engine/transmission combinations. The Borg-Warner T-10 gear box was replaced by a new General Motors built Muncie four-speed. Three-speed manual (with or without overdrive) and Powerglide transmissions were carried over from 1963.

The Chevelle was offered in 13 models, beginning with the base 300 series. Next came a sport coupe and convertible, plus a sedan and two station wagons. Top models were the Malibu Super Sports. A fourth series was the reborn El Camino.

Like full-size Super Sports, Chevelle SS models came standard with bucket seats, vinyl upholstery and a console with Powerglide or a four-speed.

SS insignia, inside and out, also distinguished Super Sport models. Exterior trim on Malibu Super Sports differed from conventional Malibus. Among Chevelle's seven interior colors, two were available only in Super Sports. Chevelles came in 15 exterior colors, with Goldenwood Yellow exclusive to Super Sports. Super Sports cost $162 more than comparable non-SS models, so that the $2,695 Chevelle Malibu V-8 convertible coupe cost $2,857 when ordered with SS equipment.

Styling was neutral, since Chevrolet was aiming for volume, rather than the enthusiast market. Sales for the year amounted to 142,000 Chevelle sixes and 196,250 Chevelle V-8s. The 1964 Chevelle Malibu V-8 convertible coupe cost $2,484 when ordered with a base V-8. The new line competed with Buick-Olds-Pontiac intermediates and clashed head on with the Ford Fairlane, Mercury Comet and Dodge Dart.

Chevelle engines began with the 120 horsepower 194 cubic inch six and added a 155 horsepower 230 cubic inch six, plus 195 and 220 horsepower versions of the 283 cubic inch V-8. A 327 cubic inch V-8 option was approved by management in mid-1964. It came in 250 and 300 horsepower versions.

For 1965, Chevelle was lengthened by 2.7 inches and lowered about an inch. There were minor chassis refinements, but Malibu SS models were the most noticeably changed. Revised moldings, insignia and a partly blacked-out grille distinguished 1965 Chevelle Super Sports.

An hydraulic lifter version of Corvette's 350 horsepower 327 cubic inch V-8 was offered in Malibu and Malibu SS models in mid-1965. For the dragstrip, a few 365 horsepower versions of the 327 were also built.

Chevrolet's new 396 cubic inch V-8, intended for 1966 models, went into 201 of the 1965 Super Sports. SS-396 Chevelles came standard with the Muncie four-speed. Motor Trend (July, 1965) found a 1965 Malibu SS-396 capable of 0-to-60 in 6.7 seconds. It flew through the quarter-mile at 95 miles per hour in 15.3 seconds. Chevrolet produced 152,650 Chevelles in 1965.

For 1966, Chevelle Super Sports came with a 396 having 325 standard or 360 optional horsepower. The big-block 396 engine was not available in other Chevelle models, except the El Camino Custom, which could also be optioned with SS equipment, minus emblems.

For 1966, Chevelle Super Sport convertibles and coupes came with a 396 cubic inch V-8 having 325 standard or 360 optional horsepower. The big-block 396 engine was not available in other Chevelles. (Old Cars)

Chevelles were restyled for 1966, but still had a 115-inch wheelbase. Malibu and SS coupes and convertibles, except for trim and identification, shared the same body. That included a new roof line with a flat rear window. This provided improved rearward vision. The SS-396 coupe cost $2,776, just $292 more than the Malibu sport coupe. The bucket seats and special wheelcovers, that had been standard SS equipment, now cost extra. SS features included simulated hood air intakes, a partly blacked-out grille and distinctive trim and insignia on SS-396 cars. Red stripe 7.75 x 14 tires or optional ($53.60) whitewalls went on six-inch rims.

Chevelles with manual gear boxes and bucket seat cars with console-equipped automatics, came with floor shifts. Most SS-396 had these options. The 1966 Chevelle SS-396 ran a quarter-mile in 14.66 seconds at 99.88 miles per hour.

In mid-1966, Chevrolet offered a 327 cubic inch 350 horsepower V-8 for the Malibu. Chevelle production climbed to 412,000 in 1966.

For 1967, Chevelle was face-lifted again. It had a new horizontal grille and horizontal theme in the rear. This put the taillights flush with the back of the quarter panels. Super Sports were distinguished from everyday Malibus by SS-396 emblems, a black-accented grille, SS lettering on the quarter panels, wheelhouse moldings, distinct body sill moldings, color-keyed body stripes and simulated hood air intakes.

Super Sports cost $285 more than regular Mailibus in 1967. They came standard with Firestone Wide-Oval F70 x 14 tires on six-inch rims. These tires were a $64.10 option for the 1967 El Camino. Super Sports and Chevelles shared hub caps, which could be replaced with four wheelcover options. Rally-style covers were part of a $79 front-disc brake option.

Bucket seats ($113) remained optional in 1967, even in SS cars. The tach-and-gauges ($79) option was carried over from 1966. The 325 horsepower 396 V-8 was standard in Super Sports and a $182.95 option in El Caminos. A 350 horsepower 396 cubic inch V-8 was optional in SS ($105.35) or El Camino ($290.55) models. Optional in Chevelle Super Sports was a 375 horsepower ($476) version of the 396.

Motor Trend, in July 1967, compared 325 and 375 horsepower Chevelle SS-396 models and found the hotter SS-396 about a second faster both from 0-to-60 and in the quarter-mile. The 325 horsepower had Powerglide, the 375 a close-ratio four-speed. The 325 horsepower went from 0-to-60 miles per hour in 7.5 seconds versus the quicker six seconds of the hotter car.

Chevelle was redesigned for 1968. Most models rode on a new 112 inch wheelbase. Four-door models, including wagons, had a 116 inch wheelbase. Though sharing its body and chassis with the standard Malibu, the SS-396 Chevelle was elevated to a distinct model in 1968. A new luxury four-door wagon, the Concours, was added to the Chevelle line.

Fender lines on the new 1968 Chevelles were sleeker and less boxy than in prior years. The hardtops had fastback roofs. New hidden windshield wipers came standard on SS-396 and Concours models. All 1968 Chevrolets had new side-marker lights in the fenders. Rally wheels became optional for all Chevelles and wheel options were expanded to include wire wheelcovers and two mag styles.

Fender lines on the new 1968 Chevelles were sleeker and less boxy than in prior years. The hardtops had fastback roofs. (Charles Webb)

Super Sports had blacked-out grilles, new rear panels and taillights, black lower-body paint, quarter-panel chrome, Firestone Wide-Oval tires and optional bodyside striping that was made standard on SS-396 Chevelles at mid-year. SS-396 grille insignia, SS emblems front and rear and 396 fender emblems were continued in 1968.

Chevelle SS-396s came standard with the 325 horsepower engine. Optional 350 horsepower (hotter cam) and 375 horsepower versions were available. Chevelles still came standard with drum brakes, but, in 1968, got finned front drums to aid cooling. Sintered metallic linings were optional, as were front discs. Chevrolet sold over 400,000 Chevelles in 1968, leading Motor Trend to call it, "America's biggest-selling super car."

Power front disc brakes became standard on 1969 Chevelles. This same year, GM discontinued "butterfly" vent windows. This change gave all models a cleaner look. Super Sports were no longer a distinct model-option package available on any coupe or convertible. An anti-theft, self-locking steering wheel became standard on all GM cars in 1969.

Engines and transmissions were mostly unchanged from 1968. However, Powerglide was dropped in 1969 in favor of the three-speed Turbo-Hydramatic gearbox.

Car and Driver (January, 1969) compared a 325 horsepower Chevelle SS-396 with automatic transmission to the Ford Cobra, Mercury Cyclone CJ, Pontiac GTO Judge, Dodge Super Bee and Plymouth Hemi Road Runner. If based solely on ride quality and quietness, they said Chevelle would have been the overall winner. The Chevelle had a 14.41 second quarter-mile time, versus the first-place Hemi Road Runner's 13.54 seconds. Chevelle went from 0-to-60 in 5.8 seconds, versus the Road Runner's 5.1 seconds.

In 1970, the Chevelle reached its peak with the SS-454 model. Its optional ($321) engine was a 450 horsepower 454 cubic inch V-8 derived from the Corvette's 427 block. The big-block 454 was shared with Monte Carlo in 1970 and had either 10.25:1 or 11.25:1 compression. Both had a solid-lifter cam and the Corvette's large exhaust values and Holley four-barrel.

Though options mandatory with the 450 horsepower engine booted the SS-454 Chevelle's price to over $4,000, its performance, by any era's standards, was awesome. Quarter-mile times were in the 13 second range and close to the 427 Corvette's performances.

The SS-396 Chevelle came standard with 350 horsepower or optional with 375 horsepower. Chevrolet bored some 396 big-blocks to 402 cubic inches, but horsepower ratings were 350 and 375, just as in the 396. (There was also a 402 cubic inch version of the Chevrolet small-block V-8, which was not a real high-performance engine.)

The SS-396 Chevelle came standard with 350 horsepower or optional with 375 horsepower in 1970. Chevrolet bored some 396 big-blocks to 402 cubic inches, but horsepower ratings were 350 and 375, just as in the SS-396. (Chevrolet)

Two four-speeds and Turbo-Hydramatic transmissions were available with these engines. The SS option consisted of blacked-out grille with SS emblems, domed hood with hood pins, wheelhouse moldings, rear bumper SS identification, chromed exhaust outlets, SS-396 or SS-454 fender emblems, Firestone Wide-Oval tires and interior SS insignia.

Sport coupes and convertibles could be SS-optioned, as could the El Camino, which could also be 454-equipped. Super Sports had distinct instrument panels and a new hood-and-deck stripe option that came standard with the $147.65 extra cowl-induction hood. Built-into-the-windshield radio antennas were rirst offered in 1970, too. Vinyl roof covers were still offered, as were 15 exterior and seven two-tone colors.

Government-mandated emission controls and insurance surcharges forced compression ratios down in 1971. The hottest Chevelle SS-454 now delivered 425 horsepower. Chevelle was slightly restyled for 1971, but the SS option was essentially unchanged from 1970. New mag style sport wheels, white-letter tires, power front disc brakes and remote-control outside rearview mirrors were included in the SS option at $357.

For 1971, Chevelle and Chevelle SS cosmetics were essentially carried over from 1970. Vinyl roof covers were now available in black, brown, navy, green and white. Power tops became standard on convertibles.

A blacked-out grille, Rally wheels, special body striping and decal identification went into a new "Heavy Chevy" model added to the Chevelle line. It was essentially a Malibu sport coupe with decals on it. Heavy Chevys could be optioned with 307 and 400 cubic inch V-8s.

A blacked-out grille, Rally wheels, special body striping and decal identification went into a new "Heavy Chevy" model added to the Chevelle line for 1971. (Terry Boyce)

There were few changes for 1972, the year the last Chevelle convertible was built. SS equipment was still optional only with convertibles and Sport Coupes, but now any Chevelle V-8 could be ordered with these SS models. A 270 horsepower 454 (which came standard with M-22 four-speed) was an option exclusive to SS cars. A three-speed manual gear box came standard with 305 or 307 cubic inch V-88. A heavy-duty three-speed was standard for the 402 cubic inch V-8.

An all-new Chevelle was unveiled in 1973, riding on a 113-inch wheelbase. Both the Malibu sport coupe and station wagon could be optioned with SS equipment. A 165 or 205 net-horsepower 350 or 245 net-horsepower 454 were available.

The SS option was dropped from the Chevelle line (except El Caminos) at the end of 1973, but a new luxury Laguna model was introduced. Laguna borrowed the SS theme and used 350, 400 and 454 cubic inch engines until 1976, when the 454 was discontinued.

Chevelle was down-sized and completely re-engineered for 1978. Its full-frame construction and rear drive layout were clearly dated by late-1970s standards. In fact, in 1977 the Chevelle (which wasn't officially retired until 1984) passed the mid-sized family car mantle onto Chevrolet's new front-drive A-body car, the Celebrity. Though El Caminos continued to be offered with optional Super Sport trim in 1985, the intermediate-sized personal-luxury Monte Carlo resurrected the SS package in its 1983 Monte Carlo SS.

Since Monte Carlo was the only Chevrolet on NASCAR's eligibility list, it was a natural for Chevrolet to introduce a distinct SS model. A 175 horsepower 305 cubic inch V-8, with four-barrel carburetion and a 9.5:1 compression ratio, came standard. The Monte Carlo SS came with Chevrolet's F-41 sport-suspension, front and rear stabilizer bars and wide Goodyear Eagle GT tires on styled-steel wheels. It sold for $10,249.

In 1986 El Camino introduced a distinct El Camino SS model. It came standard with an F41 sport-suspension package and choice of fuel-injected V-6 or 150 horsepower four-barrel V-8. Transmissions included three- or four-speed automatics. The base price was $9,886.

John Z. DeLorean and Pontiac

By Bill Siuru

Almost everyone in America has heard of John DeLorean because of his ill-fated auto manufacturing venture and an infamous cocaine bust. Forgotten, perhaps, are the many contributions he made towards changing the image of Pontiac from an "old lady's" car to one of spirit, performance and youth.

In 1956, DeLorean moved from the soon-to-be-defunct Packard Motor Car Company, where he was head of research and development, to start his brilliant career at General Motors.

In late 1958, Pontiac (under the leadership of managers like Semon "Bunkie" Knudsen and Elliot "Pete" Estes) had already started its image transformation. The first cars designed under this new philosophy were the spirited Bonnevilles and the "Wide-Track" Pontiacs of 1959. In the 1960s, Pontiac would produce some great cars that would capture the youth and performance oriented markets, benefiting the entire Pontiac line. John DeLorean was a major player in the conception and promotion of most of these great Pontiacs of the 1960s.

His influence was first felt as head of Pontiac's advanced engineering department, before becoming Pontiac's chief engineer in 1962. By 1965, he was the general manager of Pontiac Motor Division. He then influenced all aspects of the product line, including engineering, styling and marketing. His influence at Pontiac was felt through personal contributions and innovations and through the inspiration and leadership of those who worked for him.

In the late 1950s, most Detroit automakers were in the midst of developing compact cars. At Pontiac, the job was given to DeLorean and his engineers. The result was the 1961 Pontiac Tempest, a rather interesting and pioneering vehicle. It was not quite as unique as Chevrolet's Corvair. It was not as conventional as the Buick Skylark and Oldsmobile F-85, cars with which the Tempest shared its unit-body construction.

For an economical four-cylinder engine, Pontiac's 389 cubic inch V-8 was cut in half. The car had four-wheel independent suspension and a rear-mounted transaxle, something that would not be seen on another car until Porsche's 924s and 928s in the mid-1970s. Then, there was the unique flexible "rope" driveshaft and a dash-mounted transmission selector.

Up to that point, the Tempest was probably DeLorean's greatest engineering achievement. The car earned Motor Trend's "Car of the Year Award" and was praised in all the other car magazines. However, like other innovative motor vehicles, it was not without its faults. The car had a tendency to oversteer and was somewhat tricky to handle on wet roads. The rope driveshaft was also noisy. Even DeLorean said "It sounded like it was carrying a half-a-trunk load of rolling rocks." However, the unique driveshaft and transaxle eliminated the intrusive transmission hump. The Tempest was the best selling car in Pontiac's 1961 line up and was a key factor to pushing Pontiac into third place in 1961 auto sales.

The 1964 LeMans coupe was the basis for the GTO which ushered in the muscle car era. This one with a 326 cubic inch V-8 belongs to Mike Reinbold. (John Gunnell)

The Pontiac GTO showed that Pontiac had not only arrived on the performance scene, but that it was leading the pack. The 1964 Pontiac Tempest GTO was really the first of the muscle cars; vehicles created by stuffing large engines into relatively lightweight cars.

It is hard to pinpoint who was the originator of the GTO concept, but DeLorean and Jim Wangers (a young ad agency account executive) were the ones who capitilized on it. DeLorean picked the name, Grand Torismo Omologato, for its racing connotation, and he was a key factor in the GTO's heavy-duty suspension and sporty styling.

In 1964 and 1965, the GTO was an option package available on the Tempest Lemans two-door Sport Coupe, hardtop and convertible. For around $300 more than the Lemans, you got a stiffer suspension, a 389 cubic inch V-8, floorshift, dual exhausts and premium tires. A four-speed transmission was $188 more and, for another $75, you got metallic brake linings, limited-slip differential and heavy-duty radiator. Naturally, there were distinctive GTO trim items and more options in the accessory catalog. Pontiac described the option list "as long as your arm and twice as hairy."

There is an interesting reason why the GTO was not full-fledged series until 1966. In 1963, high-level GM management wanted to play down the racing and performance image. Thus, they banned the use of engines of over 330 cubic inches in mid-sized cars such as the Tempest. Pontiac got around this by offering the 389 cubic inch V-8 as an option. Top management was mad when they found out about the GTO subterfuge, but not furious enough to stop production, especially when they saw the sales figures.

Originally, Pontiac planned on 5,000 GTOs for 1964, but before the year was out over, 32,000 had been produced. Had it not been for the persistence of DeLorean and Wangers in pushing for greater GTO production, there would have been nowhere near enough 1964 GTOs to satisfy the demand.

When DeLorean took over as Pontiac's general manager, he gave Jim Wangers practically free rein in the promotion of the GTO. Soon, a singing group called Ronnie and the Daytonas had a hit record titled, "Little GTO" and Jan and Dean were singing "My Mighty GTO." GTO-labeled items, all the way from Cologne to Thom McCann sports shoes were selling like hot-cakes.

The GTO craze was on and, if the young people were too young or too poor to buy a GTO, at least the name Pontiac was embedded in their minds. This was something Pontiac hoped to capitalize on when the young folks were ready to buy a new car. 1966 was the best year for the GTO with 96,946 units sold. The GTO hardtop was the fourth best-selling Pontiac model. The team of DeLorean and Wangers had a winner.

Next, Pontiac launched a car called the Grand Prix. Whereas the GTO ushered in the muscle car era, the Grand Prix started the popular-priced, personal luxury car trend. There had been earlier personal luxury models, such as the Chrysler 300, Lincoln Continental, Ford Thunderbird and Cadillac Eldorado, but these were limited-edition cars priced above what the average buyer could afford. The initial Grand Prix, of 1962, was the brainchild of "Pete" Estes and DeLorean.

The 1966 Catalina 2+2 was a big reflection of the Pontiac high-performance image. (PMD)

When Estes and DeLorean proposed the "clean look" Grand Prix design to GM management, in order to obtain funds for tooling, they were flatly refused. Not wanting to give up an idea that had real potential, they proceeded to build a 1962 Grand Prix with what was available.

They started with a Catalina-based Ventura two-door hardtop (pre-production photographs even showed the car with Ventura script plates). They removed some of the exterior chrome, added bucket seats and a center console and adorned the car with distinctive trim. It was an instant success, with over 30,000 units sold the first year. For 1963, Pontiac got the tooling to make the Grand Prix a unique design, with styling that set it apart from the rest of the Pontiacs. In the next few years, the Grand Prix would be one of Pontiac's top-selling models.

The Grand Prix was not only a looker, but a performer as well. Grand Prix models could be equipped with Pontiac's biggest engines including the 421 cubic inch HO powerhouse with Tri-Power induction. These cars were among the fastest on the road. They performed quite well, in keeping with Pontiac's image of the 1960s.

Before DeLorean left Pontiac in 1969, the completely new 1969 Grand Prix was introduced. This Grand Prix was built on its exclusive 118 inch wheelbase chassis. Being several hundred pounds lighter than the previous year's model, it was now considered an intermediate-sized car. Pontiac claimed it had the longest hood of any production car in history.

The 1969 Grand Prix featured a 350 horsepower 400 cubic inch V-8 as standard equipment. It was one of the first cars to have a radio antenna embedded in the windshield, an idea promoted by DeLorean. However, he was the first to admit that the Grand Prix gave less-than-desired performance as it got along in years. The 1969 version was, far and away, the single best-selling 1969 Pontiac model with nearly 112,500 sales.

When DeLorean unveiled Pontiac's pony Car, the Firebird, in February 1967, he made a big deal of the fact that the car was "aimed directly at the largest growing segment of the automobile industry ... the youth market" and that it "is a car tailored to Pontiac's 'think young' marketing approach."

The Grand Prix was completely revamped for 1969, DeLorean's last year at Pontiac. It was the division's best-seller that year. (PMD)

As many know, the Chevrolet Camaro and Pontiac Firebird share the same basic body, as well as many other components. However, the Firebird did get different front end styling and a tighter suspension system that resulted in better handling. The base Firebird was only $200 more than the comparable Camaro.

It was mainly through DeLorean's persistence that GM management allowed Pontiac to build its version of GM's pony car. Otherwise, the Camaro, alone, would have had to go head-to-head against Ford's Mustang. It was a wise decision for GM and Pontiac because more than 82,000 of the 1967 Firebirds hardtop and convertible were sold, though produced for only half-a-year.

In keeping with tradition, Pontiac offered the performance-oriented Firebird buyer a long list of options. There were five engine and three transmission choices. This gave a total of 17 engine/transmission combinations to provide everything from economy to all-out brute performance. Engines ranged from Pontiac's unique six-cylinder overhead cam unit to the 400 cubic inch V-8 that put out 335 horsepower.

Probably, the ultimate performance car to come from Pontiac during DeLorean's tenure was the Firebird Trans Am. The Trans Am was a street racer with impressive handling obtained through its staggered shocks, a one-inch diameter front sway bar, quick steering and seven inch wide wheels. It came equipped with a 400 cubic inch, 335 horsepower Ram Air V-8. The Trans Am was quite distinctive, with its front fender air extractors, functional hood scoops, special decals and rear spoiler. You could have only one color in 1969 (Cameo White with blue stripes) unless you worked for Hot Rod, which tested a silver prototype. Lucerne Blue with white stripes was the sole alternative from 1970 to 1972. Thereafter, color choices were expanded. Only 697 Trans Ams, including just eight convertibles, were made in 1969. The low number was partly due to its mid-year introduction. By 1975, one out of every four Firebirds sold was a Trans Am.

In 1969, DeLorean left Pontiac to become the general manager of Chevrolet. He left quite a legacy behind. He had completed Pontiac's transformation from an "old lady's" car division to the most performance-oriented automaker in Detroit.

By DeLorean's own account, Pontiac became GM's most innovative division, accounting for three-fourths of the corporation's innovations between 1962 and 1969. These new ideas included Endura bumpers, concealed windshield wipers, an overhead-cam six, squared-off headlights and clean body lines devoid of unneeded chrome.

However, DeLorean's greatest contribution probably was his youthful outlook. He had a great desire to make Pontiacs appeal to the young and the young at heart.

Mystery of JFK's Lincoln solved

By Phil Skinner

A couple of years ago, we read a story in Old Cars Weekly that presented several interesting theories about a mystery surrounding the Lincoln that President John F. Kennedy was riding in the day that he was assassinated in Dallas, Texas. The question was, why did the well-known 1961 Lincoln Continental parade phaeton have a 1962 Lincoln front end? At that time, despite much discussion, there was still a question as to how and when the Lincoln had received a facelift.

In order to get the real facts, I contacted Mr. Calvin Beauregard. This gentleman worked for, and is now retired from, Ford Motor Company's Special Vehicles Division. Beauregard was in charge of the famous car, which is usually referred to as the "Kennedy Lincoln."

This photo shows the 1961 Presidential Lincoln, which was internally known at Ford as the X-100, with the removable roof sections used in the car's original open-or-closed parade car configuration. (Ford)

"When Ford Motor Company originally built the presidential car in early 1961, it was finished in navy blue and had the body work done by the custom firm of Hess & Eisenhardt," Mr. Beauregard told us. "The car had special 15 inch wheels, while the stock Lincolns had 14 inch (wheels). We, at first, began to use 1956 and 1957 Lincoln Continental Mark II wheelcovers, but those kept getting lost or broken and were a bit expensive, even for Ford, to replace.

"The car was continually getting chipped and dinged and, so, it was brought back to Dearborn for repaints. In the late fall of 1961, the new 1962 front bumper and grille were added, during one of these repaints. At the same time, we started using wheelcovers from the 1956 Lincoln Capri, since they were a bit more accessible and still fit the 15 inch wheels. The color was also changed, during one of these repaints, to dark Presidential Blue."

This photo shows the car during the initial construction/modification process which changed it from a stock Lincoln Continental convertible into the X-100. It had the standard 1961 Lincoln Continental grille at this time. (Ford)

Here's a front view of the car after it was repainted and fitted with a 1962-style replacement grille. The car went back to the factory for modifications both before and after the Kennedy assassination. (Ford)

After that fateful day in November 1963, the car was once again shipped back to Dearborn, Michigan. Then, it was sent on to Hess & Eisenhardt, in Ohio, for the addition of more plating and a permanent, solid roof.

As the car continued to be used, further updates occurred. In 1965, new style wheelcovers were added to replace the 1956 Capri's wheelcovers. A new 1962 front bumper was added. The old one had special bumper guards, with integral red lights, that had been removed. A special wiring circuit was installed so that the high-beam headlights could be replaced with red ones which could be flashed on and off for parades and motorcades.

During the Johnson and Nixon administrations, the 1961 Lincoln provided rides for many famous world leaders. Ford Motor Company was only loaning the car to the White House, though. When it was finally retired from service, the company donated the Lincoln to the Henry Ford Museum in Dearborn. That's where it is still on display today.

Calvin Beauregard worked for over 25 years in the Special Vehicles Division of Ford Motor Company. He personally served as a driver for countless American VIPS and foreign dignitaries who visited the United States in the mid-1960s. Calvin is one of few American fathers who has family snapshots of his kids riding and playing in the back seat of a presidential limousine.

This 1962 Lincoln Continental is a different car that was specially ordered by the White House in 1961. It also has a special "bubble top" roof. It was used for transporting visiting heads of states and dignitaries and was acquired by the Imperial Palace Auto Collection in April 1985. (Ford)

It is also interesting to point out that the so-called "Kennedy Lincoln" was not the only Lincoln Continental used by John F. Kennedy. There were several others, a number of which still survive in museums and private collections.

Calvin Beauregard is the owner of one of the other cars, a 1962 Lincoln covertible that was assigned to the White House staff for Mrs. John F. Kennedy. He also owns a 1968 Lincoln convertible parade car, which was one of only two built by Ford. The Imperial Palace Auto Collection, of Las Vegas, Nevada, owns (or did own) a bubble top 1962 Lincoln parade car used to transport visiting heads of states and dignitaries. This car was acquired by the Imperial Palace in April 1985. There is also a white Lincoln White House staff car in the collection of the National Automobile Museum in Reno, Nevada. It was sometimes used by John F. Kennedy.

Ike's "bubble top" Lincoln was well-known

By Tom LaMarre

The world knew him as a general and president, but maybe he should have been an auto designer, too. It was Dwight Eisenhower who suggested that a bubble top be added to the 1950 Lincoln Cosmopolitan parade car.

President Eisenhower used the 1950 Lincoln "bubble top" without incident in many parades.. (Photo courtesy Eisenhower Library)

A fleet of 19 Lincolns was delivered to the government in 1950, including a four-door convertible built in Raymond H. Dietrich's Grand Rapids, Michigan shop. A June 1950 press release noted:

"The long, low, custom-built convertible is painted black and has white sidewall tires. It has cherry-red and black genuine leather upholstery, a tan top and two comfortable folding seats. An unusual feature of the car is the use of chrome fender side moldings on the rear side as well as the front fenders.

"The car is equipped with special disappearing steps on each side of the rear fenders for the secret service men who guard the president. Special chrome hand grips on the rear quarter panels serve as supports for the president's guards."

President Eisenhower is pictured riding in the 1950 Lincoln "bubble top" with other officials. (Photo courtesy Eisenhower Library)

The car, which replaced the "Sunshine Special," was designed under the direction of Harold T. Youngren, vice-president of engineering at Ford. But four years later, President Eisenhower had some ideas of his own. Why not add a plexiglass roof, so people could still see him in bad weather? So it was back to Dearborn for the 20 foot-long Lincoln.

No doubt there was some grumbling among the engineers who, four years earlier, had to devise a special automatic top for the car because of its length. Their solution, in 1954, was to couple the plexiglass roof section with a removable canvas section over the driver's compartment. It was a form of protection, for the driver, that was reminiscent of the town cars of the Classic car era.

General Eisenhower liked automobiles. He was given a ride in the Buick LeSabre dream car in the early 1950s before he was president. Later, he helped redesign the "bubble top" Lincoln. (Photo courtesy Eisenhower Library)

The clear top was the finishing touch to a car that was already described as the most luxurious auto in the country. It had an electrically-controlled glass partition separating the driver and passenger compartments, separate heaters and radios for the front and back (did the driver listen to Elvis, while Ike turned in Montovani) and gold plating for all metal trim in the passenger compartment. An intercom linked passenger and chauffeur. The retractable steps at the rear of the car extended 11.1 inches from beneath the bumpers. Standard equipment should have included sunglasses, since the secret service men were probably blinded by the glare from the chrome band around the continental spare.

The one-of-a-kind Lincoln rolled up 100,000 miles for three presidents: Truman, Eisenhower and Kennedy. That's a lot of parades. After the car's well- earned retirement, in 1961, it was returned to the Ford Motor Company. The automaker eventually donated it to the Henry Ford Museum.

1950 Lincoln Cosmopolitan "bubble top."

Ike riding in his family's antique electric car.

SPECIFICATIONS

1950 Lincoln presidential parade car by Dietrich
Engine: .... 337 cubic inch V-8
HP: 152
Trans: .... Hydra-Matic
Overall Length: .... 20 ft.
Wheelbase: .... 145 in.
Weight:.................................... 6,450 lbs.
Tires:.. 8.20 x 15

President Dwight D. Eisenhower waves to the Pennsylvania Avenue crowd en route to his inaugural in the 1950 Lincoln "bubble top."

COLLECTIONS,
COLLECTORS,
COLLECTING

Safe driving this summer

By James M. Flammang

Modern technology has made driving so easy. Maybe it's too easy. All that it takes to drive today is turning the key in the ignition to fire up the engine, stepping gently on the gas to go and shifting a simple lever to change automatic gear ranges or back up. We even have a power source to help turn the steering wheel and can hit a power brake pedal to stop quickly and safely.

All these conveniences and power assists are taken for granted by most drivers today. It's easy for them to forget the potential for trouble developing when they are driving current-model vehicles. Troubles can, and do, appear on new cars, of course. However, when they do, it comes almost as a bizarre surprise.

Not so with old cars! The fact that more effort and concentration are required to drive them properly tends to make us a little more aware that the car is, after all, just a machine. It's nothing more than a conglomeration of precision parts in constant motion. Any one of those parts could give out at any time.

A starter motor is hard to overlook when, to operate it, you have to step on a foot pedal, pull a control cable or even push a separate button on the dash. And it's even tougher to ignore the mechanics of starting the engine when you have to apply muscle to a hand-crank.

Similarly, you feel a lot closer to the drive line when shifting gears regularly by hand with either a floor shift or column lever, using the clutch for each change. All the more so, if yours is an unsynchronized transmission, known fondly as a "crash box," for self-evident reasons.

Then too, most pre-1950s cars, at least, have a full complement of instruments on the dash, rather than the "idiot lights" and minimal gauges that have grown common in later years.

All these factors, combined with the noisier operation of many early engines, the harsher riding qualities of most and the higher-up driving position of full-size old autos, mean you will generally be more aware that you're driving a car rather than steering it. You know you're surrounded by components that can break down.

Still, it's easy to forget for a minute, when tooling your old beast down a rural highway, that you're sitting in an old car rather than a contemporary model. Sometimes, it comes as a shock to see other drivers and passengers turn to look at you, until you suddenly realize that they're admiring your car, rather than your good looks,

Safety rule number one, then, is to remember what you're driving and remain attentive at all times. After all, most of your car's parts are old, even if it's sporting a frame-up restoration. Moreover, a 1935 Plymouth does not respond in the same way as a 1986 Omni. And the power steering "feel" of a 1954 Dodge is far removed from that of manual steering of any vintage. Letting yourself be lulled into forgetting what you're driving is asking for serious trouble. Treat those old parts with respect, and there's no reason why they should not keep going and going. Abuse the old car and its ancient components, and you're taking a chance.

Regular maintenance is an important safeguard to safe summer driving. The "complete car service" offered by the Firestone store in this early postwar photo included lubrication, fuel and tires. Check all three when traveling in your collector car. (Firestone)

Every old car, too, has its quirks and eccentricities. Some shift levers have to be manipulated in a precise way to avoid gear clash. A clutch may have to be engaged ever-so-slowly (or in some cases, rapidly) to ensure a smooth takeoff. Certain engines must be kept below limits in speed, or outside temperatures, to avoid overheating. And nearly every car has its own unique procedure for starting the engine in the morning. It's often a process that differs from that recommended in the owner's manual.

One old Studebaker Hawk, for example, absolutely refused to start unless the gas pedal was pumped four or five times. Nothing was wrong with the fuel system, as far as I could determine. The owner's manual, like most such books, warned against pumping the gas pedal. But, ignoring this quirk meant the car wouldn't fire at all and would have to sit for an hour before making a second try.

A worn out straight eight Pontiac, which did have serious carburetor problems, could only be started by pumping the gas pedal as fast as I could move my foot. Once started, it ran beautifully. However, without that blinding fast foot syncopation, the engine would remain idle forever. A certain Oldsmobile Rocket 88, on the other hand, fired swiftly each morning, but was utterly impossible to start once the engine had warmed up. The solution this time? Never shut the engine off, unless I knew I wouldn't need to start it again for an hour. Even when changing a tire at roadside, I kept the motor running. Foolish, but practical.

The author's worn out straight eight Pontiac had carburetor problems. It could only be started by pumping the gas real fast, but once started, ran beautifully. (Old Cars)

A certain Oldsmobile Rocket 88, similar to this 1955 four-door sedan, fired swiftly each morning, but was utterly impossible to kick over once the engine had warmed up. (Ken Buttolph)

Worst of all was my first car, a 1948 Chevrolet coupe. It wouldn't fire electrically at all. It had to be pushed to start it. How did I manage that when alone, as was often the case? Why, just get it rolling by hand, jump in, and "pop" the clutch in the time-honored manner. Except, there was one minor problem; gears on the Chevrolet's vacuum shift wouldn't move unless the engine was running. So, I had to leave it in first gear every time I parked it, then use the bumper jack to hold down the clutch pedal, push it down the street, jump into the driver's seat, ease my foot onto the clutch, remove said bumper jack and, finally, pop the clutch to get it running. And you think you had troubles starting on chilly mornings!

Most of us who owned older cars in our teenage years ... especially cars in less than pristine condition ... learned many of these tricks and devious (and, indeed, unsafe practices). But still, there's quite a few of today's newer old-car enthusiasts who never went through the "beater-car" stage. These are the younger folk who have always driven well-maintained, late-model autos; cars which nearly always started in the morning and rarely faltered on the road. They must train themselves to recognize the potential dangers when they take up with oldies.

The author's first car, a 1948 Chevrolet coupe, wouldn't fire electrically at all. It had to be pushed to start it and probably wound up in a wrecking yard like this one. (Old Cars)

Those of us who've had the scary experience of stepping on a brake pedal only to find no resistance there, are not likely to ever have that feeling. And we'll be most prepared to deal with it, if that ever happens when driving an old car. If you've ever snapped a tie rod and suddenly lost all or part of your steering control, as happened to me with a 1950 Ford (fortunately, it was moving slowly at the time), the thought of such potential disasters is permanently etched somewhere in the back of your mind.

Anyone who has experienced a tire blow-out at highway speed will have a healthy respect for the frailties of tires, even though the modern versions are far less likely to blow. And the driver who has spent more than one dark night stalled by the side of a lonely road with an inoperative old car will have developed an unshakeable feeling for the fallibility of machinery in general.

Those old car motorists who've never experienced any or many of such misfortunes and calamities, should at least be made aware of them. Let's hope that you will never have a driveshaft drop out of your car on the way to work (as happened to a friend with his 1951 Studebaker). Let's hope you avoid having an oil line rupture at the the pressure gauge, thus sending a potent stream of filthy oil onto your new suit (which happened to another friend on his way to a big party with a heavy date). Such tragedies do happen, though, and are more likely to occur on a car with six figures on the odometer and many years of trusty service. They can happen even if that car has been renovated, restored and even remanufactured.

No, this doesn't mean you should spend your time behind the wheel with a sense of imminent doom in mind. Don't spend your entire vacation staring at your temperature gauge, hoping for an imperceptible nudge away from absolute normal so you can yell "Aha!" and have your fears realized. Old cars can and should be fun to drive. Even the potential of disaster can add a degree of perverse pleasure to your outings, provided you remain relaxed and aware and psychologically prepared for whatever might occur.

Too much knowledge and familiarity, like too little, can be dangerous. Some of us who have spent many years around tired old cars never can quite relax. Though, we are confident that we can handle sudden emergencies and deal with failures that might come up, we worry about every little noise. We constantly feel the steering wheel for traces of tiny vibrations and sniff the air for suspicious mechanical aromas. That can mean there is little energy left to enjoy the trip in an old car.

Safe summer driving in an old car is greatly enhanced if you travel in a group. This tour included 51 cars owned by members of the Northern California Imperial Owners Club and the California Region of the Cadillac-LaSalle Club. (Hugo Steccati)

Insuring collector cars

By Janet K. Brice

You've bought your dream car. You've scrounged around for parts, enlisted the help of family and friends, spent every spare moment and poured every dime into restoring that beautiful antique car.

You've cleaned it, shined it, tuned it and obtained the registration. Now, you're ready to take your pride and joy for a spin. There's one thing: before you take that Sunday afternoon drive or enter that parade, don't forget to give your insurance agent a call. You definitely should be covered for at least liability, to protect your investment against physical damage.

In many cases, the liability insurance premium would be the same as for any other auto you drive. However, some companies will give you a break on antique cars. For example, one company charges 40 percent of the private passenger auto rate (subject to minimum premiums) for antique autos used primarily for exhibitions, club activities, parades and other functions of public interest, with occasional use for other purposes. Classic cars are usually rated the same as any private passenger auto.

Before you take that Sunday afternoon drive or enter that parade, don't forget to give your insurance agent a call. Your collector car definitely should be covered to protect your investment against physical damage. (National Motor Museum)

Most insurance companies will require supporting coverage. For instance, they will want to write your other personal auto business as well. Liability is only part of the package. It covers the people you might injure or the property you might damage.

You may also want coverage in case (heaven forbid) your collector car is damaged. Obtaining physical damage coverage for your antique or collectible car is a little more complicated than it is for a late-model car, but it can be done.

Collision protects against damage to your car if you collide with another vehicle. You'll also be covered for collision with a tree, mail box, house, etc. This 1937 DeSoto hit a Long Island, New York garage. (Jim Fitchett)

Physical damage coverage consists of comprehensive and collision. Comprehensive includes fire, wind, theft, glass breakage, vandalism and animal collision. (Theft of personal property not permanently installed would probably be covered under your homeowner's insurance policy.)

Collision insurance covers damage to your car if you collide with another vehicle and you are at fault or if it's the other party's fault and he or she is uninsured. You'd also be covered for collision with a tree, mail box, etc.

Before a company provides insurance coverage on a 25-year-old car, they'll want to know it's value and condition. They will definitely want one or more color photographs and will very likely request an appraisal from a reputable expert. They will then insure the vehicle for the stated value. The value for some vehicles may be significantly greater than for vehicles of comparable make and model because of special construction, limited production, fine workmanship and so on.

Physical damage for an antique auto may be written on a named peril basis. The vehicle would only be covered for the perils specified in the policy such as fire, lightning, cyclone, tornado, windstorm, collision, derailment, overturning of transporting conveyances, collapse of bridges, collision or upset of vehicle, theft, hailstorm, vandalism and malicious mischief. As an alternative, you may be able to have an all-risk policy for physical damage. This would cover virtually anything that could happen, with certain specified exclusions. A deductible of $50 or $100 is usually required, with other deductibles optional.

Physical damage coverage may be written on a named peril basis. Perils that could be specified include upset of vehicle, fires, lightning, storms, collision, derailment, overturning of transporting conveyances, collapse of bridges, theft, vandalism and malicious mischief.

Companies generally frown on clients adding their antique cars to their policies for a parade or show and, then, deleting them when the event is over. Your best bet would be to cover your car for the entire summer. During the winter months, you can delete all coverages except comprehensive.

If you have a really elegant car ... a Rolls Royce for instance ... it is not likely that a standard insurance company will want to write a policy for it. In that case, you will have to go to a specialty insurance provider.

Call your insurance agent to find out what's available and what type of policy is most suitable for your particular situation. Your agent may have to shop around a little, but once you've worked out the details, you can go out and enjoy your car with peace of mind.

Flooding is another peril that car collectors might want to write into their insurance policies. (Old Cars)

Standard policies do not cover damage in motorsports competition. If you plan to enter your vehicle in vintage auto races, you will need special insurance coverage designed for such activity. It's available. (Old Cars)

Happy trailering to you

Driving collector cars to and from shows is considered part of the fun by many hobbyists. Increasingly, however, collectors are using other means of transporting their prized possessions.

The main reason for this is the preservation of the vehicles themselves. Cars which are driven or brought along via tow bar are likely to suffer wear and tear on tires and mechanical systems as well as exposure to road hazards. On the other hand, a car which is comfortably perched atop or inside of a trailer can be protected from bugs, stones and melted tar.

Rapid escalation in the value of many collector cars in recent years has led some owners to protect their investments by using trailers.

What, then, are some of the factors to be considered when buying a trailer? Price is the first thought of most trailer buyers. While enclosed trailers provide the most protection, they also tend to be the most expensive to purchase and to tow. Beware of paying too little for a trailer, however.

While enclosed trailers provide the most protection, they also tend to be the most expensive to purchase and to tow. (Bruce Litton Trailers)

The collector needs a trailer capable of transporting the largest vehicle in his/her collection. Factors to be considered are axle load capacity, bearings, tire load ratings, platform length and adequacy of brakes. (Jer-rdan Trailers)

It is also recommended that the tow vehicle be left attached to the trailer while loading and unloading. Many states offer information on trailer regulations for free. (Old Cars)

A good rule is to buy a rig whose specifications qualify it for the job it is expected to perform. For a collector, this means a trailer capable of transporting the largest vehicle in his/her collection. Factors to be considered here are the load capacity of axles and bearings, tire load ratings, platform length and width and adequacy of brakes. Also, old car hobbyists tend to favor double axle trailers because of their generally greater load capacities, self-supporting feature, better balance and greater safety in the event of tire failure.

If these items are given proper consideration, overloading can be avoided. Overloading can lead to unsafe trailer operation due to excessive wear, and possible breakdown, of trailer components.

Trailer quality may vary with price, but the buyer should pay particular attention to certain features. Basic trailer design is one of these. Is the trailer engineered soundly? Will it actually perform as it is intended to? The grade of materials used should be considered as well as fit and finish.

Trailers constructed almost entirely of aluminum are available. While generally higher in initial cost, these offer the advantages of lighter weight and greater ease of maintenance. Additional preferred features are self-storing ramps, high quality lighting systems, leaf springs with equalizers, and removable fenders to ease loading and unloading.

Trailer manufacturers offer the following suggestions for safe trailering. First, trailer overloading should always be avoided. Next, the load vehicle weight should be balanced front to rear as nearly as possible. The trailered vehicle must be secured against movement on the trailer, while being transported. This can best be done through the use of chains, cables, or, more recently, special rachet-type tie-down straps. It is also recommended that the tow vehicle be left attached to the trailer while loading and unloading. Many states offer information on trailer regulations, as well as trailering tips, through their state patrols or departments of transportation.

An appropriate tow vehicle is essential to trouble-free trailering. Despite the general down-sizing of new vehicles in recent years, there are still some tow vehicles on the market which are large and powerful enough to lend themselves "to collector car trailering. A less expensive and more attractive alternative, especially to old car fans, is the abundance of large, powerful cars and trucks of the mid-to-late 1970s, which is still out there.

Whatever the choice of tow vehicle, however, it should be properly equipped and strong enough to do the job. Recommended here are heavy-duty cooling components for both transmission and engine, heavy-duty springs and shock absorbers and frame-mounted, rather than bumper-mounted, trailer hitches.

The final key to to happy trailering is frequent monitoring of the entire rig while on the road. This can be done while stopping for food, fuel or any other reason. It works best if it is a systematic procedure. The tow vehicle should have its vital fluid levels checked and topped up, if necessary. Trailer ball and safety chain connections should be checked and adjusted, if need be. Tie-down devices should be examined and adjusted. All the while this is going on, any obvious problems with tire pressures may be noted and dealt with. Finally, and very importantly, the lighting system should be thoroughly checked and any malfunction corrected.

A satisfactory trailering experience boils down to buying the best equipment your wallet will allow and exercising good sense in its use.

Happy trailering to you!

Continental kits were popular on Fords

By John Lee

The invention of the balloon tire, a milestone in automotive history, brought with it a problem: When they get holes in them, balloon tires go flat.

Therefore, along with the balloon tire came the spare tire or, in the early days, two or three spare tires. The designer's problem was where to put the spares.

Generally, spare tires were attached to the side or rear of the car. Later, they were worked into the design, being placed in wells in the front fenders or enclosed in steel covers on the back of the car.

Still later, the enclosed trunk compartment became a handy place to stash the spare tire. So it was with Ford stylists, in 1937, when all their models had enclosed trunks. The spare was stowed out of sight. Designers brushed off their hands and said, "That's that!"

Less than three years later Edsel Ford, Henry Ford's son, decided he wanted a specially-designed car to impress his country club friends. What happened? In 1939, the Lincoln Continental was born. It had (you guessed it) the spare tire attached to the rear. It was mounted on the outside of the bustle-back trunk compartment!

The 1940 Lincoln Continental, designed by Edsel Ford, started the continental tire craze. (Lincoln)

The Lincoln Continental emerged, after World War II, with modernized styling (actually previewed on 1942 models). An exposed spare was a prominent part of its appearance. When the sporty Willys Jeepster came on the scene with a similar appendage, everyone wanted a tire on the back of their car.

By the mid-1950s, the kits were elaborate with tire covers and massive bumper extensions, as on this 1955 Ford Crown Victoria. (Old Cars)

The aftermarket responded by making kits available for attaching a spare to the tail end of about any car. Continental kits (so-called after Edsel's creation that prompted the revival) provided bumper bracket extensions, wider gravel shields, tire covers and mounting brackets that permitted them to be tilted back for access to the trunk.

The square auto designs introduced for 1949 lent themselves to the addition of continental kits much better than the rounded lines of previous models. More kits were probably added to the 1949-1951 "shoe box" Fords than any other car. Ford owners sought to set their vehicles apart from millions of others and make them look more expensive than they were.

The "Coronado Deck" was a tire-shaped appendage attached to the trunk lid giving the impression it contained the spare. It got a lot of exposure on the 1953 Indianapolis 500 pace car and copies sold by dealers. (Old Cars)

The continental kit enjoyed such a run of popularity, during the early 1950s, that it became standard on some models and a factory option on others. Ford even produced a modified version of it, as an accessory on 1953 models, and carried it over for 1954. Known as the "Coronado Deck," the tire-shaped appendage merely attached to the trunk lid and gave the appearance that it contained the spare tire. The option got a lot of exposure by being used on the 1953 Indianapolis 500 pace car and the convertible copies that were sold by dealers.

Available for the handsome-looking 1957 Ford Fairlane 500 was a continental tire with matching v-shaped trim moldings and two-tone finish. (Old Cars)

Continental kits were popular on the 1957-1959 Ford Skyliner Retractables since a rear-mounted spare allowed more space inside the luggage bin for luggage. This is a 1959 model. (Old Cars)

The Continental kit's popularity increased. It got a boost in 1956, when Ford made the exposed wheel standard equipment on the Thunderbird and brought out the new Continental Mark II, which had a deck design suggestive of the exposed-spare styling of the previous Continental.

Ford offered a true, extended bumper continental kit as an option from 1956 to 1960. Accessory houses did a good business in them, too. They were particularly welcome on the 1957-1959 retractable hardtops, as they got the bulky spare tire out of the trunk (where it monopolized most of the minimal storage space) and moved it to the outside rear.

Offering the continental kit option on the 1960 Ford was probably a mistake. It didn't blend with the new styling and not many were installed. As far as Ford was concerned, the continental kit went into remission in the early 1960s. The pseudo spare tire styling gimmick was revived on the Lincoln Continental, later in the decade. It remains a part of its design to this day.

Most quality kits have a swing-out mechanism to permit access to the trunk lid lock and luggage compartment. (Old Cars)

As styling cycles go, the continental kit came back in the late 1970s with models for contemporary cars. Now "connie kits" for many earlier models are also back in production. It's still possible to give your Ford a continental flavor.

Continental Enterprises, of Kelowna, British Columbia, started building reproduction continental tire kits over a decade ago. "My brother and I started years ago," said Sam Borenstein, the founder of the company.

According to Borenstein, individual kits don't sell in big numbers now. The secret is having a lot of them. "In the early days, the kits we made were for 1952 Chevrolets, 1954 Fords, 1955 Chevrolets and 1955-1956 Fords. They were reproductions of aftermarket designs," Borenstein says. "It wasn't until six years later that I had money for expensive tooling and dies."

Rare books shop

T.E. Warth, Esquire, Automotive Books is the name of a new small business. Surprisingly to some, the owner is a transplanted Englishman who gave America its largest car-books company.

In 1967, when Tom Warth left his job with Prudential Insurance in Minneapolis, even he didn't dream that his side line of selling British auto magazines would become a giant operation. Twenty years later, Tom found himself the owner of a retailing and publishing firm that shipped as many as 10,000 books in a single day.

Classic Motorbooks/Motorbooks International, of Osceola, Wisconsin, was definitely flourishing, but Warth's personal interest in rare books was riding in the back seat. That's when he decided to make a change.

Warth (center) was the founder of Classic Motorbooks/Motorbooks International and is seen in this early 1980s photo with his former Motorbooks staff.

After finding capable people to take over the Osceola operation, Tom rented an empty shop in his home town of Marine-on-St. Croix, Minnesota and hung a small shingle outside the door. He was back in the rare book trade.

"Our objective is to be able to supply any post-World War II book on automotive-related subjects," explained Warth. "If we do not have title on hand, we will search for it throughout the world."

The business is based on the fact that only about one-third of the titles that Classic Motorbooks has cataloged over the years are still in print. However, people building new automotive libraries want obsolete books. Tom knew there was a strong demand for out-of-print titles.

Tom Warth sells rare automotive books in Marine on St. Croix, Minnesota. He has also published a guide to the values of vintage automotive books. (John Gunnell)

Hundreds of books no longer available in the retail market already line the shelves of the homey little shop. But, if a certain desired title is not on hand, a computer-aided search for good used copies can be initiated. The shop is located at 13 Lumberyard Shops, Marine on St. Croix, MN 55047. It can be reached by phoning (612) 433-5744 or faxing (612) 433-5012.

Warth and his employees will begin a search with no obligation to the customer. Therefore, if you request a certain book and stumble upon a copy at a flea market, you're free to go ahead and buy it. If you don't locate the book and one turns up through the search, it will generally cost at least twice the amount it originally retailed for, with a minimum charge of $30.

Since opening the shop, Warth has also compiled and published his own research project ... a book focusing on the value of vintage books on vintage cars. The 1993 edition of The Car Book Value Guide features a guide to 5,000 automotive book titles sorted alphabetically, by author and by subject and provides estimates of what each book is worth. In addition, Warth throws in his current stock list for free with every order for the $19.95 book.

The company specializes in searching for books only. Sales literature, shop manuals or owner's handbooks are not included, since there are many hobby vendors willing to help out in those areas. If you are not seeking a particular title, but like old books in general, the shop (about 30 minutes northeast of Minneapolis) is open for browsing on Wednesday between 10 a.m. and 4 p.m. If you're going to be in the area at another time, the shop may be open by chance or appointments can be made. A telephone message machine is also left on during regular Monday-Friday business hours, to take messages from potential customers.

After one year of operation, Warth is convinced that his new small business is going to get big. "We didn't make a fantastic profit," he noted. "But, we did make enough to equip the shop, hire a staff and build up an inventory to satisfy the ever growing demand for rare automotive books."

Warth is a genuine car enthusiast and the owner of a Cobra, a vintage Citroen and this Jaguar sport coupe. (John Gunnell)

Model cars of today are geared to tomorrow's drivers

Toy vehicles have been fixtures in toy chests around the world from the time real automobiles were invented. Throughout the years of changing styles, materials and construction techniques, children of all ages have continued to make model car collecting a growth industry.

No company knows that better than Matchbox Cars U.S.A. Last year, Matchbox sold more cars than General Motors, Ford Motor Company and Chrysler Corporation combined. Of course, a toy car maker doesn't face the same problems that the "Big 3" do.

"We've never had a recall; we have no smog problems, no safety problems," said Larry Wood, a designer of Mattel's "Hot Wheels" cars. Wood spent three years as a Ford designer, before joining the number two toy car maker and is happy he switched. "When I worked in Detroit, I did a few door handles and taillights. So far I've done every Hot Wheels car since 1968."

The 1938 Lagonda was model number Y-11 in the Matchbox "Models of Yesteryear" series of the 1970s.

Wood does keep an eye on car styling coming from the "Motor City," and elsewhere around the world, trying to anticipate future trends. "If Detroit or Japan or Germany come out with an exciting car or different profile, we take a look at it," he said. "I think they have gone a little more conservative in the last few years," he added. "Now kids seem to like the standard sporty cars.

Wood's competition follows the trends just as closely. "If we see a trend developing in auto design, we will stay with the trend and capture it in our cars," said Jim Walsh, Matchbox marketing director. Matchbox was impressed enough by Ford's Taurus/Sable design, that it copied the look for its 1/64-scale die-cast miniatures. "Obviously the Ford Taurus is a pretty sleek design, something that's caught on with the public," adds Walsh.

It's obvious that miniature cars are a hit with the public. Consider that the number 3

Also included in the "Models of Yesteryear" series was the classic 1928 Mercedes Benz 'SS.'

There are approximately 6,000 members of Match-box collectors clubs seeking miniatures like this 1934 Riley from the "Models of Yesteryear" line.

Kids favor sports cars, like the Matchbox number 32 Maserati Bora, but military and construction vehi-cles are favorites, too.

A craftsman patternmaker checks a critical mea-surement on the hand-carved wooden patterns for a new Matchbox series scale model at the Lesney fac-tory.

A finely cut steel portion of the mold for a new Matchbox model is hand-fitted and rough castings are taken to ensure the continued accuracy of the mold-making.

toy car maker, Lewis Galoob Toys Incorporated, expected to sell 45 million vehicles in 1988, its second year in the toy car marketplace. Their Micro Machines are only 1-1/4 inches long, smaller than Hot Wheels or Matchbox toys. Galoob is now selling toy cars that change color in the sun, which is a departure from the firm's realistic offerings.

"Kids are not crazy for fantasy," said marketing manager Marjorie Forrest. "They don't want a car that doesn't look like a car. Kids today are very sophisticated," she added. "They know what a (Lamborghini) Countach is and what a Rolls-Royce is." Forrest echoed Larry Wood's opinion that kids favor sports cars, but added military and construction vehicles to their favorites.

Wood also points out that kids are not the only buyers. He sees just as many adult pur-chasers, but adds that kids tend to choose what they see on television, such as the Ferrari Testarossa seen on "Miami Vice."

Matchbox's Walsh says that kids also lean toward American made cars, because of what they see on the streets. It is a loyalty that can carry over into adulthood. "If they happen to like four-wheel drive cars as a kid, there's a strong possibility they'll like four-wheel vehicles as an adult," he said. "In my opinion, if you like a particular type of car as a kid, you're apt to grow up and like them."

That's music to the ears of the real automakers, in Detroit, who usually do not charge their toy counterparts any royalties. "Anytime you get your product in the mind of the car buyer or a young person, you enhance your reputation," said Chrysler's B.F. Mullins. "We think it does a lot of good. You get involved in a lot of shelf space in department stores. It also gets young people involved in your product. The bottom line is consideration of your product," he concluded. When Chrysler introduced its Dodge Caravan and Plymouth Voyager minivans, it handed out Matchbox versions as souvenirs to the press.

Ford officials take models made of their vehicles very seriously. "We want it (a toy) to be very authentic," said Ford's David Krupp. "We want it to be accurate in every detail, We consider this child a future car buyer."

While children are still the primary market, the toy makers know that collectors are also part of their market. Jim Walsh stated that there are about 20,000 Matchbox collectors in the United States. They sell and trade the vehicles, with some fetching as much as $200. Worldwide, there are approximately 6,000 members of organized Matchbox toy car collectors clubs.

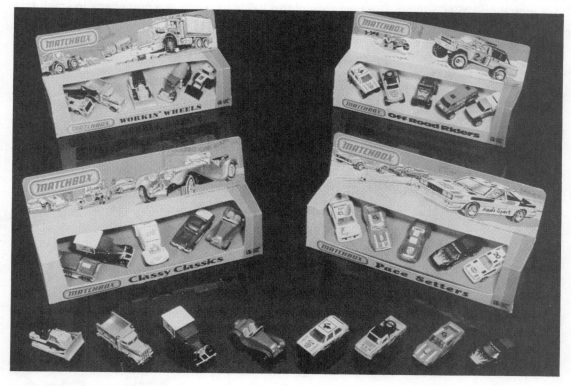

The Matchbox "Super Sets" were aimed at some of strongest areas of collector interest including: (clockwise from top right) off-road vehicles; sports-racing cars; classics; and construction vehicles.

Franklin Mint's "Classics of Fifties" well done

By Pat Chappell

They're called "Classic Cars of the Fifties," and the Franklin Mint has them. A full dozen miniature versions of classic 1950s cars, from a 3-7/8-inch long copy of the 1957 Corvette to a 5-1/4-inch long 1959 Cadillac. The best cars of the 1950s have made a comeback in small size.

They're called Classic Cars of the '50s and the Franklin Mint has them.

This dozen from the 1950s is not the beginning of the Franklin Mint's die-cast precision models, nor is it the end. From 1986 on, a 1907 Rolls-Royce Silver Ghost, a 1930 Duesenberg J Derham tourster, a 1935 Mercedes-Benz 500K Special Roadster, a 1938 Jaguar SS-100 and a 1954 Mercedes-Benz 300 SL gull-wing, all in 1:24 scale, were produced. Most recently, a "Classics of the Golden Era" series of a dozen 1:43 scale models was announced. It included a 1928 Hispano-Suiza and a 1931 Bugatti Royale.

Starting as a direct response company selling commemorative coins and medals, The Franklin Mint has become the world's largest creator of fine, heirloom-quality collectibles. Its emphasis is on originally designed, upscale products distributed directly and exclusively by the company.

With international offices in 18 countries and four continents, The Franklin Mint employs 4,300 people worldwide. Five distinct marketing divisions conceive, design and execute products from heirloom dolls to artistic firearms and weapons; jewelry to finely bound books; and historic coins and medals to precision model die-cast metal automobiles. Each year, The Franklin Mint adds about 100 products to its ever-changing 300-item line.

The "Classic Cars of the Fifties" series includes a dozen well-selected precision models in 1:43 scale. Besides the 1959 Cadillac Eldorado, 1956 Ford Thunderbird, 1957 Corvette and 1958 Edsel on the product brochure's cover, there is a 1950 Ford woodie station wagon, 1950 Chrysler Town & Country Newport hardtop, 1951 Mercury Monterey two-door sedan, 1953 Buick Skylark convertible, 1953 Packard Caribbean convertible, 1953 Studebaker Starliner coupe, 1955 Chevrolet Bel Air convertible and a 1956 Continental Mark II.

Having an active interest in postwar collector cars, we contacted The Franklin Mint's public relations department to see if we could examine these precision models first hand. Eventually, we had the opportunity to visit The Franklin Mint and speak with them about the "Classic Cars of the Fifties." The Franklin Mint is not a part of the United States Mint, as some assume. However, it is the world's largest private mint.

The mint picked a winner for the first offering in its "Classic Cars of the Fifties" series, when this line of models was originally released. It was a Venetian red and shoreline beige 1957 fuel-injected Corvette. The second model in the series featured the "grinning" front bumper and chrome wire wheels of the 1953 Buick Skylark. The 1956 Lincoln Continental Mark II became the third car to be replicated in the series.

The first model in the series was a red 1957 Corvette.

Jack Wilkie, the mint's director of public relations, is an automobile enthusiast. He remembers the cars from the 1950s, which he describes as the "golden age of collector cars," when they were brand new. Wilkie explained how the idea for this series of model was generated in 1986. It was test-marketed with a preliminary mailing, in March 1987, that drew a tremendous response. It seemed to have the potential to be one of the Franklin Mint's biggest sellers, even surpassing the very popular collector chess sets.

With the model of the fuel-injected 1957 Corvette sitting on his desk, marketing director Dan Schutzman explained how the precision models program was focused directly toward a marketing area "between the inexpensive toy-like car models and the one-of-a-kind pricy models."

This is where The Franklin Mint is aiming its model cars program, with the goal of offering the best available product replica, for the money, in that market niche. Schutzman explained, "That market has expanded, beyond just car enthusiasts and collectors, to the masses of people who just like cars."

After the 12 postwar automobiles to model were selected, contacts were made with car collectors throughout the United States. The idea was to find pristine, show-quality, factory original examples of the real cars. The Franklin Mint's staff, including photographers and engineers, went to where the cars were located. They took hundreds of photographs and measurements. They even put each car on a hydraulic lift to check for undercarriage detailing.

Returning to The Franklin Mint studios in Franklin Center, Pennsylvania, they went to work hand-sculpturing "master models" of each car. They used these to create the special tooling from which matching sets of precision steel dies could be drawn. With The Franklin Mint manufacturing and owning the tooling, a world-wide search ensued for a combination of the best model makers, the best skilled labor and the best price in the marketplace.

While visiting The Franklin Mint, we had an opportunity to see one of the largest photographic studios we've ever seen where the entire series of 1950s car models was assembled. They were still in prototype form at that time. As any admirer of handsome automobiles would, we wanted to touch and feel them, but that was not possible. We remarked on the proportions and the accuracy of the scaled-down size; on how very small the Corvette looked beside the 1956 Continental Mark II and the 1959 Cadillac. The relative proportions were like those the full-sized cars would have illustrated when parked side by side.

We wanted to take the 1957 Corvette model home with us that day; the one on Dan Schutzman's desk. However, he didn't have the removable hardtop handy just then. Several days later, our own Corvette arrived from The Franklin Mint. It was complete with a top. The styrofoam molded shipping box served as its garage. We set it up on display and had an opportunity to study it.

Looking at the precision model from the perspective of a Chevrolet enthusiast and historian, we felt the overall proportion of this replica was excellent. There seemed to be no distortion at all. We gave it good marks for quality of paint finish. It was smoothly finished and there was no evidence of roughness or irregularities in the application of the paint on the metal body. We were also impressed with the display options, the doors and the hood that opened and shut, and the removable hardtop.

The Corvette has many functional features that are detailed to look authentic.

We really looked forward to the arrival of the other 11 models, the wall display shelf and the binder that contained reprints of original ads and specifications. One by one, the first dozen Classic Cars of the Fifties models became available to the public.

This past July, we were on our way to cover the National Corvette Restorers Society convention in nearby Lancaster, Pennsylvania. Thinking that collector cars receive their most accurate appraisal in the judging arena, we decided to take the Franklin Mint precision model with us and enter it in its own "unofficial" judging session. We hoped to get genuine input from representative owners, judges and restorers who belonged to this society of 8,000 collectors of 1953-1972 Corvettes.

Over 100 full-sized Corvettes were assembled at an indoor tennis facility, in Lancaster, Pennsylvania, for the first day of judging. We had an opportunity to circulate among the owners, judges and restorers. They seemed amazed and pleased with the Corvette precision model.

We had a chance to meet with an owner of a similarly-colored 1957 Corvette in the judging area. He agreed the miniature was a good representation of the full-sized Corvette and liked the authentic color. He remarked that Venetian Red is a very difficult color to match and that, in competition judging, it was not unusual to see several rather slight variations of the color.

We had lunch with a couple of Corvette restorers, Sara Blake and Joe Myers from Ft. Myers, Florida. They had just finished a 1955 Corvette restoration. By the end of the meet, this car would receive NCRS's top honor, the Duntov Award of Excellence. A few other owners and judges gathered near us and all scrutinized The Franklin Mint's Corvette.

There was much enthusiasm about examining the little model firsthand. Good marks were given for its proportion and translation to the 1:43 scale, which agreed with the positive comments we had received earlier.

One of the latest 1950s models is a red and white 1957 Ford Skyliner.

Men, boys and the price of their toys

By LeRoi "Tex" Smith

You know the saying about men, boys and the price of toys. Fortunately, it's true. Nowhere is this more apparent than in the hobby of automotive toys. We can all vividly remember the first toy car, truck or tractor that made such an indelible impression. Usually, it was owned by someone else or sat on the dime store counter. It was shiny and impossibly expensive and we wanted it in the worst of ways.

We can all vividly remember the first toy car, truck or tractor that made such an indelible impression. (Old Cars)

Now that we can have them, those wonderful dreams of yesterday can't be found. At least, not easily found. And, certainly, not found at the dime store. Oh, there are toy cars, trucks and tractors, but, for me at least, a plastic throw-away is not nearly the same as a "real" toy ... something heavy and substantial ... something made of metal and rubber.

194

A plastic throw-away is not nearly the same as a heavy and substantial old toy made of metal, or in this case, rubber. (Gabriel R. Delobbe)

So, we wander through the antique shops and swap meets and moan under the strain of price tags far beyond what we are willing to pay. And, we continue to yearn for the possessions of someone else, there on a counter.

With luck, you can find discarded toy trucks where they were thrown away 10, 20 and 40 years ago...the dumps on abandoned farms and ranches. (Old Cars)

In recent years, I've devised a remedy. In many ways, it is a solution far more satisfactory than merely plunking down the money. In my part of the mountainous west, rust is not the scurrilous plague it is elsewhere. So, I go out and find discarded toy cars, trucks and tractors right where they were thrown away 10, 20 and 40 years ago. I scrounge the dumps of abandoned farms and ranches.

Farmers never used a central, community dump. Instead, they had a private trash pile somewhere on their property (usually in a depression or on an erosion bank.) These are very easy to spot, because everything ended up there, from household trash to farm junk in general.

Rural America is dotted with these private goldmines and, even if such a mine has been picked over by the bottle-and-such collectors, the chances are prime that poor-condition toys remain.

These are the gems I haul home and resurrect. Since most of these toys are made of metal ... either sheet metal or cast metal ... they are almost always rusty and, usually, bent. Many times, there will be small parts missing. And, almost always, the tires and wheels will be gone. They are perfect projects for restoration.

Most old toys are made of metal (sheet metal like this Cadillac or cast metal) and they are almost always rusty and bent. (Dennis Doty)

I generally start a toy rebuild by sand blasting or acid dipping the unit. I'm no chemist, so I don't know what acid is best. I just go down to the drugstore and get some "muriatic" stuff and put it in a plastic container deep enough to immerse the toy. Then, I keep a close watch on the toy and remove it before the acid has a chance to destroy the good metal. More often, I fill my small, Sears, Roebuck & Co. sandblasting gun (the kind with a small quart-size cup for the sand) and very carefully do a number on the metal.

I don't care how pitted the metal is or how much of the metal is missing. Just as long as there is enough for a pattern.

Most of the toys are not so much bent, as they are simply pushed out of shape (usually, by other trash having been heaved on the pile). I very carefully push the toy back into shape and, then, use a small body hammer to reshape the bent metal. The workbench vise is enough of a solid work station to hammer against. This is painstaking work and, because of the rust, you must go slowly and easily. As a guide, a really misshapen toy car will usually take about one hour or less to straighten.

It is possible to do the straightening before sand blasting, but the results just don't seem to be as good. They're not as "clean," anyway.

Once the toy is straightened, missing pieces can be cut from 22- or 24-gauge sheet metal. Lots of times, things like headlights or grilles, and so on are gone. If you are after absolute authenticity, you need some kind of book or pictures to go by. I don't worry that much about being a purist and I make up what seems, to me, would have been right. Regular tin snips trim the metal and you work it, in the vise, with the body hammer. Patience is the key to success.

Once all the small parts necessary for the body are in place, you can reconstruct missing pieces of the main body. Suppose a portion of one side has been lost to rust. Simply use a piece of lightweight cardboard as a backing for the missing area. Tape this inside the body and flush up against the side you are repairing. Now, mix up some fiberglass resin and thin glass cloth. Patch the area and build it up with any of the common body fillers. You do all the finishing and shaping with sandpaper and ordinary hand-files. Remove the cardboard backing.

For the most part, I don't have to make such extensive repairs. I use ordinary body shop metal finishing techniques, even on deeply rusted surfaces. I spray on a coat of the new metal etching primers and let this set a day or so. This is followed by plastic filler, which is sanded glass-smooth. You can do this on the inside of the metal as well.

Before the final paint is applied, attention is turned to the wheels and tires. I have a lot of toys around without tires and wheels, simply because I didn't know where to get replacements. I found out about Julian Thomas, P.O. Box 405, Fenton, Michigan 48430 (Ph: 313-629-8707). Apparently, he offers tires and wheels for toys. Hooray!

Anyway, before final paint application, remove the original wheel axles. They are usually nothing more than lengths of wire bradded at either end outside the body. I just cut the old axles away and make up new ones, generally from welding rod stock. A neat trick I've learned is that I don't have to brad the wire after replacement; a dab of Loc-Tite metal mending compound will do.

There is a two-part, black-colored system I've been using to weld everything from aluminum cylinder heads to exhaust manifolds. It's called Loc-Weld and it really works. I've also used it to mend broken sections of toy bodies, where it can be built up on the inside without showing too much. Now that I know where to get tires and wheels, everything takes on an entirely new meaning.

The final paint is applied before the axles, wheels and tires are installed permanently. The better the paint job, the better I like my restoration. So, I have been using the best paint possible. Sticking with special two-part etching primers (most of these come from two German companies, Sikkens and Glasruit), I use the same brand final finish; always urethane! It finishes far superior to anything else I've tried, although it's expensive. The key is to find an area painter who uses it. Then, I have the models ready to paint when he is going to paint a car with the same kind of expensive materials.

Sometimes, I have to be content with a color not exactly to my demands, but since the painter just sprays it while he is spraying the big vehicle (at no cost to me) I can be very tolerant. These paints require color-sanding with 1,000-grit paper and final compound polishing, but the results are superior.

Recently, I've been experimenting with rust converter products like Fertan and Jenolite. If the metal isn't badly corroded, I just brush off the converter and finish over the top. This isn't the same as just knocking off rust, but it is quicker.

Doing toy restoration is really a fun process, especially if I intersperse it with one of the full-scale building projects that seem to be ever at hand. But, to be perfectly honest, I think the scrounging in long-forgotten dumps is the best part of the adventure.

Toy restoration is really fun when you restore a toy to look, for example, like that full-size woodie you own.
(Old Cars)

Peter Helck: a tribute

By Keith Marvin

Famous automotive artist Peter Helck was referred to as "painter's painter." Peter Helck died on April 22, 1988. He was 94.

Helck, a victim of failing eyesight, had not painted for several years prior to his death. However, he was still considered the dean of American automotive illustrators of the 20th century. He was a prolific artist who was admired by many people.

"Nobody can take his place," said fellow automotive artist Jack Juratovic. "He was an inspiration to automotive and fine art. If you had to pick fifty 20th century artists, he'd be in the top half."

"He was the greatest artist in the world on automotive subjects," said Helck's longtime associate and friend, Henry Austin Clark Jr., of Long Island, New York, who has passed away since Helck's death.

Helck began his journey to an artistic career in 1912 at the Art Students League in New York City. He subsequently studied privately under a variety of noted artists.

"Bourque's Winning Model R Knox at the Bridgeport Hill Climb in 1909," by Peter Helck. (Courtesy Antique Automobile)

Working as an advertising illustrator for almost 50 years, Helck acquired awards and much recognition in the process. His works of commerical and fine art have appeared in countless publications, including two major award-winning art books of his own. His paintings and drawings can be found in the collections of the Metropolitan Museum of Art in New York, the Carnegie Institute in Pittsburgh, the Congressional Library in Washington, the Philadelphia Museum of Fine Arts, the Long Island Automotive Museum in New York and the New Britain Museum of American Art in New Britain, Connecticut, among others.

Helck was also a founding member of the Automotive Fine Arts Society and was actively involved in the Veteran Motor Car Club of America, the Antique Automobile Club of America and the Horseless Carriage Club of America.

The Peter Helck award is given to the best race car from the Circle of Vintage Racers at the Meadow Brook Historic Races and Meadow Brook Concours in Michigan. Beginning in 1988, a bust of Helck has served as a perpetual trophy for the event. Miniatures of the bust have been given to the winners.

Hall Carpenter racing his record-breaking Chalmers touring car against a steam locomotive, as captured on canvas by Peter Helck. (Courtesy Antique Automobile)

"The Night Before the Big Race" was painted by Peter Helck and depicts last-minute preparations on a Thomas race car driven by LeBlon at Mineola. (Courtesy Antique Automobile)

Museum for Irish Transport Treasures

By John A. Gunnell

Back in 1907, Philip Somerville-Large initiated an ambitious project to assemble a luxury car, in Ireland. He formed Somerville-Large & Company, in Kilcullen (a city in County Kildare) to produce a machine using parts sourced from England, France and Belgium.

In his New Encyclopedia of Motorcars 1885 to the Present, Nick Georgano mentions that the one prototype built ... at a cost of £2,000 in 1907 ... had a 3-litre six-cylinder Gnome engine, a Malicet et Blin chassis and a touring body by Salmons of Newport Pagnell. Georgano also mentions that the car still exists in Ireland today.

This one-of-a-kind 1907 Silver Stream is the star of the show at the Transport Treasures Museum in Killarney, Ireland. (John Gunnell)

The museum's 1914 Wolseley was seen in the movie "The Blue Max." Curator Lucey is considered a Wolseley expert. (John Gunnell)

The second floor of the museum has an exhibit of license plates, dealer signs, antique bicycles and an American built Model T. (John Gunnell)

It does indeed! In fact, with only 600-700 original miles, it became the centerpiece of an auto museum that opened in the city of Killarney, a major Irish tourist town.

"We not only have the car, but every scrap of information and all the sales catalogs," said Denis Lucey, a former veterinarian who has been collecting veteran cars for 30-35 years and is now curator of the Killarney Museum of Irish Transport located at Scotts Gardens.

In addition to the rare Silver Stream, the "Transport Treasures of Ireland" collection lays claim to the world's first bicycle, plus such attractions as the Countess Markiewicz car, a Wolseley used in the movie "Blue Max" and an 1898 Benz Velo Comfortable which it bills as "The Car of the Century."

Lucey revealed that the Benz was the property of a Dr. Colahan, who owned the first car brought to Ireland. In 1907, it was sold at a public auction for 10 shillings and, later, it was abandoned in the city of Tipperary. A complete restoration was finished in 1986, in celebration of the 100th anniversary of Mercedes Benz.

Lucey believes this car is the oldest Vanden Plas in captivity. It's a 1904 model with natural wood fenders. (John Gunnell)

Another rare automobile on display is a 1904 Vanden Plas touring car with a 50/60 horsepower seven-litre engine, which Lucey believes to be the earliest surviving example of the marque anywhere in the world. The Belgian firm would become a well known coach-maker and the Vanden Plas name was later used on an English offshoot automobile built from 1960-1980.

Also on exhibition at the two-story museum, are 10-15 more veteran and vintage cars including a Mercedes 540K cabriolet, Mercedes gull-wing, Model A and Model T Fords and a small, right-hand drive European Ford (it looks like a scaled-down early V-8 model) that was purchased from an Irish farmer and left unrestored. Plus, more than 1,000 transportation-related items are on display, such as advertising signs, petrol pumps, lamps, wheels, model engines, stationary engines, magazines, rally programs and registration books dating from 1900.

The new museum was the idea of a Killarney businessman who owns the Glen Eagle Hotel & Country Club. He approached Lucey with the concept, putting Denis totally in charge of the curatorial aspect, while the hotelier retained the "business" responsibilities.

The address of the museum is Scotts Gardens, Killarney, County Kerry, Ireland and the phone number is (064) 31870, extension 285.

The Transport Treasures Museum's rare 1898 Benz Velo Comfortable. (John Gunnell)

An American visitor looks over the Mercedes 540K Cabriolet housed in the museum in Killarney, Ireland. (John Gunnell)

Imperial Palace
Auto Collection

By Phil Skinner

When Ralph Engelstad, owner of the Imperial Palace Hotel/Casino in Las Vegas, Nevada decided to collect a few cars of unique historical interest, he never thought that the collection would end up numbering over 500 vehicles. From the purchase of his first collectible car, a 1929 Ford Model A coupe, to one of his most expensive, a 1939 Mercedes-Benz G-4, he has taken a personal interest in each and every one.

Not only cars, but trucks, motorcycles and tractors are a part of this huge collection. With over 200 vehicles on display daily, the collection is housed in a specially enclosed top floor garage, atop the parking structure of the Imperial Palace complex, located on the "Strip" in Las Vegas.

Ralph Engelstad takes the wheel of a Model T Ford pie wagon advertising his auto collection. (Las Vegas News Bureau)

As the guest of the collection, one first enters the lobby and is greeted by a pair of familiar-looking Model T occupants, full-size replicas of Stan Laurel and Oliver Hardy. Because the collection has so many cars and limited room to display them, the cars are changed periodically. So, over the years, Stan and Ollie have been seen with several different Ts.

Many of the cars in the collection are, or were, the type we used to see as every day transportation. Quite a few of the vehicles were once owned or occupied by famous, or infamous, notables.

Cars of note include one of three 1952 Chrysler parade phaetons. You may look at this car and say, "It's a 1955 Chrysler, not a 1952!" According to Richie Clyne, the collection's administrator, this happens on many occasions. The phaetons were originally built in 1952, as 1952 models, and then updated by Chrysler in 1955.

The collection includes classics like this Packard, plus antiques, special-interest cars, Milestones and unusual vehicles. (Old Cars)

Even the most knowledgeable old car buff may be surprised at some of the cars on display, such as Father Divine's 1937 custom-bodied Duesenberg. This car was ordered from the Bohmann & Schwartz coachbuilders by a man known only as "Brother John." Some other unique vehicles one may see include the 1941 Chrysler Newport dual-cowl phaeton Indy Pace Car or the 1933 Pierce-Arrow Silver Arrow, one of five built. Certainly unusual in design is a Mohs SafariKar. It has a door that pushes out from the side of the vehicle, to keep charging animals at a safe distance.

Imperial Palace spokesman Steve Radulovich said that some of Ralph Englestad's favorite cars are those that were related to the noted personalities. One is Howard Hughes' 1953 Chrysler New Yorker four-door sedan with sealed windows and an air filtering system that cost more than the car. Today, the car shows only 1,533 miles on the odometer. It is prominently displayed near some of Henry Ford's contributions to the automotive world.

Featured here are several unique Model Ts, including one with a snow-tractor attachment and a restored Fordson Tractor. Also of interest to early V-8 Ford lovers is a working display chassis of a 1946 Ford. It was used as a prop at car shows and as a mechanical training tool for returning World War II veterans. A 1940 Lincoln town car, with a 1946 front end, which had been assigned to Mrs. Henry Ford, is also proudly displayed in the collection.

To set off the cars and trucks, there are accessories such as antique gas pumps to be seen. (Old Cars)

The oldest vehicle in the collection is an 1897 Haynes-Apperson. It is one of several in this special assemblage built prior to 1900. One of the newest cars on display at the Imperial Palace is a stainless steel bodied DeLorean. Sitting just down the aisle from this 1980s loser, is a loser from the 1950s, a 1958 Edsel Pacer convertible. One car recently brought to the public's attention is the Tucker, a gorgeous maroon example of which is proudly displayed.

Richie Clyne related an especially intimate moment in Mr. Engelstad's life. "Las Vegas is a 24-hour-a-day place and the gaming goes on around the clock. The city never sleeps, but the collection does close its door at night," he told us, "On many an occasion, in the wee hours of the morning, I have had to visit the collection for one reason or another. There, in the pre-dawn hours, among his sleeping beauties, will be Ralph Engelstad. He'll be taking time from his schedule to walk among and admire his garage full of great cars."

The Imperial Palace is open 24 hours a day, but the collection operates for only 14 hours, from 9:30 am to 11:30 pm. One of the most complete automotive related gift shops is also operated in the lobby of the collection.

With a total of over 500 vehicles, there is a constant rotation of displays, making a second, third and fourth trip just as much fun and interesting as the first. All these facts show why Old Cars, in its "Top 10," issue cited The Imperial Palace Auto Collection as one of the 10 best in the world.

Television heroes and their wheels

By Bill Siuru

There have been some important "supporting actors" in television shows through the years. These are the cars, and sometimes trucks, driven by the stars of the shows.

Sometimes they have been the source of laughs, like Howard Cunningham's 1947 DeSoto Suburban in "Happy Days." Others have played a more serious role, such as the Corvette driven by George Maharis and Martin Milner down "Route 66."

Sean Connery, in his role as secret agent James Bond, used a gadget-laden Aston-Martin to chase crooks. It now belongs to a collector in New Jersey.

207

Passport Transport hauled several of George Barris' Hollywood cars to auction. They included (front) "Far-rah's Foxy Vette" and (rear, left-to-right) the Green Hornet's "Black Beauty," Liberace's Cadillac, Zsa Zsa Gabor's Rolls and the Batmobile. (Courtesy Bob Pass)

Actor Adam West, in his super-hero costume, makes a flying leap into the cockpit of the "Batmobile."

Some vehicles were chosen to mirror the images of their drivers. Who can forget an unkempt Peter Falk getting out of an equally unkempt Peuguot 203 convertible in Columbo?" In contrast, there was Roger Moore (as Simon Templar) driving a saintly white Volvo 1800 coupe in "The Saint." Maxwell Smart was seen arriving at Control headquarters, on "Get Smart," in a variety of contemporary sports cars, including a Sunbeam Tiger, Volkswagen Karmann-Ghia, and Opel GT.

Other cars and personalities that seemed to go together included Sergeant Bilko and his Cadillac convertible, Mary Tyler Moore and her Mustangs, the huge Lincoln Continentals used by private-eye Cannon and the 1960 Dodge Dart convertible cherished by Sergeant Carter on "Gomer Pyle USMC." Then, there was Jack Benny and his Maxwell. It was seldom seen, but frequently talked about.

Some cars were built specially for television series like the Batmobile used on "Batman" and the "Green Hornet's" Black Beauty. The Batmobile started life as the Lincoln Futura, a Ford Motor Company dream car. It was modified by George Barris, a world-renowned car customizer. The Black Beauty was a customized mid-1960s Chrysler Imperial.

The Monkeemobile was used by "The Monkees." It was based on a Pontiac GTO. One of these cars wound up in Hollywood. Another went to Puerto Rico, where a hotel used it as a tourist bus. Last year, it was sold in a United States government auction for $500!

"The Munsters" television stars had their specially-built Munster Koach. There was also a film called "Munsters Go Home," featuring the same Barris-built vehicle. The surrey with the fringe on top used on "Fantasy Island" was a converted Plymouth Volare station wagon.

The "Munster Koach" was seen both on television and in the movies. It was also built by George Barris.

209

While some Hollywood vehicles are just for fun, others had to do serious work. When it came to 18-wheelers, "Movin' On" featured a 1975 Kenworth. GMCs and Kenworths were seen on the earlier trucking series "Cannonball." A Kenworth was also used on "B.J. and the Bear." On a smaller scale, "Sanford and Son" used a 1951 Ford pickup in their junk business.

As for taxis, "Amos and Andy" used a 1939 Plymouth for Amos' Fresh Air Cab, while "Taxi" used the more typical Checkers. The "ambulance" on "M*A*S*H" was a 1954 Ford bus.

While we're on working cars, we can't forget police cars. No police or detective story is complete without its high-speed chase. Jack Webb (alias Joe Friday) used a 1955 Ford in the early "Dragnet" series. The "Sheriff of Cochise" didn't ride a horse. He chased the bad guys in a rather plush 1956 Chrysler station wagon complete with built-in door holsters. Incidently, "Sky King" had a similar Chrysler wagon.

Broderick Crawford, on "Highway Patrol," used a variety of patrol cars. They included a 1954 Oldsmobile, 1955-1957 Buicks, 1957-1958 Mercurys and 1957-1959 Dodges. Some were the same types of cars actually used by California Highway Patrol officers.

"Car 54" was a Plymouth. Plymouth and AMC Matador police cars were used on the police action series "Adam 12." Tin toy versions of some of these cars were produced in Japan and the United States. Many of these toys have become valuable collectibles today.

Jeeps have been popular with television characters. Pat Brady drove Nellybelle, a Jeep, on "Roy Rogers" when everyone else rode horses. "Cade's County" also used a Jeep. Naturally, military Jeeps were seen on war stories like "Rat Patrol, M*A*S*H" and "Combat." Jeeps were used in "Wonder Woman," because of its World War II setting. Mindy owned a Jeep CJ5 on "Mork and Mindy." A fancy Jeep surrey was seen on "Surfside Six." Speaking of wartime series, prewar Mercedes-Benzs and Horches were used on "Hogan's Heroes."

Old cars have played a major role in several series, even having episodes written around them. Model A and T Fords have been especially popular. An abundance of Model As were part of "The Waltons." They ranged from roadsters and coupes to pickups and panel trucks. Eve Arden was driven to school in Walter Denton's Model A in "Our Miss Brooks" and the "Real McCoys" drove a Model A phaeton. "My Mother the Car" was not really a 1928 Porter, as the story said, but a Model T Ford in disguise.

The "Hillbillies" arrived in Beverly Hills driving an over-loaded pickup truck that was made from a converted Oldsmobile.

210

The Clampetts' truck on "The Beverly Hillbillies" was an early 1920s Oldsmobile. Soon to be released is a movie version of the Beverly Hillbillies. An old car is included. It is also an Oldsmobile designed as an almost exact replica of the television car.

On television, "The Addams Family" drove a 1932 Chrysler dual-cowl phaeton. In the more recent movie version, the car was a Packard.

Actor Robert Stack, as crime-buster Elliot Ness, used an abundance of vintage tin, as did the crooks that he battled. Cadillacs, Lincolns, LaSalles and Buicks were seen on "The Untouchables" television show. A recent "Untouchables" movie was also loaded with a variety of vintage vehicles.

A neat 1940 Packard Darrin was seen on "Banacek." What else could be used on "The Bearcats" but a Stutz Bearcat? However, it was not a real one. The car was a replica and it was equipped with a gatling gun.

Some television car makes went the same way their television shows did ... to oblivion. "Superman's" Lois Lane drove an early 1950s Nash Rambler convertible. Nashes were also used by Captain Braddock on "Racket Squad" and by "Mr. & Mrs. North."

"Laverne & Shirley's" car was a 1953 Hudson convertible and Howard Cunningham traded his DeSoto in on a Studebaker on "Happy Days." When Barney came back for a class reunion on "The Andy Griffith Show," he arrived in an Edsel convertible.

Television cars seem to take a greater beating in each episode. For example: "The Dukes of Hazzard's" Dodge Chargers, Harry Fox's Cadillac sedan, Colt Sever's GMC four-wheel drive pickup and the red Coyote kit car on "Hardcastle & McCormick" were driven hard almost every week. Nevertheless, several examples survived. We have seen "General Lee's" that the Dukes used on television in several shows and the Coyote was saved by a Wisconsin collector who occasionally exhibits it.

Inventor Doc Brown (Christopher Lloyd) explains the workings of his DeLorean time machine to a fascinated Marty McFly (Michael J. Fox).

Alternatives to dealer purchases

By Bill Siuru

When you are in the market for a new car, traditionally you go to the dealer who specializes in the make you want. However, there have been some attempts by automakers to use other outlets to sell their cars. These have included mail order and sales through department, appliance, or hardware stores.

Almost as soon as Andrew L. Dyke opened the world's first auto parts store and mail order enterprise, in St. Louis in 1899, he started selling his Dyke cars through the mail. While Dyke cars could be purchased already assembled, the kit cars came in a large pine box. For $275 f.o.b. St. Louis, you got the basics of a one-cylinder, two-passenger car. The kit included, in the words of the catalog, "a six horsepower motor, flexible reach-less running gear with radiator, brass pump, pump socket and gasoline needle valve."

Almost as soon as Andrew L. Dyke opened the world's first auto parts store and mail order enterprise in St. Louis in 1899, he started selling his Dyke cars through the mail. This is a 1902 model. (Old Cars)

Besides assembling the parts from the box, the new Dyke owner had to "finish the castings," hire a blacksmith to forge and fit pieces, and make the water and fuel tank. Building a body, painting and upholstering were also the new owner's responsibility, all of which added about $100 to the price.

Dykes were sold between 1902 and 1904. Then A.L. Dyke went on to other things, such as writing the first auto repair manual for do-it-yourselfers and establishing the first correspondence course for auto mechanics.

In 1891, Richard Warren Sears started his mail order business with a 32-page catalog that included mainly watches, plus some jewelry and sewing machines. By 1900, this catalog carried almost everything an American of the time needed, including horse-drawn buggies. So, it was only logical that the horseless carriage be a Sears, Roebuck and Company item, which it was, beginning in 1908.

The Sears Motor Buggy sold for only $375 and came "shipped and crated so as to secure the lowest possible freight rate." The Sears wasn't a great car, with its flat twin-cylinder engine, tiller steering and top speed of only 25 miles per hour. Later, a closed model, the "Cozy Cab" was added. However, the company lost $80,000 on this venture. That was a tidy sum for the time and it got out of the auto business in 1912.

The Sears Motor Buggy sold for only $375 and came "shipped and crated so as to secure the lowest possible freight rate." Seen here is the 1911 Model G runabout. (Henry Austin Clark, Jr.)

In 1933-1934, Continental Motors, the world-famous independent engine manufacturer, took a flyer in the automobile manufacturing business. Its four- and six-cylinder cars went by the names Beacon, Flyer and Ace. Prices started at $335. While the prices were right for those depression-era times, apparently the car wasn't. Only 4,293 units sold before production ceased.

Continental attempted to sell their cars through the mail, with local garages handling delivery and service. The car was also marketed through selected department stores, such as Gimbels in New York. Continental's failure can be attributed to their cars' old styling. They were just revamped versions of the 1931-1932 DeVaux, which was another marque that failed. The new marketing scheme couldn't change the vehicle's unpopularity.

Continental got out of the car making business. It went back to what it did best, making internal combustion engines for just about every application.

Powell Crosley Jr., who made his millions in the radio and refrigerator business, decided to build a car that could be sold alongside his appliances in hardware and appliance stores. Thus, the idea behind the Crosley evolved. It was the most successful mini-car to be sold in the United States before the import invasion of the 1950s.

The first Crosleys, with their air-cooled, two-cylinder, 12 horsepower engines and 80 inch wheelbases appeared in 1939. Before the war broke out, about 5,000 Crosleys were sold. Powell Crosley found that appliance and hardware stores were not the place to sell cars.

After World War II, the Crosley returned with a new body style and 26-1/2 horsepower engine. Sales of the Crosley were relatively brisk in the car-starved postwar years. Some 81,000 postwar Crosleys were sold before sales stopped in mid-1952. All in all, Crosley lost $3 million on the venture.

You can hardly pick up a 1950s or 1960s copy of magazines like Popular Science or Mechanix Illustrated without seeing an ad for the King Midget, America's most successful mail order and kit car. The Midget Motor Company was founded in Athens, Ohio by Claud Dry and Dale Orcutti, Their 1947-1950 King Midget was a single-seat car with a one-cylinder, air-cooled, six horsepower Wisconsin engine. Early versions had the appearance of a midget racer. At a price of $270 for the kit, it was advertised as the "world's lowest priced car."

In 1958, there was another King Midget redesign with tailfins for the taillights and doors for passengers. Horsepower from the Wisconsin power plant went up to 9-1/2. The price was then over $950. (Old Cars)

In 1951, the King Midget was up-rated to a two-passenger roadster and horsepower from the one-cylinder engine increased to 7-1/2 (later 8-1/2). In 1958, there was another redesign including tailfins for the taillights (like other contemporary cars), plus doors. Horsepower from the Wisconsin power plant went up to 9-1/2. The price was then over $950.

In 1967, the King Midget entered the "horsepower race" when a single-cylinder 12 horsepower Kohler engine was offered. Production ceased in 1969, after 5,000 King Midgets, in both kit and assembled form, had been made. The 24 years of continuous production is a record for a mail order car company.

In 1952, Sears, Roebuck and Company got back into the automobile marketing business. This time it happened with its Allstate model. The Allstate was essentially a Henry J "clone," with minor changes to the exterior trim and a major upgrading of the interior. The car was sold only in Sears' car and accessory parts stores in the southeastern United States. Naturally, it was equipped with Sears-brand spare tires, batteries and spark plugs.

In 1952, Sears, Roebuck and Company got back into the automobile marketing business. This time it happened with its Allstate model. The Allstate was a "clone" of the Kaiser-built Henry J. (Applegate & Applegate)

The Allstate two-door sedan was offered in standard and deluxe versions with either a four- or six-cylinder engine. Prices started at just under $1,400, and were within a few dollars of those of comparable Henry J models. Sears' second try at selling cars also ended in failure, with only 2,363 Allstates sold in 1952 and 1953. This failure can be attributed to a number of factors, including the limited sales area, a Henry J-based car (at a time when sales of that marque were on the downswing), plus the simple fact that people didn't want to buy a car from a department store.

Today, while new cars are being displayed in shopping malls, you usually have to go down to your local dealer to buy them. However, there are an abundance of kit cars, ranging from replicars of the quaint MG-TD to the awesome AC Cobra 427, that you can purchase by sending your order through the mail.

WRITERS' LICENSE

Speaking of Chevys...

1953 was a great year for Chevrolet

By Pat Chappell

Speaking of Chevys, we've always enjoyed going to car shows and looking at vintage Chevys. And we've always been attracted to good-looking 1953 Chevy Bel Airs.

The present day worship of 1955-1957 "Hot Ones" and 1958-1964 "Late Greats" has thrown Chevys of the early 1950s into the back row. This seems a proper time to look back some 35 years and see what was happening in America back then.

Part of the brand new image for 1953 was the brand new Corvette. It became a rare collector car, since only 300 were built. (Chevrolet)

The date was November 4, 1952. General Dwight D. Eisenhower had just defeated Adlai E. Stevenson in the presidential elections. Shortly, a Republican administration would take over for the first time in 24 years. We'd been listening to Johnnie Ray's "Cry." We'd seen Rocky Marciano knock out "Jersey" Joe Walcott in the world heavyweight championship bout. We'd seen the New York Yankees defeat the Brooklyn Dodgers 4-3 in the 49th annual World Series.

Somewhere in the midst of those events, Chevrolet announced its "Entirely new through and through" 1953 model line up from east to west and north to south. Those were the days when dealership windows were wrapped in gigantic ads hiding the new product right until announcement time. Then, floodlights bathed the fall skies and lured families to showrooms on Main Street U.S.A. where salesmen dispensed free Cokes, gimmicky souvenirs and new cars.

The 1953 Chevrolet Two-Ten four-door station wagon was an attractive utility vehicle. (Chevrolet)

It was an era when automotive manufacturers were making up for time lost during World War II and the Korean conflict. Major postwar changes, after the initial one for Chevrolet in 1949, evolved in a head-over-heels fashion. The years 1953-1954; 1955-1957; 1958; and 1959 saw major re-designs.

The changes for 1953 included dressy interior and exterior appointments flourishing in the new Bel Air series, the evolution of two-tone paint combinations on the lower body of the car and windshield and backlight development in a wraparound fashion. It was the year we saw the end of the "Cast-iron Wonder" (when coupled with Powerglide), as well as the phase-out of the 216.5 cubic inch six, which was replaced by the 235.5 cubic inch engine in passenger cars. A new image was evolving. Chevrolet was changing from a staid, conservative mode of transportation to a youthful-looking and hotly-powered piece of machinery. Motor Trend featured Chevy's turnabout in its road test headline, in mid-1953, as the "perennial favorite, long America's best girl, Chevrolet hopes to stay in that coveted spot with curvaceous new bodies (and) a Powerglide transmission that takes off without beating its wings ...!"

In 1950, Chevrolet beat Ford and Plymouth to the draw with two firsts: an optional two-speed automatic transmission (called Powerglide) and pillarless hardtop styling in the Bel Air Sport Coupe. The models for 1951 and 1952 followed with minor styling and engineering changes. However, the immediate success of the 1950 Bel Air caused management to extend that name to an entire car line by 1953. It included, not only the Sport Coupe, but two- and four-door sedans and a convertible.

Chevrolet cranked out 247,284 of its new-for-1953 Bel Air four-door sedans. Previously, all Bel Airs were Sport Coupes. (Chevrolet)

Options were becoming available, too. Power steering made its debut in 1953. The trend of power options in the low-priced field predicted the future, for soon we would be able to order power brakes, power windows and power seats. The list grew longer with the advent of the V-8 engine in 1955 and air conditioning!

Motor Trend, then (and collectors now), who drive 1953 Chevys, extol the roominess and comfort of these models. The cars were equipped with well-placed arm rests; there was scads of arm, leg and head room. The back seat and trunk were cavernous by today's standards. The trunk was more accessible than it had been before. The sill was much lower, too. This was a definite plus when loading and unloading baggage and groceries.

The ride was considered improved over that of 1952 and Motor Trend's 350 mile jaunt to San Diego found passengers and driver all quite rested at the end of their trip. Favorable comments came forth about Chevy's handling for 1953 and, even though the car was 250 pounds heavier than in 1952, brake stopping distances were improved.

Motor Trend's tested performance fared better than in 1952: Acceleration from 10 to 60 miles per hour was two seconds faster, at 19.9 seconds. In the 30 to 60 miles per hour range, time was cut by three seconds to 13.6. Remember we are talking about an automobile with a 235.5 six-cylinder engine that was 250 pounds heavier than its 1952 model.

If only one claim were to be made of the 1953 Chevy, it would have been in the category of endurance. That, after all, was Chevy's middle name in those years. Try as they might, the team of Motor Trend scribes (Woron, Potter, Molson, Hoeppner, Bodley and Lodge) could not wear out the Chevy. They all took turns at the wheel. While believing that "considerable mileage over all types of roads and by different drivers usually results in some service being required on a car at the end of a test," their conclusion was, "the Chevy didn't require this."

Perhaps that statement said it all then. Perhaps it's all we really need to say today about the 1953 Chevy's durability!

This 1953 Chevrolet Two-Ten four-door sedan was an excellent buy at the modest price of $1,761. (Chevrolet)

By June 9, 1953, the 29 millionth Chevrolet rolled off the assembly line at Kansas City, Missouri. By the end of the year, calendar year production of Chevrolets totaled 1,477,287. The total was up almost 600,000 units from 1952's total of 877,947. Once again, for the 18th straight year, Chevrolet led Ford. The margin was now over 293,000 units. In fact, Chevrolet production had been higher only once before in history. That happened in 1950, it being the year of the introduction of the Bel Air and Powerglide.

We must remember that "The Hot One" of 1955-1957 had not yet made its appearance. We had yet to feel the impact of Ed Cole and his team. The "New Look, New Life, New Everything" theme of 1955 could be seen only through a crystal ball held by Chevrolet's designers. What 1953 sales brochures proclaimed to be "Entirely new through and through" was, at the time, an honest assertion. 1953 was but another benchmark for Chevrolet. The company built reliable, yet attractive automobiles, in which almost a million and a half people invested their faith and money.

Speaking of Chevys...

Shades of the '50s!

By Pat Chappell

Speaking of Chevys, it is interesting to note that the entire segment of devotees to the automotive past represents an estimated following of a million people. And those hobbyists are prepared not only to collect and restore certain models from a century of automobile production, but to seek out all sorts of associated memorabilia as well.

The memorabilia possibilities are endless: T-shirts, posters, mugs, calendars, greeting cards, advertisements, music and a variety of promotional material dating to the year of said auto are collected.

As the decade changed from the war-dominated 1940s, we were buying 1950 Chevy Bel Air hardtops. (Chevrolet)

We bury ourselves in this one particular hobby, but we are in search of something that crosses over into many other interests. Our interest moves where people are following the trend to recapture their past or that of their parents or their grandparents. The truth is, throughout the United States (and many other parts of the world) this reaching back to another time ... this worshipping the past and appreciating its part in history ... is being acted out in many different scenarios.

We remember a television show called "Our World." As we watched it and listened to it, we were catapulted back to the fall of 1949. Bits and pieces of that year were tossed at us: We were smoking Camels and listening to "That Lucky Old Sun" by Frankie Laine. We were buying a ranch house in nearby Levittown, Pennsylvania for $8,000 and seeing the New York Yankees beat the Brooklyn Dodgers in the World Series. We were buying 1950 Chevy Bel Air hardtops and gathering around a new piece of furniture, called television, to listen to and watch "Studio One," "The Milton Berle Show" and the "Roller Derby."

The television set, which brought a new form of entertainment into one million American living rooms in that year, became ... as one historian noted ... "an altar around which to gather."

Television brought a new form of entertainment into one million American living rooms. One historian called it "an altar around which to gather." This exhibit at the National Automobile Museum in Reno, Nevada honors its impact.

Another type of product that has become a nostalgia item with a large and enthusiastic following is Coca-Cola related merchandise. (Institute of Outdoor Advertising)

Departing momentarily from the automotive hobby, we'd like to pay homage to other collectors who, in many ways, parallel our own automotive interest. One friend of ours, from Florida, not only has a serious interest in 1956 Chevys (including an ambulance and an airport limo), but owns two other fine collections. The first is an American Flyer scale-model train layout with sets of trains that fill up an entire room. The other is a Coca-Cola room loaded with associated memorabilia. It's one of the finest tributes to that century-old product we've ever seen.

Another friend, who resides in New Jersey, lives in a New England "saltbox" house and has an actual carousel pony (taken right off a merry-go-round) in the den. Then, there's the couple we know who belong to a roller coaster club and travel throughout the United States "coasting" in amusement parks and theme parks.

Back in the 1950s, automakers seemed prouder of their products and made a big deal of promoting them with lively billboard art. (Institute of Outdoor Advertising)

We have been witness to history being recreated in Colonial Williamsburg, Virginia and the tremendous impact that has had on our 20th century world. There are now cities that issue exterior and interior design guidelines for buildings.

223

Juke boxes and the records they hold are also gaining collectibility among America's nostalgia buffs. (John Gunnell)

More recently, many nostalgia buffs have been seeking entry back into the Victorian era. There's a revival which has generated considerable interest within the past decade. The Victorian craze has spilled over into fashion, jewelry, furniture and housing. A Victorian Society has been founded in Philadelphia, with the old customs of lawn parties and tea dances being recreated. This often occurs in the company of a splendid assemblage of vintage brass and Classic automobiles.

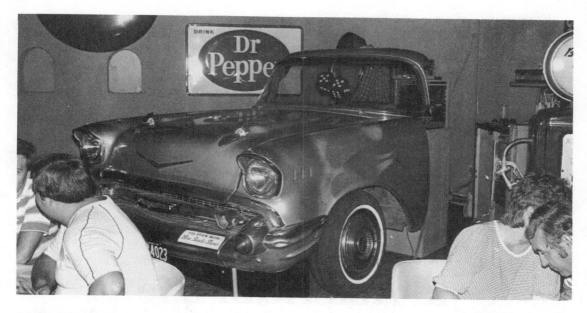

A 1957 Chevy serves as the dee jay's turntable at "Blue Suede Shoes," a 1950s nostalgia nightclub located in Chicago, Illinois. (John Gunnell)

One of the most influential elements of past times is the recording artists and music associated with them. Recently, focus has been on the music of the 1940s, 1950s and 1960s. The Four Lads perform as the original group, launched in 1950, and sing such hits as "The Things We Did Last Summer" and "No, Not Much." The movie "The Big Chill" brought back the Motown Sound. The Beach Boys celebrate their 25th anniversary "beach partying" in concert in snowbound cities all over the country.

Clever recording company executives are profiting by reissuing old LPs in record numbers. The vintage sounds, a potpourri of 1940s, 1950s and 1960s tunes, are revived as appropriate background music to sock hops or 1950s and 1960s style dance parties. Movies like "Radio Days," "Back to the Future," "Peggy Sue Got Married" and "Stand By Me" are capitalizing on the good sounds of the past as they reincarnate them.

One wonders what we will be collecting from the 1980s. However, one doesn't have to wonder for long. It seems Charles J. Jordan has answered our question with a book called What to Save from the 1980s. It was published by Fawcett Columbine and priced at $6.95.

Turntable built into '57 Chevy ragtop.

As a writer about antique and collectible items for Yankee magazine (10 years) and editor of Collectible Illustrated (five years), he is considered a walking encyclopedia of trivia. Jordan sets three guidelines for what comprises memorability or collectibility: importance of an event; quirkiness of an item; and nostalgia associated with a person, place or thing.

Some of his suggestions about what to collect from the 1980s are: anything related to the royal wedding of Prince Charles and Lady Di; Kermit the Frog merchandise; Halley's Comet memorabilia; Rubik's Cube; and Cabbage Patch Kids.

We wonder about collectible autos, especially Chevys of the 1980s. Certainly, Camaros and Corvettes will be collectible as will convertibles, in any form. What about the demise of the Chevette? Or first-year Beretta and Corsair models (they were released in mid-March of 1987 as 1988 models). What others do you think are bound to become collectible?

Speaking of Chevys...

The Automobile
in American Life

By Pat Chappell

Speaking of Chevys, we had the chance to see several good-looking ones at the grand opening of "The Automobile in American Life" exhibition in the Henry Ford Museum (HFM) several years ago. It was a spectacular event and an opportunity for the world's major automotive corporations to unite in presenting the history of the automobile and to show how it changed the lives of Americans, plus many people overseas as well.

Along with stylists, engineers, heads of affiliated industries, collectors, media and automotive press (including publishers, editors, writers and artists), we enjoyed being part of the gala affair.

An artist's conception of "The Automobile in American Life" exhibit at the Henry Ford Museum & Greenfield Village in Dearborn, Michigan. Several historic Chevrolets are among the 100 vehicles on exhibit. (Henry Ford Museum)

General Motor's Chevrolet was but a segment of this historical celebration honoring the automobile as it has affected the lives of many. However, we'll focus on Chevy's contribution, as interpreted by those many individuals on the museum staff who put the exhibit together. Congratulations are definitely in order for such a magnificent undertaking.

As the exhibit was in the process of being assembled, this column concentrated on a couple of Chevys which had been selected for the display. The novel, but unsuccessful, "copper-cooled" engined 1923 Superior coupe and the 1929 International Series AC Chevrolet sedan, running Chevy's first six-cylinder overhead valve engine were two of them. In addition, a 1960 Corvair shared the focal point of the display.

Historical perspective was part of the exhibit. For example, regarding the Corvair, the display reminded us that this innovative rear-engined car "fueled the mid-1960s consumer movement and became the main argument in Ralph Nader's successful 1965 campaign to create government-mandated safety regulations."

A group of over 30 vehicles made up what the museum's director of public affairs, Donald Adams, referred to as "the intellectual spine." Indeed, this multi-level display of the evolution of technology of the American automobile and its industry, was the backbone of the entire exhibition, which included over 100 total vehicles. All of the cars were specifically selected for their contribution to the evolution of the industry.

We were greeted by a very effective presentation to the right front of the museum: A 1956 Chevy Bel Air convertible, finished in Twilight Turquoise and India Ivory. It reposed, top-down and ready for curb service, before a 26 foot high 1960s McDonald's Speedee Restaurant sign transported from Madison Heights, Michigan. This sign was used at a restaurant that was the 146th in McDonald's system. The company now operates well over 10,000 restaurants worldwide.

We were reminded of the dated attributes of the 1956 Chevy (although we still feel it looks good) as we read the descriptive placard in front of it: "The pleasant, but heavy chrome-laden styling ... with plenty of airplane motifs typifying the 1950s era."

Probably one of Chevrolet's most significant automobiles in its 75 year history, the 1955 Bel Air Sport Coupe in contemporary colors of coral and shadow gray, was highlighted in the "Vehicles Illustrating the Evolution of the Automobile's Appearance" section. Once again, we had the opportunity to study its tastefully integrated styling. Chevrolet's general marketing manager, Thomas A. Staudt, presented this 1955 Chevrolet to the Henry Ford Museum to commemorate Chevrolet's 75th anniversary.

The year 1955 was also represented by a Corvette roadster, displayed in the "Getting Away From It All" area. This particular 1955 Corvette surely could "get away" with its all-new high-performance overhead valve V-8 engine. The fiberglass beauty, which had originated as a six-cylinder entry in 1953, had come into its own by 1955. It was in good company "speeding along" with a 1932 Ford hot rod, a 1949 MG TC roadster and a 1951 Crosley "Hot Shot" at the exhibit. This grouping of vehicles was interpreted, by people at Henry Ford Museum, as an illustration of "the exhilaration of speed and the freedom associated with motion."

It was a thrill for us to attend the grand opening on a moonlit Friday evening in Dearborn, Michigan. The event was enhanced by tasteful amenities: floodlights focusing on the museum entrance; celebrities stepping from luxurious vehicles; champagne; an orchestra playing the fabulous "big band" sounds; six-foot high floral arrangements; and an automotive ice sculpture, which by evening's end had melted into what appeared to be a new styling exercise almost global in flavor.

Most of all, it was an evening representing the best of all things remembered: In the company of a diner; a drive-in movie; and a service station where "service" was once given freely and free-of-charge. The design landmarks of General Motors' past were present. We'd seen them in pictures, but never "in the flesh." They included: Harley Earl's 1927 LaSalle; the 1939 Buick "Y Job" (GM's first design concept car); the 1951 Buick LeSabre (first postwar American "dream car"); and the 1958 Firebird III.

The grand opening, as a good friend remarked, "was a once-in a-lifetime event!" We'd recommend visiting the exhibit now, which is still in place. Then, you'll have more time left to go back again and again!

Speaking of Chevys...

An ode to the 1950s Chevrolets

By Pat Chappell

Speaking of Chevys, many enthusiasts feel the ones that were built in the 1950s were probably among the most memorable of all. And the changes which occurred during that decade, from the 1950 Bel Air to the 1959 Impala, were more than you would think could be crammed into one 10 year period.

In the 1950s, Chevrolet designers were intrigued with the idea of giving their cars aircraft styling motifs, such as tailfins. (Chevrolet)

Next time you are at a car show, check out the number of 1950s Chevys. Remember, we write here only of full-sized Chevys, seven years of Corvettes and several interesting truck forms, including sedan deliveries, Cameo Carriers and El Caminos. The Corvairs, Chevy IIs, Novas, Super Sports and Camaros had not yet surfaced.

The cars of the 1950s were really fabulous. This seemed especially true since, in the decade before, car production had halted. No cars were manufactured during World War II, from early 1942 until midyear 1945. Most 1946 to 1948 cars were warmed-over face-lifts of prewar autos.

From 1949 to 1954, engineering and styling changes were gradually made. By 1955 we were witnessing the full impact of an evolution in styling and engineering. A metamorphosis was occurring, ushering in an era which was to go down as "the golden age" or "the modern classic" era.

As we look back to the 1950s, it was a period which didn't just begin on January 1, 1950 and end abruptly on December 31, 1959. In reality it grew out of the late 1940s and spilled over into the early 1960s.

Indeed, much of the commercial 1950s memorabilia, which is marketed in the 1980s, covers a span of almost two decades as it dips into what came before and spills over into what followed.

In the 1950s, the world was a happy place, so safe motoring was depicted as the peak of happiness. (Institute of Outdoor Advertising)

Was it all really so fabulous in the 1950s ... for those of us who were there then? Some of the memories being manufactured, packaged and sold to us today are better than they ever were the first time around. We tend to agree with one chronicler of the era who defines these nostalgic products as "a plethora of artifacts that reinterpret some feature of 1950s design in 1980s terms."

Recently an advertisement crossed our desk for a new aerosol air freshener compressed inside an attractive dispenser. The copy accompanying the art work in that ad began, "Remember the smell of..." and four illustrations depicted the scents.

One showed a young, sweet-looking blonde woman smelling the lilacs; next a 1950s homemaker was removing two loaves of cinnamon clove bread from a 1950s oven. Then a damsel was relaxing in a hammock, idly spinning one of those tiny paper umbrellas one finds garnishing a tropical drink called "Hawaiian Islands." Finally, there was a young mom, with her idyllic female offspring smiling, sniffing and almost cheering over the "fresh linen" smell of a hung-out wash. Well...

One nice thing about the 1950s was the fact that most service stations promoted use of their restrooms, instead of padlocking them. (Institute of Outdoor Advertising)

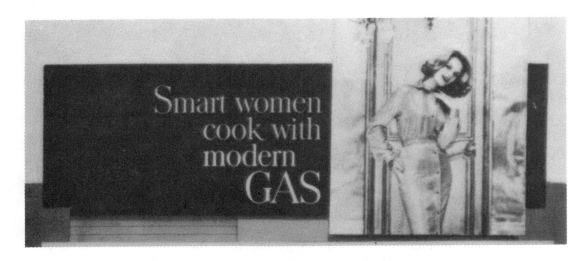

Even when cooking in the kitchen, the ideal woman depicted in 1950s billboard art seemed ready to win awards for beauty and fashion. (Institue of Outdoor Advertising)

There never was time to smell the lilacs or the roses. "Homebaked" cinnamon clove bread was "baked from scratch" because only a few packaged mixes were available. Even those were limited to a couple of awfully gritty concoctions. (We remember one called Joy which wasn't.)

The closest we ever got to the Hawaiian Islands was watching "Hawaiian Eye" when it appeared on television and the fresh hang-out-the-linen laundry chore was a never-ending one. It included washing, spinning, drying on the line, taking it down, starching and finally ironing it.

And the clothes we wore! Humorist Erma Bombeck remembers the 1950s as "a nothing decade, style-wise ... women dragged around in Dior-length skirts looking like Russian street cleaners." Another 1980s scribe recalled men's undershirts, "You wore them because you were told they kept you cooler in the summer and warmer in the winter. It made no sense, but in the 1950s you did what you were told."

Then there was television ... in the homes of a lucky few. In its infancy, it could be watched on a teensy, weensy set in black and white only. The author remembers coming home from school one weekend to find "color." Not really living color, but a transparent tinted piece of plastic. It was carefully placed over the television screen. Green was the color of grass at the bottom, blue was the color of sky at the top and all else in between was beige, the color of skin. Ha! It looked simply awful because the people's faces were this unreal color, which never seemed to cover both their arms and legs at the same time.

But there were drive-in movies, tons of them. Clearly, we remember them because they originated on the East Coast in 1933. Only a few have survived to celebrate their 60th birthday.

There we were, in the late 1940s and 1950s, sitting in cars that were lined up in front of a giant screen, waiting for dusk. Of course, dusk finally came, after what seemed an endless parade of "sizzlin' hot" hot dogs dancing across the screen. The in-car speakers, many of which didn't work at all, were loaded with static. Then, there were previews ... anywhere from five to 10 of them ... advertising coming attractions, such as "Death in the Bat Cave" or "Nightmares of the Nerds." Added to that was a ton of mosquitoes. In fact, those insects are especially giagantic in New Jersey, where the drive-in movie was born. Other elements included a sticky hot night, several tired and hot screaming kids and ... well, you've got the picture.

Still, we keep coming back to the cars and we do have such wonderful memories of them.

Sometime this summer we'll get together with a couple of friends who have Chevys from the 1950s. We'll go to one of the last drive-in movies in the area, where we'll line up those Chevys in a row with their chrome glistening and their paint shining. We'll watch the "sizzlin hot" hot dogs dance across the screen one more time and we'll munch on popcorn, while we listen to the scratchy in-car speaker. And we'll probably see "Funny Farm" and "Police Academy V." But, it won't really matter what the flick is. We'll be "Lost in the 1950s" one more time!

Kids were always spic and span back in the 1950s, long before anyone heard of teen gangs and cults. (Institute of Outdoor Advertising)

Speaking of Chevys...

"Child of the magnificent ghosts"

By Pat Chappell

Speaking of Chevys, a tremendous amount of money has been spent by the Chevrolet Motor Division on advertising and literature over the years. As the automotive hobby expands, not only are the cars being collected, but the literature about them is too.

When we attended the recent National Corvette Restorers Society (NCRS) Convention, we had an opportunity to take in a couple of seminars where this field of specialization was examined in relation to Chevrolet's sports car.

Bill Lester, who knows all there is to know about collecting Corvette literature, spoke of the value of Corvette press release packets, product training kits, "fingertip facts" books, dealer presentation albums, mailers, posters, postcards and all sorts of sales literature and brochures. "Why, there is even an International Literature Society," he informed us, "and a lot of these people collect literature who don't even have the cars the literature is written about." So, it appears that if you have the literature and the car, it is indeed the best of both worlds.

Hardly a flea market goes by that we don't sort through automotive literature, while our partner in this "adventure-land-in-flea markets" digs through trays, bins, boxes and barrels of old car parts. And though we've never had the pleasure of owning a Corvette, we've been very fond of some of the interesting and, yes, exciting promotional material written by Chevrolet's advertising agency Campbell-Ewald.

In fact, the Corvette is now the oldest nameplate in the Chevrolet line up and, as a result, has one of the longest continuing advertising campaigns of any car born 40 years ago. That is incredible, isn't it?

"Child of the Magnificent Ghosts" was an evocative slogan.

"For Experts Only" was the lead-in for a Corvette ad in the March 1955 issue of Motor Trend.

Wins at Pebble Beach were highlighted in the ad that Motor Trend carried in August 1956.

Check page 11 in the May 1956 issue of Motor Trend for this sizzling Corvette advertisement.

"Bring on the hay bales!" was the challenge that was issued in Motor Trend during June 1956.

"The Real McCoy" was a ad slogan designed to convince imported sports car buffs that America had a genuine contender. It appeared in Motor Trend in July 1956.

"The Winnah" was a simple message to hype the 1963 Corvette split-window coupe in this February 1963 Hot Rod magazine ad. (John Gunnell collection)

"FI = 1 H.P. per CU. IN. x 283" was Chevy's mathematical way of promoting its new Corvette fuel-injection system in 1957. (John Gunnell collection)

"What do you mean, practical?" asked an advertisement for the Corvette appearing in Motor Trend's April 1955 edition.

TIGER!

A Corvette is no tame kitten.

Sure, it can purr softly and gently as any household tabby, idling along in the sun. But even so, you catch a hint — a certain lithe competence in the way it moves, an undertone of raw power in the velvety exhaust.

For this one is a tiger! Under its sleek hood beats a savage heart — the steel-sheathed fury of 195 V8 horsepower. Its broad tread clings to the road with an incredible footsureness. And its 16-to-1 steering ratio, the taloned grip of its huge brakes, give it lightning-fast reflexes.

It is a tiger — but an obedient tiger. This fury of acceleration, these whiplash reflexes, are servant to the slightest nudge of your foot, the fractional pressure of your fingers. Your eye and your nerves command these steel muscles with an absoluteness you have never even dreamed.

True, this car can slip through the tangle of traffic with effortless serenity, its special Powerglide transmission metering out a faultless flow of power. In its foam-rubber seats, its deep floor-carpeting, its glove-soft upholstery, are the true marks of luxury.

But the tiger is always there . . . just under the surface. And, if there is fire in your blood . . . if your heart soars to the harsh music of excitement . . . this is the car that was meant for you. Corvette is its name. And *action* is its business. . . . Chevrolet Division of General Motors, Detroit 2, Michigan.

CHEVROLET CORVETTE

MOTOR TREND/AUGUST 1955 9

"Tiger!" was enough to get the Corvette message across in this early (August 1955) Corvette advertisement written by ace ad man Barney Clark.

We attended another seminar at the NCRS Convention and heard Jerry Burton, of Campbell-Ewald, speak about Corvette advertising through the years. Burton, who joined the company in 1983, represents a more recent generation in advertising and is credited with the Chevrolet Division's latest and most successful slogan, "The Heartbeat of America ... Today's Chevrolet." He is currently editor of Corvette Quarterly, which will supersede the former Corvette News.

In order to trace Corvette ads from the beginning, Burton got in touch with Barney Clark. He was responsible for putting together those wonderful, early ads some 30 years ago. After having him on the phone for an hour, Burton told us, "I wish I'd called him years earlier."

One of our favorite ads of all time is the classic one written by Barney Clark entitled "Child of the magnificent ghosts." It recalled the sports cars of yore with a sketch of a Mercer raceabout, in the puff of a dream, behind a 1955 Corvette. Clark's passionate words lured many down to the nearest Chevy dealership. They may or may not have bought a Corvette, but through his words, they could harken back to: "Years ago (when) this land knew cars that were fabricated out of sheer excitement. Magnificent cars that uttered flame and rolling thunder from exhaust pipes as big as your forearm, and came towering down through the summer dust of American roads like the Day of Judgement ... And so, today, they have an inheritor ... for the Chevrolet Corvette reflects, in modern guise, the splendor of their breed."

With this one beautiful exception, there is no such thing as a true American sports car.

'69 Corvette *CHEVROLET*

In 1969, Chevrolet was still pushing the Stingray Corvette as a "true American Sportscar" with this Hot Rod advertisement. (John Gunnell collection)

If that didn't do it, there was another Barney Clark ad which simply said "TIGER!" It showed a driver at the wheel of a 1955 Corvette and featured just a few words of description to the right. It told us, "the tiger is always there ... just under the surface. And, if there is fire in your blood ... if your heart soars to the harsh music of excitement ... this is the car that was meant for you. Corvette is its name. And action is its business...."

Those were the words of one of the first Corvette copywriters, one whom Jerry Burton describes as "a passionate, brilliant and very knowledgeable guy." A writer who was a wordsmith of the highest order and whose job it was to put words together that said something important to us, such as the Corvette ad: "Let it talk! The Chevrolet Corvette speaks your language; why not hear what it has to say? Hear it whisper on the straightaway... sigh gently as it smooths a turn ... laugh a little as it levels out a hill ... speak of planes and wild blue yonders as it ghosts into a valley...."

The ads were to continue being written in that remarkable style for a time. Ads like "Loaded For Bear," "Bring on the Hay Bales" and "The Real McCoy."

Recently, a friend who worked with Barney Clark wrote us, "You would have been fascinated by him. There was that rhythm in his work, an accuracy in his choice of words and a grandeur about them that swept you up and carried you along."

There was something super fine about those advertisements. They were a brilliant send-off for an advertising program which grew and adapted to the following generations, as did the car itself, throughout 40 great years.

The tradition established by Clark continued, capturing our imagination and stimulating our senses with magical words such as "What Happened to Gravity," "Wolf in Wolf's Clothing," "Why Men Leave Home" and "Beware the Red Bowtie."

Ford Motor Company's 1933 commercial cars

By Peter Winnewisser

The year 1933 was an up and down one for the Ford. On the up side, it was Ford's 30th year and marked production of the 21 millionth car and the opening of Greenfield Village.

To stimulate sales, Ford introduced the graceful Model 40 with updated 112-inch chassis, V-8 option and longer, more streamlined body. By year's end, sales, including trucks and Lincolns, rose almost 10 percent.

On the down side, the higher total revealed a decreasing share of market. Chevrolet outproduced Ford (481,134 to 334,969). Plymouth, although still trailing, more than doubled 1932 output. This, along with a strong showing by Dodge, helped the four Chrysler makes outsell Ford in total units. Ford hung on to nose out Chrysler in world production (including trucks) by a scant 2,000 units. It wasn't a great showing. Even more disquieting was news that Ford's percentage of the low-priced field dropped from 37 percent to 30 percent. The loss of sales leadership in trucks, to Chevrolet (for the first time in five years) didn't help.

But, 1933 is a memorable year for truck buffs for two reasons: Scarcity and styling. Trucks and commercial cars from 1933 are rare. Not many survive and, when they appear, they get attention. Scarcity enhances the value of survivors.

The styling is noteworthy because it reflected little change from 1932. The late James K. Wagner, in his book Ford Trucks Since 1905 (Crestline Publishing) said, "This marked the first time since 1926, when the Model T was restyled and the truck was left unchanged, that the company's passenger and commercial vehicle styling deviated from a common theme. Starting with the 1933 model year, however, the appearance of Ford cars and trucks would follow diverging paths. Only on rare occasions, in the future, would current models of both resemble each other."

Truck and commercial car lines for 1933 included the Model 46 on the 112-inch car chassis and the Model BB 1-1/2-ton on 131-1/2 or 157-inch wheelbases. We'll examine the commercial cars and leave the larger trucks for later.

Designed for light deliveries were five models in the commercial car: Sedan delivery, deluxe panel delivery, standard panel delivery, pickup and station wagon. The sedan delivery and station wagon were assembled with Model 40 passenger car sheet metal. The pickup and the two panel deliveries had the 1932 Model B style body components adapted to the longer 112-inch wheelbase. All five had right-hand sidemounts. Pickups and panel deliveries had the horn relocated to the headlight bar, like Model As.

In addition to the extended 112-inch wheelbase, all 1933 commercial cars utilized the new X-type, double-drop frame in which the X section ran the full length of the side rails.

This double thickness was designed to reduce flexing and relieve torsional stresses, increasing the life expectancy of chassis and body.

Other features included the straddle-mounted driving pinion, four double-acting hydraulic shock absorbers, a 14-gallon electrically-welded terneplate rear-mounted fuel tank and 17-inch steel spoke wheels equipped with 5:50 x 17 balloon tires.

The commercial cars came with either the standard 50 horsepower four with new counter-balanced crankshaft or, for an extra $50, with a new 75 horsepower V-8. The latter was the popular choice.

Ford was proud of its V-8 motor and distributed thousands of brochures that highlighted the construction and dependability of this engine. Among the advantages stressed were the all-aluminum cylinder heads, one-piece casting of cylinder block and crankcase, special hard alloy exhaust valve set inserts, large bearing areas, down-draft carburetor with accelerator pump, heat-treated aluminum alloy open-skirt pistons, 65 pound 90-degree throw crankshaft and automatic spark control with vacuum brake.

These features produced an engine which delivered in excess of 75 usable brake horsepower at 3800 rpm. Ford said, contrary to common practice, that this was done with all engine accessories (water pumps, fan and generator) being driven by the engine in their normal manner.

Rough use for a rarity. This 1933 Ford commercial car was obviously used commercially and pretty hard, too. Though strong and sturdy, the small trucks were not really designed to carry loads this big. (Texaco Archives)

Here's a brief summary of the Ford commercial cars that were available for 1933:

The commercial car chassis came with standard equipment that included a four-cylinder engine, a complete electrical system, an instrument panel, head and tail lamps, a stop light, coincidental steering and ignition lock and tools. Five steel spoke wheels and four balloon tires were provided, along with front fenders, running boards, a fender well spare wheel carrier, a 14-gallon fuel tank and dash, cowl and hood assemblies. The chassis was priced at $320.

The Sedan Delivery was also known as Type 46-850. Its price was $520 freight-on-board (F.O.B.) Dearborn, Michigan. All exposed bright metal was rustless (stainless) steel. There were two folding bucket seats, with the driver's seat being adjustable. A large cowl ventilator, an insulated dash, adjustable sun visors, a jute pad beneath the floor mat and a passenger car type instrument panel were standard features. A sturdy, single rear door swung on three heavy hinges. The rear door glass could be lowered. Production came to 2,296 of the body style with the V-8 and 2,153 with the four-cylinder engine.

The so-called "New Ford" Station Wagon was the Type 46-860, priced at $640 with a V-8. It had two-tone maple paneling and seated eight passengers, including the driver. The rear and two center bucket seats were removable. The tailgate was supported by covered drop chains and provided a large luggage deck when lowered. Weather protection was provided by close-fitting side curtains, with the curtains in the sides of the rear compartment operating in slide channels. The curtains were designed to be stored in the ceiling, when not in use. All seats were finished in two-tone black/brown colonial grain artificial leather. Production peaked at 1,654 wagons with the V-8 and 359 with the four-cylinder motor.

The pickup was available with either an open or closed cab. The open cab "roadster pickup" could be completely enclosed with the side curtains, which were standard equipment. (Old Cars)

The pickup was officially Ford's Type 46-830 commercial model. It was available with either an open or closed cab. The open cab could be completely enclosed with the side curtains, which were standard equipment. The top was unsnapped and removed, with the irons, as a unit. Sides and flare boards were of rigid steel construction, with a heavy steel floor panel mounted over a wood sub-floor. The floor had pressed-in skid stops. The full-width tailgate was equipped with covered drop chains. Sockets at each end of the flare boards allowed the use of small stake racks, advertising panels or special tops. Production of pickups included 33,748 Closed Cab V-8s and 14,815 Closed Cabs with the four-cylinder egine. Open Cab model production totaled 308 with the V-8 and 202 with the four. Base prices were: Open Cab - $420; Closed Cab - $430.

Type 46-820 was the standard panel delivery with a body of rugged, dust-proof construction. It had a rigid, all-steel, one-piece rear end assembly assuring the permanent fit of rear doors. The interior was finished with hardwood slats along the sides and a dome light in the center of the insulated roof. The panel delivery floor was made of hardwood with metal skid strips. Its body had a glossy satin finish. Only a driver's seat was provided as standard equipment, but an optional passenger seat was available. Production hit 1,021 with a V-8 and 1,923 with the four. Its selling price was $510.

Last, but not least, comes the deluxe panel delivery, Type 46-820. Body lines were similar to the standard model. It had a highly-polished finish, rustless steel cowl lights, chromium-plated rear view mirror, windshield wiper blade and front bumper. The interior side panels were made of Masonite. The insulated roof was lined with artificial leather and had a dome light. The deluxe panel was priced only $20 above the standard panel delivery. Its production came to 846 with V-8s and 1,274 with a four-cylinder engine.

Ford's 1933 deluxe panel featured lines similar to the standard model. It had a highly-polished finish, rustless steel cowl lights, chrome-plated rear view mirror, windshield wiper blade and front bumper. (Old Cars)

Watching the Fords Go by...

Aerodynamic styling marked FoMoCo prototypes

By Peter Winnewisser

In the fall of 1982, Ford unveiled the softly curved aerodynamic look on its Thunderbird models. It was a gamble for the company, a move away from " me-too-ism" in the direction Ford stylists believed the American public wanted to go.

Not everyone agreed. "We don't believe as Ford does, in going from chipped granite to jelly beans in one year," said Charles M. Jordan, General Motors (GM) design director in Car and Driver, July 1984.

As it turned out, Ford was right. The American public quickly caught up with the new aero look. "That one gutsy move," said Car and Driver, drew every eye to Ford, changed antipathy to anticipation and launched the revitalization of Ford's ravaged North American Automotive Operations."

Ford pursued its advantage, in late 1985, by introducing the Mercury Sable and Ford Taurus. Developed over a five-year period at the cost of $3 billion, Taurus and Sable are the most aerodynamic cars in their class. They were an instant hit and, with them, Ford seized not only the industry styling leadership, but also, for the first time since Model T's heyday in 1924, beat GM's profit margin.

"The 'bubble' shape," recalls Road & Track in its 1987 Buyer's Guide, "was diametrically opposed to GM's crisp-line styling and it was a gamble whether the public would accept the aesthetics. But, now Ford's stock is up, GM's is down and it's a good bet that the record sales of Taurus/Sable had much to do with this."

With Taurus and Sable, aerodynamic styling is no longer an "in" phrase reserved to auto enthusiasts, car kooks and stylists. It's a concept for average Mr. and Mrs. America.

In laymen's terms, aerodynamics means a streamlined look designed to reduce the wind resistance of car bodies, so they will slice the air with a minimum of drag. "It tranquilizes the airflow," said long-time aerodynamic advocate Alex Tremulis of Ventura, California. "The cars become slippery and require less horsepower to get there."

The aero look is not a new idea at Ford. Tremulis pioneered aerodynamic research for the company from 1952 to 1963 as head of its advanced styling area. During this period, two advanced concepts in aerodynamics were designed for testing and performance. They were the Ford Mexico and the Gyron.

The story of the Ford Mexico begins with the failure of a Thunderbird during Daytona SpeedWeeks in 1955. The T-bird suddenly stood on its nose, went upside down for 1,500 feet and came to a stop. An embarrassed Henry Ford II discussed the failure with Tremulis. He was told that the problem was too much lift. This neutralized the weight over the rear wheels, causing the car to flip.

As a result of this conversation, Ford gave Tremulis the green light to design and build a "zero lift" automobile. In a five-day crash program, from drawing board to a clay model "slicked" and ready for casting, Tremulis produced an ultra-streamlined aerodynamic coupe designed to use T-bird components. It was named the "Mexico" in hope that it could race in the Pan American races, if these were ever revived.

The Mexico was a three-eighths scale (seven foot long) non-drivable fiberglass model. It was super-streamlined, with rear fender fins for stability at high speeds. Air for cooling the radiator entered frontal scoops, passing out through two wide louvers in the car's elongated nose. Outside exhaust tubing permitted an exceptionally low car body.

Tests on the Mexico, done in the wind tunnel at the University of Maryland, were considered an aerodynamic breakthrough. With a flush underpan, the car eliminated any semblance of high aerodynamic lift and demonstrated it was capable of attaining 200 miles per hour with just 240 horsepower at the wheels.

Innovative ideas, no matter how well documented, do not always get a favorable hearing. Such was the case with the Mexico. The wind tunnel report was completely ignored. In a lengthy interview with Thunderbird Illustrated, in 1975, Tremulis commented on this sad ending.

"This car could have conceivably set a world's record for two-passenger sports cars with today's high-performance engines. Unfortunately, this aerodynamic philosophy was sadly misunderstood by the styling management at that time."

Tremulis recalls the Mexico as one of the most beautiful cars he has ever done. "I didn't deliberately design it to be a beautiful automobile," he says. "If it was a beautiful automobile, it was only because it obeyed the laws of aerodynamics. It was honest, it had sheer integrity and function. If there was any beauty, it was the by-product of function. This is what makes design. Function dictates form. That is what makes airplanes beautiful. I never saw a horrible-looking airplane in my life, unless it was a big, ugly cargo ship. If it looks good, it is good." (See Thunderbird Illustrated, Spring 1975 for more detailed coverage of the story of the Ford Mexico.)

The Gyron, a novel experiment in future automotive styling, was designed by Ford Motor Company.

Another advanced aerodynamic car developed at Ford was named the Gyron. It had a delta shape and two running wheels, instead of the customary four. This marked it as a radical departure in automotive styling. The Gyron was 209 inches long. It had a low silhouette, centered around a plastic canopy covering the passenger compartment. Its appearance suggested extremely high aerodynamic efficiency.

Stylists envisioned that a gyroscope, no larger than two-feet in diameter, would be sufficient to stabilize the vehicle with its two wheels set in tandem. Two small outrigger wheels. mounted toward the rear on each side of the car, were retractable. They could be lowered automatically, to balance the two-seater when the gyroscope was inactive or until it had gained enough momentum to provide stability.

Other novel ideas incorporated into Gyron included a built-in computer, a viewing screen and, instead of a steering wheel, a steering dial located between the seats. This dial, combined with the provision for individual accelerator and brake pads, permitted steering from either seat.

Labeled by Thunderbird Illustrated as the "'guru of advanced automobile thinking for generations," Alex Tremulis, at age 73, was still a practicing designer and advocate of aerodynamics. Several years ago, a car that Tremulis designed ran for 200 miles on less than two gallons of gasoline at an average 55 miles per hour.

Besides his 11 years at Ford and many years as a consultant, Tremulis also styled for Duesenberg Corporation, Briggs Body Company, Custom Motors, American Bantam and the United States Air Force. In 1947, he joined Preston Tucker at Tucker Motors Corporation and styled the Tucker Torpedo. Later, he created a 105 inch wheelbase streamlined Kaiser for Kaiser-Frazer. This car was another that was really ahead of its time.

In 1982, Alex Tremulis was inducted into the Automotive Hall of Fame. His achievements, however, were famous long before then.

Watching the Fords Go by...

A Model T potpourri

By Peter Winnewisser

Model T postcards

In its heyday, in the 1920s, the Model T Ford was the most popular car in the world. For a generation or more it was "family" to millions of people. It had such universal appeal that around it grew a folklore, a mystique, that no other automobile has ever approached.

Contrary to what some think, the final story on this remarkable car has not been written. There is much about the Model T, its times and the people who drive it that remains to be chronicled. Here's a look at a Model T potpourri.

Poking fun at the Ford during the teens and 1920s, funny anecdotes, jokes and one-liners about the Model T were all the rage. Since postcards were in vogue in those days, it was natural that a number of these jokes and sayings would appear on the cards that Americans were mailing to each other in great numbers.

This postcard recommends a "rocky" cure for a sick Ford.

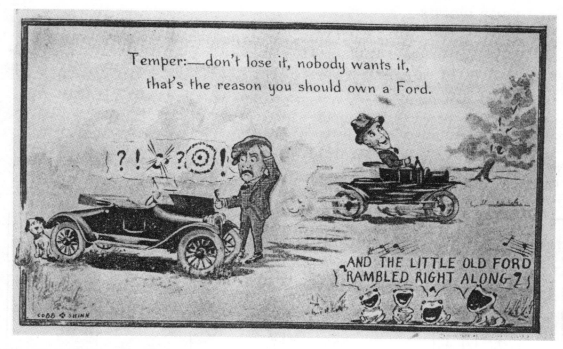

Many Model T postcards had a positive tone.

Some of these "Ford Comic Postcards," as they are called today, included caricatures of Fords and their owners, along with some gentle humor that was as often positive as it was negative. Others were without illustration and carried brief, pithy statements such as:

"One of Ford's blessings. He made walking a pleasure."

"New use for bathtub. An easy way to wash your Ford. Put it in the tub and turn on the water."

"Always carry a can opener in your Ford so you can get out if it turns turtle."

It's typically American to joke about what we appreciate most. The Model T Ford did not escape this honor.

Rattles were always a fun thing to poke fun at.

Ford code words

"Code" is a word most frequently associated with the Central Intelligence Agency, police work and espionage thrillers. "But," says Peter Shay, of Canastota, New York, "did you know that, during Model T days, the Ford Motor Company used a code system to identify parts and the instructions for entering and shipping them?"

Shay forwarded a February 1, 1917 price list of parts which lists all Ford parts, their prices and their code names. The purpose of the code system was to cut expenses, expedite ordering and make the purchase of parts more convenient for customers.

A typical coded entry would read as follows: "Toperig eight Carat three Dispark for car No. 2841." Translated, this reads as an order for eight push rods no. 3058 and three transmission band springs no. 3425.

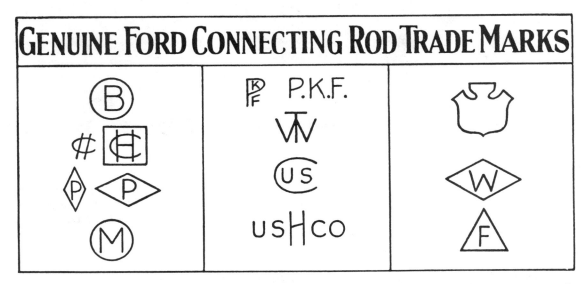

In addition to code names for parts, code-like symbols were used to identify Genuine Ford connecting rods.

The code words were evidently chosen at random and many are not even real words. There is no correlation of a particular word to a part, other than an alphabetical one. The use of "hernia" to describe a starting crank was probably a coincidence, although a humorous one at that.

Here is a random sampling of parts and their code words:

1917 radiator	Honey
Universal joint assembly	Ashore
Front wheel	Becomb
Cylinder head	Cabin
Carburetor	Mire
Pliers	Paddy
Oil can	Paxos

So, here is some advice for Model T owners. The next time your Ford won't start, get out the paddy and paxos, adjust your mire and give your hernia a good turn.

Tale of the old Model T

There are probably as many stories about the Model T Ford as there were owners, and there were millions of them. Ward O'Hara writes "The Storyteller," a popular history column in The Citizen, a newspaper published in Auburn, New York. He hopes, someday, to write a book of Model T stories. One of his favorite tales is a true story from the 1920s, originally told by a friend named Allyn Schoonmaker, who is now deceased. It is printed here with the kind permission of O'Hara and The Citizen.

Big cars couldn't keep up with a Ford, this card hints.

"Well, to get on with Allyn's story, it happened this way. He was driving to Oneonta one Sunday when he glanced upward and, to his astonishment, beheld a Model T Ford sitting astride the telegraph wires. In the car was the driver sitting in a middle position, not daring to move left or right as the Ford tilted either way in its precarious position if he moved.

"You older people will remember that telegraph lines used to frequently follow the railroads, and the station agent was the telegraph operator. They were not just two wires on a pole, but often were two or three cross arms carrying a dozen wires. Some of the wires had snapped but enough held to keep the driver and his flivver hanging about 20 feet above the earth's surface.

"Well, I'm sure the question in readers' minds is how did the vehicle come to be up there. Allyn explained that there was an overhead crossing above the telegraph lines and railroad. You went up an incline to cross the bridge at a right angle to the lines and railroad. The driver had failed to negotiate the sharp turn going up the incline, went through the guard rail, sailed through the air, and landed astride said telegraph lines, from which he was now swaying. Someone summoned two tow trucks to the scene, but their drivers could only remove their hats and scratch their heads with no solution to the problem above.

"Seems to me, the telegraph messages must have gotten pretty well garbled that day. Well, when Allyn came back through the town nearest the scene of the spectacular accident, he found, via a newspaper account, that the railroad had to be summoned to send in a crane on a flatcar to remove the hapless driver and his Model T.

"I will bet you the best drivers of today couldn't imitate that stunt. The best car driving stunts you see on television cannot equal Allyn's story, for theirs are faked and his was for real. It happened way back in the 1920s."

Ford accessories

Wheels and beds were among the thousands of gadgets and accessories developed for the Model T. There was the Smith Expanded Wheel and the All-In-One Folding Ford Bed. The wheel was manufactured by Smith Wheel Incorporated of Syracuse, New York. The bed was made by Outers Equipment Company, of Milwaukee, Wisconsin.

A flyer distributed by Smith Wheel boasted that its product was superior to other wheels, because it was not affected by moisture, as in the case of wooden wheels. It also did not stretch out of shape, as wire wheel spokes tended to do, and the metal did not fatigue, as was the case for disc wheels.

Smith Wheels for Fords, the company claimed, were attractive, easy to wash, secure, noiseless, economical and lasting. "In appearance," said the company, "the Smith Expanded Wheel is the aristocrat of the road."

Turning a Model T into a camper was easy with the handy folding Ford bed. At bedtime, the back seat cushion was pushed forward under the steering wheel and a small 4-1/2 inch by four-foot package, weighing only 14 pounds, unrolled. Sturdy, unbreakable oak frames, with double strength canvas stretched between, were set up inside the car. This assembly was strong enough to hold two 250-pound persons.

With the All-In-One Auto Cot, a Model T was easily turned into a cozy cabin in less than four minutes. The price was only $14.50 fob Milwaukee.

Old Henry Ford created a phenomenon when he created the Model T. Here he is with a 1919 edition with New York dealer (demonstration) license plates. (Courtesy Ford Archives)

1953 Ford was the last of the flatheads

By Peter Winnewisser

There's a special place in the hearts of Ford collectors for the 1953 Ford. It was a 50th anniversary model and the last of the flathead V-8 Fords. To commemorate that year, each 1953 Ford carries the Ford crest in the center of the steering wheel hub with the words "50th Anniversary 1903-1953."

All 1953 Fords utilized 1952 bodies with moderate styling changes. Most apparent was a revised grille, with a larger horizontal bar and three vertical stripes on either side of a large chrome bullet. The bar wrapped around the front edges of the fenders.

Other cosmetic changes included rectangular parking lights, an additional chrome molding on the rear fenders, a new jet-plane hood ornament, smart plastic-lensed, jet style taillights and a brand new bright metal handle with lock cylinder and dust shield on the rear deck lid.

A choice of three lines, 11 body styles and 18 models offered prospective customers a wide range from which to choose the 1953 Ford suited to their needs. At the base trim level, the Mainline series included four body styles: Tudor sedan, Fordor sedan, business coupe and Ranch wagon. The middle range Customline also had four models: Tudor sedan, Fordor sedan, Club Coupe and Country Sedan (station wagon). The top of the line Crestline featured the Sunliner convertible, Country Squire wagon and Victoria hardtop.

Body color and upholstery combinations were based on 12 single-tone and 14 two-tone colors, all keyed to "Fordcraft" upholstery fabrics: Leather, vinyl and Saddletax (vinyl). In all, there were more than 200 body style, color and upholstery combinations, up from 80 in 1952.

The three Crestline models and the Custom-line Country sedan were available only with a V-8 engine. The others came with the buyer's choice of either a V-8 or six.

Advertised as the only V-8 in the low-price field, Ford's final flathead boasted a 7.2:1 compression ratio and produced 110 horsepower at 3800 rpm. This compares with the 65 horsepower at 3400 rpm and a 5.5:1 compression ratio of the first V-8 in 1932.

The other engine option for 1953 was the six-cylinder, inline, overhead-valve type "Mileage-Maker Six." It was rated at 101 horsepower at 3500 rpm with a 7.0:1 compression ratio.

Both engines came with a standard three-speed manual transmission. Automatic overdrive was $108 option. Also a variable was Ford-O-Matic automatic transmission at $184. In June 1953, Master Guide power steering was introduced for the first time on the Ford.

Motor Trend for May 1953 reported on its test of a 1953 Ford V-8 Customline Fordor sedan equipped with Ford-O-Matic transmission. It rated the car at an average top speed of 86.5 miles per hour, fuel consumption at 18.7 miles per gallon and gave it high marks for handling and roadability.

Fifty Years Forward on the American Road

Beauty is only <u>half</u> the picture!

OF COURSE they're proud of the beauty of their car. We think you would be, too. But we wish we could give you the rest of the picture —take you over a Ford car, step-by-step, and point out some of its quality features.

First, we'd call your attention to a detail of body construction. We'd show you that there isn't a single exposed seam to catch and hold water. It costs more to build bodies this way but the weather stays out, the paint stays on and the beauty lasts.

Next we'd show you the way the doors fit, and we'd let you hear that good solid sound when they close. You'd see that each door is weather-stripped with a band of sealed foam rubber. Then we'd show you how easily the doors unlatch by just the pressure of your thumb on a button in the door handle. And, show you, too, how the Silent Doorman holds

the front doors open in your choice of two positions, two-thirds or full open.

Now we'd ask you to Test Drive it and let you *feel* some of the things about the Ford car that you can't see. First off you'll notice the "hushed" silence in which you travel and, then, the relaxed comfort you enjoy. (Ford engines, both V-8 and Six, are actually so quiet you can barely hear them as you drive along.) Ford bodies, too, are "quiet"... floor, roof and body panels are "sound deadened." Even the body bolts are insulated. As to the comfort ... well, you can see that the seats are sofa-wide. But

you can't see the heavy foam-rubber padding over non-sag springs underneath that fine upholstery. These quality "extras" are standard comforts in all models.

Another item we'd point out would be the paint. Did you know that it is baked-on enamel ... baked on over a complete rustproofing treatment? That's why Fords *keep* their fresh, youthful look far longer.

Why don't you get the whole Ford quality picture firsthand? Your Ford Dealer will be proud to let you see, Value Check, and Test Drive the 1953 Ford.

Ford
Worth more when you buy it
Worth more when you sell it

"Beauty is only half the picture!" states this advertisement for the 1953 Ford Crestline Victoria. Note the one-piece curved windshield and the rear quarter windows that roll out of sight. Also note the "Golden Anniversary" symbol in the ad, below the car's right front wheel. (Old Cars)

A choice of three lines and 11 body styles offered prospective customers a wide range from which to choose the 1953 Ford suited to their needs. This ad also promoted the line's 41 "Worth More" features. (Old Cars)

"In our test," said Motor Trend, "we gave this new 'miracle ride' a workout driving rutted, bumpy roads; taking dips at a fast clip; traveling winding mountain roads with numerous sharp curves. Our car took the rutted roads in its stride and took all dips without bottoming and with minimum oscillation after rebound. No side sway or body motion was noticed during the rebound. In the mountains the steering was light and positive, and the car hugged the road well with no tire squeal on the turns taken deliberately at above average speeds."

Motor Trend attributes the improved ride and cornering ability of the 1953 Ford to the use of small cone-shaped rubber stops, which served as bumpers between each front wheel control arm and the chassis frame, and new support plates. Others (see Robert Ackerson, The Best of Old Cars Weekly, Volume Six) point to the re-valved rear shocks and softer semi-elliptical rear leaf springs as important changes that contribute to the golden anniversary car's better road qualities.

Based on January sale figures, Ford started 1953 looking good in its race to catch Chevrolet. There was hope in some quarters that the Ford car would finally regain the sales lead it last enjoyed in 1935. But it was not to be. Still, Ford managed to build nearly 1.25 million cars, up almost 50 percent from 1952 and only 110,000 units behind Chevrolet. It was a strong showing and solidified the company's position as the second ranked firm in the industry.

Ford advertised that two 1953 Fords could be had for the price of one of the more expensive "fine" models.

Make the picture perfect with a "Travelized" Ford!

There's nothing like a sweet-running Ford to make those carefree summer trips *perfect*.

The best way to make certain your Ford's in "trip-top" shape for all that driving you're going to give it, is to have it checked and "Travelized" *now*—before you go away.

If replacement parts are needed, be sure to insist on the parts that are made *right* for your Ford—Genuine Ford Parts. They're made to the same specifications set by the men who originally built your Ford. They're given exhaustive tests before they're approved for manufacture. And they're *made right* to work right to last longer in your Ford!

GENUINE Ford PARTS

SURE SIGNS OF SAVINGS

Ford SERVICE

Wherever you go for service insist on Genuine Ford Parts

Among the genuine Ford parts used in 1953 models were revised suspension componentry and under-the-hood improvements. In June 1953, Master Guide power steering was introduced for the first time on the Ford. (Old Cars)

253

Al Stuebing's 1953 Ford Mainline 6 four-door sedan got 27.03 miles per gallon in the AAA supervised Mobilgas Economy Run. The contest covered 1,206 miles from Los Angeles, California to Twin Falls, Idaho. (Old Cars)

Watching the Fords Go by...

The best is yet to be!

By Peter Winnewisser

Ford hobbyists and anyone interested in the automobile story anxiously looked forward to the publication of two books destined to be milestones in the recording of Ford history. The first was a Ford corporate history. The second was the biography of Henry Ford II. Both were authored by Dr. David Lewis, professor of business history at the University of Michigan.

Professors Allan Nevins and Frank Ernest Hill completed a three-volume corporate history of Ford in 1963. Their hefty, 1,910-page trilogy covered the Ford story from the birth of Henry Ford to 1962. All three volumes went out of print and came to be considered collector's items.

In 1987, Ford Motor Company entered into an agreement with the University of Michigan to update the history of Ford as a worldwide multi-national corporation. Lewis was selected to lead the university's team in this effort. He was relieved of his teaching responsibility, through 1990, so that he could devote himself to the very special project.

Ford also established a corporate history office, under the direction of Robert D. Isom, to coordinate the project and assist Lewis and his team with the research. The Ford Archives, other company records and interviews with active and retired Ford employees provided the primary basis for the updated history of the company.

Lewis picked up the story in 1956, about the time Ford went public, and brought it to the present. He completed the research and wrote the book in 1989. The date for publication was the fall of 1990.

After reading Lee Iacocca's autobiography a few years ago, I was left with the strong feeling that I wanted to hear, as Paul Harvey is fond of saying, "the rest of the story." Iacocca was not very complimentary about Henry Ford II. Yet, Ford, perhaps following the philosophy of his famous saying, "never complain, never explain," did not respond by revealing his reasons for firing Iacocca.

The "rest of the story" was included in the biography of Henry Ford II which Lewis wrote. The book was based on Ford's memoirs, as recorded in conversations between Lewis and the auto magnate during the period from 1980 to 1987. By prior agreement, it couldn't be published until September 1990, three years after Ford's death.

In this columnist's opinion, there was no one better suited for the task of bringing these two books to us than David Lewis. He is acknowledged worldwide as a leading historian of the automotive industry and the foremost authority on Henry Ford, the Ford Motor Company and the Ford family. In addition to more than 400 published articles, his credits include the award-winning study, "The Public Image of Henry Ford" (1976) and "The Automobile in American Culture," which he edited for the Michigan Quarterly Review in 1980. "Ford Country," a compilation of selected items from more than 3,000 articles which have appeared in a magazine column that he writes over the past 13 years, was published last year.

Lewis traces his interest in Henry Ford to his work for Ford, in 1953, developing historical material for use in conjunction with the company's 50th anniversary celebration. "I found it so fascinating and so vast that it has been my principal research interest ever since."

Listed in "Who's Who in America," Lewis received his bachelor's degree in journalism at the University of Illinois in 1948. He has a master's degree in public relations from Boston University and a master's and doctorate in economic history from the University of Michigan.

In 1965, at the age of 38, Lewis left a promising career in public relations at General Motors to follow his first love: writing about Ford. He took up duties as a teacher and writer at the University of Michigan where today he is professor of business history. For Lewis it was a great move. "I have the best job in the world," he is fond of saying. "It enables me to do what I love most, research and write about Henry Ford and the Ford Motor Company."

Prior to his stint at General Motors from 1959 to 1965, Lewis worked as a reporter, editor and public relations representative. He was part of Ford's public relations staff at Dearborn, Michigan from 1952 to 1955.

Lewis and his wife, Yuri, live in Ann Arbor, Michigan. They have four children: Kim, Leilani, Sumiko and Lance. As might be expected from a "Ford man," his favorite car is a Ford; a 1921 Model T touring which he says he will keep as long as he lives.

A while ago, David Lewis compiled a list of his favorite things which he shared with this columnist. "The basic ingredients for happiness," he wrote, "are good health, a job that you like and that likes you, and to love and be loved. If one has these three things, he/she has 97 percent or more of that which makes for happiness. But, one's favorite things make a pleasant life even more pleasant."

Lewis concluded his list with a favorite thing that captures the spirit of this remarkably talented man. One of his favorite things, he said, is "looking forward to the delights of the wondrous and splendid years that lie ahead, and won't you come along with me, for the very best is yet to be!"

Although much of his life and writing lie behind him, we can look forward to significant contributions in the field of Ford history from David Lewis in the future. The Ford corporate history and the biography of Henry Ford II were but the beginning of what lies ahead. The very best is yet to be!

Dr. David Lewis (standing with dark jacket) presents fellow automotive historian Ralph Dunwoodie with an award at the Society of Automotive Historians banquet. (Old Cars)

Today Ford is a lot more than cars...
it's a Control Center for astronauts circling
the earth...an electronic machine
that reads 36,000 zip-coded addresses an hour.
The Mariner IV antenna sending back
the first pictures from Mars...
a laser beam that creates 10 million volts
out of thin air...Philco refrigerators...
medical research...guided missiles.
It's a company that goes where good ideas take it.

"And to think I started all that."

Ford Motor Company advertisements, such as this one, have long reflected a concern with the importance of corporate history. Professor David L. Lewis, a noted automotive historian, has spent much of his life researching the Dearborn, Michigan firm's roots. (Old Cars)

Collecting Chryslers...

Bottling up one-horse-per-cube Chevrolet myths

By Dave Duricy, Jr.

A press release for a whisky decanter that's a replica of a 1957 Chevrolet Bel Air two-door hardtop stated the 1957 Bel Air was the "first American production car to achieve one horse-power from every cubic inch of engine displacement." This statement is erroneous and vexing to MoPar fans.

The first cars to break the one horsepower per cubic inch barrier were Chrysler products. The original, offered in 1956, was the Chrysler 300B. (Chrysler)

The magnificent Chrysler 300B was a masterpiece of styling and engineering with a 354 cubic inch hemi V-8 with stiffened valve springs, high-lift camshaft and a 3.94 x 3.36 inch bore and stroke. (Chrysler)

The first cars to break the one horsepower per cubic inch barrier were Chrysler products. The original, offered in 1956, was the Chrysler 300B. This magnificent car, a masterpiece of styling and engineering, was sold standard with a 354 cubic inch hemi V-8 with stiffened valve springs, high-lift camshaft and a 3.94 x 3.36 inch bore and stroke. This engine delivered 340 horsepower at 5200 rpm. However, a 10:1 compression ratio was optional. It raised horsepower to 355, one for each cubic inch.

This Chrysler 300B's standard engine delivered 340 horsepower at 5200 rpm. However, a 10:1 compression ratio was optional. It raised horsepower to 355, one for each cubic inch. (Chrysler)

When the 1957 Bel Air appeared, so did an aggressive DeSoto Adventurer. The Adventurer was the latest in styling and the latest in power. Hurling the handsomely tail-finned and two-toned Adventurer body shell down America's highways was a standard equipment 354 cubic inch hemi V-8 pumping out 354 horsepower. The bore and stroke of this engine were 3.80 x 3.80 inches. Atop the cast iron engine block was a Carter dual-quad induction system. Compression ratio was 9.25:1. The Adventurer was the first American car to offer one horsepower per cubic inch as standard equipment. The Chrysler 300B and 1957 Bel Air offered one horsepower per cubic inch as optional equipment.

The 1957 Bel Air is an automobile surrounded by myth. This has been inadvertently perpetuated by public relations people. Why this is so, is hard for non-Chevrolet lovers to understand.

The Bel Air, and the other Chevrolets of that model-year, were cleverly restyled, but they were actually revamped and recycled variations of an all-new car introduced in 1955. The power plant promoted in Chevrolet ads was called the "small-block" and developed a performance heritage. However, as we have said, it was not the first to exceed one horsepower per cubic inch.

The muscle-bound MoPar power plants propelling the 300B and DeSoto Adventurer utilized shear size and brawn to achieve their remarkable power ratings. The Chevrolet engine relied on fuel-injection and solid valve lifters.

Sized at 283 cubic inches, the Chevrolet power plant had less displacement than the MoPar engines. Of course, it is not entirely fair to compare a low-priced Chevrolet to DeSotos and Chryslers that sold in the medium- to upper-price ranges.

One must always keep in mind that the 283 cubic inch Chevrolet power plant was an outstanding development, even though it was not the remarkable "first" that legend and lore have made it out to be. Most MoPar fans feel that Chrysler Corporation set the industry standards for truly impressive engineering.

This doesn't mean that the 1957 Bel Air isn't deserving of immortalization in the form of a porcelain whiskey decanter.

MoPar fans can be satisfied with the knowledge that their favorite company was the first producer of a one horsepower per cubic inch engine and slotted it into exciting, vibrant and lasting automobiles.

Maybe someday, the Embossograph Company, which plans, designs and produces decanters for Beam Distilleries, will decide to make its publicity releases ring a bit truer and tool up to produce a decanter honoring the Chrysler 300 letter car or DeSoto Adventurer.

1957 DeSoto Adventurer

Collecting Chryslers...

The forgotten alternative

By Dave Duricy, Jr.

Chrysler research on turbine-powered vehicles began before World War II and culminated May 14, 1963 at the Essex House, in New York City, in the form of a stylish black on bronze hardtop coupe.

This car, the product of four generations of lab experiments, cross-country endurance tests and limited public exposure was displayed before reporters. With great fanfare, it was announced that some lucky motorists might have the opportunity to operate a turbine car for three months, allowing Chrysler to gather consumer evaluations of a turbine-powered automobile used in real driving situations.

The Chrysler Turbine car held great promise. Its turbine power plant required little or no maintenance. It operated with no vibration and was capable of running on virtually any fuel, everything from kerosene to jet fuel, while providing the driver with a behavior similar to a piston engine.

A 1945 research and development grant from the United States Navy to create a turbo-prop airplane engine greatly established Chrysler's interest in automotive applications of the turbine.

Prior to the war, Chrysler had flirted with the idea of a turbine-powered car. However, materials capable of withstanding the extreme internal temperatures of the turbine were few and expensive. The United States Navy grant provided Chrysler with access to materials and purpose to explore turbine engines.

Though the Navy project terminated in 1949, with the development of a turbo-prop capable of performing just as economically as a conventional unit, Chrysler turned turbine research toward use in automobiles.

The company made rapid success. Chrysler was the first American manufacturer to place a turbine in an automobile. This took place, in March 1954, when the motor was installed in a two-tone Plymouth hardtop.

The little Plymouth's turbine was advanced in that its turbine utilized a heat exchanger, which increased fuel economy and reduced exhaust temperature by exchanging heat from initial exhaust with incoming air to increase gas temperature. This reduced the burner's job.

In 1955, Chrysler brought out another turbine car. Again, the engine was installed in a Plymouth. This car was never publicly displayed.

In March 1956, a Chrysler turbine installed in a Plymouth sedan made the first transcontinental trip for a turbine. The car traveled 3,020 miles in four days on its journey from New York to Los Angeles. It averaged 13 miles per gallon with no turbine failure. However, an intake casting and a faulty bearing in a reducing gear both malfunctioned.

Plymouth's greatest contribution to the turbine program was the fact that it was operated exactly like a piston-engined car.

A third-generation turbine appeared and was installed in a 1962 Dart. It made another cross-country cross-ing, outperforming its piston-engined traveling companion under the most adverse conditions. (Chrysler)

More trips were made in turbine cars. A 1959 Plymouth made the trek from Detroit to New York, utilizing advances in Chrysler metallurgy and greater engine efficiency.

A third-generation turbine appeared and was installed in a 1962 Dart. It made another cross-country crossing, outperforming its piston-engined traveling companion under the most adverse conditions. More amazing was the installation of the turbine into the Dodge Turbo Truck, a medium-duty truck of hefty proportions. The turbine demonstrated its strength in a 290 mile run, from Detroit to Chicago, in the Turbo Truck.

The 1962 Dart turbine car was joined by a Fury Turbo. They both toured the country as part of an exhibit asking spectators, "Do you like the idea of a turbine and would you buy one?" (Chrysler)

The 1962 Dart turbine car was joined by a Fury Turbo. They both toured the country as part of an exhibit asking spectators, "Do you like the idea of a turbine and would you buy one?" Thirty percent responded with yes; 54 percent with a definite maybe. The decision was made, after such enthusiastic public support, to build 50 turbine cars for consumer evaluation.

Built by Ghia of Italy and Chrysler, with styling by Elwood Engel, the 50 1963 turbine cars were beautiful machines. Each was done in bronze. Most had a black vinyl top. (Chrysler)

Built by Ghia of Italy and Chrysler, with styling by Elwood Engel, the 50 1963 turbine cars were beautiful machines. Each was done in bronze. Most had a black vinyl top. All were outfitted with a four-place, leather bucket seat interior (also bronze in color).

Running the length of the cabin was an elaborate metal-tone console adorned with turbine style decorations. The console contained a glove box for the rear seat, power window switches and a host of other controls.

The dashboard was composed of three circular pods positioned directly in front of the driver. A smooth shelf extended from these pods, in front of the passenger seat, and gently swept into the door. The steering wheel was elegant and slim, with a full horn ring and two spokes.

Each Turbine Car was fitted with every available luxury item, including power steering, power brakes, power windows and automatic transmission. Most important was the fourth-generation turbine under its hood.

On October 29, 1963, in Chicago, Mr. Lynn A. Townsend, president of Chrysler, handed the keys of the first turbine car to the first evaluators, a young couple named Mr. and Mrs. Richard E. Vlaha.

Everyone loves DeSotos ...
or just about everyone

By Dave Duricy, Jr.

"Collecting Chryslers" once visited Jack Stevens and his beautiful DeSoto called "Iron-sides." We also described a handsome 1958 DeSoto Fireflite, that was discovered buried deep in a garage. The connection between these two cars, other than both being blue and both being of late 1950s vintage, was the fact that both were in remarkable original condition.

The writer suggested one reason for this was that DeSoto built its cars well. Apparently, the editor of another publication begrudged DeSoto this honor. He condemned the entire Chrysler Corporation line of late 1950s automobiles, calling them "rolling rust buckets."

This is an all too common mistake about Virgil Exner's "finned fantasies." It is not entirely deserved. Granted, Chrysler experienced serious quality control problems early in model year 1957, when it rushed its revolutionary designs into production. However, quality was much improved as the decade wore on.

No automaker, especially among the "Big 3," can claim truly outstanding construction quality back then. Even the grand dame of the industry, Studebaker-Packard, suffered from severe quality control problems in the last years of Packard, not to mention Studebaker's difficulties.

Chrysler's late 1950s models, especially DeSotos, have been attacked by historians. DeSotos of 1957-1959 have been described as, "totally unwanted automobiles that were roundly rejected by buyers because of outrageous styling and poor quality."

That a car sold in low numbers is not an absolute indicator of poor quality. There were other factors contributing to DeSoto's demise. A 1957 economic recession put the damper on sales of mid- to upper-market automobiles. This was DeSoto's already small marketing niche.

DeSoto was also plagued by rumors of discontinuation and feeling pressure, from above. The Chrysler Windsor intruded, quite successfully, into the same sales territory. This rendered DeSoto "non-essential."

There were buyers who wanted and loved DeSotos. And the cars were, indeed, built to last. Several readers wrote in with stories and photos proving this.

Eddie Smith's pride and joy helps illustrate DeSoto durability. Eddie's gorgeous Firedome two-door hardtop was purchased from the original owner. It has 98,800 miles on it. Eddie also owns a 1957 Fireflite.

Barbara Tripson has a 1959 DeSoto Firesweep two-door hardtop that was in her family since new. Her father purchased the beige and white car from the showroom floor. He gave it to her mother as a Valentine's Day present (which certainly beats the heck out of a greeting card and a few candy hearts). Despite the car's age, it was still in great condition when Barbara and her husband inherited it. They cleaned it and had a mechanic go over it. Now, the car is just about as good as new.

Last, but not least, is Jim DiGregorio's 1957 DeSoto Adventurer, which is depicted in the accompanying photographs that he sent us. This black and gold beauty is one of several exquisite Chrysler products included in DiGregorio's collection of mid-1950s cars.

The 1957 DeSoto Adventurer was a high-powered, performance car. The Adventurer hardtop coupe was introduced two months after the other cars in the regular DeSoto line. (Jim DiGregorio)

Standard Adventurer equipment included TorqueFlite push-button automatic transmission, power brakes and a padded dashboard. Only 1,650 hardtops were built, along with just 300 convertibles. (Jim DiGregorio)

The Adventurer featured a 345 cubic inch V-8 engine with 9.25:1 compression and dual four-barrel Carter carburetors that produced 345 horsepower at 5200 rpm. (Jim DiGregorio)

All Adventurers came with dual exhausts, dual rear mount radio antennas and dual headlamps, which had recently been legalized in all states. Sales in 1957 were the third highest in the history of DeSoto. (Jim DiGregorio)

Collecting Chryslers...

1963 Chrysler Turbine Car

By Dave Duricy, Jr.

In 1963, Chrysler Corporation initiated a bold program in which motorists across the country were enlisted to evaluate its latest experimental Turbine Cars on a regular, everyday driving basis. The first testers of the 1963 Chrysler Turbine Car were Mr. and Mrs. Richard Vlaha. They were followed by 203 participants who were chosen from over 30,000 people who had volunteered. Those selected were picked for various reasons, including geographic area and type of everyday car use (must own an automobile). Participants had to have valid driver's licenses.

They represented 128 major population centers and 48 states. Each participant had use of a car for three months. They were expected to maintain its appearance, protect it from harm, pay for fuel and relate their experiences. Chrysler handled mechanical malfunctions (there were few). After three months, the cars went to other testers.

The Turbine Car looked conventional enough, but it would operate on almost any fuel. It had no pistons, radiator or carburetor. The jets at the rear were for appearance only. (Chrysler Historical)

Driving was done exactly as one drove a conventional auto. However, the starting procedure was somewhat different. Testers were instructed to first place the transmission lever in the "idle" position and push down to engage the "park/start" position. As with any car, a turn of the key started the turbine engine. Drivers were told that, within a few seconds, the inlet temperature gauge would read 1200-degrees and the tachometer would show 22,000 rpm. Chrysler said these two readings "indicate that the engine is started." Imagine having to look at the dashboard to know a car is running. Now, that's smooth!

Results of the testing were fascinating. One-third of the users were dissatisfied with acceleration from standstill. Others said the cars had exceptional acceleration at freeway speeds.

Gas mileage was considered poor. However, much time was spent demonstrating to friends, with stop/start driving, which is not conducive to good mileage in any car. Several testers had driven economy cars before. They were unaccustomed to a full-size car with high performance.

It would be safe to assume that overall mileage of the Turbine Cars was in the neighborhood of 13 miles per gallon, as the first cross-country turbine-powered Plymouth achieved that mileage without the many improvements of the 1963 Chrysler version.

A majority of users were impressed with the sound of turbine power and its quiet behavior. Strangely, though, 25 percent mentioned annoying engine noise. All were pleased with vibration-free operation, the prospect of no maintenance and the ability to use any fuel.

Chrysler experienced some minor problems with the starting mechanisms. They only lasted for 20,000 miles. Engineers were confident they could more than double that life span.

The Turbine Car's controls were simple. The dials showed temperature, speed and revolutions per minute. (Chrysler Historical)

Turbine power held great promise. It offered decent performance and decent economy, with the prospect of much better fuel mileage. Another plus was a virtually maintenance-free engine, with few moving parts, that was highly dependable and capable of running on the cheapest of fuels. It was unaffected by severe cold and needed no anti-freeze. It provided almost instant heat in the interior. It was quiet and smooth, almost the perfect power source.

With all these things going for it, it's strange that after extensive consumer testing, little was heard of the turbine.

Many who followed the 50 cars were puzzled and disappointed when a production version didn't appear. It is unclear why Chrysler never went all the way with it. Some automotive historians declared the turbine dead or a failure.

It is known that the turbine program was finally canceled after the government ceased to offer assistance when Ronald Reagan entered office and looked for budget cuts. High manufacturing costs and high emissions of nitrogen oxides (something Chrysler felt it could correct) are the only clear reasons for the turbine's demise.

In my opinion, the turbine didn't deserve to die. Many have cited the highly efficient piston engines of today as reason enough not to resurrect the turbine. There is fault with that thinking.

A turbine promises sure starting in cold weather. How many engines today can make that claim? A turbine doesn't stall. Many owners of today's high-performance, high-efficiency piston engines frequently complain of stalling. One tank full of bad gas and today's piston-engined car is sick with clogged fuel injectors. A turbine can run on any fuel at any time.

Today's piston engines seek out performance with carefully planned gear and weight ratios. They may be fast off the line, but don't provide power for every situation. A turbine could provide performance like that of the old, big-cube V-8s.

Some cite high fuel consumption as a reason not to utilize the turbine engine. The engine in today's average Chrysler Fifth Avenue/New Yorker can only promise 17 miles per gallon in real life. In 1956, a turbine produced 13 miles per gallon without the benefit of weight reduction, down-sizing or aerodynamics. Imagine what a turbine could do today!

If a turbine requires no maintenance, oil or anti-freeze and makes no vibration and little noise, wouldn't it be worth an extra gallon or two of fuel? Besides, Chrysler has made strides, since 1963, toward better fuel economy in the turbine.

Chrysler said the technology of its 1963 turbine was extraordinarily simple. Such a car should be easy for mechanics to work on. How simple are today's piston power plants to service? Today, entire engines have to be removed to change a simple belt.

Before condemning turbines, we have to remember what we expect from cars. America picked the auto as its favorite mode of transportation. But, the car is an inherently dangerous, wasteful and expensive form of transit. So, we might as well use cars that give us comfort, performance and dependability.

If econoboxes are to become the sole mode of transportation, one might as well throw away all cars ever built and replace them with mass transit vehicles. The original idea behind the car was personal mobility. How mobile does one feel inside a rickety compact, with their knees pressed against their nose and no power or style? You may be able to get 30 miles per gallon, but under such conditions, who wants to?

There was something rousing to Chrysler enthusiasts about the Turbine Car program. The project symbolized all that was good about Chrysler. Here was a project whose sole purpose was to produce a safe, economical, automobile that offered the ultimate in carefree motoring.

Chrysler encountered numerous engineering problems and conquered virtually every one with skill and determination.

Those 50 wonderful Turbine Cars, with their snazzy turbine style headlamp bezels and taillight assemblies held an aura of "futurama" of what could have come next. One can almost see that sleek, turbine silhouette appear on the horizon with headlamps blazing. In the dim of twilight, the bronze finish glows. The car approaches, rushes past, making only the whisper-like sound of turbine power.

Collecting Chryslers...

Amazing slant sixes

By Dave Duricy, Jr.

The slant six is one of Chrysler's famous engineering feats. It has powered everything from trucks to big cars. Perhaps, its most famous use is in the little MoPars called "America's Mercedes"; the Plymouth Valiant and the Dodge Dart.

There is a dynamic club devoted to this engine. The Slant Six Club of America publishes a quarterly magazine called Slant Six News. There's a regular column called "Amazing Stories." It relates the tales of members who experience amazing events in slant sixes. Their stories usually revolve around the astonishing durability of the slant six and eerie tales of engines that run when all conditions are against them.

This 1963 Plymouth Valiant advertisement featured the V-200 station wagon and some of the available equipment, including the slant six engine. (Old Cars)

Doug Dutra, creator of "Amazing Stories," wrote of an amusing adventure. He took his 1963 wagon on a camping trip. It had 202,000 miles on its 198 cubic inch slant six. Before departure, he brought the car to a quick oil change shop. It was given the works. A few hours later, Doug was in the middle of nowhere, when his oil light came on.

Quickly, he shut off the engine and coasted to the side of the road. After looking under the hood and replacing the dipstick, Doug saw a black puddle under the engine. He put a coffee cup under the drip, to save as much oil as possible. In doing this, the problem was discovered. The shop hadn't tightened the drain plug. It fell out.

Necessity is the mother of invention. Doug found a stick and whittled it to a size to fit the hole. With his makeshift plug installed, he needed oil. Doug had one quart. He recovered just half a coffee cup full from the engine. Not enough. After driving 100 feet, the oil light came on. What to do? Doug remembered the salad oil in his camping gear. In went all 16 ounces.

The slant six powered 1963 Valiant V-100 two-door sedan got 26.26 miles per gallon in the Mobil Economy Run. (Old Cars)

A similar advertisement for the 1963 Plymouth Valiant Signet 200 two-door hardtop moved the slant six to the top of the features shown on the left side of the photo. (Old Cars)

Doug drove 20 miles to the next town. He stayed below 45 miles per hour and stopped at the first gas station for an oil change. He paid $5 for a used drain plug from one of the station owner's "project cars."

The slant six was back on the road, hardly the worse for wear. Doug now does his own oil changes and carries two quarts of oil in the car.

Jerry Almond had another story to tell about the durable little motor. Shortly after having his 1966 Dodge D-100 pickup's 225 cubic inch slant six overhauled, Almond knocked a pinhole in his radiator.

This accident occurred just before a trip that Almond was planning to pick up a performance car to restore. He needed the truck to tow it. All nearby radiator shops were closed.

Jerry's father-in-law suggested putting two tablespoons of black pepper in the radiator. Jerry did. Amazingly it sealed the leak. The truck completed its mission towing a trailer twice its size.

"Amazing Stories" has described other interesting feats, such as an emergency tune-up done with a pocket knife and a car climbing 75 miles up Mount Whitney (near Death Valley) on empty. Such feats are common to die-hard slant six owners.

The slant six is a fantastic engine. The Slant Six Club even has a "200,000 Miler's Club."

Readers wishing to join the Slant Six Club of America and tell a few "Amazing Stories" of their own are welcome. Write Jack Poehler, PO Box 4414, Salem, OR 97302. Ownership of a slant six is not required.

Another car available with the slant six was the 1965 Dodge Dart GT. The slant six is certainly one of Chrysler's famous engineering feats. It has also powered everything from trucks to big cars. (Chrysler Historical)

1963-1966 Darts: The little Imperials from Dodge

By Dave Duricy, Jr.

When thinking of 1960s Dodges, one usually visualizes a sleek 1966 or 1967 Charger or a Super Bee. Rarely does the name Dart spring to mind.

Overshadowed by their glitzy and glamorous brethren, the 1963-1966 Darts have been largely overlooked by the hobby, which is a shame, since gem-like compacts were a hit when new and are still nifty today.

In 1963, the all-new Dart line appeared as a replacement for the not-so-successful Dodge Lancer of 1961-1962. The Lancer was based on the contemporary Valiant and bore an extremely strong resemblance to it. This lack of individuality was perhaps the greatest single reason for the Lancer's failure.

The new Dart solved this problem. Though still a close cousin to the Valiant, the new Dart appeared distinctively Dodge and offered a bit more car, as one would expect from the marque.

The Dart's wheelbase was 111 inches, five more than Valiant's, though the wagons used the Valiant's 106 inch wheelbase. An overall length of 195.9 inches (wagons 190.2) made the new Darts "big" compared to many competitive compacts. Their extra size was well utilized in the areas of cargo carrying ability, styling and driving comfort.

The new Darts boasted an impressive trunk volume of 30.2 cubic feet and interiors with enough space to carry six passengers. A clever Dart ad from 1963 displayed two Dart sedans, one with six gentlemen inside, the other with six young ladies. The copy read: "Room for six of one or half a dozen of the other."

Dart styling, which varied little during this four-year cycle, was quite good. Though not in league with that of the 1955 Chrysler C300 or the LeBaron- bodied Imperials of the 1930s, it was a balanced, purposeful-looking and pleasing design.

The Dart name originated on a line of full-size Dodges characterized by budget prices and wide range of body styles, as advertised in this 1961 announcement. (Old Cars)

In 1964, the ad theme used a 1950s "Kidillac" pedal car to cleverly emphasize the Dart's roominess, compared to other compact cars. (Old Cars)

Ads for the all-new 1963 Dodge Dart stressed the amount of room inside the passenger compartment and luggage "containment" areas. (Old Cars)

The Premier models wore prominent headlight bezels that protruded slightly from the fenders and grille, creating a look that resembled the face of the Chrysler Turbine Car. Body sides were clean and smooth and rear styling was neat and tidy. However, perhaps the most striking styling element of the Dart was its distinguished roofline.

The rear roof pillar was thick and nicely angled to create a decidedly formal air. This touch of class, accompanied by a remarkably high construction quality and comfort level, made the Darts, especially the top of the line GTs, appear to be more like "little Imperials" than just compact Dodges.

The Dart's beauty was more than skin deep. Initially the Darts, offered in 170, 270 and GT trim levels, were all powered by the famous slant six. Standard was the 170 cubic inch six, while the larger 225 cubic inch unit was an option. Horsepower was 101 and 145 respectively.

These engines combined rugged dependability with excellent gas mileage (as high as 24 miles per gallon with the 225 and optional TorqueFlite automatic transmission) and adequate go power.

So confident was Chrysler Corporation of the new Dart, that it gave the car a five-year, 50,000-mile warranty. This warranty was one of Chrysler's more famous creations. Combined with the Dart's good overall design, it caused sales to reach 153,992 cars, an excellent volume. Dodge ads proudly announced that sales of its compact models had risen 109 percent over previous totals.

A good portion of this volume was made up of the snazzy Dart GTs. This car line, comprised of a hardtop and a convertible, offered a spiffy bucket seat interior with better-than-average appointments.

Though the GT offered no different drive train specifications from those of its lesser line mates (as its GT name would seem to indicate), it did provide a sporty environment in which the Dart's inherently good ride and handling could be appreciated.

The GT's 1963 sales of 34,227 indicated that the Dart series was successfully received by the buying public as an upper-market "large" compact.

Throughout its 1963-1966 production run, the Dart experienced evolutionary changes rather than revolutionary ones. The most notable improvements were in additional engines options, especially their application in the GT series.

For 1964, the Dart got a shot in the arm. Newly available to the line was a 273.5 cubic inch V-8 with wedge-shaped combustion chambers. The new engine offered 180 horsepower and 0-to-60 mile per hour times of 10 seconds. Though such performance is not earth shattering, the engine could be made to tool around rather snappily.

Accompanying the new engine were minor trim changes. Most notable was a new convex grille that resembled the blade guard of an electric razor. The public saw a good thing becoming even better and Dart sales rose to 193,035. GTs accounted for 49,830 of this total.

Since Ford had trotted out the Mustang (with its pretense of performance) in 1964, Dodge modified the Dart's optional small-block V-8 with a wilder cam and a four-barrel carburetor for 1965. Also, the GT could now be had with a special heavy-duty suspension option and a four-speed floor shifted manual transmission. With this new hopped-up engine, the GT could really dart from 0-to-60 miles per hour in 8.2 seconds.

The fun continued with the 1966 models. Dart styling was squared up with a new rectangular grille and rectangular headlamp bezels that did away with the vague resemblance to the Chrysler Turbine Car. Otherwise the car was left essentially alone.

Darts, especially the GT, had developed into truly superior transportation. However, production went down. Only 176,027 Darts were made, 30,041 of which were GTs.

Though the Darts and Dart GT arrived with completely new body structures and styling in 1967, they had lost some of the class that had characterized the pleasant 1963-1966 versions.

The New GT was a brazen number called GTS that used its new body structure to accept bigger power plants such as the 330 horsepower, 383 cubic inch V-8. It was a much more muscular and potent machine than its predecessor.

A new grille added richness to the "stamp-out-cramped-compacts" sized 1965 Dodge Dart. (Old Cars)

The survival rate of the first-generation Darts has been good. Occasionally, a well worn example can be seen cruising down the highway. Though many Darts have seen mileage well over the 100,000 mark, this should not deter a hobbyist from considering a Dart for his collection.

All Darts were built with durability in mind, and engine parts are still widely available today. The Darts, especially the GTs, have a certain appeal that shines through even the roughest examples. Cleaned up and sparkling, the Darts are down right enchanting, especially when compared to their 1960s Ford and General Motors compact contemporaries.

These Darts have a certain status and stand out against today's horde of collectible 1964-1966 Mustangs. They're simply more car than either Falcons or comparable Chevrolets, plus they enjoy an excellent reputation, unlike the Corvair's "Unsafe At Any Speed" dark cloud, which still lingers.

The first-generation Darts are worthy candidates for your attention and offer a driving pleasure that could only have come from Dodge.

Collecting Chryslers...

The VIP: A very impressive Plymouth

By Dave Duricy, Jr.

In 1965, Chevrolet and Ford both introduced new top-of-the-line models that attempted to offer their buyers automotive luxury at low-line prices. At Chevrolet the new model was the Caprice; at Ford it was the LTD. Both brought added success to their respective manufacturers.

Though it already had the Sport Fury (long recognized as a sporty and luxurious offering) and the prestigious-sounding Fury III, Plymouth felt it needed a new model to counteract the Caprice and LTD. The new Plymouth, introduced in 1966, was called the VIP.

The VIP created some confusion at the top of the Plymouth line, since it competed with the Sport Fury and Fury III for the same customers. The VIP was priced similarly to the Sport Fury, though it came in a four-door hardtop body style that wasn't offered as a Sport Fury. The Fury III hardtop sedan was also a handsome car that came with an excellent selection of standard equipment and a generous options list.

The Fury III was easily made into a plush automobile, comparable to both the Caprice and LTD. The VIP was very alluring, even if it did compete with its siblings.

Early in its first year, the VIP was offered only as a four-door hardtop, but, later, a two-door hardtop was added. Appointments and equipment were exceptionally good and combined with styling that emphasized a limousine-type aura. The VIP was an honest, capable and high-quality automobile.

Though unmistakably based on the Fury, with its 119-inch wheelbase and decidedly Fury-like silhouette, the VIP offered slight styling extras that the 1966 dealer brochure said added a "distinctive styling approach."

Among these extra touches were body side moldings that contained a thin insert surfaced with a wood-grain finish. This treatment was also applied to the base of the very formal rear roof pillars.

The roof was a critical exterior design element of the VIP. Vinyl covering was, though not standard, strongly recommended. It was available in black or white. Rarely was the VIP illustrated minus the vinyl top treatment. This is not surprising, since the roof covering added to the limousine look that Plymouth had tried so hard to create. Further enhancing the formal look was a pretty roof pillar badge. It was done in gold-tone with the name VIP, in bold letters, surrounded by swirly gold flourishes.

The interior, as had been true with many big Chrysler products through the years, was the VIP's most beautiful feature. It certainly created the atmosphere of a VIP lounge. Big, handsome, cushy, sofa-style seats were standard. Both front and rear seats had pull-down arm rests. Front seats were framed at the sides and the bottom with a chrome and woodgrain trim piece that added to the luxurious look. Attractive chromium door assist handles were provided and set against a woodgrain base.

Premium features such as cigar lighters, front and rear, and rear cabin reading lights set into the roof pillars, were standard. They helped create VIP's image of an executive express.

An express the VIP could certainly be, with its standard 230 horsepower 318 cubic inch V-8. Heftier power plants were available, ranging from the 270 horsepower 383 cubic inch V-8 with two-barrel carburetor to the big and bad 365 horsepower 440 cubic inch four-barrel V-8 with dual exhausts. Since the VIP was equipped with torsion bar front suspension, its road handling was naturally superior.

What was perhaps the VIP's most appealing asset was its options list. A VIP could be equipped to satisfy virtually any taste. It could be customized by selecting any one (or two for two-toning), of 18 exterior colors, many of which were metallic.

The cloth and vinyl interiors could be had in red, blue or black. Of course, there was a full compliment of optional accessories: Auto Pilot, 'Tilt-a-Scope' steering wheel, air conditioning and rear window defogger, to name just a few.

Sales of the 1966 VIP were nothing to be ashamed of: 12,058 four-doors left the showrooms, along with 5,158 two-doors. Production was probably hampered by the VIP's sibling rivalries with other Furies and an all-too-successful campaign by Plymouth to give it an expensive image.

The VIP model was continued into 1967 and treated to new sheet metal, as were the rest of the full-size-Plymouths. This 1967 model was probably the most beautiful of all the VIPs. (Chrysler Historical)

The model was continued into 1967 and treated to new sheet metal, as were the rest of the full-size Plymouths. This 1967 model was probably the most beautiful of all the VIPs. So handsome and "rich" looking was the VIP, that it succeeded in looking more "imperial" than that year's Imperial.

The starchy formal lines of 1966 were softened a bit. The formal roof line of the four-door was relaxed, to create an elegant sporty look. A full-length wheel hub-level body side molding ran along the length of the car, emphasizing its size. Color offerings were expanded to 21 choices and the two-door VIP was now a nifty "fast top" with dual front seats.

Inside, decoration was shuffled about and new fabrics and vinyls were used. They had a very faint gold fleck. Copper was added as a new upholstery color, while leather was now an interior option.

Seemingly unimportant, but surprisingly effective in altering the VIPs appearance, were four different types of wheel treatments. All were very attractive, ranging from slotted wheel covers to handsome mag wheels. The ability to fashion the VIP to one's liking had not been lost with the coming of 1967. There was still a wonderful options list.

VIP production did not change dramatically from the previous year: 7,912 two-doors and 10,830 four-doors.

Sadly, 1968 was the last year for the VIP. The 1968 edition was little changed from 1967. An unfortunate shuffle slightly marred the front end, but otherwise the VIP was just as desirable as it had been in the past.

The interior was toned down slightly and was probably the most tasteful of all the VIP interiors. Seats were still opulently cushioned and finished. Interior use of artificial wood trim had been restrained, as Plymouth relied more on generous amounts of tufted vinyl to create a plush appearance. The interior was still distinguished by exclusive ornamentation, such as the fancy VIP badges on the doors.

While it lasted, the VIP model line was fabulous. It truly succeeded in offering premium luxury at a standard line price. It offered a level of customization that has been all but lost today. It had a certain prestige that its Ford and Chevrolet competitors lacked. The VIP was one very impressive Plymouth.

This is the 1967 Fury VIP with its rakish roof. It featured a more formal appearing rear window treatment for 1967. (Plymouth)

A little off center:
The Plymouth XNR

By Dave Duricy, Jr.

In 1960 Virgil Exner was nearing the end of his reign as head of design at Chrysler Corporation. He would leave behind him an impressive styling history, one that helped Chrysler shake its mid-1950s stagnation with the glamorous new 1955 models. He then catapulted the firm to design leadership with his dazzling 1957 modes.

While Exner's production designs zipped about the roads of America, he produced a substantial number of memorable show cars that illustrated to what further extent Chrysler engineering and styling could be taken. The lineage of Exner show cars began with his formal and dashing European look 1950 Plymouth XX-500 sedan. The Plymouth was followed by a burly grand tourer of classic elegance, the 1951 Chrysler K310. It featured full radius wheel cutouts, long hood/short deck configuration and curvaceous, flowing fender lines. Exner then produced what was hoped to become the MoPar sports car to answer the Corvette, the 1954 DeSoto Adventurer.

The Adventurer was styled similarly to the K310 and would have existed on a much higher plane than the Corvette, had it been placed in production. Sitting on a 111-inch wheelbase and powered by a DeSoto hemi V-8, the coupe would have been no slouch. Inside, the Adventurer was an honest four-seater, with four-place bucket seats covered in black leather, a radical departure for 1954. These sumptuous seats were accompanied by a satin-finish aluminum dashboard, complete with round gauges.

Enormous wire wheels and external exhausts set off the Adventurer package. The model was seriously considered for production, but Chrysler's dim fortunes in 1954, plus its all important plans for 1955, pushed the DeSoto aside. However, the idea of a MoPar sports car just wouldn't die.

One of Exner's standout show car designs for 1955 was a muscular two-seat convertible, the Chrysler Falcon. With Ford's debut of the Thunderbird, Chrysler was again seduced into contemplating a sports car. The Falcon had squarer lines than its immediate show car predecessors and wore them extremely well. Edges were rounded off, giving the car its strong look, while its headlights were set within concave areas on either side of the pronounced heart-shaped grille. The front end configuration gave the Falcon a vicious look, perfectly complementing the low stance of the car.

With standing quarter-mile times of 17.5 seconds (at 82 miles per hour) achieved with two-speed PowerFlite automatic transmission and sparkling handling, the Falcon was eagerly awaited in Chrysler showrooms. However, it wasn't to be.

Chrysler built only three examples, then dismissed the project. Perhaps the introduction of the Chrysler 300 took care of any need for a corporate image car. Later MoPar models, such as the production DeSoto Adventurer, Plymouth Fury and Dodge D-500/D-501, certainly established Chrysler's mastery of speed and performance much more economically and practically than a special two-seat sports car.

That wasn't the end of the MoPar sports car, however. Exner still had one wild, very wild, card up his sleeve. It was the beautifully bizarre Plymouth XNR, conceived for 1960. The XNR represented a new direction in Exner's styling philosophy. He had tired of the tailfin that had so distinguished Chrysler's cars. He appeared to be moving away from the svelte curves of his previous exercises. Instead, he was experimenting with heavy sheet metal sculpturing, pronounced fender lines and asymmetrical motifs.

These characteristics can be found in Exner's aborted plans for the corporation's 1962 models. From Plymouth to Imperial, long hoods and sloping rear decks were to be ordained. The initial 1959 DeSoto mock-up epitomized Exner's vision. The rear fenders were characterized by a deeply-sculpted character line that began at the taillight, ran up to below the rear side glass, angled up, and then swept back to the taillight. Stylists called this rakish protrusion the "chicken wing." The front fenders were highlighted by a highly exaggerated "blade" that ran from the headlight to midway through the doors.

The XNR was the most bizarre expression of the new look. It was a sports car in the most serious sense and illustrated this via a design emphasis on the driver and a traditional sporting drive train. (Chrysler Historical)

The XNR was the most bizarre expression of the new look. It was a sports car in the most serious sense and illustrated this via a design emphasis on the driver and a traditional sporting drivetrain.

The nifty, new compact Valiant had appeared for 1960, wearing Exner's "new look." They were powered by the now famous slant six engine, coupled to a manual three-speed transmission. The XNR used the Valiant's mechanicals with, so Chrysler claimed, no modifications.

Indeed, powered by the 170 cubic inch slant six, but much faster than the 101 horsepower power plant would allow, the XNR slant six must have had some sort of modifications that permitted the engine to produce speeds well over 120 miles per hour. It has been suggested by slant six experts that the XNR was equipped with an early edition of the Hyper-Pak engine option that was used on Daytona race cars. Either way, the power train was production-suitable, functional and effective.

Functional and effective could also describe the style. Since the XNR was conceived as a racer, the driver was the focus of attention. The passenger seat was covered by a metal tonneau and set four inches lower than the driver's, so that the passenger would not project into the air stream. Clearly intended for only occasional use, the passenger side of the car was fitted with a tiny auxiliary windshield that could be flipped up for protection.

The hood was dominated by a huge air scoop that sat on the left side of the hood, running its whole length. The bulge continued into the driver's area, to compose the instrument hood over the dashboard. A small curved glass windshield sat atop the scoop and ran around to the top of the driver's door. The radical off-center theme was continued by a huge fin that began at the driver's head rest and flared back in a dramatic sweep. This treatment was conceived to subdue the winds that would otherwise be disrupted by the driver's head.

Out back, the off-center fin was made part of the bumper assembly by a huge "nerf" style cross-shaped chrome bar. In front, the XNR predicted Chrysler's future with a loop style bumper that enclosed the grille and headlights. This treatment would be seen on all full-size Chrysler products in 1969.

Front fenders were accentuated by wild blades that stuck out a good three inches from the body and could have functionally served as splash guards. The lower body lines were remarkably similar to the Valiant's, with the rear fender kick up, round wheel cutouts and dramatic front fenders emphasized.

Inside, the XNR was all business. Simple black leather seats were employed, along with a no nonsense dashboard and three-spoke steering wheel. Zippered storage bags were found on the aluminum door panels, to carry small items. The glove box was detachable and could serve as a camera case. A small storage area was found inside the huge fin. It was accessible from behind the headrest and was, probably, the only space appropriate for stowing a golf club.

Ghia constructed the 195.2 inch by 71 inch Plymouth marvel for Chrysler. The XNR was well-received on the show circuit. Because of its exceedingly practical power plant, it seemed that the XNR might find its way into production. It didn't and it's probably just as well. It would have lost much of its wild nature. For one thing, it would have needed a roof and a proper windshield. There's half the fun right out the window. Any attempt to civilize the wild thing would have created an aesthetic disaster.

Ghia, however, did try to tame Exner's design into a production car, twice. The first was called Asimmetrica and the other the St. Regis. Both were embarrassing and comical, when compared to the XNR.

The daring XNR slipped away. It was last seen in the pages of National Geographic in May 1969. A photo showed the XNR flying along some road in Kuwait with what would appear to be a sheik at the wheel. Virgil Exner left Chrysler Corporation in 1961.

Ghia, however, did try to tame Exner's design into a production car, twice. The first was called Asimmetrica and the other the St. Regis. Both were embarrassing and comical, when compared to the XNR. (The Auction)

One for the Road...

Lincoln Continentals

By Henry Austin Clark, Jr.

Interest in the Lincoln Continental started with your writer, when the first ones appeared on the road and at the auto shows in 1939 and 1940, but it was not until much later that we owned one.

The car was conceived by Edsel Ford, as a derivation of the Lincoln Zephyr, after a trip to Europe in 1938. There, he observed the interesting cars being built in England, France and Germany. Lincoln styling was done in the Design Department under E.T. Gregoire. A one-tenth scale model of the Continental was made by George E. Adams. The Mark I, as it was called, had only minor changes through 1942. It was updated, after the war, and continued through 1948. It has been described as "the last Classic car built in the United States."

The 1942 Lincoln Continental Mark I cabriolet sported a slightly revised grille, but no major styling changes. (Ford)

The only drawback of the Mark I was its V-12 engine, same as the Zephyr. It was under-powered and developed problems, including excessive oil consumption. Many were replaced by V-8 engines. We once acquired, for $75, a V-12 that was being converted to marine use. We let a friend have it to replace a bad one in her very fine-looking 1942 cabriolet. It solved her problem and the car lived on.

The Mark II was introduced in the fall of 1955 as a 1956 model and was continued only through 1957. We have owned two fairly good examples of this model. It was the most exclusive of Continentals and the least popular, probably because it was expensive. It had a specially-assembled Lincoln V-8 engine and was much more powerful than the regular Lincoln. It had an acceleration of 0-to-60 miles per hour in 11 seconds, which is a very fast getaway. We did not keep either car very long, but enjoyed them at the time.

The expensive Mark II Continental was released in 1956 and continued in 1957. (Ford)

Only two Lincoln Continental Mark II convertibles were built and both are different. This is the one made for Mrs. William Clay Ford. (Ford)

There was one Mark II cabriolet designed and built for Mrs. William Clay Ford. It was a very beautiful car. In the late 1970s, we attended the Arkansas Diamond Tour, organized by the Rockefeller Museum of Automobiles in Morrilton, Arkansas. This beautiful 1956 convertible was on the tour and belonged to a man from Iowa. We got a good photograph of it and later made a postcard of the car.

The first new Lincoln Continental that we bought was not a Mark model. It was a four-door sedan that was the first of a series with new and sleeker styling. It was our first-line car and we drove it over a 100,000 miles. It was as fine an automobile as we ever had in our family.

In more recent years, the Continental Mark III appeared, first with the 1969 model. We were immediately taken by storm and bought one. It is a magnificent car and performs as well as it looks. The styling is a compromise between classic and modern. It still has the simulated spare tire mount in the rear of the trunk lid and the long hood. There is an improved shell-type radiator grille. The overall design recaptured the prestige as the most desired and sought-after personal luxury car that was available. It was available with all sorts of extra options and standard equipment, including a tape player, as well as a radio. It is, of course, a two-door car, but is very comfortable in front or rear. Actually, it is the second one we have owned, the first having been used up more or less in an accident that could have been very serious, except for the rugged construction on the Continental.

The late Henry Austin Clark, Jr., a renowned automotive historian, was the proud owner of two 1969 Continental Mark III coupes. (Henry Austin Clark)

When our Mark III was laid up with mechanical problems, the New York parking lot attendants regularly asked about the health of our Mark. No other car has ever had this sort of attention. We planned to take her to a restoration shop, where the owner had two of his own.

Aside from Continentals, we have owned at least two other outstanding Lincoln models and have driven them many miles. The first was a 1953 Cosmopolitan four-door sedan, which we purchased new that year. This was a very handsome and lively car, as well as most comfortable. Of course, it was one of the lot known as the "Mexican Road Race Lincolns," which acquitted themselves better than most any other car in those most arduous events. There are days when we wish we still had it now.

Our favorite older Lincoln, and one that we had in the garage at home was the 1929 Model L sport phaeton. This car has a dual cowl and dual windshield, so the rear seat passengers are just as well protected from the weather as those in the front. It was acquired, as we have written before, at a coffee stop on the cross country tour for the March of Dimes in January 1956. We had been riding, as one of the organizers of the project, in a GM car loaned to the March of Dimes. It was driven by a March of Dimes chap who couldn't drive and wouldn't let us take the wheel. After one close escape in New Jersey, we made the coffee stop in eastern Pennsylvania and heard the owner of this car, which had joined this Pony Express type of run at the New Jersey/Pennsylvania line, say that he had put up his Lincoln for sale. Having watched the car since it joined and being in great need of wheels, a bargain was struck at the county line and we drove it on the first overnight stop ahead. The owner brought the trunk with fitted suitcase that evening, and we motored happily on to California with hardly a bit of trouble. Another year we toured it out to Pikes Peak for a Glidden Tour. I guess it is fair to say that we are hooked on Lincolns, as well as on Continentals.

The Lincoln Continental Mark III, introduced in February 1968 as a 1969 model, had the classic lines of the 1940 Mark I at left rear and 1956 Mark II at right rear. (Ford Motor Company)

One for the Road...

Ugly ducklings

By Henry Austin Clark, Jr.

We have all had favorite old cars that we thought of as beautiful, but what about the others ... those the least handsome? Let us call them the "ugly ducklings." Also let's divide them into three age periods.

The first of these would be the gas and brass era, up to the start of World War I in 1914. This is the hardest era from which to pick ugly cars, but we have owned a few and know of others.

The first and oldest is the 1899 Parisienne Victoria Combination. It had a single-cylinder air-cooled DeDion engine mounted on the front axle. The front axle swung from side to side, for steering, by using a tiller. Behind was a body that looked very much like an Atlantic City rolling deck chair. The machine was located up the Hudson in Goshen, New York. It took a number of visits to be able to buy it in 1954. Restoration of the engine and driving gear was done by Joe Tracy of Vanderbilt Cup fame (he did the fastest lap in the 1906 race in the Locomobile). Over 20 years later, it went to friend Ed Berry, who finished the restoration into a state of excellence, if not of beauty.

Next in order of age is the 1906 Success Auto Buggy, easily the most optimistically named vehicle of all time. It was strictly a horse-type buggy, although the axle did not swing and it steered with a wheel. Since it had high wheels with steel tires, we hardly ever ran the thing. We just let people look at it on the museum floor.

A strange little prewar machine was the Imp cyclecar. A 1914 model is shown. We found a 1913 version. (John Conde)

The last strange little machine in this age group would be the 1913 Imp cyclecar. We found it on Long Island, in poor shape, and never kept it for restoration. The friends we gave it to did do it up in good shape and it made the 1984 Glidden Tour at French Lick, Indiana with flying colors.

Going on to the period largely between the two World Wars, the first vehicle that comes to mind is the 1919 Sizaire & Naudin French limousine. It was obviously designed as a taxicab of a slightly later type than the famous Battle of the Marne fleet that carried allied soldiers to the front. We had some interesting experiences with this rare "frog" machine.

Easily the ugliest of the American cars of the 1920s were the sloping-hood Franklins. (Old Cars)

Easily the ugliest of the American cars of the 1920s were the sloping-hood Franklins. We owned one or more of these cars at one time or another, but never restored and used one. On the annual Franklin Trek to upstate New York, fine examples of almost all years of the Franklin can be seen. We attended in 1974 and photographed various cars. Bill Harrah always came with a load of cars, as that was one of his favorite makes.

Now we'll go to the post World War II period, on up to 25 years ago, starting with the first production of new vehicles after the end of the war. The year 1945 was not yet over when it was announced that Willys would be producing a civilian model of the famous Jeep. The dealer for the New York area was Hearn's Department Store in the Bronx and we hastened over there to place our order.

During our service in the United States Navy, we had learned to like the Jeep and we surely wanted one to take home. In the early spring of 1946, we received word that ours had arrived and we picked it up, post haste, with a box trailer. Our first other purchase was a snow plow and the next was a wrecker crane, specially down-sized for the Jeep. All these items were an unqualified success and it was only last winter that we let the Jeep go to an old friend and neighbor. He keeps an eye on the remains of our museum, which has been closed for seven years. The adventures with the Jeep were endless and would fill many column inches, but it was one machine we really loved. And as anyone can see, the Jeep was not a thing of beauty.

One of our very favorite little cars of unusual design was the 1959 Fiat "Jolly" Beach Car. It was built on the fairly common Fiat 600 chassis and was arranged with wicker seats and no doors. It was strictly for fair weather operation, such as going down to the beach at a summer resort. With the help of an old friend, we obtained one as a gift for our wife and even got a special license plate with her initials on it WHC-2.

One of our very favorite little cars of unusual design was the 1959 Fiat "Jolly" Beach Car.

There was little protection from the weather, although it did have a windshield and a canvas top. On examination, it cannot really be called ugly, but it certainly is a duckling, especially when being passed where there are puddles. We had lots of fun with this machine for many years ... probably more than she had. It was certainly ideal summer transportation in Southampton.

Undoubtedly, the most popular ugly duckling of the postwar period has been the Volkswagen Beetle. Shortly before it went out of production in Germany, the total numbers built exceeded the 15 million-plus cars that were built of the Ford Model T from 1909 to 1927. We never did own one of the Volkswagen Beetles, but we did have a pop-top camper that we used to take to the flea market in Hershey.

When we were on a vacation trip, a couple of winters ago, in Acapulco in Mexico, we saw new Beetles at Volkswagen agencies in the area. It seems that they are still making them down south of the border and selling them, too!

One for the Road...

Brass and Gas Tours

By Henry Austin Clark, Jr.

One of the most elite parts of the old car hobby is the touring on country roads with pre-war cars on organized tours. These are called brass and gas tours, brass standing for the material from which the lamps and trim are made on most pre-1916 cars and gas being the vapor used to burn in the headlights. About 1913, nickel-plated trim started to take over and the entire appearance of cars changed.

Hobby touring activities rekindle memories of the grand tours that motorists did in the pioneer days of the automobile. This scene was from an American Automobile Association "Sealed Bonnet Contest" circa 1912. (Davis B. Hillmer)

The New England Brass and Gas Tours of the Veteran Motor Car Club of America started officially with the 1966 tour out of Woodstock, Vermont, followed by two others with the same hub in 1970 and 1973. However, the first Vermont Brass and Gas activities were the Fall Foliage Meets in Brattleboro. They took place in the early 1950s, early in October. We attended a few of these and particularly remember 1955. We were persuaded to lead the March of Dimes Coast-to-Coast Relay, in January 1956, an event we will never forget. However, that is another story altogether.

The press car from a 1909 automobile tour co-sponsored by the New York Herald and the Atlanta Journal. (Davis B. Hillmer)

This is a report on the 1987 event, held from June 27 through July 3 out of Ellsworth, Maine, reviewing the highlights, as well as the parts that we found to be amusing. There were five days of touring, most starting from the Holiday Inn, with a few starting from the nearby Colonial Inn.

Our favorite touring day was the first on Monday, most of which was on Desert Island. That is the second largest island in North America, behind only Long Island. The route encompassed the entire island and we were pleased to discover that it passed the driveway to the summer residence of our youngest daughter. Needless to say, we stopped and invited our crew of seven, including our support vehicle, to lunch. A quick trip to the nearest village for supplies made this possible.

The afternoon stop was at the Seal Cove Auto Museum, showing the huge private collection of Richard Paine. We visit it each summer, to look at old favorites from the collections of James Melton, Sam Scher and many others. We were surprised to see at least three of our own old cars, including the 1907 Locomobile which we sold at auction last October. It had been at Paine's only a week and was owned by him.

Tuesday's tour was in the opposite direction, to Old Town, Maine, a spot famous for its canoe factory. There, we were given a tour of the plant. We did make the official lunch stop this day at the Knights of Columbus Hall, where we were treated well.

On Wednesday, our daughter came over from North East Harbor to make the run with us. This was a shorter day of driving and a good time was had by all. In the evening, there was a power boat cruise to the dinner location and return. We took the last of the three shifts and returned to Bar Harbor with the sunset in full glory. Many of the old cars had to light their gas lights for the trip back to Ellsworth.

Thursday's long tour went down over Deer Isle, a trip of 100 miles, including the return heading south, and a bit west, from Ellsworth. It was a delightful trip over country back roads and over the historic Deer Isle Bridge. It was long, but well worth it.

Thursday evening was the auction of old car stuff brought by the entrants, the material being taken to the auction site after the day's touring. We had thought the material was to be contributed and it was a pleasant surprise when we found that the person bringing the stuff got the money. Even after buying a couple of nice pieces of literature and bidding on three of our nine items, we came out a hundred bucks or better ahead. The auctioneer, Don Meyer, was seemingly tireless and the sale ended well after 10 pm. The settling up went on until midnight. A great but rugged day it was.

Friday was the last day of touring and it dawned with threatening weather. After three days of beautiful, cool, sunny outlook, rain was predicted. However, it never rained. Nevertheless, we took the short route, which led east from Ellsworth to another part of the Maine coast from Winter Harbor to Millbridge. At the first place, we were invited to make a stop for coffee and donuts at their Yacht Club. This was a most pleasant stop, with vintage sail boats anchored nearby. The Clubhouse itself was a vintage and beautiful building. The lunch stop was at the Red Barn Restaurant in Millbridge, after which we took the short way back to Ellsworth. Back at the Holiday Inn, we helped load our 1912 Simplex on the 48 foot box trailer. It was to ride with another Simplex and the 1912 Cadillac of the owner of the rig on the trip home.

We certainly enjoyed the 1987 Brass and Gas Tour. This one was the first time that VMCCA and Horseless Carriage Club of America have combined to sponsor a national event of both clubs. They should be encouraged to do it again.

Touring in vintage cars is great fun. This tour featured 11 Simplex four-cylinder cars that converged on Glen Cove, New York in 1984. (Henry Austin Clark, Jr.)

Unimproved roads challenged early tourists.

Cars on tour with 1917 New York plates.

Tourabouts were perfect for touring.

These people toured in 1906.

A 1914 road tour featuring (l. to r.) a Scripps-Booth, a Krit, a Moses Break cart and a Paige. (Jimmy John)

One for the Road...

Auto literature

By Henry Austin Clark, Jr.

The collecting of literature relating to early automobiles is an important part of the old car hobby and should be practiced to some extent by all collectors. At the least one should find and save items relating to one's own car or cars.

In the case of your columnist, looking for old car material started when we were very young and the first find was in the family bookcase at home. It was a hardbound book and, on the cover, it said: The Locomobile Book. On the spine was written, "The car of 1912." There were 210 pages six inches wide and eight inches tall. Altogether it was, and is, as fine an automobile catalog as we have ever seen.

About the same time, in 1929, we were given a new book of travel and adventure fiction called The Mascot Goes Across. It was about two boys who buy a 1913 Ford Model T sedan at an auction for five dollars and drive it, on a dare, to California from the Boston area. We still have this one as well.

In the 1930s, we went to the New York Auto Shows and would always gather catalogs on the then-new cars. Somehow these accumulations did not survive our moves and growing up.

After World War II, we started to collect old cars in earnest, adding to the very few we had before the war. Then we started to look for old car paper material, wherever it was to be found.

There were two old men who helped us by finding stuff that we could buy. One lived in the lower east side in New York and seldom bathed. We would meet by our car to do business outside his house. The other lived in Astoria on Long Island and drank. He would call from one of his saloons, usually at night.

One night, the drinker directed us to a second-hand magazine store on 13th Street, near Sixth Avenue, where he said we would find some Horseless Age magazines. We went there and were told that they had none of that title, but there was a large shipment of bound volumes of other motoring publications sent by a library in Chicago. Was it for sale? Not until unpacked and checked, but we were able to make an offer and take it in our station wagon, which it filled.

The next night, our friend called from the saloon and said that the light had been bad and he meant to say to go to 43rd Street. We went there and, sure enough, there were some copies of Horseless Age, the earliest of all motoring magazines (including Autocar of England.)

We have been fortunate in being able to acquire several large collections of material, which formed the backbone of our library. The first of these came from the estate of an early inventor by the name of A.E. Osborne. The deal was arranged by the late Gordon Ayer, who used to work with us. The cost was $4,000. The material filled a two-ton moving van and took hours to unload. There were books, catalogs and periodicals galore. It was a fine purchase.

Another great acquisition came almost by accident. We had been at a viewing of four vehicles to be auctioned out of a New York City carriage house on East 57th Street. There was a 1912 Pierce-Arrow limousine, a 1923 coupe-sedan of the same make and a 1938 Buick convertible, plus a large horse-drawn carriage. A hopeful bidder on the last item was wondering how to get it home to Long Island. We gave him our card and told him our large trailer would carry it.

He did not buy it, as some big money from Texas was at the auction. We did buy the 1923 Pierce, and a friend got the 1912, which we did get to haul home to Connecticut for him. The unhappy bidder kept our card. Ten years later, he called to say that he was settling the estate of his uncle, Captain John Jay Ide, and that there were a lot of early auto catalogs and the like. Would we be interested?

Of course we were interested. We met him at the warehouse. We filled the station wagon and gave him a ride home with the small lot of items he wanted. A week later, he called again to say there was another warehouse and did we have anything larger than the station wagon? This time we used our three-quarter-ton stake truck and we came away loaded. Again, the price was a ride home to Long Island, hardly out of our way.

Captain Ide was a United States Naval Reserve captain who was on active duty between the wars and who reported on the buildup of Nazi air power. He was a most important agent, taking many trips to Europe on this job, where he used to visit the salons and collect European catalogs of fine cars and custom coachwork. His favorite cars were Hispano-Suizas and be wrote articles on coachwork for American magazines.

We have been fortunate in being able to acquire several fine collections of early photographs, mostly with the help of friends. Two of these were in good organized condition and we were able to keep them in that form.

We were able to buy the Albert Mecham Collection, complete with the negatives. We could order prints only of the other collection, photos by Ed Waterman. We ordered all he had and he would send a batch every week or so. When he died, we were unable to make contact to get the negatives. However, we do have a fine set of prints, almost all of racing in America, which he had taken when he was quite young. Another great lot of photos came from the Locomobile factory, in Bridgeport, Connecticut, and these include negatives up to 8 x 10 inches in size.

Other lots of literature and photos are either too small or contain too many items to go into, but they all add up to a large total. We have been able to help many collectors with information on their own cars and various authors with illustrations for their books and articles. It was a source of great satisfaction to be able to do so.

Now our museum in Southampton, New York is permanently closed. We have given the library to the Henry Ford Museum, but we have lifetime use of the material.

The collecting of all kinds of literature related to early automobiles is an important part of the old car hobby.

One for the Road...

Old fire engines

By Henry Austin Clark, Jr.

Our interest in fire engines started many years ago. One of our earliest memories is of watching the 1913 American-LaFrance hook and ladder, belonging to the Southampton Fire Department, get stuck in a private hedge. The truck was trying to get into a narrow driveway, leading to a barn in the north edge of the village.

This was in the late 1920s, when the truck still had solid, dual rear tires. These were later changed to large pneumatics, with different wheels, of course. Much later we owned this machine for over 30 years. The Southampton Fire Department gave it to our museum on our opening day, August 27, 1948 and we returned it to them after we closed.

The first fire engine that we owned was our 1920 Ford-LaFrance, which we bought in Huntington, Long Island in 1940. The Ford-LaFrance was in running condition at the time. Unfortunately, we tried to tow it to the World's Fair Meet that same year and learned, the hard way, that you do not tow a Model T (in this case a TT).

The rear end broke up after about 10 miles and had to be replaced. We put in a Ruxtell axle, which is probably still there. It gave the advantage of two speed ratios. This machine we restored after the museum opened, giving it the livery of our own "Sandy Hollow Fire Department."

Bill Pritchard ran a small paint shop in the village and he was a consummate artist with gold leaf and decorations. He did all of our engines, making each one a thing of beauty. His first big job was the 1913 hook and ladder, which was kept in Southampton livery. All the others became Sandy Hollow Fire Department livery. That was a local name for the neighborhood of the museum. It was also called the old horse burying ground, but that would not fit on the hood of a fire engine.

The chief's car, our 1915 Ford runabout, was actually the first old car in our collection, having been found in Pittsfield, Massachusetts, in the spring of 1940, while I was a freshman at Harvard. The original touring body was poor and incomplete, so we were happy to locate a much better runabout body to replace it. It was also much more suitable for a chief's car.

We still recall driving it from the point of purchase, over the road, to Cambridge. We were followed by a young woman from Smith, Massachusetts driving in our 1935 Ford everyday car. We had managed to get the license plates on a Saturday morning in Albany, based on an affidavit made on the back of an envelope. Things were more relaxed then.

This machine has joined the hook and ladder in the antique division of Southampton's fire department and has been redone in their livery. As a member of that fine group, we are still allowed to drive "Emaline," as we have always called her.

The most popular engine in our Sandy Hollow Fire Department was the 1911 American-LaFrance hose truck. It had benches on each side in the rear to carry a number of passengers. It had little or no fire fighting equipment when we bought it in New England, many years ago, after the museum was open. We used it mostly to carry visiting kids around the museum grounds and through the "Wilderness Road" down in the back of our grounds. It was also very popular for parades, in particular the July 4 event in Southampton.

My favorite load was a Dixieland band called the "South Hampton Dixie, Racing and Clambake Society." We would have a concert at the museum right after the parade and the Coke machine would offer free beer. In the end, this great machine went to England and we do not know how it is today.

The most impressive and elegant piece we ever owned was the 1911 Seagrave six-cylinder, 80 horsepower chemical hose truck. Originally it was part of the fire department of Bucyrus, Ohio and we acquired it by mail from a gentleman there. He sent professional photographs that showed it to be in fine original condition. The purchase price, in the spring of 1950, was $350. That was complete with lamps and accessories. It cost more than that for freight.

The seller arranged to have it loaded into an end-loading box car. The chocking was wiped out during the trip and the rear step was crushed against the end of the car. This was due, we figured, to "humping" of the freight car. It had to be unloaded in Westhampton, the nearest spot where an end-loading car could be unloaded. We were able to start the engine and drive it eastward to Southampton. We ran out of gas part way, as we only put in five gallons. In all, it was quite an adventure.

A restoration was done by Bill Pritchard, who did his all-time best job in putting on the gold leaf and striping, making it into Sandy Hollow livery. We were lucky to find a firm that could supply and mount new solid tires all around, as the originals were completely shot. My main regret is that we did not get to use this great machine nearly as much as it deserved. Of course, one needed King Kong to crank it or it had to be towed. The LaFrance's engine started much easier.

During the early 1950s we were developing a set of paintings of our vehicles to be made into color prints, with Leslie Saalburg doing the artwork. He used the Seagrave, making it the property of Engine 16 of the New York Fire Department, better known as F.D.N.Y. We still have a supply of the prints.

In 1963, we sold the Seagrave to Bill Harrah. He had it for years in his collection, retaining our livery. It is now the property of Mike Silvera of South Lake Tahoe, California. We were delighted to see it, in full color, on the cover of a 1987 copy of Engine! Engine! That is the name of the magazine of the Society for the Preservation and Appreciation of Antique Motorized Fire Apparatus in America (SPAAMFAA). The address is 7249 Buckley Road, Syracuse, New York 13212.

All that is now left of the Sandy Hollow Fire Department are the badges of the chief and of the approximately 75 captains, all good friends of ours. One told us that it still works to avoid speeding tickets!

One for the Road...

Car model names

By Henry Austin Clark, Jr.

These days there are more and more strange names inscribed on modern automobiles to indicate their models. Some of these are impressive, some are amusing, but many are past understanding.

Though few early cars had model names, this 1904 Peerless "Green Dragon" was an exception. (Henry Austin Clark, Jr.)

In the very early days, only a few makes used interesting names for their models instead of letters, numbers or a combination thereof. Here are a few examples: In 1904 Knox had a Lenox and a Tudor designation for their one- and two-cylinder models, respectively. Lenox was a pleasant town in Massachusetts, but the Tudor designation had no relation to its body style.

In 1907, Rolls-Royce introduced what was to become its most famous model, the Silver Ghost. The Phantom followed in the 1920s and 1930s and, then, other mysterious figures such as the Silver Wraith.

The 1909 Rolls-Royce "Silver Ghost" Roi des Belges touring car by Barker. (Henry Austin Clark, Jr.)

Phantom was another famous Rolls-Royce name. This is a 1929 Phantom I "Derby" phaeton by Brewster. (Henry Austin Clark, Jr.)

In 1909 and 1910, Lozier had a Briarcliff model named after a pleasant village up the Hudson River and, in 1911, they added the Lakewood. It was named after a posh New Jersey resort.

In 1910 one of the pioneer firms, Apperson, started calling their touring model a Jack Rabbit, but about the only other pre-World War I maker to use names for models was American, who called their underslung five-passenger touring the Traveler and the seven-passenger the Tourist. In the years between the wars, the use of names for car models increased slowly, but we will pass over the details at this time for reasons of brevity.

The model names of the last few years can be divided into almost 10 classifications. As we drive around almost anywhere in the United States, we can see numerous examples. Of course there are still some makes that use only letters and numbers.

Let us take people as the first group. Among the adventurous are the Plymouth Voyager, Chevrolet Cavalier and Dodge Wayfarer. Occupations include the Ferrari Boxer, Ford Escort and the Isuzu Trooper, as well as the Dodge Diplomat. Indians are people, too, and Jeep has its Cherokee and Commanche as examples.

After people, come animals. Of these, the most popular are the horses. A favorite is the well known Ford Mustang. They also have promoted the Bronco for off-the-road applications. The Pinto seems to have expired, as has the AMC Pacer. Your writer has a fondness for the last, after attending its introduction at Palm Springs some years ago. It was the greatest car introduction party we have ever attended.

No less exciting are the wild animals. Mercury seems to have the majority with its Cougar, Lynx and Sable, but the Dodge Ram is almost as wild. Wild birds are another variety. There are the Buick Skylark and the Pontiac Firebird, plus of course the best of all, the Ford Thunderbird. Only the first of these is non-fictional.

Races and race tracks are very popular name sources. Pontiac seems to have the lead with Grand Prix, Grand Am and, of course, Le Mans. There is less confusion about the race circuits with the Dodge Daytona, Jaguar Sebring and Porsche Targa. We may have missed others, but for sure no car has been named after the Bridgehampton Race Circuit.

Another favorite category has been resorts and fancy places, starting with Knox and Lozier. Today's entries include the Chevrolet Malibu, Mercury Capri and Cadillac's Seville and Eldorado, plus of course the Rolls-Royce Corniche. That last is for a road on the Riviera, near Monte Carlo, both of which names have been used.

City streets have been used, as with Buick's Park Avenue and Chrysler's Fifth Avenue, but it is likely that, after October 1988, no car will be called a "Wall Street." Chrysler also named a car for our least favorite summer resort, Newport, and they named one of their great cars, the Imperial of the late 1960s, after our most favorite such place, Southampton. We had one of these and loved it.

Several marques have been named after horses, with the Ford Mustang the most famous. This is a 1968 Shelby GT500KR version. (Henry Austin Clark, Jr.)

Cars named after birds include the Sky Hawk, Skylark, Falcon, Blue Goose and the Thunderbird, of which a 1959 model is depicted. (Henry Austin Clark, Jr.)

Many classic Cadillacs, like this 1933 Town Car, carried the name Fleetwood after the Pennsylvania home of Fleetwood Body Company. (Henry Austin Clark, Jr.)

In the Classic car era, the names of custom body builders were regularly included in the complete name of a particular car, usually at the end after "by," such as with our 1929 Lincoln sport phaeton by Locke. Today there are at least three custom builders, each of which has been absorbed by car makers who now used their names as model names. These included Cadillac with Fleetwood, whose plant was in the Pennsylvania town of that name, Chrysler with LeBaron and most recently Jaguar with Vanden Plas, which had its main plant in Belgium and another in England. Also Volkswagen has acquired Ghia, which built its Karmann Ghia in Italy. This was the fancy companion to the little Beetle we know so well.

Anyone who looks at cars today can see more than a dozen model names which mean a variety of things that have no relation to cars, going from weather conditions to emotions, including some that have no meaning at all. Perhaps this is better than naming a car after a traffic ticket, as with the Chevrolet Citation.

Probably the most prominent model name, along with the Mustang, is the Corvette. This Chevrolet product started out to be in 1953 a manufactured version of a Motorama Dream Car. It made an immediate hit and has been so ever since. We owned a 1963 split-window coupe and loved it dearly. It had to be disposed of because of the need to keep a driver's license. We even received a summons for a moving violation from a meter maid on a scooter. Just to be seen in the car made one a moving target for the law. The Corvette was more than a model, it was a thing unto itself and all models are today prized by many collectors.

Probably the best known name of all time among American models is the Chevrolet Corvette. This is a third-year 1955 model. (Henry Austin Clark, Jr.)

Cars we had fun with

By Henry Austin Clark, Jr.

This column is about the cars that we found were the most fun to drive, the ones with which we had the most enjoyable experiences. They are not the oldest, the fastest, the rarest or the most desirable, just the most fun.

Taking them in order of date, the first would have to be our 1915 Ford Model T runabout. We made this into the chief's car for the Sandy Hollow Fire Department at the Long Island Auto Museum, now closed for almost eight years. We bought this machine in the spring of 1937 as a college freshman in Cambridge, Massachusetts.

The car was in Pittsfield, at the other end of the state. Somehow, over one weekend, we were able to get it running, get it registered over the border in Albany, and drive it back to college. The original touring body was poor, it lacked cushions and top, so we found a good runabout body with all the missing parts and converted it.

We used it in club events and for general early motoring until World War II. After the war and when the auto museum was opened in 1948, we used it a lot. With its Sandy Hollow livery, it was a popular item in July 4th parades in Southampton. One always has a fond feeling for one's first old car.

Another prewar fun car was our 1934 Austin London taxicab, which always turned heads whenever it appeared on the street. We got it in 1953 and had it restored by Gus Reuter in 1955. This was well before London cabs became a fad in New York City. We kept it ready to go when we had the Carnival of Cars, in 1954, on Times Square. We saved a spot in our car elevator to park it for easy accessibility. It is amazing how many people would try to hail it for a ride. One chap asked to try the wheel when we had it at the Bridgehampton Road Races in 1961. Since his name was Sterling Moss, we figured he was competent in an Austin, so we let him.

Passing World War II, the "Big One" as Archie Bunker called it, our thoughts ran to sports cars. One of the first popular vehicles of that type to be imported here from England was the MG Type TC. We acquired a 1949 MG Type TC, which still sits in our garage, although it belongs to our younger daughter. The body style is called Midget, but it holds two full-sized people in fine comfort. Performance is adequate, with the small four-cylinder engine, but the road handling is the high point of MG.

In the early days of Bridgehampton, dozens of MGs were raced, but now they are considered vintage sports cars. We have driven ours in some special events, but most of its use has been just for fun. It is right-hand drive, as a proper British machine should be, and still stands ready to go, either for a long ride or a trip down to the neighborhood pub.

In 1953, we acquired an Austin-Healey model 100-4 sports roadster, which was a much greater performer than the MG. It was a streamlined beauty. I bought it for my wife. She enjoyed it for years, until we went to the 1970 New York Show and saw our first 1971 Datsun

240Z. They were in immediate demand and advertised for $5,995 new in the New York Times ($3,995 used). Thanks to a good friend who sold cars part-time, in an agency in Brooklyn, we were able to get one for our daughter. It was a beautiful, light yellow sports coupe. It would catch the eye of any traffic cop. We did manage to get our hands on it for some drives of great pleasure.

Probably our favorite fun car of all time was the 1959 Fiat "Jolly" Beach Car. This was definitely a summer car for good weather only. It had wicker seats for four and a white cloth top with a three-inch-high fringe all around. Luggage went under the hood and the little four-cylinder engine was in the back, along with the other things such as transmission and differential. The Jolly is not shown in the regular Fiat 600 catalog folder, although the other body styles (including the convertible with an opening roof and the Multipla, which can carry six people or be made into a bed for two) are shown in detail.

In 1959, when we had purchased the Jolly, the state of New York introduced the practice of allowing people with clean driving records to reserve special license plates with their initials. We tried to get one with WHC, as I wanted to give the Jolly to my wife, Wally, as a 15th wedding anniversary present. Much to our delight, the Commissioner of Motor Vehicles let us have WHC-2 for the Jolly. We were quick to transfer the registration and get the special plates.

We no longer have the Jolly or the special plates. We do know that the Jolly has gone to a good friend with a winter home in Florida. There, it fits in perfectly. We cannot recall how we lost plate number WHC-2.

We have written in the past about our 1957 Fiat 600 "Eden Roc" Yacht Tender, built on the same chassis. It was bought off the floor of the Turin or Paris Automobile Show by Henry Ford II, who used it in Southampton for a season or two. When he turned it in on another vehicle, we were able to trace it and get it ourselves. We had lots of fun with that one, too, probably more than Henry the Deuce did.

Probably our favorite fun car of all time was the 1959 Fiat "Jolly" Beach Car. This was definitely a summer car for good weather only. It had wicker seats for four and a white cloth top with a three-inch-high fringe all around.

The rise and fall of automotive museums

By Henry Austin Clark, Jr.

The other day we received a postcard from Missouri asking about the Long Island Auto Museum. We answered with an old postcard of the building, stating that it had closed on September 11 1980, after nearly a third of a century of operation. We then started to wonder about other auto museums and how long they lasted.

The first one we visited was the Museum of Antique Autos in Princeton, Massachusetts, just north of Worcester. This was when I was a student at Harvard. The occasion was an early Veteran Motor Car Club of America run to there, from the Boston area. This may have been the very first auto museum that was not part of a more general museum, such as the automobile collection at the Smithsonian Institution in Washington.

The best known of the early museums was that of James Melton, the nationally known opera singer. He opened it on Route 7 in Norwalk, Connecticut in 1948. (That was the same year we opened our museum.) Several years later, he moved it to Hypoluxo, Florida, south of Palm Beach.

Top left: The Swigart Museum is located in Huntingdon, Pennsylvania. Top right: A 1916 Scripps Booth from the Swigart Museum. Bottom left: A rare 1908 Studebaker electric truck from Bill Swigart's collection. Bottom right: This car in the Swigart Museum is a 1920 Carroll.

Another private collection that was opened to the public was the collection of William E. Swigart of Huntingdon, Pennsylvania. After his death in 1949, his son, Bill Jr., erected a new building in which to display the cars as an adjunct to an insurance business. That opened in 1957.

The former Briggs Cunningham Automotive Museum in Costa Mesa, California was in the news a few years back. Briggs, who lived earlier in Florida and Connecticut, not only collected cars with an emphasis on racing, but also manufactured racing cars under his own name. He had more than 80 cars when he moved to California in 1962. In 1987, he sold his collection to the son of an old friend and racing companion, Miles Collier Jr. The collection was moved to Naples, Florida.

The Cunningham collection, added to that of Miles Collier, is housed in a fine new building. Not all of the cars will be there, but many important pieces will be on display. The Cunningham Bugatti Royale has been reported as sold. Our son visited the Collier Museum before the official opening and was shown around by Mr. Collier. He spent lots of time with him, to his great pleasure.

A major collection in the Midwest was started by the Thompson Products Company at their factory in downtown Cleveland, Ohio. Frederick C. Crawford was president of the company, which is now known as TRW, Incorporated. He arranged to have the collection given to the Western Reserve Historical Society and was instrumental in organizing a fund-raising campaign to provide a beautiful new building to house the automobiles.

We were involved in this operation since the gift of the collection about 1959 and we were invited, by Fred Crawford, to help in its organization. We have photographed many of the automobiles and have had postcards made for sale there. With a strong parent organization and much local support, the future of the Frederick Crawford Auto-Aviation Museum seems to be safe, with a long and happy future.

There are a number of other museums with collections of note, which have special connections or locations that make them worthy of attention. Time and space limitations do not permit going into detail on them, but let us mention a few that come to mind.

The Antique Auto Museum of Massachusetts, at Larz Anderson Park in Brookline, had a long history of involvement with the Veteran Motor Car Club of America. This is the club with which we have been most intimately involved, even being its president at one time.

The Indianapolis Motor Speedway Museum is one we have visited and which is of great interest. Naturally, its thrust is towards the Indianapolis 500 and it does a fine job covering that specialty. Our racing interest was mostly related to sports cars and Bridgehampton, but it is good to see how the sport is operated properly.

As we all know, the largest collection of automobiles in this country, and probably in the world, was gathered together by the late William F. Harrah, and was on display at Harrah's Automobile Collection in Reno, Nevada. We visited it several times, sold cars

In Las Vegas, the place for car collectors to visit is the Imperial Palace Auto Collection at the Imperial Palace Hotel and Casino. (John Gunnell)

The Museum of Automobiles is in Petit Jean, Arkansas. President Bill Clinton keeps his Mustang there.

to Bill Harrah and admired his undertaking greatly. After his death, the casino was sold to Holiday Inns and they started to liquidate some of the collection.

The William F. Harrah Foundation has moved some of the great cars from the collection to a new museum alongside the Truckee River in downtown Reno. They are open as the National Automobile Museum and have done a great job showcasing the vehicles in street scenes and theme rooms. We wish them every success in carrying on the name of the world's greatest collector of old cars.

The William F. Harrah Foundation moved many great cars to a new museum in downtown Reno. They are open as the National Automobile Museum and have done a great job showcasing the vehicles in street scenes and theme rooms. (John Gunnell)

Several years back, the Behring Museum opened in Danville, California, in the hills east of San Francisco Bay. When we were at Pebble Beach, we stayed over an extra day to get an early look at what has to be the most striking auto museum building ever created. The 70,000 square-foot granite, steel and glass museum opened to the public on September 6, 1988 with what they described as a "$100 million collection of rare Classic automobiles." The collection features cars from 1897 to 1987 and leans towards the exotic and custom creations. We were happy to see a couple of old friends among the cars, including an 1898 Leon Bollee Tri-car and our old 1933 Pierce Silver Arrow ... one of the six built.

We acquired the Silver Arrow from the private collection of D. Cameron Peck in Chicago, Illinois. He was one of the great early collectors with many extraordinary cars. The Behring Museum is situated in a development covering 7,500 acres in the rolling hills, much of which is already completed.

One of the pleasures left to us after the closing of our Long Island Auto Museum eight years ago was meeting someone who recalls, with pleasure, the day that he visited our quonset hut building, in Southampton, on eastern Long Island and who, consequently, became interested in old cars. That is what happened this very morning, at a local meet of the Horseless Carriage Club of America, on a beach here on Long Island. It was a good event, too, with many beautiful cars. But meeting this gentleman made it a perfect day.

One for the Road extra...

Cars are stars at the National Automobile Museum

By the Old Cars staff

They were discovered by Hollywood and starred in numerous movies. More than props, automobiles drove into the celebrity spotlight and became stars in their own right. In Reno, Nevada, a glimpse of these stars and cars owned by celebrities is as easy as a stroll through the National Automobile Museum (NAM).

Red Skelton and Orson Wells shared movies with the uncomfortable 1890 Philion. This vehicle, one of the oldest existing American-built automobiles, was featured in "Excuse My Dust" with Skelton and in "The Magnificent Ambersons" with Wells.

"Not many cars can compete with the awkward ride of a Philion," said NAM executive director Jackie Frady. "The ride was rough, since its metal wheels do not have rubber tires and the steam boiler, which is placed between the front and back seats, insured a hot ride."

Even at the auto's full speed, a breeze would not provide respite from the warmth. Its top speed was eight miles per hour, but designer Achille Philion, who created the vehicle while on the circus circuit in 1890, never drove the Philion for any length of time. It was merely incorporated into his act.

In 1923, Walter Chrysler took control of the prosperous Maxwell firm and merged "the Good Maxwell" into his own line. The 1925 Maxwell was the last known by that name. It was succeeded by a four-cylinder Chrysler and it ultimately became the Plymouth line, in 1928. Despite its disappearance, the Maxwell became a household word through frequent mentions on Jack Benny's radio programs during the 1930s and 1940s. Benny also used this car for his casino stage shows in the 1960s.

Al Jolson's 1933 Cadillac all-weather phaeton is another car exhibited at the National Automobile Museum. This $8,000 Classic featured a V-16 engine. In 1933, production of this engine was limited to 400 custom-built cars available on special order only. Jolson's all-weather phaeton, number 56 in production, is painted black. It has a Fleetwood custom body and six wire wheels, including two spares mounted in fender well carriers and decorated with metal tire covers.

The black, sleek and sinister 1938 Phantom Corsair starred as the Flying Wombat in the 1938 film "The Young in Heart" starring Douglas Fairbanks, Jr. This prototype was built at a cost of $24,000 and sported an aerodynamic design, front-wheel-drive and a Cord Lycoming V-8 engine.

Like many celebrities, this automobile shouts eccentricity. It has no appendages, no fenders or running boards and door handles are non-existent. Seating up to six passengers, this roomy vehicle gave new meaning to a joy ride. It could accelerate to speeds of 115 miles per hour. Originally, designer H.J. Heinz and Maurice Swartz planned to mass produce this model for a retail price of $12,500. Unfortunately, Heinz passed away and so did the chance of the Phantom Corsair's production.

The 1941 Chrysler Newport is a rare experimental car with an unusual dual-cowl phaeton body. Its original owners were Dan Topping, former owner of the New York Yankees, and his wife Lana Turner, the actress. The car features an all-aluminum body, concealed headlamps, folding windshield and hide-away top. Topping further customized the car by replacing the Chrysler engine and transmission with those from a Cadillac. He also personalized it by having his name cast into the cylinder heads and hubcaps and his initials placed on the grill. The Newports were the last dual cowl phaetons built by LeBaron and, of the original six produced, only four are known to exist.

While the National Automobile Museum's 1948 Tucker missed its chance to star in the movie "Tucker," the rare vehicle (number 32 of 51 produced) exudes a presence worthy of any celebrity. The car illustrates the futuristic thinking of Preston Tucker with its rear engine, automatic transmission, padded dash, pop out windshield and armored passenger compartments.

"Rust" Heinz, of the H.J. Heinz "57 Varieties" family, designed this streamlined Phantom Corsair based on a Cord. (NAM)

Lana Turner's husband, H.J. Topping, owned the New York Yankees and this 1941 Chrysler Newport parade phaeton, one of six built. (NAM)

The controversial story surrounding the Tucker and its manufacturer were immortalized in a movie by the same name. In the late 1940s, Tucker was involved in a costly court battle with the Securities and Exchange Commission, in which he was charged with fraud and regulation violations. Although Tucker was vindicated, his money, cars and plant were gone. His factory and everything in it was auctioned off, in 1950, for 18 cents on the dollar.

The Tucker was noted for its innovative design, but too few were produced to prove its performance. Some rare units in private collections, however, are reportedly running well 40 years later.

James Dean's cool hot rod in "Rebel Without a Cause" was a 1949 Mercury. It contributed to Dean's image of reckless abandon in this 1955 classic motion picture. Slightly customized for the movie, the "Merc" had its hood nosed and trunk decked.

In spite of these few alterations, the car retained its original flair, setting lower to the ground, wider and longer than previous Mercurys. While the 1949 Merc is seen as a hip hot rod, the designers extolled its benefits as the perfect business or family vehicle. "It has a smartly-styled body that turns glances into gazes. The wide, comfortable seats hold six king-size passengers ... with plenty of room for anyone to snooze in the rear seat," the advertisements touted.

Television audiences became acquainted with the model, in 1949, when Mercury sponsored the Ed Sullivan variety show "Toast of the Town." The 1949 Mercury marked a significant change in the line. With a $1,978 price tag, the car was targeted at the medium-priced market and more than 301,000 were produced. It was one of the first cars to use the new, low-pressure, super balloon tires.

"Few cars have developed such a 'cult' following," Frady said. "It is one of the most famous movie cars in history." One reason for its notoriety was James Dean's untimely death, in a car accident, one month prior to the release of "Rebel Without a Cause."

Actor James Dean drove this 1949 Mercury in the 1955 movie "Rebel Without a Cause." It has become one of the most famous movie cars in history. It's one of 200 cars on exhibit at the William F. Harrah Foundation's National Automobile Museum. (NAM)

Cars, like this Studebaker Hawk GT, are exhibited in street scenes that capture the flavor of life in different eras. (John Gunnell)

John Wayne's 1953 Corvette is also in the Reno collection. A small, fast naval vessel, Corvette seemed an appropriate name as well for Chevrolet's new sports car. Chevrolet built the first Corvette as a "dream car" to display at the General Motors' Motorama, in New York City, in January 1953. The car created such tremendous interest that Chevrolet pushed ahead and put the car into production that June. Approximately 300 "Vettes" were produced in 1953, at a $3,523 sticker price. That year, John Wayne purchased the 51st Corvette built. Having a difficult time fitting his tall frame into the Corvette, Wayne later gave it to his friend, Ward Bond.

The National Automobile Museum's 1961 Ghia hardtop model, L6.4, was originally purchased by Frank Sinatra and was the first of its type sold in the United States. Twenty-six Ghias were produced and sold for about $15,000 each. The Ghia was the "in car" of its day. In fact, a Rolls-Royce was the status symbol for those who could not acquire a Ghia. This handsome car utilized the superb styling skills of Chrysler's Virgil Exner to keep with the original Dual-Ghia front theme.

However, it was mated to an especially sleek coupe body, capped with a semi-fastback roof and large glass areas.

The Cadillac Eldorado was as much of an Elvis Presley trademark as his "shake, rattle and roll" gyrations and his skin-tight costumes. The 1973 Cadillac custom Eldorado Coupe was a 38th birthday gift to Elvis from his father, Vernon Presley. Elvis drove the car until June, 1973. Then, he gave it, as a gift, to his karate instructor. Selling for $10,002 with its white exterior and white interior, the Cadillac weighs 4,897 pounds. It has an overhead valve V-8 engine with 235 horsepower.

A 1962 Lincoln Continental convertible that was part of the White House fleet assigned to John F. Kennedy is among the cars at the National Automobile Museum. (John Gunnell)

Ab Jenkins' 1937 Cord 812 Beverly Sedan is another of the personality cars that Bill Harrah collected, which are now at the National Automobile Museum in Reno, Nevada. (John Gunnell)

In addition to these cars, visitors to the National Automobile Museum can admire former autos of the rich and famous. Other cars on display include: 1912 Baker owned by Andy Griffith; a 1922 Dodge owned by Mrs. Jean MacArthur (General MacArthur's wife); Mary Pickford's 1928 Ford; Sammy Davis, Jr.'s 1935 Duesenberg (Replica); John F. Kennedy's 1962 Lincoln Continental; the Smothers Brother's 1965 Lotus Ford; Elliot Gould's 1948 Lincoln Continental Coupe; and Florence Henderson's 1966 Oldsmobile Toronado.

The National Automobile Museum, located on the corner of Mill and Lake streets in downtown Reno, is within easy walking distance from hotels and casinos. The museum covers more than 100,000 square feet. It features a theater presentation, four period street scenes, the acousti-guide tour system, specialty shops and the Wheels Roadhouse Cafe.

It is open daily from 9:30 am to 5:30 pm, except Thanksgiving and Christmas days. Ample parking is available at the east entrance of the complex. For more information call (702) 333-9300.

Race driver Ray Crawford was the "piloto" of this 1954 Lincoln when it ran in the Mexican Road Races 40 years ago. (John Gunnell)

Dr. Nathan Ostich went 359.7 miles per hour with his 1961 Flying Caduceus at the Bonneville Salt Flats in Utah. (John Gunnell)

Futurist Buckminster Fuller created the Dymaxion in 1934. It's another of the famous cars in the collection. (John Gunnell)

1911 Franklin Averell Special Speed Car built for S. G. Averell to use in Puerto Rico. (John Gunnell)

One for the Road...

Vanderbilt Cup Races

By Henry Austin Clark, Jr.

We have had an interest in the early Vanderbilt Cup Races, since childhood, for a number of reasons. For one thing, our father had attended at least one race in person, probably in 1908. He recalled the Long Island Motor Parkway, which became the main part of the course that year.

Living on Long Island, close to the location of the races from 1904 through 1910, is a second reason to be interested.

Another, and even more compelling, reason is that we had a chance to get to know more than one of the original drivers. The one we knew best was Joseph Tracy, who did the fastest lap in 1906, although he did not win. Next was George H. Robertson, who won in 1908 and whose son we still see regularly.

In 1904, 1905 and 1906, the races were run on the public roads of this area, although not the same each year. After much public outcry over the commotions of 1906, Nassau County closed the roads to racing. At that time William K. Vanderbilt Jr., the power behind the races, raised money to begin work on the Long Island Motor Parkway. However, construction was not completed in time for a 1907 race.

The Motor Parkway was sufficiently completed for it to be used as the main part of the course for the 1908 race, with the return part on public roads. This was enough to allow permission of the authorities to run the 1908 Vanderbilt Cup Race. The race was run on October 23, 1908. The 80th anniversary of the event was celebrated on Sunday, October 24, 1988, by the Long Island Old Car Club Chapter of the New York York Region of the Veteran Motor Car Club of America (VMCCA).

The 1909 and 1910 races were also run on the course that included the Long Island Motor Parkway, but the cars were restricted to production models with engines from 301 cubic inches to 600 cubic inches of displacement, taking away its international status. The great days were over.

The 1911 race was held in Savannah, Georgia and the 1912 in Milwaukee, Wisconsin, where local enthusiasm was not a disappointment. The race then went to California, where the last three races were held in 1914, 1915 and 1916. We have spent less time researching these, as our main interest lies in the Long Island contests.

Over the years, we have searched for literature about the Vanderbilts and have had a degree of success. Probably the scarcest of all items are the original programs, which were issued at the races themselves. We have managed to find a few of these, but not all. Of course, they only give information known before the start of each race and nothing on the results.

Most helpful, of course, are the written reports in the various motoring periodicals such as The Automobile, MoTor, Horseless Age and the like. We have good runs of all of these, and a few others which also have some coverage. Of less use, but of interest to read, are two volumes entitled Log Of My Motor. One covers 1899 to 1908 and the other covers 1908 to 1911. Both were done by William K. Vanderbilt, Jr. They cover his extensive trips around Europe in his passenger cars, but make no mention of the races bearing his name.

Probably the best book on the races is Peter Helck's work The Checkered Flag. It was published in 1961, but went out of print and is nearly impossible to find, except in libraries. It covers everything from the Gordon Bennett Race of 1903 through the Vanderbilts, plus the Grand Prix races of 1916. If you ever find one for sale, grab it. If you can look at one of a friend, do so at length. Also, Peter Helck's book Great Auto Races, published in 1975, is worth having.

Most of our efforts at collecting Vanderbilt Cup Race matter relates to photographs of the races, of which we have been rather fortunate in finding enough to make up an album of copies for each race. Most of these photos have appeared in small lots, mostly borrowed from friends. We have made copy negatives in pairs, one for the owner of the photo and one for our collection. Peter Helck had the largest collection we were able to borrow, but there were a few others as well.

The 1908 Vanderbilt Cup Race from a painting by Peter Helck. George Robertson, on Locomobile number 16, leads H.J. Kilpatrick, on the Hotchkiss, around a turn on the 23.46 mile course, part of which was the new Long Island Motor Parkway. Robertson's win was the first by any American car and driver in any international race. (Painting from the collection of Lew Gotthainer as photographed by Henry Austin Clark, Jr.)

Of course, we have bought Vanderbilt Cup Race photos where we could find them for sale, but not often. Over the years we have been able to purchase several large collections of photos of early automobiles, some of which included Vanderbilt Cup Race material. In one case, the photographer, long retired, would not sell his negatives, but would make prints. He did the entire lot for us, delivering a dozen or so, at a time, over several years. Later on, he did sell the negatives (or his estate did), but we missed out on purchasing them. However, we have all of his prints, some of which are of the races.

In 1936 and 1937, there were two Vanderbilt Cup Revivals at Roosevelt Raceway, a course built on the site of the 1908-1910 races. We attended one of these, probably in 1937. George Robertson was the manager of that operation. He did pace laps in the famous Locomobile, called "Old 16," on these occasions. Later, in 1941, Peter Helck was able to buy the racer from Mr. Sessions, who had made castings for Locomobile and had saved the car from its retirement. Now that Peter is gone, his son Jerry has the car and had it at the 80th anniversary gathering.

Undoubtedly, the most interesting part of our research would be the interviews which we had with those who lived and were involved in part of that Vanderbilt Cup Races era, such as Peter Helck.

The one whom we knew best and were able to spend the most time with was Joe Tracy. Each summer, he would come out to Southampton and spend a couple of months with us, at our auto museum. We would get him a room in Bridgehampton, in an old boarding house that he liked, and he would devote himself to turn-of-the-century mechanical restoration projects on very early vehicles or engines; the same sort of work he did at his winter quarters in Astoria, New York. This gave us lots of time to get together and talk Vanderbilt Cup Races.

Next came George Robertson. He ran all the early races, but is best known for his win with the first American car in 1908. We did not know him as well, but used to see him whenever possible. Now we see his son, Crawford, who has made his father's material available to us for copying. Joe had given us lots of his photos and the like and never forgot doing the fastest lap in 1906.

Sagas of the Old West...

Imperial Palace
Auto Collection

By Bruce Fagan

The third time's the charm. You've probably heard that old saw as often as I have. I must say that I have found a certain relevance to it.

On my initial visit to the Imperial Palace Auto Collection, during the first National Automotive Journalists Association (NAJA) conference in 1984, I wasn't really too impressed by it. Sure, they had some nice cars, but so what? I, like most of you, am quite used to seeing nice cars.

I was more upset by some misidentification I found as to car dating and owners: A 1932 Chrysler identified as a 1931, plus an error as to who Tommy Manville was (and I used to see him drive around Westchester, New York before and after the war). There was also an error related to Mrs. Charles Howard and her 1932 Buick limousine.

Mrs. Howard's initials on the car read "AHZ." I'm quite possibly the only person who saw that and knew that those initials stood for "Anita Zabala Howard." Zabala was her maiden name. I knew her parents. In fact, we rented their home on Rodeo Drive, in Beverly Hills, in 1934-1935. Anita's older sister married Charles Howard's son. Of course, I called these errors to the attention of those in charge. As of December, 1986 they still existed.

My second visit, during the second conference in 1985, still left me unimpressed. I did appreciate that the cars on display ran the gamut from early antiques to more or less contemporary cars. Also, there were some commercial vehicles included. I think I enjoyed the visit to the restoration shop the most.

The first thing to hit my eye there was an old, old friend: W.C. Fields' 1938 Cadillac V-16 limousine. While it was still maroon, it was a slightly different shade than I recalled. I knew both of Fields' Cadillac V-16s well. His coupe belonged to a next-door neighbor and was parked in the garage next to my 1938 Cadillac 75 coupe for more than two years. Another old friend, then undergoing restoration, was Lindy Bothwell's ex-Czarina of Russia 1914 Rolls-Royce Silver Ghost Town Car.

For some reason, on my third visit, in December, 1986, the whole museum came alive to me. Now, I think it is a very good museum and a darned nice collection. It is well and attractively laid out. There are some really lovely antiques. Lindy's "Ghost" is now on display and identified as "Ex-Czar of Russia." When I knew it, it was a light green; now it's a royal purple.

An "old friend" was W.C. Fields' 1938 Cadillac V-16 limousine. While it was still maroon, it was possibly a slightly different shade than years ago. (Old Cars)

There are also some very nice cars of the latter teens and early 1920s at the Imperial Palace. I was particularly impressed by two utterly magnificent Pierce-Arrows of the late teens. What handsome cars! I'd be delighted to own either one. Of course there are Classics, too, including three Duesies, one of which was Father Divine's "Throne Car." Not to mention Cadillacs and Packards and Pierces.

There are nice "ordinary" cars, too: Fords from the T days and before, up through postwar cars. As before, there are commercial vehicles, too. And motorcycles. You might not find your own particular pet there. After all, they can't have everything in a display of 200 cars. But, you'll probably find something pretty close. All in all, a very good representative collection that is well and attractively displayed.

One very nice thing about this museum is that you don't have to go some distance to see it. In fact, you don't even have to go outside the hotel, in possibly inclement weather, to get there. You just take an elevator, inside the hotel, that lets you out on the top floor of their guest parking garage. Then, you are there!

Fagan enjoyed his visit to the Imperial Palace's restoration shop. Here is a Mercedes body undergoing restoration there. (Old Cars)

After three visits, Fagan recommends visiting the Imperial Palace. Here's one of the many Duesenbergs exhibited there. (Old Cars)

As I indicated earlier, I do have some criticism. I do wish that they would correct those glaringly wrong mis-identifications that I've mentioned. In all too many instances, I noted cars in the 1920s and very early 1930s painted in metallics. All wrong! But, maybe it makes it more colorful and attractive for the run-of-the-mill tourist. I guess I really don't mind Bothwell's 1914 Ghost being painted purple, instead of the green I knew for so many years. Who knows what color it was when the Russian royal family owned it?

This may well be a rash suggestion and the museum personnel may well hate me for it, but I'll make it anyway. If you are ever there and you can convince them you are a real and genuine enthusiast, maybe you'll be able to talk them into letting you go through their restoration shop. It would be a nice way to cap the museum visit.

Sagas of the Old West...

The changing museum picture

By Bruce Fagan

"Once upon a time..." we out here in the West had a couple of the finest automotive museums that you could ever hope to find.

One was the largest and most comprehensive collection that ever existed. It started with the antiques and progressed through all the years up to and including our present postwar period. Of course, it was the Harrah's Automobile Collection in Reno, Nevada. Many of the cars were of genuine historic importance ... either the only existing one or one of only two or three in the world. While the primary thrust was automotive, this collection included all forms of transportation: There were airplanes, boats and steam trains. I expect that there were also horse-drawn vehicles, although I don't honestly recall. Maybe the only thing missing was a Roman chariot! There may even have been one.

Some of that superb collection is long gone now. It is scattered to the four winds. Years ago, everyone knew it was worth a trip from the East Coast just to see the rarities and the goodies.

The William F. Harrah Foundation's National Automobile Museum in downtown Reno, Nevada, still has many one-of-a-kind cars, such as the 1930 "Orchid" Packard. (John Gunnell)

315

(Editor's note: Now, there is a fresh, new museum in downtown Reno, alongside the Truckee River. It's officially known as The William F. Harrah Foundation National Automobile Museum. There are fewer cars (planes, trains and chariots) than there was years ago. However, we recently visited there and found the selection and they way they are displayed to be very pleasing; well worth a trip from Iola, Wisconsin and most other points east.)

Briggs Cunningham's collection was a highly personal one. Briggs was very much a long-time car enthusiast, especially with sports cars. Well before World War II, Briggs and the Collier brothers were very active in the sports car field.

I first saw the nucleus of the Cunningham museum, in 1957, at Briggs' place in Connecticut. I remember a few of the cars from that day: An 8-Liter Bentley, a Rolls-Royce Phantom III sedan, a Phantom II roadster (formerly Betty Carstairs'). Then Briggs moved to the West Coast and decided to set up a museum in Newport Beach, California.

Sometime in the latter 1960s, Stan Sedgwick, long-time president of the Bentley Drivers Club, was out here as Briggs' guest. So, Briggs put on a little luncheon, in Stan's honor, at the museum's site to-be. In this way, Stan could get to meet all of us local club members. However, I never did visit the Briggs Cunningham Auto Collection once it was set up, until 1986. It was a fine collection, with a heavy emphasis on sports and racing cars. After all, Briggs did participate in a number of the LeMans 24-Hour Races.

Now, of course, that museum is gone, too. It was sold to the son/nephew of the Collier brothers and relocated back East; to Florida this time. Some of the cars were dispersed. For example, Briggs' Bugatti Royale, one of the prettiest of them all, was auctioned by Christie's in England.

One of the two Bugatti Royales that Briggs Cunningham brought into this country was in the D. Cameron Peck Collection when this photo was taken in the 1950s. It later went into Tom Monaghan's Dominos Pizza Collection in Ann Arbor, Michigan. (Don McCrau photo via Bruce Fagan)

A few years after the war, Briggs returned from a trip to Europe with two Royales included in his "luggage." At that time in our hobby, I don't suppose that either of those Royales cost him much over a $1,000 or so each. He immediately sold one to Cameron Peck. It subsequently changed hands a few times in the intervening years, winding up at Harrah's. It sold for $6.5 million. Then Tom Monaghan bought it for $8.1 million. Now that Briggs' other Royale has been sold, I'm left wondering what that other Royale from the Harrah's Automobile Collection will sell for. That's the one that you, any of you, could have bought in the very early 1950s for a mere $1,000. Talk about appreciation! Or is it inflation?

This saga does not purport to be an overview of all the car museums around, past and present, as I've only been to a very few. But, do you ever wonder how many of these museums will be around for your children and your grandchildren to see? Blessed few of those currently viewable, I'd say.

The Henry Ford Museum & Greenfield Village, outside Detroit, will most likely still be there. It is eminently worth viewing. The Smithsonian, in Washington, D.C., will still be there for those grand kids of yours to see what thrilled you. Wonder what they'll think of our cars come the year 2025 or 2050?

The city of Los Angeles has an Industrial Museum that includes a car collection. That's another one that will still be there many years down the line. There may well be other tax-supported museums in other cities and states that will well survive those of you reading this now. The Blackhawk Collection out here in the San Francisco area, has set up a museum in conjunction with the University of California. That one could also be a survivor.

Although I never visited them, I can look back at a lot of collections and museums that have since closed their doors. One of the earliest, and the finest, was the Cameron Peck collection. He dissolved it many years ago.

Singer James Melton had a museum. It was first in Connecticut and then in Florida. Upon his death, it was acquired by Winthrop Rockefeller and was moved to Arkansas. Upon Rockefeller's death, it was dispersed. Some of the cars wound up at Harrah's.

Henry Austin Clark Jr. had his Long Island Museum. It's now been closed for some years. Gene Zimmerman had a goodly collection back East. It's now gone, too. Gabe Ingram had his California collection and museum out in Cucamonga and then moved it to the Santa Monica Pier. Neither location lasted very long. I'm sure all of you can remember others that are now just memories.

Frankly, I think we all owe a great debt to those enthusiasts who set up those museums. It gives us and the general public a chance to see a lot of first-rate cars. I cannot believe that any of those museums were ever financially successful. It's my belief that they were all subsidized by their owners. I doubt if the admissions collected even paid for the maintenance of the building and the salaries of attendants.

Nevada does have another good museum collection. It's the one at the Imperial Palace Hotel. Will it still be there 20 or 30 years down the line? Time will tell, but it sure seems likely.

The Merle Norman Classic Beauty Collection at San Sylmar (near Los Angeles), California showcases Jack Nethercutt's cars in a lavish setting. It's definitely worth visiting, but advanced reservations are required. (MNCBC)

In the Los Angeles area, we have the Nethercutt Collection. Jack Nethercutt does have some very fine cars, but only a few are on display at any one time. While it is, theoretically, a public museum, it is not all that easy to get in to see it. Jack is now in his mid 70s. What happens to this collection once he departs?

The museum building is owned by Merle Norman Cosmetics, a company wholly owned by Jack. Jack personally owns all the cars and, I guess, everything else in the building. I expect that one of these days, that collection will be another one to be dispersed to the four winds.

My advice? I guess it's simple. See them while they're still here!

Sagas of the Old West...

Greta Garbo's Duesie!

By Bruce Fagan

Back in the very early 1930s, and again in the mid-1930s, I spent a couple of years in the Hollywood-Beverly Hills, California area. I then moved there, permanently, in 1940.

Even in the 1930s, I was (as were all other kids of that time) interested in cars, though I was not the kind of an enthusiast (nut) that I've since become. However, in the 1930s, you just never heeded the Packards, the Cadillacs and the Lincolns you passed in the streets, unless they had very unusual bodies or were driven by Jean Harlow or Thelma Todd. In those days, though, you might deign to glance at a Duesie.

Maybe, because I came from a theatrical family, I did note seeing a celebrity driving a car, especially a Duesie. I can recall seeing Gary Cooper, Lupe Velez and Richard Arlen in their Duesies. I remember hearing a high school classmate, Joe E. Brown's son, complain because the "old man" wouldn't let him drive his Duesie. I also recall sometimes seeing pictures of the stars, with their cars, in fan magazines.

I cannot state that I was so interested that I tried to find out all the local personages who had Duesies (or any other fine car for that matter). By the same token, I certainly did not recall ever seeing Greta Garbo in a Duesenberg or even hearing that she owned one, which certainly does not mean that she didn't.

In the early days of our hobby, none of us, so far as I can recall, was even the slightest bit interested about the original owners of our cars. We didn't know and we didn't care. But today, a famous owner seems to make it more valuable. And often, such "ownership" is deliberately quite false. A 1940 Buick convertible sedan was, for a short time, touted as having been built for Shirley Temple. There's the myth of the "Lucky Luciano Lincoln," too.

A former Packard of mine is, so I hear, claimed to be an ex-George Raft car. Not so, as far as I ever knew! Of course, I never bothered checking as to the original owner. Based on what little I knew of that car, I might have accepted that Dick Powell, Joan Blondell or Warren William was the owner, but not George Raft.

Then, there's the Ty Power Duesie. Yes, it is true that he did own it. But it was over 20 years old when he first acquired it as a well-used car that had innumerable owners. In all fairness, Ty was a genuine old car and sports car enthusiast, owning several fine examples in both categories.

As of the time I'm writing this "Saga," I couldn't prove or disprove Greta Garbo's ownership of any Duesenberg. To confirm my knowledge, or lack thereof, I checked with a friend of mine. He not only grew up in the film colony, but is also a long-time Duesenberg enthusiast. He, too, could not recall ever hearing that Garbo had a Duesie. He used to help out at Bob Roberts, the shop where everybody took their Duesies for service after the factory dealer closed up. He had no recollection of ever seeing this car there.

I did know the so-called Greta Garbo Duesenberg slightly. In fact, I had driven it. Back about 1957, it belonged to a friend of mine named Fred Prophet. He owned the restaurant facilities in General Motors plants and that made him a very wealthy man. I first knew him in 1945. In 1946, when we were both in New York City, I saw a very attractive Delage coupe in a used car place on Broadway, around 53rd Street.

I told Fred about the car and he promptly bought it for about $5,000. Used cars were very expensive during, and right after, the war. Fred subsequently came to the West Coast, moving first to Beverly Hills, then Bel-Aire and, finally, to Santa Barbara. He had a fine Delahaye drop-head that he loaned to Gabe Ingram for Gabe's car museum on the Santa Monica Pier. I drove it from Fred's home to the museum. French coachwork left a bad taste in my mouth after that experience. You had to have one of those sliding bolts on the doors to keep them from flying open while you drove.

Fred Prophet had a beautiful and very rakish Rolls-Royce Phantom III two-passenger coupe with a body by Inskip. It was a really rare, one off car. However, he didn't like having to shift gears. So, he had a new (probably 1955) Cadillac engine and Hydra-Matic transmission installed. I sold the Rolls engine for him. It went to Ham Greenough, in Santa Barabara, for $500. Hammy later sold that Phantom III sedan to Jack Nethercutt.

Back around 1957, our local Classic Car Club of America chapter had a meeting up at the Santa Barbara Biltmore. While there, I called Fred. He had bought the Avery Brundage home. Do you remember Avery Brundage? He was the long-time head of the American Olympic Committee. The home was in Montecito.

Fred suggested that I come up and drive his Duesenberg down to the Biltmore for all the other enthusiasts to see. So, I drove up to Fred's. It was only a mile or so away. Bob Gottlieb went with me. We chatted a bit with Fred and then drove his car back down to the hotel. There, the hotel's publicity people took a picture of the car with me driving and Gottlieb beside me.

Writer/historian Bruce Fagan drove the Greta Garbo Duesenberg in 1957, but didn't know that it had been owned by the famous actress until he contacted the late Ray Wolff, a marque historian, in the late 1980s.

Now, I do know that Fred never said a word about this being the ex-Greta Garbo car, if he even knew. As I mentioned earlier, in those days we just did not care a whit about something like that. Probably, Fred only knew the name of the person he'd bought the car from; if he even remembered! He would have had no interest in its earlier history. My pictures, which are undoubtedly much sharper than the reproductions on newsprint, do show that this Duesie was in really superb condition.

To follow up on the car's history, I was put in touch with Ray Wolff. He was, undoubtedly, one of the leading Duesenberg historians. Ray saved me from really putting my foot in my mouth and making a most grievous error. He confirmed that this car was first owned by Greta Garbo. She bought it under her real name, Greta Gustavson, in Paris. It is one of either two or three cars with nearly identical bodies. One is or was owned by, as I recall Ray Wolff telling me, the Nizam of Hyderabad.

The Garbo car's chassis was probably sent to France in 1931, then subsequently bodied. It was shown at the 1932 Paris Auto Show, so my supposition is that Garbo bought it after the show. When Garbo sold it could be in 1932 or in 1939. It was most difficult trying to pin down information from that time and that place, even for such a careful historian as Ray Wolff.

In addition, Ray Wolff's records showed that Fred Prophet did, indeed, own this car in 1957. He bought it from Jim Hoe. Hoe sold the car to Fred Prophet, at the end of 1957, for $5,500.

While there is no question that this is the ex-Greta Garbo car, it is also very true that she never had it in Hollywood. Therefore, we "Hollywoodites" never saw her in it hereabouts.

Sagas of the Old West...

Back when our Classics were "pre-owned"

By Bruce Fagan

Shortly after my friend lent me that 1938 Kelley Blue Book, our local newspaper had an interesting and pertinent item in its "50 Years Ago" column. It was a February 15, 1938 report by the American Petroleum Industries on the typical American auto owner.

The report covered the entire United States. The typical 1938 car owner had an income of $30 a week or less. He drove a used car worth $238. Only one car owner in three owned or had owned a new car. Families with incomes of $30 a week or less owned 55 percent of all cars; families earning $20 a week or less owned 34 percent of all cars. Less than two percent of all cars were owned by families with incomes of $100 a week or more. And this typical motorist drove 9,615 miles a year.

Think about it. Let some of those figures sink in. How many of you would even consider working for $20 a day, let alone a week? Even $40 a day is just barely the current minimum wage. Twenty dollars a week ... that's just barely $1,000 a year. Thirty dollars a week is only $1,500 a year, which was a pretty good yearly salary then. It was enough to raise a family on. In that bracket, you didn't live well, but you were halfway comfortable. Today, that $1,500 is merely a pretty good bi-weekly salary.

Let's go back to our 1938 Kelley Blue Book where we started. On today's market, probably the cheapest used car you can buy is a Yugo. From all I've heard, they're a mighty poor excuse for an automobile. They sold new for $3,990. With extras, dealer prep and taxes, figure $6,000 out of the showroom door. (Editor's note: According to 1993 Used Car Prices, by Pace Publications, current Yugo GV used car prices are: 1986 model at $550; 1987 model at $700; 1988 model at $850; 1989 model at $1,075; and 1991 model at $1,425). Now let's look at some vintage prices.

First, we'll look at the very best cars that you could buy around the end of 1938. If you bought a used 1938 Packard then, it would run you about $2,400. That compared to a delivered price of $4,155 for a brand new 1939 Packard 12-cylinder sedan (less whatever new-car discount you could talk the dealer into).

You don't like Packards? Okay, let's look at Cadillacs. The 1939s weren't out yet, so we can only look at 1938s. A Cadillac 75 series sedan cost $3,380 delivered in Los Angeles, less a discount. A Cadillac V-16 sedan went for $5,490. On the other hand, either of these cars, in used condition, would have been cheaper ... about $1,800 for the 75 and $2,450 for the V-16.

How about Pierce-Arrow? Well, as you may know, 1938 was the company's last year. A new Pierce eight-cylinder sedan ran $4,064 out of the dealer's door. The V-12 was $4,668.50. Why that 50 cents was tagged on is beyond me, but I note that all the Pierce 12s had that extra 50 cents added on. (Maybe that was their profit.) The 1938 Pierce eight, as a used car with maybe 5,000-8,000 miles on it, would cost you something like $1,750. The pre-owned Pierce 12 would cost you only $150-$200 more.

This means that 55 years ago, the finest, most luxurious cars that you could buy (remember that Duesenberg, Cord and Auburn were out of business and that a Rolls-Royce or Mercedes were scarcely viable options) cost less than the cheapest automobiles on the market today.

When you consider the so-called medium-priced cars of that day, like the Buick, Chrysler, Oldsmobile, DeSoto, Lincoln-Zephyr, Nash eight or Packard 120, the price differential is even more obvious. When you get to the cheap cars, like Ford, Chevrolet and Plymouth, it becomes almost staggering.

A 1939 Buick Special sedan (yes, the 1939 Buicks were available by then) was only $1,247 delivered. The big Roadmaster was all of $1,832. A Cadillac 60 series sedan was yours for $2,015. A Chrysler eight-cylinder sedan ran you $1,413. A DeSoto was $1,131.55 (there's those odd pennies again!) A Hudson Eight was $1,280, while a LaSalle was $1,608. And a Lincoln-Zephyr was $1,602.10, as opposed to a Packard 120 at $1,597. In addition, you had the Studebaker President, priced at just $1,338. Of course, we're talking about the standard "family car" or least expensive four-door sedan in the line.

Now, on to the so-called "cheapies." Today, there really is no such thing as a regular Ford or Chevrolet or Plymouth. Each of these makes now comes in a number of different lines ranging from sub-compact to today's version of a "standard six-cylinder" car. Fifty years ago, there was only one Ford, Chevrolet or Plymouth. You could get it as either the "standard" or the "Deluxe" model. The Deluxe cost you $50 or so more, but it included things like two windshield wipers, two taillights, two sun visors, maybe a cigar lighter, and a few other goodies, depending upon make. Oh yes, Ford did have a third option ... their little 60 horsepower model.

A Chevrolet sedan cost you $885 for the standard and $952 for the Deluxe. Plymouth was $882.90 for the standard and $953.90 for the DeLuxe. A Ford V8-60 would cost you $886.60, while the standard 85 horsepower V-8 was $912.80. The Deluxe version cost $974.60. (Gosh, Fords were kind of pricey, weren't they?)

The 1938 Oldsmobile eight four-door sedan sold for more than the Oldsmobile six when both were introduced at the start of the season. (Old Cars)

Within a few years, the pre-owned 1938 Oldsmobile six had a "blue book" value higher than that of the eight. (Old Cars)

If all these cars were too expensive, you could buy an American Bantam (Austin) coupe for only $549 ... delivered. Granted, it wasn't much of a family car, but neither is a Yugo.

Another interesting thing that I discovered in going through the 1938 Kelley Blue Book was that once the cars were three or four years old, the initially more expensive version was sometimes the cheaper one. As one example, an Oldsmobile six-cylinder, as a used car, was worth more than an Oldsmobile eight. (In a 1935 edition, the six was worth about $15 more than the eight.)

This price differential was understandable. If you were a family man, making $25-$30 a week, you needed a "new" car. You'd like an Oldsmobile eight, but the six would burn less gas than the eight. It also had smaller tires, which cost less to replace. In addition, it was cheaper to get a six-cylinder engine serviced, than it was to fix up an eight. Thus, the used Oldsmobile six was worth a slight premium over the eight. Of course, you'd save enough in a few months, on gas alone, to pay that difference.

One last comment. Back in 1937, I was a Cord salesman in New Rochelle, New York. Back then, a 1937 sedan would have cost about $2,700, with the convertible being $100-$200 more. However, at the end of 1938, the 1937s models were worth $850-$900 for the sedan and $50-$75 more for the convertible.

Somewhere West of Laramie...

Introduction to the Forty-Niner

By Tim Howley

You can say all you want about today's superior automobiles with their high technology design and engineering, efficient use of energy and space and sports car handling and performance. They all lack one simple element of the cars I knew as a boy ... showmanship.

Back in the swinging 1940s, new cars were introduced with all the ballyhoo of Barnum & Bailey. New car introduction time was a national event. And, of all the new cars to be ceremoniously unveiled in the early postwar years, none ever dazzled the public like the 1949 Ford. It was Henry Ford II's first great visible accomplishment and he spared no expense on the trumpets.

The event was built up in the press like the Second Coming, which it was in a sense. When the car finally appeared, on June 18, 1948, at some 7,500 Ford dealers, it received the greatest reception since the Model A. It is estimated that some 28 million viewed the great postwar "Tin Lizzie" during its first three days of public showing.

I'm sorry to say I was not among the throngs. Having viewed the first photos in a Minneapolis newspaper, June 17-18, my dad decided to load his fishing gear in the trunk of our smiling 1946 Ford club coupe and head for the lake. His comment to me was, "Young Henry is plum nuts if he thinks we're going to buy a contraption like that." A 1949 Ford fan my father was not.

I finally did get a look at the wondrous "Forty-Niner" a few weeks later, at the Ford dealer show room in Pine City, Minnesota. It was a metallic Club Custom four-door displayed in the front room of an old brick building that went back to the Model T. It seemed hardly an appropriate stage for the Ford of the future. Yet, to me at age 13, it was like viewing an ethereal chariot of the gods on a pedestal set in heaven. It mattered little that the manager was so humble or that the simple flathead V-8 still breathed underneath this modern Ford bonnet. Here was a Ford of my boyhood dreams, as new from stem to stern as 45 rpm records and 12-1/2-inch screen televisions; as alluring and mysterious as Heddy Lamarr and Maureen O'Hara.

Debut at the Waldorf

Maybe some of you readers were lucky enough to attend the gala grand entrance at the Waldorf Astoria in New York. The great show was designed by Walter Dorwin Teague, who had done all the spectacular Ford shows since 1933. It started as a press showing, beginning on June 8, with all the top Ford executives on the scene, shaking hands and raising drinks. Then, on June 18, the doors were flung open for the public.

The 1949 Ford Custom two-door sedan showed off the new postwar styling very nicely. (Old Cars)

It was just one of a dozen or more such shows staged in major cities all around the country, but it was by far and away the most lavish. Now, one might ask why the new Fords were introduced in June 1948, when September-October is traditional new-car introduction time. Well, considering the deplorable financial condition of the Ford Motor Company in the mid-1940s and the archaic state of the 1946-1948 models, young Henry wanted to waste no time in getting the "long overdue" postwar Ford into the showrooms and on the streets. A debut at the Waldorf was the most dramatic way possible to make up for lost time.

As you came out of the elevator on the Ford show level, you went straight ahead, to the East Foyer, where you saw six quarter-sized models of the 1949 Ford. Each was a precision replica in every detail. The models were faithful to the original, even in interior design and details. They lacked only engines and running gear. I've often wondered about these models. Have any of them survived? Or were they destroyed, like most of the full-sized show cars of the 1950s, which was typical Henry Ford II's policy at the time?

To the right end of the model display was the "Forty-Niner" exhibit. This was an old-time California prospector, dipping gold nuggets from a stream of running water, and passing out souvenirs. To the left of the model cars was a picnic scene with live bathing beauties. They were "caught" in a sudden rain storm with a bright red 1949 Ford convertible. As the first drop of rain hit, the top came up and the "windows automatically closed," which was a neat trick, since Ford did not offer power windows, to my knowledge, until 1954.

You passed from this room into a hallway of testing machines and, then, into a big ballroom. Here there was a merry-go-round of Ford body styles and a Ferris wheel with two full-sized chassis, twisting and turning as they revolved. In this room, you also found cut-away engines and special exhibits demonstrating the instrument panel, brakes, ventilating system, new suspension and overdrive. In the far back room, called the West Foyer, were additional exhibits showing the living room comfort of the new Fords, plus special engineering exhibits. In all, there were 34 motors operating the exhibits, plus pumps for the water exhibits. There were 54 live models, actors and actresses and 75 members of the narrator crew, all as part of a total work force of some 300 people.

On the other sides of the elevators, three more large rooms contained exhibits of the new Lincolns, Lincoln Cosmopolitans and Mercurys. In these rooms, like the Ford rooms, there was paper sculpture everywhere. But, there were very few moving exhibits for the senior cars. Young Henry wanted all of the energy and attention directed toward the Fords. The 1949 Lincoln had been introduced in showrooms on April 22 and the Mercury on April 29. Both these makes were ready much earlier than the Ford.

Behind the Scenes

There's an interesting story behind all these cars. The Ford, Mercury and Lincoln had all been designed and put into clay by 1945. But, Ernest R. "Ernie" Breech decided to bump them all up a notch and introduce a totally new 1949 Ford. He reasoned, very wisely, that "this company will be judged on the next Ford it produces." Therefore, the 118-inch wheelbase Ford became the Mercury, pushing the Mercury up to the 121-inch wheelbase Lincoln chassis. The 125-inch wheelbase Lincoln then became the Lincoln Cosmopolitan. The compact, 97-inch wheelbase Ford project car secretly under development, then went overseas. It become the French Vedette. The Lincoln Continental project was abandoned altogether. In my own opinion, the 1949 Mercury was the best of the crop in every respect.

But, was the 1949 Ford really new? From a styling standpoint, definitely. About the only similarity between the 1948 and 1949 models was the 114-inch wheelbase. There was an all-new ladder-type frame and a new slab-sided body that proved to be a real trendsetter. The model line up was the same as in 1948, except that the coupe now shared its body shell with the club coupe. The station wagon was the most changed model of all. It was now a two-door, instead of a four-door, and the former all-wood body was replaced with a combination metal-and-wood body designed for greater durability and a more contemporary look.

Like the 1948 Fords, the new 1949 models came in two series. They were now called the Standard and Custom lines. Both offered a choice of flathead six or flathead V-8 power.

Since the 18 month crash program to develop the 1949 Ford (project X-2900) allowed no time for radical engine change, the 239.4 cubic inch flathead V-8 was greatly refined. It still had the same bore, stroke and 100 horsepower rating, but with much-needed improvements. The old distributor, driven directly off the camshaft, was exchanged for one located above the head, on the right-hand front cylinder bank. It was shaft-and-gear driven. The cooling system allowed water from a new, larger radiator to be pumped straight back to the rear of the block, without any baffling. Oil consumption was cut through the use of improved rings and solid valve lifters. Intake and exhaust manifolding was improved. Finally, the engine mountings were better cushioned.

For the first time in Ford history, the antiquated buggy transverse springing was gone. The front suspension consisted of wishbone coils with telescopic shocks mounted in the center. The rear suspension became the longitudinal semi-elliptic leaf type. Torque tube drive was tossed out in favor of Hotchkiss drive. The new-for-Ford ladder type frame provided for a lower body silhouette, without sacrificing headroom. The engine was shoved forward five inches. The seats were moved forward so that the back seat was no longer over the rear axle. Ford called the total result "Midship Ride," a clever advertising slogan for simply catching up the with rest of the Detroit fleet. Brakes were improved. Overall, the car handled, rode and performed better than the 1948 model, but not to the degree that the publicity and advertising led buyers to believe.

Just to show you how fast the 1949 Ford was developed, this car was not even finalized until a top-level executive conference in July, 1946. By July, 1947, the first hand-built models were put on the test track. The first production models were coming off the line in April, 1948. It was a record to that date. It formerly took about 2-1/2 years to develop any radically new car.

While I never did attend any of the gala events, I had one of the most memorable experiences of my childhood in connection with a 1949 Ford.

On a brisk, sunny, Saturday morning in February, 1949, my dad took me to the Highland Park Ford Plant. We watched the shiny new Fords come together on the line. I will never forget my boyhood fascination with watching thousands of parts converge from feeder lines and overhead conveyors. And there, at the end of the line, we heard that familiar Ford starter whine, as the bouncing new babies came to life.

The one I remember most that day was a bright red convertible. I rather suspect that my own interest in car collecting started on that Saturday morning. I collected every brochure they had, every tiny nut and bolt they would give me, even the sand briquettes from which they made the glass. Later, at home, I started a collection of 1949 Ford models, 1949 Ford ads and all the issues of Ford Times pertaining to the 1949 model. I wish I had it all now.

After our tour of the assembly plant, I lured my dad into the plant showroom where a dark blue Custom four-door sedan was on display. Dad looked at the $2,000 price tag and jumped back in dismay.

"For that pile of junk," he mumbled in disgust. "I only paid $1,295 for the 1946. Tim, Henry Ford is trying to rob us all blind." After that morning at Highland Park, my father was totally convinced that Ford would eventually go right down the tubes with this one. "You just wait and see, Timbo," he warned. "Three years from now, these new Fords will all be on the junk pile and people will be buying back the old Fords they traded in. If this one doesn't put the company out of business, it will put Henry out of a job."

My dad was like a lot of Americans at the time. In his eyes, old Henry Ford could do no wrong and young Henry could do no right. He was right about the quality control of the new car. The doors and the trunk lid fit so poorly that there were numerous complaints of dust and rain getting into the car. The bodies were mounted to the frames very poorly. And, just all kinds of weird problems developed, especially during the first few months of the model run.

But, what a show it was at a time when showmanship still sold cars. A total of 1,118,308 units were produced and they, at least, ran well enough to put the Ford Motor Company back on its feet. The bodies were a mess, but the faithful flathead V-8 never missed a beat and the faithful flathead six was pretty popular that year, too.

You will not find very many 1949 Fords left to collect now. It was a combination of being loved to death and being driven right into the ground. These are not really hot collector cars, even today. But, they were a benchmark in Ford history. No car in history ever promised so much postwar happiness and prosperity or delivered it in such simple and beautiful style.

The 1949 Ford was not the first slab-sided car, but it was the first to start the trend to slab sides and squared-off lines. The fenders came all the way up to the window sills and hood line with no break and not even the slightest vestige of a front or rear fender. (The very squared-off bustle back was another 1949 Ford first.)

By the mid-1950s, this was the standard automobile styling of the industry. It is, in fact, the standard styling motif of nearly all automobiles worldwide today. And the Forty-Niner introduced it!

One of the most collectible Forty-Niners is the woodie station wagon. (Old Cars)

Somewhere West of Laramie...

My Chrysler girlfriend

By Tim Howley

Diane Rosacker wasn't just another teenage romance. She was my number one high school heartthrob.

Glamorous as Marilyn Monroe. Witty as Carole Lombard. Sophisticated as Grace Kelly. Intriguing as Ingrid Bergman. Little wonder that the guys lined up to her door on the corner of St. Anthony Boulevard and McKinley Street, in northeast Minneapolis, all the way to Lowery Avenue.

I was about two blocks back in line, but did manage to get three dates with her in late 1950. The romance of my mind continued throughout high school and Diane always kept me dangling, which only added to the glamor and intrigue. She was my original girl from "Somewhere West of Laramie," long before I ever heard of Ned Jordan or the girl on the sassy pony riding lean and ragged.

The 1947 Chrysler New Yorker four-door sedan.

I literally worshipped the ground Diane walked on, or more accurately, the carriage in which she rode. It was a dark blue 1947 Chrysler New Yorker four-door sedan. I believe her aunt bought it originally and sold it to Diane's father, Art Rosacker, in about 1949. I remember riding in it only once, when her aunt had just bought it. She took a bunch of us kids to Long Lake for an afternoon swim. I can still remember the utter silence and comfort of the brand new Chrysler and the smoothness of the Fluid Drive. I can almost sense the new-car aroma, mingled with the wet freshness of a bunch of skinny little Cub Scouts, in bathing trunks and towels, taking warm comfort in those royal blue broadcloth seats. They were fit for a king.

The Rosackers, to this day, own Rosacker's Rose Acres Florists on Stinson Boulevard. Art was one of the original three brothers who operated the business for years. Art drove the elegant Chrysler for as long as I knew Diane, which was from 1950 to 1956. Not that he couldn't afford anything newer. The Rosackers could have bought all of Stinson and St. Anthony Boulevards if they wanted to. Old Art just happened to like that particular car. And for good reason.

Chryslers of the 1946-1948 era, especially the eights, were probably the most well-engineered and long-lived cars that I knew as a boy. There were a lot of them sold to begin with because, being more expensive than Fords, Plymouths and Chevrolets, there was no long waiting list. Also, being offered in four series, they covered a wide range of markets from upper-medium price to upper- upper price.

Chrysler out-produced Cadillac by more than two to one for all three model years. Estimated production was 83,310 for 1946, 119,260 for 1947 and 130,110 for 1948. The Chryslers seemed to outlive Lincolns, Buicks ... even Packards. I can remember still seeing them on Minneapolis streets in the early 1960s. No rust, no tarnished chrome, no worn out seats. Maybe the paint was a little faded, but they still looked like they were ready to go another decade or more.

I might have thought such sturdy cars would still be on the roads of California, when I came here in 1968. They were not. I rather suspect that conservative Chryslers of that era were a lot more popular with the Germans and Scandinavians in the upper Midwest, than with the flamboyant California types. What was distinction for Art Rosacker, must have been anathema for even Ronald Reagan and Regis Tomey, although Bob Hope and Ray Milland drove Chrysler Town & Countrys.

Early postwar Chryslers had their origins in the 1940 models. These cars were introduced the year that Walter P. Chrysler died. K.T. Keller then became Chrysler president. His cars were as conservative as his pinstripe suits and tall enough that a man could sit on "chair high" seats, even in the back compartment, wearing his Adam hat. Keller seemed to like the kind of elegance that was almost a throwback to 18th century English and French carriages. The 1946-1948 models, in particular, had a kind of old world charm that almost made you think Marie Antoinette would descend from one. Or, in my own fantasies, young "Lady Diane" just back from England on the Queen Mary.

Wheelbases for the postwar models were set down in 1941: 127.5 inches for the New Yorker and Saratoga, 121.5 inches for the Royal and Windsor. In 1942, the running boards disappeared beneath the doors and the massive front end took on the 1946 shape. For 1942, horizontal grille bars were extended right along to the sides. These same "speed streaks" were also repeated on the rear fenders of some models. My friend Bill Lindstrom's mother had a 1942 Chrysler Royal club coupe, not only a "black-out" model, but black as well. The instrument panel was all mottled plastic in sickly yellows and greens. At the time, I thought it was a pretty ugly car, but I sure wouldn't mind having it now.

The 1946 face-lift was a great improvement. The egg crate grille was an industry trend at the time in higher priced cars and resisted only by the lesser Packards. On Chryslers, it probably came off the best. Whitewall tires were scarce at the time, so Chrysler answered with steel or white plastic "doughnuts" hung around the hubcaps. As I recall, 1946 interiors offered less color selection than 1947 and 1948. I don't think the elegant blues, greens and maroons and bright "Highlander Plaids" arrived until a bit later. The 1946-1948 Chrysler instrument panel was one of the most ornate in the industry. The mottled effect of the plastic was replaced with mono-tones, polished to perfection. There was lots of dash chrome; so much it was almost a chore reading the gauges. So good was that early postwar Chrysler plastic that I have seen steering wheels on cars in wrecking yards, 25 years later, that were in perfect condition with not a crack anywhere!

Chrysler had quite a line up of postwar models. A business coupe with a trunk big enough to sleep in was offered in all four series. A now rare two-door sedan was also offered in all series, as was a Club Coupe. The convertible was offered in the Windsor and New Yorker series, but not the Saratoga and Royal. An eight-passenger commercial limo, on a 139.5-inch wheelbase, was offered as a Royal and Windsor, but not a Saratoga or New Yorker. In addition, there was a Crown Imperial limousine on a 145.5-inch wheelbase. Added in 1948 was an eight-passenger sedan. I remember going to my grandfather's funeral in a 1947 Crown Imperial limousine. Grandpa, born in County Slago, Ireland, was as strong as a Chrysler himself. He never drove a car in his life and died, at age 94, in 1949.

The most unique of all Chryslers then, and the most desirable now, is the Town & Country. It was offered as a four-door sedan on the shorter wheelbase and a convertible on the longer wheelbase. About 100 of the earlier four-doors were eight-cylinder models. All the later ones were sixes. Evidently, none of the four-doors were sold before January 1947. I believe all of the convertibles were eights.

A 1947 Chrysler Town & Country.

Quite a line up of Town & Countrys had originally been planned, including a two-door brougham, a roadster and a hardtop. One brougham and seven hardtops were built experimentally. I wonder if any still exist. These were the first pillarless postwar hardtops, preceding the 1949 Buick Riviera by three years. The Town & Country frame was white ash with mahogany veneer inserts. Unlike the Ford Sportsman, the Chrysler Town & Country bodies were metal-reinforced. In 1948, the veneer panels were replaced with a woodgrain decal called Di-Noc.

Power for the New Yorker and Saratoga series and Town & Country convertibles was supplied by Chrysler's venerable 323.5 cubic inch L-head eight-cylinder engine, which was introduced way back with the 1934 Airflow Imperial. Through the years, Chrysler kept upping the horsepower and compression ratios and making camshaft and manifold changes, but it was still the same engine.

From 1939 through 1941, there were three different horsepower versions of this engine. From 1942 on, there was only one version. It was rated at 135 horsepower through 1950, when it finally bowed out to the 1951 Chrysler hemi overhead valve V-8. The 250.6 cubic inch L-head six was introduced in 1942, but its basic engineering goes back farther. It was standard on the Royal, Windsor and Town & Country sedan.

The low-revving, "luxury cruiser" eight was coupled with Chrysler's famous Fluid Drive, which had long been standard on the Crown Imperial. Until 1949, it was still optional on all other models.

Looking back, Fluid Drive seems to be a kind of Rube Goldberg device. It was primitive in design, slow in the lower speed ranges and prone to break down. Actually, it was extremely dependable in its day. The troubles occurred mostly in much older and higher mileage cars. Fluid Drive was a combination of a conventional clutch with a torque converter and electric shifting circuits. With Fluid Drive, you only had to depress the clutch once, when starting out or when shifting from low to high or from high back to low.

Admittedly it was very slow up to five to six miles per hour. After that, it provided adequate, although not outstanding acceleration. Right around 15 miles per hour, you would let up on the accelerator and the transmission kicked into high gear. It was improved in 1949 and was continued up through 1953 (on some models into 1954.)

The 1947-1948 Chryslers are nearly impossible to distinguish from 1946 models, except by the trained eye. It will spot changes in fender trim, hubcaps, wheels, carburetors and instruments. In 1947, Chrysler added the Traveler to the Windsor series. This was Chrysler's version of the DeSoto Suburban. Riding only on a 121.5-inch wheelbase, instead of a choice of 121.5-inch or 139.5-inch wheelbases, it lacked the Suburban's optional roomier model. It also lacked most of the Suburban's station wagon-like features. However, it did sport a luggage rack.

I had one personal experience with a Chrysler of this period as a collector car. In 1967, a friend called and told me he was passing on buying a 1948 Chrysler Town & Country convertible for $500, because it had a blown engine. He said he would have bought it, at several times the price, if it were a Ford Sportsman. The car was located in El Sobrante, a suburb north of Oakland, California. I decided to have a look.

What I found was an all-original car, excellent body and wood, fair interior and a thrown rod. I bought it, had it towed to my home in San Rafael and did the wood restoration. A year later, overbought on cars and pressed for garage space, I sold it (for a small profit) to one Warren Young in the Los Angeles area. He located another engine, restored the car and showed it. Chrysler Town & Countrys were real sleepers in the early 1970s, compared to Ford Sportsman models. I sold it just before prices skyrocketed. That same car now, as I bought it, would be worth in excess of $10,000. Restored, they are worth more than $30,000 today.

This one reputedly had a Hollywood celebrity history, although I never checked into it. Could I have let Clark Gable's Town & Country slip right through my hands?

I haven't the vaguest idea of what happened to Art Rosacker's New Yorker sedan or, for that matter, Diane and the entire family. I think they moved to Florida in about 1957. Old Art is, very possibly, still driving the Chrysler. Diane will forever be the enigma of all my teenage girlfriends. Vanished without a trace into the land "Somewhere West of Laramie." Or, possibly in Diane's case, into the Bermuda Triangle.

A couple of years ago an identical Chrysler sedan turned up in San Rafael. It was all original, had about 70,000 miles, and was desperately looking for a home for about $3,000. It was a nice car, but, being a 1947 Chrysler and a four-door sedan at that, buyers were hardly swarming all over it.

I get a lot of surprising "fan mail." Maybe Diane will read this, write and send a picture of her dad and the car.

Postwar Hudsons

By Tim Howley

Over the years, a few Hudson enthusiasts have written to me asking what I have against their cars. It seems that I seldom, if ever, write about Hudsons.

It's not what I have against Hudsons. It's what my mother had against them many years ago. Late in 1947, my Uncle John Howley bought a beautiful two-tone green "step down" Hudson four-door sedan, probably a Commodore Eight. Uncle John was the yardmaster for the Northern Pacific Railroad's northside Minneapolis office and he always drove fine cars, mostly Chrysler products. But in the late 1940s, there was this brief Hudson episode.

Uncle John invited us all up to his lovely home on Xerxes Avenue for a ride in the new Hudson. I remember it as an incredibly handsome and wide automobile and quiet as Grant's tomb. It was at night and the magnificent Hudson dashboard was all aglow. I think that Hudson had just about the best-looking dashboard of any car of the era, because it was such a throwback to the classic 1930s dash and it wouldn't spill. The ride was that steady and smooth.

On the way home from Uncle John's, mother spent the entire trip in the humble 1946 Ford, running down Uncle John and the rest of dad's Irish family. If Uncle John bought a Hudson, it was probably an overpriced and pretentious car, she concluded.

Two years later, my cousin, Tommy Genadek, bought a 1950 Hudson sedan. Again, my mother went into one of her sermons. "Where do they get the kind of money to buy a car like that? Nothing but poor shanty Irish like the rest of Bill's bunch. Should be driving Fords and Chevrolets."

No, Mother did not like the more expensive cars in those days. She liked her transportation simple and church-going. Since there were now two Hudsons in the family, they became the cars she criticized most. Fat, overblown, pretentious and Protestant. Thus, I had mighty few childhood experiences with these fine automobiles. It is only in very recent years that I have come to appreciate their many fine qualities, although, admittedly, with deep pangs of childhood guilt. The car that I missed out on, in its day, was quite a machine. I wouldn't mind owning one of them now.

The 1948 Hudson was inspired in part by World War II aircraft designs. (Hudson built a section of the B-29 fuselage.) But, it was also inspired by those World War II drawings of "Cars of the Future." Two more practical influences were European designs and mono-body construction. The Chrysler Airflow had a unit body. Lincoln-Zephyr was of unitized construction and Lincoln was continued as such through 1948. Nash went unitized in 1941. Hudson had been experimenting with it since 1937 and finally decided 1948 was the target year. Oddly enough, Hudson management bought a 1942 Buick Super two-door to show stylists and engineers that this was the car they wanted to beat.

The designing of the 1948 Hudson began in earnest in 1945. Some of the sketches show how advanced the car really was. One radical proposal had the grille set high between the headlights. From the front, it almost looks like a 1964-1/2 Mustang. There was a sleek phaeton proposed, but it never got off the drawing board. There were other proposals, with much more glass area than the final product. Hudson's engineering staff held far more influence with management, than the small, and rather unstructured, design department working under Frank Spring. Designers were still considered the dreamers and dawdlers in those days. So, what finally emerged as the 1948 Step-Down Hudson was a car that came more out of engineering, than design. And, yet, it was and still is, a remarkably good design.

This was the first American mass-production car to cradle the passengers between the frame side rails. It was wider than it was high and was very likely the safest and best-handling car of its day. The engine and seats were moved forward. The floor wells were as low as the bottom of the main frame side rails.

This was an expensive car to put into production. It cost about $16 million. It ended up several hundred pounds heavier than the 1947 models and was so costly to build that, by the end of the 1948 model run, the price was 36 percent higher. That was probably Hudson's greatest drawback. The average man admired it greatly. The cost pushed it out of his price range. It suffered from a problem inherent to unitized cars, especially in those days. The tooling was so expensive that a manufacturer could make major body styling changes, even after three years. The 1948 Hudson body was continued through 1954.

The six-cylinder engine was entirely new and was called the Hudson Super Six. It had the largest displacement and highest horsepower of any American-built six to that date. It was engineered for performance comparable to the venerable Hudson eight. It was of traditional L-head design with a 3-9/16 inch bore and a 4-3/8 inch stroke. Displacement was 262 cubic inches. It produced 121 horsepower at 4,000 rpm. The standard compression ratio was 6.5:1. With an optional aluminum head, you could have a 7:1 compression ratio. The eight-cylinder engine was not at all new. It had been around since 1932 and had been rated at 128 horsepower since 1940. It had a three inch bore, 4-1/2 inch stroke and the compression ratio was 6.5:1 (again 7:1 with the optional aluminum head). Displacement was 254.4 cubic inches.

The 1948 Hudsons were offered in four series: Super Six and Commodore Six and the Super Eight and Commodore Eight, all with the same body on the same 124-inch wheelbase. The Super models had rather plain interiors, but the Commodore models were beautifully finished, inside, with the finest broadcloths. The Super Six had the greatest selection of models, including a three-passenger coupe, a Brougham two-door sedan, a club coupe and a Brougham convertible. The Super Eight came in a four-door sedan and Club Coupe only. The Commodore Six and Eight were offered in a Club Coupe, four-door sedan and Brougham convertible coupe. No production figures have been given by model, except for the convertibles (88 Super Sixes, 48 Commodore Sixes and 64 Commodore Eights).

A Super Six four-door sedan listed for $2,222, compared to $1,729 for the 1947 model. A Commodore Eight listed for $2,514, compared to $1,972 for 1947. The Super Six four-door sedan weight was up from 3,110 pounds to 3,500 pounds. The Commodore Eight weight was up from 3,330 pounds to 3,600 pounds. Overdrive was a popular option at $101. There was Vacumotive Drive (an automatic clutch) for $44 extra and a DriveMaster vacuum-electric automatic shifter, including Vacumotive Drive, for $112 extra.

Despite problems in obtaining materials and supplies, due mainly to supplier strikes, Hudson managed to get their all-new postwar Step-Down car into showrooms on October 12, 1947. Even though the designers felt the car fell short of their original plans, dealers and the public were wild about it. It may have been the first car ever advertised on television. It received excellent press reviews. I can remember Bob Hope's jokes: "How does the Chinaman describe the new Hudson? A One-A-Swung-Lo." Or, "This is the first time in history that Ford and Chevrolet owners have been stepping down into higher priced car." 1948 model year sales were 117,200, about 25,000 more than 1947.

The most visible change, for 1949, was greatly improved interiors in Supers. There were now two tones of wood graining on the dashboards. There was simulated leather grain just below the window sills.

1949 models were introduced quietly in October, 1948. Outward appearances were very little changed. Under the Six's hood there was now an optional 7.12:1 compression head, improved lubrication, and a larger capacity cooling system. A Brougham two-door sedan was added to the Commodore Six and Super Eight series, but not to the Commodore Eight series. The most visible change for 1949 was greatly improved interiors in Supers. There were now two tones of wood graining on the dashboards. There was simulated leather grain just below the window sills. Leather grain was also put on the armrests and the ledge of the side recesses. Production for Hudson's 40th anniversary year was 159,100.

The big news for 1950 was the addition of the lower-priced Pacemaker series with a five-inch shorter wheelbase and 6-1/2-inch shorter overall length. The Super Six engine was reduced to 232 cubic inches for the Pacemaker. Horsepower was 112. The compression ratio was 6.7:1 standard, 7.2:1 optional.

The Pacemakers were offered in two series, the Pacemaker and the Pacemaker Deluxe, the latter being a mid-year addition. Both series included a Club Coupe, Brougham two-door, four-door and a Brougham convertible coupe. The price of a Pacemaker four-door was $1,933, against $2,105 for a Super Six and $2,282 for a Commodore Six.

The Pacemaker was introduced in November, 1949. The senior Hudsons did not come out until February, 1950. The major change was a horsepower and compression ratio increase, in the standard Six, to keep it a step ahead of the Pacemaker. There was also the introduction of a closed type of pressure cooling system in all Hudson cars. Another big Hudson improvement that year was Super-Matic Drive. This was actually the Drive-Master setup with overdrive added. Vacumotive Drive (the automatic clutch) was no longer available.

What saved Hudson from falling even further down the ladder in 1950 was the Pacemaker. It accounted for about half of total production. It's easy to tell a 1950 Hudson from a 1948 or 1949. There is an upside down "V" in the grille.

Total 1950 Hudson production was 121,408 and the firm slipped from 11th place to 13th in the industry. Two key problems were lack of really low-priced cars and the lack of an overhead valve V-8 engine. What saved Hudson from falling even further down the ladder in 1950 was the Pacemaker. It accounted for about half of total production. It's easy to tell a 1950 Hudson from a 1948 or 1949. There is an upside down "V" in the grille.

Nine Hudsons were entered in the first Mexican Road Race, held May 5-9, 1950. The first car to start was a 1950 Hudson driven by a Mexican "piloto." It never finished. The oldest car in the race was a 1937 Hudson, another Mexican-driven entry. It developed clutch and transmission trouble and dropped out after the second leg. Lou Figaro wrecked his 1950 Hudson on a sharp curve south of Pueblo. The Mono-bilt body probably saved his life. Other Hudsons met with lesser road fates and mechanical failures. Only Charles Fraley, of Columbus, Ohio, finished. His 1948 Hudson, car number 20, came in 39th. His co-pilot was Reggie McFee, who became quite a driver in his own right. Hudson may have eaten a lot of dust down in Mexico, but its greatest racing history was yet to be written, after the fabulous Hornet came along in 1951.

I also had my own Hudson revenge of sorts. If there was any group that my mother disliked more than my dad's brothers and sisters, it was my own girlfriends. In college, I had a girlfriend named Ginny McCoy. She owned a two-tone blue 1952 Hudson Hornet Club Coupe. It was a real classy car and Ginny loved to drive it. As a matter of fact, on all our dates, Ginny would pick me up, at the dormitory where I stayed, in that fantastic Hudson. I do not know what happened to Ginny's Hudson, but I do know what happened to Ginny. She moved to Florida.

Somewhere West of Laramie...

Hooray for the coral-and-gray 1955 Chevrolet

By Tim Howley

My father was always a Ford man, although at one point he owned a fine 1950 Packard. In 1954 he bought a new Ford, and that fall the new 1955 Chevrolet came out. My Ford father became an instant Chevrolet fan. He made me a proposition. If I would trade in my 1953 Bel Air convertible on a new 1955 hardtop, he would pay the difference.

In the summer of 1955, Dad and I went down to Hennen Chevrolet in Forest Lake, Minnesota. Hubert Hennen was an old family friend and I think he practically fell dead on his showroom floor when my father actually came in to buy a new Chevrolet. But, he did have a suggestion.

Hennen said that my 1953 convertible would not depreciate any further by fall. If we waited until the end of the 1955 model run, he could get us a very good deal on a 1955 model. However, he could not guarantee the color. I remember I made a long list of colors I liked: Red and white, turquoise and white, coral and gray, yellow and white and several others.

The car came in the last week of September. It was a coral and gray Bel Air hardtop with a six-cylinder engine, standard transmission and quite a lot of accessories. The factory price was $2,067. That must have been picked up at Detroit.

In Minneapolis, they were nowhere near that cheap. Our car came from the assembly plant in Janesville, Wisconsin and there was about $400 in shipping and dealer preparation. My car, as delivered, was about $2,700 list. I distinctly remember that Hennen allowed us $1,700 for the 1953 convertible, because the difference that dad paid was right around $1,000.

I drove that 1955 Chevrolet for 3-1/2 more years or about 60,000 miles. It was an adventure all the way and it was the real beginning of my own lifelong automobile affair.

The 1955 Chevrolet was, of course, Ed Cole's baby and he really turned a sow's ear into a silk purse overnight. A callow teenage youth couldn't have chosen a better first new car in 1955. The fact that it was a six wasn't really all that bad.

The frame was entirely new and much of it was enclosed in the rocker sill. Actually, the body, especially in the cowl area, carried most of the strengthening. The whole car was lighter than 1954 models. For example, a 1955 Bel Air six hardtop weighed 3,195 pounds against 3,300 pounds for the 1954 model. The V-8 engine was, surprisingly, 30 pounds lighter than the six. The 1955 cars was several inches lower, too.

The 1955 design was so good that the car even looked pleasing in the simple 150 utility sedan. It had the Ferrari grille, the wraparound windshield and the teardrop headlights with speedlines that carried into the front fenders. It looked like a baby Cadillac.

Most of the interiors in the Bel Air series matched the two-tone exteriors. That year, Chevrolet introduced a new dielectric process for embossing vinyl, and it was extremely well done. The dash panel, patterned after the Corvette, was another classic styling touch. Good design and high quality were just everywhere in that little car. The vinyl headliner even had stainless steel bows over the seams, for a nice convertible touch.

As in 1954, the convertible was offered only in the Bel Air series, the "210" ragtop having been dropped in mid-1953. There was also a gold "anniversary" model. It was patterned after a gold Bel Air hardtop that became the 50 millionth car built by General Motors. This maintained a tradition, as the corporation's 25th millionth car was a silver 1940 Chevrolet. The original gold Bel Air appeared in a Flint, Michigan parade and some experts say a specific number of look-alikes were built. I have only seen one, painted gold with white trim and sporting a beautiful and special gold and white interior.

Underneath all 1955 Chevrolet models was a new ball joint front suspension. But, the best news of all in 1955 was the new Chevrolet overhead valve V-8. The only reason that my car was a six was that I commuted 60 miles (round-trip) daily to the University of Minnesota. So, gas was a real consideration, even at 26.9 cents per gallon. My six averaged around 20 miles per gallon on the highway and about 16 around town.

Originally, Chevrolet had been working on a V-8 along the Cadillac V-8's lines, but Ed Cole chose, wisely, to start from scratch and design something simple and lightweight, like the rest of the car. Obviously, he had modifications in mind. The 1955 Chevrolet V-8 was 265 cubic inches and had an 8:1 compression ratio. It developed 162 horsepower, without modifications. With the optional Power Pack, the horsepower was up to 180. I know it has been written that this engine was ultimately bored out to 400 cubic inches. I find it hard to believe that it was the same engine block, but am first to confess that I am not a Chevrolet high-performance authority.

In the January, 1955 issue of Motor Trend, Walt Woron wrote up his test of a 1955 Chevrolet 210 four-door sedan with Powerglide transmission. He wrote in part: "Our heads are buzzing, because there are so many good features about the car. It has exceptional handling qualities for an American production car. Its acceleration is better than all the top performance cars of 1954. Its ride is improved over last year's model. The general workmanship is excellent....

"This 1955 Chevrolet doesn't let the moss grow under its feet either. An average of 97.3 miles per hour is not only adequate in itself, a good five miles per hour faster than last year's car, but is faster than any other 1954 cars in its class. The overdrive should be slightly faster and, when that's coupled with the 180 horsepower engine, the Chevrolet should easily break 100 miles per hour.

"Acceleration-wise, this car's got it, too. Can you imagine a Chevrolet outdigging every 1954 car, but Cadillac and Buick Century, and being able to stay with Chrysler, Lincoln and Oldsmobile?"

The 0-to-60 time was 12.3 seconds. A standing quarter-mile took 19 seconds at 71 miles per hour. They were even impressed with the braking, which was considered pretty fair in 1954. In 1,241 miles of driving, Motor Trend averaged 14.5 miles per gallon. At a steady 60 miles per hour, the gas mileage was 15.8. That's not at all bad for a V-8 with an automatic transmission ... especially in 1955.

Motor Trend concluded, "The new Chevrolet is quite a combination with particular credit going to chief engineer Ed Cole and his able staff. A good looking car, plenty of top-notch performance that will constantly keep the bigger cars in track shoes, agility in traffic, sports car characteristics as far as handling is concerned, ease of driving, a ride that isn't sacrificed on the altar of roadability, better than average brakes and fair fuel economy. But, the greatest compliment we could pay this car is that our praise is so high and our criticisms so minor that we find it hard to believe it's a descendant of previous Chevrolets."

Tom McCahill of Mechanix Illustrated was almost as impressed and you have to remember that McCahill was a died-in-the-wool Lincoln man. Testing a Bel Air V-8 four-door with Powerglide, he achieved a 0-to-60 time of 14.9 seconds and a top speed of 96 miles per hour. McCahill concluded: "The new Chevrolet should stir up the dormant swashbuckle in many a drab mouse. The new Chevrolets are entirely new from hood ornament to bumperette. They are excellent road cars and have the best of the General Motors' looks. If you are an old Chevrolet man, and there are many old ones, you should be very pleased with this new offering."

Now, Uncle Tom was quick to admit he didn't have the complete Chevrolet story, because the factory didn't supply him with a stick shift or "kitted" (Power-Pack) version. It was at the 1955 Daytona SpeedWeeks, Tom's favorite event, that the 1955 Chevrolet raised hairs on his near bald head. A stock kitted Chevrolet sedan, driven by a local sheriff named Jack Tapscott, ran off with the popular price class award at 112.877 miles per hour. Later, Tapscott finished second overall, to Joe Littlejohn's 1955 Cadillac, in the acceleration trials. The Chevrolet's average speed for a measured mile from a standing start was 78.158 miles per hour. Right behind, in the third slot, was another Chevrolet, driven by Mickey Boundy to 77.519 miles per hour. Then came a Buick Century, a Chrysler 300 and another Chevrolet. My poor Lincoln was down in 25th place surrounded by Fords.

It was an amazing year for Chevrolet, starting off with a red and white Bel Air convertible as the official Indianapolis 500 Pace Car.

It was an amazing year for Chevrolet, starting off with a red and white Bel Air convertible as the official Indianapolis 500 Pace Car. Then, it was just one victory after another, with drivers like Herb Thomas, the Flock brothers and Jim Reed.

The most sweeping Chevrolet victory was at the Darlington Southern 500, on Labor Day. It was Herb Thomas first and Jim Reed second, both in Chevrolets. Then came Tim Flock, third, in a Chrylser 300, and Glen Staley, fourth, in another Chevrolet. Chevrolets driven by Jake Maness, Cotton Owens, Bill Widenhouse and Jim Massey finished seventh through 10th.

The problem with the bigger cars, especially the Chrysler 300s, was that the Firestone tires wouldn't stand up to the weight. With Ford, it was plain bad luck. Chevrolet had that special combination of lightness, handling and power that was virtually unbeatable. Motor Trend named the 1955 Chevrolet, along with the 1955 Mercury Montclair, the best handling car of the year.

How did my own little Chevrolet six stack up? Jim Lodge tested a 210 four-door sedan with the six-cylinder engine and overdrive for Motor Trend. The results: 19.3 miles per gallon over 1,608 miles and 21.9 miles per gallon at a steady 60 miles per hour. Zero-to-60 time was 15.3 seconds. A standing quarter-mile was 19.9 seconds at 70 miles per hour. Average top speed was 95.7. It was pretty close to a V-8 with Powerglide in performance, but considerably better in the economy department. I had not made such a bad choice.

What happened to my 1955 Chevrolet is kind of funny. My popularity with the young women increased three-fold over my 1953 convertible. They loved the coral and gray color. "Let's head for Judd's drive-in with Tim and his little coral and gray bomb," they'd suggest. All the money I saved on gas was spent on hamburgers, fries and malts.

The coral and gray 1955 Chevrolet color combination was promoted in several contemporary advertisements.

Somewhere West of Laramie...

More Chevrolet memories

By Tim Howley

It's kind of sad what happened to Ned Jordan, author of the immortal ad "Somewhere West of Laramie" and builder of the Jordan car.

I think the story can be told at this late date. Old Ned had his bouts with the bottle, and along about 1927, Prohibition booze got the best of him. This was one of several reasons why Ned and his wife split their Jordan stock right down the middle. Ned simply bailed out of the company and was seldom heard from again, until he began writing his column, "Ned Jordan Speaks." It appeared in Automotive News in the 1950s.

This was quite a number of years after Ned "went on the wagon" for good. I strongly suspect that, had it not been for problems in his personal life, Jordan would have been a powerful force in the world of advertising throughout the 1930s.

As things turned out, Henry Ewald, one of Ned's cronies, seized on a real opportunity. Ewald was founder of the Campbell-Ewald Advertising Agency in Detroit, which handled the Chevrolet account since March 4, 1922. The Chevrolet, at the time, was a sporty little car which was finally giving the staid, although lovable, Model T Ford some real competition. Ewald was quick to realize that the Jordan style of advertising could be applied to the Chevrolet.

With Jordan sales faltering and Ned Jordan on a two-year binge in the Caribbean, Ewald shrewdly concluded that he could ape the entire campaign for the more available and saleable Chevrolet.

Then, as now, there is nothing sacred in the world of automobile advertising. Of course, the Jordan style of advertising worked so well for Chevrolet that Henry Ford's advertising for the new Model A copied it to a degree. Henry Ewald now had the Chevrolet account for keeps. Poor Ned Jordan returned from his two-year odyssey as penniless as if he had kept his Jordan stock through the 1929 stock market crash.

Ned's advertising now is a part of American folklore. "Somewhere West of Laramie" is singled out in the Julian Watkins book, The Hundred Greatest Ads. And strangely enough, so is the entire 1955 Chevrolet advertising campaign. Not that Henry Ewald personally had anything to do with it. He was long retired and, possibly, even dead by then. But, obviously, a car as new and different as the 1955 Chevrolet required an advertising campaign as dashing as the car itself.

There were headlines such as "We've turned Old Reliable into a Flash of Fire" and "There isn't a road built that can make it breathe hard." One of the most interesting aspects of the 1955 Chevrolet ads was that they brought back line art, which had gone out of vogue in the 1940s and 1950s. The ads usually showed interstate highways winding far into the distance with a sassy 1955 Chevrolet, in the foreground, passing all the unidentified Chryslers, Lincolns and even Cadillacs. Chevrolet had the performance to be sure. But, hardly a mile of

Chevrolet's *red-hot* hill-flatteners!
162 H.P. V8 - 180 H.P. V8

See that fine fat mountain yonder?

You can iron it out, flat as a flounder . . . and easy as whistling!

Just point one of Chevrolet's special hill-flatteners at it (either the 162-h.p. "Turbo-Fire V8," or the 180-h.p. "Super Turbo-Fire"*) . . . and pull the trigger!

Barr-r-r-r-o-o-O-O-OOM!

Mister, you got you a flat mountain!

. . . At least it *feels* flat. Because these silk-and-dynamite V8's gobble up the toughest grades you can ladle out. And holler for more. They love to climb, because that's just about the only time the throttle ever comes near the floorboard.

And that's a pity. For here are engines that sing as sweetly as a dynamo . . . built to pour out a torrent of pure, vibrationless power. Big-bore V8's with the shortest stroke in the industry, designed to gulp huge breaths of fresh air and transmute it into blazing acceleration.

So most of the time they loaf. Even at the speed limit they just dream along, light and easy as a zephyr, purring out an effortless fraction of their strength.

You don't have to be an engineer to know that these are the sweetest-running V8's you ever piloted. Just drop in at your Chevrolet dealer's, point the nose at the nearest hill, and feather the throttle open. These V8's can do their own talking . . . and nobody argues with them!

SEE YOUR CHEVROLET DEALER
*Optional at extra cost.

motoramic 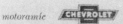   *Stealing the thunder from the high-priced cars with the most modern V8 on the road!*

Performance was stressed in 1955 Chevrolet advertising.

those idyllic interstate highways had been built in 1956. That was the year that the Eisenhower administration inaugurated the Federal Interstate Highway Program. Most of those roads in the 1955 Chevrolet ads would not be completed until most 1955 Chevrolets were long gone from the road. I can remember, in 1958, driving my 1955 Chevrolet along about 20 miles of one of those marvelous roads in southern Minnesota that ended in little more than a cow path.

My 1955 Chevrolet was not new very long. In November, 1955, not long after I took delivery on my car, the new 1956 model was introduced. Naturally, my boyhood buddy, Bobby Schwaab, had to top me by buying a brand new black and white 1956 Chevrolet Bel Air two-door hardtop with the biggest V-8 and all the power seats and power windows. I think about the only item he didn't order was air conditioning. From a performance standpoint, the 1956 Chevrolet really was one up on the beloved 1955.

The horsepower for the 1956 Super Turbo-Fire V-8 was up to 205. The ultimate 1956 engine was the same Super Turbo-Fire V-8 with dual four-barrel carburetors, which produced 225 horsepower. The boost came from a new high-lift camshaft, 9.25:1 compression ratio and a four-barrel carburetor, all standard equipment on this optional engine. Two other V-8s were also available, 162 horsepower for standard shift cars and 170 for Powerglide, same as 1955. The six got a new high-lift cam and had a 8.0:1 compression ratio. Horsepower was up to 140.

The 1956 Chevrolet with the "205" showed its colors sometime before the model was introduced. On Labor Day, 1955, Chevrolet engineer Zora Arkus-Duntov broke the old Pikes Peak record by making the 12-1/2 mile climb in 17 minutes, 24:05 seconds. The old record of 19 minutes, 25:70 seconds had stood for 21 years. The car was a pre-production, camouflaged job called the "Monte Carlo," and, later on in the year, several magazines tested this same car for their road reports. The Monte Carlo was but a promotional gimmick to demonstrate 1956 Chevrolet potential before the model was introduced. As might have been expected, the 1956 model continued to show remarkable strength in NASCAR events throughout the 1956 stock car season.

Zero-to-60 time for the "205" was 12 seconds with Powerglide and about 10 seconds with standard transmission. Motor Life claimed times as little as 8.4 seconds with stick shift and overdrive. The real power boost was in the 50-to-80 miles per hour passing range, now about 12 seconds, even with Powerglide. Motor Trend claimed the car's top speed was 108 miles per hour for an average of four runs. In anybody's book, this new Chevrolet was fast. Chevrolet's 1956 advertising slogan, "The Hot One's Even Hotter," was no idle boast.

Nobody could argue with 1956 Chevrolet performance. The styling was another matter. Going to a much more massive and conventional looking grille, which encased the new and larger parking lamps, was a major change. The plane of the hood was flattened. The hood was actually a little longer at the forward end. Chrome body moldings now swept the entire length of the car. This chrome sweep was now extended to even the lowest-priced 150 series. Taillights were greatly revised to look like those of other GM makes and the left taillight now hid the gas filler, a neat Cadillac trick for many years before.

I suppose I'll get letters on this one, but in my opinion, I think they ruined the distinctive 1955 design in an attempt to offer a car that would be more appealing to a larger group of buyers. There had been some complaints about the distinctive 1955 Chevrolet "Ferrari style" grille. Some said that even the Bel Air series looked too plain, too simple. I'm not saying that the 1956 Chevrolet was a badly trimmed car. I just feel that the original intent was lost. And I feel that it was lost even more with the 1957 model. Yet both years are still quite attractive, when you compare them to the garish 1958 and finny 1959.

The 1956 Chevrolet interiors were more attractive and durable than in 1955. A number of striking new colors and two-tone combinations were added. New models were introduced: stylish four-door hardtop and a nine-passenger Beauville station wagon. Happily, the Nomad sport-wagon was continued. So was the popular Del Ray. The 1956 Chevrolet was not quite the success of the 1955. Production was down from 1.7 million to 1.567 million. However, this could hardly be attributed to changes in design. 1955 had been a banner year for the entire industry. Chevrolet continued to lead where it really counted, outselling Ford and Plymouth. I'm sorry to say I never owned a 1956 Chevrolet, new or used. But, there was one pretty humorous 1957 Chevrolet incident. Humorous now, not then.

Loves to go...*and looks it!*
The '56 Chevrolet

The Bel Air Sport Sedan is one of two new Chevrolet 4-door hardtops. All 19 new models feature Body by Fisher.

*It's got frisky new power ... V8 or 6 ...
to make the going sweeter and the passing safer. It's
agile ... quick ... solid and sure on the road!*

This, you remember, is the car that set a new record for the Pikes Peak run. And the car that can take that tough and twisting climb in record time is bound to make *your* driving safer and more fun.

Curve ahead? You level through it with a wonderful nailed-to-the-road feeling of stability. Chevrolet's special suspension and springing see to that.

Slow car ahead? You whisk around it and back in line in seconds. Chevrolet's new high-compression power—ranging from the new "Blue-Flame 140" Six up to 225 h.p. in the new Corvette V8 engine, available at extra cost—handles that.

Quick stop called for? Nudge those oversize brakes and relax. Chevrolet's exclusive Anti-Dive braking brings you to a smooth, *heads-up* halt.

No doubt about it, this bold beauty was made for the road. Like to try it? Just see your Chevrolet dealer. . . . Chevrolet Division of General Motors, Detroit 2, Michigan.

THE HOT ONE'S EVEN HOTTER

"The Hot One's Even Hotter" was Chevrolet's 1956 sales theme.

In the fall of 1957 I met a young lady named Colleen. While she dated me regularly, she sort of let me know I was a rather drab little mouse in my coral and gray Chevrolet. At Christmas, she presented me with a miniature 1957 Chevrolet convertible. It was light blue and a note was attached reading, "If you really want to impress me, why don't you buy one of these?"

In June, 1958 I graduated from college. The world was not waiting and neither was Colleen. I took a job as a radio announcer trainee at KSUM in Fairmont, Minnesota at the, even then, rather dismal salary of $75 a week. Colleen was not at all impressed and took a vacation to California.

While she was gone, I visited a Chevrolet dealer on Lake Street in Minneapolis. One of the salesmen there was a classmate of mine. I told him of my plight with Colleen. Now, it so happened he had just gotten in a light blue 1957 Chevrolet convertible on trade. He knew about my paltry salary in Fairmont and suggested I might simply try out the car and show it to Colleen, before I went head over heels in debt.

When Colleen returned from California, I called her up and asked her for a date, saying I had a surprise for her. She also said she had a little surprise for me. I made arrangement to borrow the 1957 for the weekend and, on Saturday night, I wheeled up to Colleen's house with the top down and all. She got in the car and never so much as said a word. At the dance that night, she never even mentioned the car. After the dance, I went through the ceremony of putting up the top, still without a word from Colleen about the car. All she did was rave about her trip to California and subtly suggest what I rube I was, working for a hick radio station in Minnesota.

I finally blurted out, "I suppose you don't even like my new convertible."

"Oh, I love it," she replied. "It's just like Ed's."

"And who, might I ask, is Ed?" I inquired.

"Oh, Timmie, didn't I ever tell you? I thought you kind of got the hint at Christmas, when I gave you the model. Ed is the guy I went to see in California. We've finally decided to get married and I'll be moving out there."

Colleen was dumped at her door without a word. Utterly devastated, I spun rubber for a half block and never saw her again, from that day to this one. The following morning, I handed the keys back to the dealer and he returned the keys to my coral and gray hardtop. "I could have sold your 1955 over the weekend, Tim, customers just love the color," he said. "But, I had the funny feeling that things weren't going to exactly work out between you and Colleen; blue just isn't your color."

I kept my coral and gray Chevrolet for eight more months and my popularity with young women continued. As a matter of fact, I was driving it the night I met my wife. Yes, that was definitely my good luck car. It was ultimately traded in for a two-year-old 1957 Ford convertible. Well, you see I had to try to get one-up on Bobby Schwaab.

In the summer of 1957, Bobby pulled up in front of my house in a brand new 1957 Ford Fairlane 500 hardtop, blue and white. I couldn't believe my eyes. Ever since we were little kids, Bobby had been ridiculing my dad's Fords, reciting his ridiculous little poem, "A slab of paint, a piece of board, a hunk of tin and there's your Ford." Bobby loathed Fords or at least that's what he led me to believe. His father was a Chrysler man in the 1930s and during the World War II years.

Then, in 1949, the Schwaabs bought a new Mercury. That wasn't the same car as the lowly Ford, or so I was told. It seems that early in 1957 Bobby had taken a job as an automatic transmission mechanic with a northeast Minneapolis Ford dealer. So, naturally, the Chevrolet had to go.

Incidentally, Bobby's change kind of reflected a growing trend. 1957 was the year that Ford out-produced and out-sold Chevrolet. However, its success was not measured by a very wide margin, you can be sure.

Until about 1970, in California, those 1955-1957 Chevrolets were as common as Japanese imports are now. The cars were simply indestructible and were not nearly as prone to rusting-out as Fords of the same era. I still see a little old lady driving her all-original 1955 Chevrolet convertible on a daily basis here in San Diego. Not too long ago, I was amazed to see an all-original 1955 Chevrolet Bel Air two-door sedan parked in a "yellow zone." It was being ticketed by a San Diego meter maid just as if it were a new car. Upon close inspection, the car appeared to be in as good a condition as I remember them in Minnesota, when they were about four years old. And believe it or not, you still occasionally see them on southern California used car lots.

By the way, old Ned Jordan had his last laugh on Henry Ewald. I heard this particular story from Warren MacArthur, a New York City advertising man who Ned had worked for in his later years. Around the end of World War II, Jordan came out of seclusion. Wiley Henry Ewald commissioned him to write a biography about him, his advertising agency and the marketing success of the Chevrolet automobile.

Evidently, Jordan was rather well paid for this project and it took the major part of a year. Looking as dapper as ever, Jordan appeared in Ewald's office one day with the completed manuscript. Henry took it home, read it, and called the author back in.

"I've read your book," Ewald frowned. "Is this what I've paid you for, Ned? It's all about advertising and the Chevrolet automobile. There's really nothing in this book about me, Ned."

With a poker face, in dead seriousness, Jordan replied, "Well, you see, Henry, there isn't much about you I can write. I've interviewed quite a number of people in the industry. Nobody seems to remember that you ever did anything."

Ned Jordan was right. Now, 30 years after his death, the world still sings praises to his wonderful Jordan ads and remembers who wrote them. Henry Ewald, who made a fortune on other people's ideas, is not only long dead, but long forgotten.

The Hot One's Hotter theme was used in attractive advertisement highlighting '56 Chevrolet's record breaking climb up the Pikes Peak road. (Old Cars)

Adding a comical aspect to the performance ad theme was this advertisement depicting a "hot" fire chief's car. (Old Cars)

Somewhere West of Laramie...

More four-door sedans

By Tim Howley

During the 1930s, Ford was famous for its little four-door touring sedans with the notched trunk. They were a little more elegant than fastback sedans. Late in the 1930s, Ford sedans went to extreme aerodynamic style and this same styling theme was carried over onto the new Mercury sedans. The styling holds up well, even today. Of course, the original Lincoln-Zephyr of 1936 was a four-door sedan and the styling comes off remarkably well as late as 1948.

The original Lincoln-Zephyr of 1936 was a four-door sedan and the styling comes off remarkably well.

I have my misgivings about 1946-1948 Ford and Mercury sedans. I also know they are some of America's most popular tour cars. They have enormously large rear seating areas. However, they were so outdated when new, they seemed like 1930s cars, and this has become a definite collectible feature.

The 1949 Ford sedan, like the 1936 Lincoln-Zephyr, is an extremely good-looking car, because it was originally designed as a four-door sedan. Mercury sedans of the 1949-1951 era are big, comfortable and somewhat more affordable than the "James Dean" Mercury coupes of the same era. Try riding in the back seat of a Club Coupe or four-door sedan of that vintage for 500 miles and tell me which one you like better. For that matter, try climbing out of the back seat of any Club Coupe after a 500 mile trip, especially if you're my age.

Mercury sedans of the 1949-1951 era are big, comfortable and somewhat more affordable than the "James Dean" Mercury coupes of the same era.

Lincoln sedans of these same years are quite a bit rarer than the Mercurys and are usually no higher priced. They came in two series, the Lincoln with the Mercury body and the Lincoln Cosmopolitan sedan, with a larger body on a longer wheelbase and little rear quarter windows. Did you know that in 1949 only Lincoln built a Town Sedan?

That's what they officially called it, as if to create more nomenclature confusion. It was a four-door Cosmopolitan fastback with the little rear quarter windows and became a very rare car. I had one of those in the early 1970s and, stupidly, sold it. Well, it was "just a sedan."

Not many collectors will get excited about Plymouth, Dodge and DeSoto sedans, but they have their moments. From 1941 through 1948, Dodge and DeSoto offered Town Sedans without rear quarter windows. Plymouth offered them only in 1942, with a mere 5,821 built. From 1949 through 1952, Chrysler products offered Town Sedans. Except for the Dodge version, they were simply designated four-door sedans. The name "Town Sedan" kind of faded away in the 1950s.

Chrysler sedans through 1946, are the epitome of sedan elegance and the 1955-1956 Imperials are even more so. Chrysler always had a special way with sedan styling and comfort.

Chrysler sedans for all years through 1946 are the epitome of sedan elegance in my opinion. The Chrysler Imperials and 1955-1956 Imperials even more so. Chrysler always had a special way with sedan styling and comfort. The interiors, especially in the earlier years, remind you of English carriages.

Chrysler sedans of the 1930s up to the mid-1950s are far more plentiful than Lincolns, and often quite a bit less expensive than Cadillacs. For my money, you can't find a better tour car than an old Chrysler sedan, especially when you get into the hemi engine era, beginning with the 1951 model.

If you don't like sedans, then you must not like Packards. Back in the 1930s, America's "car of cars" was usually a black, dark blue or dark green Packard sedan. Even the lesser models were elegant-looking. Many sported side-mounted spare tires. In 1941, Packard introduced the sporty Clipper sedan, with its enormous expanses of sheet metal and fenders that swept handsomely into the front doors. For 1942, most closed model Packards took on the Clipper look and name. This handsome car did not sell too well.

Right after the war, Packard quickly slapped on new outer panels, creating the "pregnant elephant" Packards of the 1948-1951 years. These are also great tour cars. You really have to drive them and ride in them to appreciate their elegance and comfort.

The 1951 Packard is another sedan masterpiece. It was designed by the late John Reinhart, who later did the much-celebrated Continental Mark II hardtop coupe, a car that might have fared a lot better in the marketplace had it also been offered in sedan or four-door hardtop styles.

Kaisers and Frazers were originally introduced as four-doors and every one of them is collectible.

Kaisers and Frazers were originally introduced as four-doors and every one of them is collectible. Step-Down Hudsons of the 1948-1954 era are another collectible series of sedans.

But, my ultimate sedan pick would be the 1949-1951 Nash four-door, with its great gas economy. Besides, you can sleep in it. This is no slight consideration when you check out the hotel prices at most of today's regional and national collector car meets. The Nashes are real sleepers in more ways than one. They really are quite aerodynamic, in the sense that their styling does contribute significantly to their good gas economy. I saw one, restored, here on the streets of San Diego a few weeks ago. You don't see them very often anymore. I thought to myself that it was really a fairly good-looking car. Yet we used to laugh at them.

I recall that back in 1967 I was offered a Nash Airflite by a dealer in northern Minnesota. It was a very nice, original, low-mileage 1951 Ambassador Super four-door sedan. The price was only $85 and I turned it down!

"Well, nobody around here wants an old Nash sedan," the dealer explained to me. At that time, neither did I. Instead, I bought a 1959 Thunderbird for about 12 times the price, including transmission repairs. I drove the Thunderbird to California when we moved out here.

Had I driven the Nash, I could have saved enough on motel bills to more than pay for the gasoline. Think of it. I could have slept out under the stars "Somewhere West of Laramie," where the setting sun meets the wide prairie.

A year ago I finally started looking at old sedans in a new light. A friend from Orange County offered me two 1954 Lincoln Capri four-door sedans for the price of one. In fact, he even offered to trailer them both to my front door. As I explained it, nobody was biting on them at any price because they were sedans .... not convertibles or even hardtops. But, they were both really nice original cars with perfect original interiors. My wife said, "Well, they're just sedans." I thought, "That's what I've been telling myself for years. What in the world is wrong with just a nice sedan, especially when you can have two for the price of one?"

As the Arab merchant once said to the little old man, "Mister, I'll sell you a white elephant cheap." The little old man, living in an apartment, replied, "I don't have room in my apartment for a white elephant." The Arab countered, "Today only I'll sell you two white elephants for the price of one." To which the little old man replied, "Mister, you've got yourself a deal."

The 1953 (shown) and 1954 Lincoln four-door sedans let you take modern living with you. (Old Cars)

Through the Windshield...

Automotive innovations in retrospect

By Ned Comstock

In 1925, the paint had pretty well peeled off the family Buick, although the car was only two years old. What paint remained turned iridescent in the rain and rusty in the sun. It was a mess.

General Motors was having trouble with this paint, too. In 1925 the paint process took 30 days and auto production was piling up in front of the paint shops. Then, the only solution seemed to be a roof over Michigan to house the cars while the paint dried. Painting an automobile took 30 days and that was that!

"Boss" Kettering, an inventive genius who, along with Alfred Sloan, was the real architect of General Motors, had something to say about this. In the end, he said, "Duco." It was his name for a new finish that reduced the painting process from 30 days to one hour. It first appeared on Oaklands in 1925. This broke the bottleneck at the paint shop and revolutionized the auto industry.

Duco nitro-cellulose lacquer first appeared on Oaklands in 1925. This broke the bottleneck at the paint shop and revolutionized the auto industry.

As Kettering found out, before you can win a revolution you have to clean out a lot of stagnation. Smithsonian magazine recently related some of Kettering's battles, and how he won them, before his paint changed the auto world. One was a luncheon with an executive who could, if he wished, make a fine friend for the new paint. Rather, it was after lunch that the incident took place.

Following that meal, the guest returned to ask help in locating his car. "I parked it right here," he said, "where that green car is parked now. Mine was just like it, only mine was blue."

"Your car is green now," replied Kettering, who loved practical jokes. He had had his guest's blue car painted green during the lunch hour to demonstrate the new quick-drying paint. The guest drove off, surprised and pleased. Well, he was perhaps a little more surprised than pleased, but he was convinced.

The great success of Kettering's paint program makes one realize there are other developments just as important on which the auto world turned. The foremost two of these, both in which Kettering counted heavily, were the self-starter and no-knock gasoline.

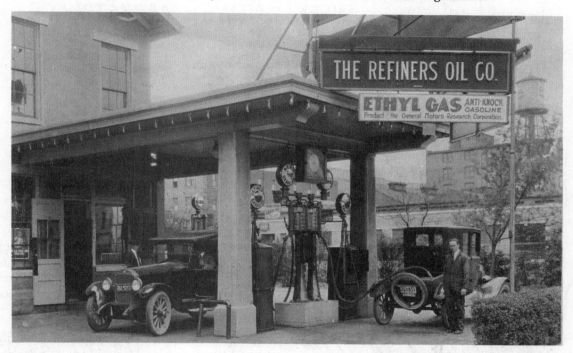

Old car engines tended to knock. This robbed the engine of power when it was most needed. "Boss" Kettering solved this problem with "no-knock" gasoline.

The self-starter explains itself. Cranking by hand is arduous and dangerous. Nobody would hand-crank, unless he has to. The technological barrier was the very heavy, short term demand for electric current by the starter motor. When Kettering's Delco company solved this, the self-starter flowed into place like manifest destiny. Cadillac was first in 1914, and Rolls Royce (let the chauffeur do the cranking) may have been last in 1919. In between, the self-starter was a $50 option on Ford Model Ts, but there were few refusals.

I learned about the other universally accepted auto extra from a chauffeur. He was the long-term driver for the family next door. He liked small boys and from him I learned (on the front seat of the family 1923 Lincoln with the sloping windshield) that you "retarded the spark" on steep hills by means of a lever on the steering column.

These, then, are three components that made the modern automobile possible: quick-drying paint, self-starting engines and no-knock gasoline.

There is a short list of other developments that made modern automobiles successful: closed cars with competitive prices; coherent styling; synchromesh gear-shifting; and all-weather ventilation.

Along with all the progress, one bolt-on extra stands out as a giant step backwards in automobile development. Hydra-Matic transmission, introduced on the 1939 Oldsmobile, made the car much more dangerous without any real advantage.

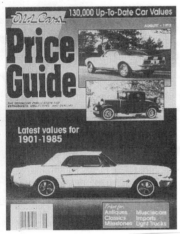